A Garland of Feminist Reflections

A Garland of Feminist Reflections

Forty Years of Religious Exploration

Rita M. Gross

UNIVERSITY OF CALIFORNIA PRESS
Berkeley · Los Angeles · London

University of California Press, one of the most
distinguished university presses in the United States,
enriches lives around the world by advancing
scholarship in the humanities, social sciences, and
natural sciences. Its activities are supported by the
UC Press Foundation and by philanthropic
contributions from individuals and institutions.
For more information, visit www.ucpress.edu.

University of California Press
Berkeley and Los Angeles, California

University of California Press, Ltd.
London, England

Library of Congress Cataloging-in-Publication Data

Gross, Rita M.
   A garland of feminist reflections: forty years of
religious exploration / Rita M. Gross.
        p.   cm.
   Includes bibliographical references.
   ISBN 978-0-520-25585-2 (cloth : alk. paper)
   ISBN 978-0-520-25586-9 (pbk. : alk. paper)
   1. Feminist theology.   2. Women— Religious
aspects.   3. Feminism—Religious aspects—
Buddhism.   4. Buddhism—Doctrines.   I. Title.
BL458.G764 2009
202.082—dc22   2008034386

Manufactured in the United States of America

17 16 15 14 13 12 11 10 09
10 9 8 7 6 5 4 3 2 1

This book is printed on Natures Book, which contains
30% post-consumer waste and meets the minimum
requirements of ANSI/NISO Z39.48–1992 (R 1997)
(Permanence of Paper).

*Dedicated to all the teachers and all the
students who have walked the paths of life,
of scholarship, and of practice with me*

Contents

PART ONE

Introductory Materials

Introducing *A Garland of Feminist Reflections*

This *Garland of Feminist Reflections* represents my lifelong concern to live deeply immersed in exploring and understanding questions of ultimate significance. It also represents my lifelong concern with how women have pursued such questions, or have been prevented from pursuing such interests by the prison of gender roles specific to their cultures. The first concern is core and the second is adventitious. Only circumstances forced me, willy-nilly, into lifelong concern with issues of sex and gender. That was not what I intended, and in an ideal world, it would not have been necessary. All these years later, I wish it would have been possible to delve deeply into questions of truth and meaning more abstractly, without so much attention to issues of sex and gender. But, given the world and the academic context into which I, a female, was immersed as a student in the 1960s, only serious, complete ignoring and denial could have permitted me to go about my work and my life pretending that sex and gender were not relevant and determinative.

THE "F" WORD: FEMINISM

As a result, throughout my academic and professional life, beginning in graduate school, I have written about and been concerned with women's religious lives. A significant portion of the 150 articles and essays I have published since 1973, the date of my first published article, have dealt with women and religion in one way or another, and the three most significant books that I have authored or edited to date also deal with women and religion.[1] Thus, it is not surprising that I have been labeled a "feminist"—whatever that might mean—and have even labeled myself a "feminist," frequently. That label has been attached to me more than I would prefer, given that it blinds many observers to other concerns and strengths that one may have.

No matter how often I have argued that feminist concerns are not special interests isolated from the general fabric of life and scholarship, the opposite has often been assumed about me and my work. An example comes to mind: some years ago I was to teach a workshop on women and Buddhism at a Buddhist meditation center. Enrollment in the program was low, and those responsible for registration began to call the members of the center. When asked if he would be attending, one man, a man with a wife and daughters, replied, "Now why would I be interested in *that!*" Changing the title of the program to "Buddhism and Gender" makes little difference.

No wonder I have resisted being labeled as someone who specializes in "women and religion." I prefer to think of myself as a scholar of religion. I especially resist being labeled a "woman scholar." I remember my frustration when, soon after I finished my PhD, one of my graduate school mentors regularly began referring to me as "one of the best new women scholars in the field." Why not simply "one of the best new scholars"?

Though I have often written about women and religion, nevertheless there is a certain accidental or reluctant quality, both about my identity as a feminist scholar and about the fact that I have written on the topic so much. The ambiguity, the edge, concerning this life's accomplishments stems from the irrationally ambiguous reaction such work receives from colleagues and from the academy. Usually, those who analyze the causes of social conditions that cause suffering, such as disease, famine, warfare, poverty, and environmental degradation, and then seek to alleviate those situations are appreciated, not vilified and marginalized. Why would those who seek to alleviate the prison of gender roles and the suffering and ignorance caused by that prison be regarded differently?

Naively, in the late 1960s, when I first began to discover the vast oversight in my field, the comparative and historical study of religion, that had been caused by its operating model of humanity, an androcentric, one-sexed model of humanity, I thought my mentors would be as excited as I was. Instead, they were upset, for the most part. One of them actually told me that an intelligent person like myself should realize that the generic masculine "covered and included the feminine," making it unnecessary to say anything about women specifically. The implication was that if I wanted to do something as redundant and unnecessary as studying the religious lives of women in a society that practiced a high level of sexual segregation (aboriginal Australia), I should not be surprised if my mentors did not approve of my work.

On the other hand, the only truly negative thing about being labeled a feminist scholar is the dismissive tone that label often carries, the way it is assumed that men and "normal" people would not be interested in what one has to say. Nevertheless, one also is part of a great movement for truth and justice. For those of us who were fortunate enough to take part in the very early phases of the second wave of feminism, in the 1960s and 1970s, there was an exhilarating feeling of momentous discovery. In those days, we really did change the landscape from what we had inherited and had been taught to believe as girls socialized in the 1950s in the United States. The paradigm shift effected by feminist scholarship in the 1970s is very straightforward and unarguably persuasive. Even though I did not exactly plan to devote much attention to matters of women and gender and, in many ways, was forced there by circumstances, still I can think of few things I could have done with my life and career that would have made more difference. Perhaps it is because feminism makes so much difference that so many people do resist its insights.

I have often argued that truly "getting" the feminist paradigm shift is like putting on a new pair of glasses crafted with a vastly improved prescription. *Everything* looks different—what we thought we knew about the culture or religion in general, what we thought we knew about men, and certainly what we knew, or more usually, did *not* know, about women. Whatever the subject matter may be, that generalization holds true. It is not as if one can deal with androcentrism in religious studies by working through the problems with scholarship on one particular religious situation or era, then move on to another subject matter and, having done one's homework, be home free. Virtually all subject matters, including some of the most abstract, will involve gendered data, and one will "see" different things, or "see" the same things differently, if one has internalized the subtle transformation of consciousness involved in the feminist paradigm shift. Whether one is working with situations as different as the scholarship on aboriginal Australian religions, issues in contemporary feminist theology, or the vast sweep of

Buddhist institutions, history, and philosophy, insights garnered from the experience of internalizing the feminist paradigm shift will change one's focus and angle of vision.

Regarding this garland of reflections, it could also be asked how one author could publish on topics as disparate as Hindu goddesses, female god-language in a Jewish context, aboriginal Australian religions, and many aspects of Buddhism. The answer is that they are all strung on a single thread—the difference it makes when one reflects in a feminist fashion. The beads on this garland are quite distinctive, even seemingly unrelated, but they are strung on a single thread—the transformation of consciousness effected by the feminist paradigm shift.

Sometimes people think that feminist scholarship would involve merely collecting and adding some data about women but that nothing else would change, as if one were filling in some blank corner in an otherwise complete painting. If that were the case, one could then return to the other parts of the painting and nothing would have changed, but they too look different now, and often various other elements of the canvas have been rearranged. Or, to switch analogies, it is often said that feminism is not about getting a piece of an already finished pie but discovering that one needs a wholly new recipe if one is to bake a successful pie at all. Both "pie" and "canvas" are very limited analogies, however. When one really gets the fact that women truly are human beings, to put the essence of feminism one way, or when one really gets the fact that any set of gender roles whatsoever is still a prison, no matter how "reformed" and "fair" it might be, to put the essence of feminism another way, conventional perspectives on virtually everything seem limited. One notices previously unnoticed androcentric innuendos everywhere, which can be very frustrating and painful. Or with enough confidence to bring them to light, things can be very amusing.

UNTANGLING THE THREADS: GENDER DOUBLESPEAK

Feminism has been defined in many ways by many people, and definitions of feminism are mutually incompatible. Like others who have written extensively on feminist issues for many years, I have my own definitions and understandings of feminism. Long ago, I learned that it is quite unwise to use the term *feminism* without first defining what I mean by it, which is why I included very succinct versions of the two definitions I have used for many years in the preceding paragraph. A formal discussion of the issues involved in what I have been calling the feminist paradigm shift will conclude this section of my introduction to this volume.

But I believe that several very tangled, confused, and confusing threads must be pulled apart before more formal definitions of feminism as the thesis that women are human beings, to quote one of my T-shirts, or the thesis that feminism is about life free from the prison of gender roles, can make sense. Always trying to reach further back into unraveling the mystery of sex and gender, I will be using Buddhist tools that were not available to me in my early writings on feminism and religion.

When Tibetan Vajrayana Buddhism deconstructs a person into elementary components, three strands—body, speech, and mind—are isolated. Much Vajrayana practice consists of transforming conventional or unenlightened body, speech, and mind into enlightened body, speech, and mind, that is to say, body, speech, and mind that manifest true human clarity and brilliance rather than a temporarily confused state. Gender norms depend entirely on body, but a person does not consist only of body; a person consists of body, speech, and mind. Thus, when gender norms are made fully determinative of one's destiny, speech and mind are ignored to give full dominance to body, as happened to me when it was expected that I would devote my life to maternity despite my preference for books over dolls. Such practices are much more thoroughgoing for women than for men. Men are expected to develop speech and mind as well as body, whereas conventional gender roles by and large define women only in terms of the potential of their bodies.

In this context, it is important to remember that for Buddhists, mind has several important meanings and is always said to be the "leader" of human activities, which means that for Buddhists mind, not body, is the primary determiner of what humans do with their lives. (This does not mean, illogically, that Buddhists have not also engaged in male-dominant institutional practices.) One meaning of *mind* in Buddhism is that mind is the sixth sense, a nonphysical sense, whose sense object is thoughts. This sixth sense and its sense objects are not equivalent to the brain. Thus, arguments about the determinative quality of hormones and differences between male and female brains are irrelevant. Those differences reside in the body, not in the mind. However, the more important meaning of *mind* in Buddhism is that mind refers to the nonconceptual awareness that sees clearly. For Buddhists, *mind* in this more important sense does not even reside in the head or the brain. It "resides," so to speak, in the heart, while body is identified with the head, and speech, quite logically, with the throat.

Therefore, paradoxically, I agree both with those who contend that gender is a rather superficial matter upon which so much energy need not be placed and with those who claim that gender is of momentous importance. The one position fuels my ambivalence about having needed to spend so much of my intellectual capital writing about sex, gender, and feminism. The other position led to all that writing and reflecting. Both positions are deeply grounded in my own experience.

On the one hand, probably nothing is so outwardly determinative of what a person is expected to be and the possibilities easily available to one as a person's biological sex. Biological sex is usually quite obvious, but the way in which sex limits human beings happens mainly because of culturally and religiously specific gender norms, dependent on speech and mind, that are built upon biological sex, not because of biological sex itself. Those gender norms impose themselves insidiously and unconsciously upon oneself, despite the fact that, at least in my experience, nothing *felt* more irrelevant to my vision of who I was and wanted to become than the gender expectations built on top of biological sex. I was interested in books, not dolls, so why was it expected that I would want to devote my life to maternity rather than intellectual and spiritual pursuits? (One might object that these are not mutually exclusive alternatives, but in the 1950s world in which I was socialized, they were presented as if they were. Furthermore, girls were not even allowed to choose between these alternatives. I was always primed for biological motherhood, and nonreproductive futures were denigrated and pitied.)

How can biological sex be both utterly determinative and utterly irrelevant? Granted, bodies are at least somewhat different. Female bodies can do things that male bodies cannot do, though I think there is less that only male bodies can do. But speech and mind can only be forced into "female" or "male" patterns by enculturation. They have no natural male or female manifestation or style, though it is often asserted that they do. In fact, most gender role socialization is accomplished by enforcing culturally defined patterns of speech and mind onto boys and girls. Simple body consciousness, by itself, does not seem to be strong enough to create strict or strong gender roles. This makes sense because so much of being human is involved with speech and mind, not body alone.

Even body is quite fluid. Male and female bodies share so much that it is now possible to turn male bodies into bodies that appear to be female and vice versa. Even without modern surgery, such sleight of body is possible, as many skilled cross-dressers can demonstrate.

The phenomenon of transgendered people, people who are sure they were born with a body of the wrong sex, further illustrates the fluidity even of body. This phenomenon should not be confused with people like me, who are physically comfortable with the sex with which they were born, but really have no affinity for or identification with the culture-specific gender roles built on top of that sex. This nonconformity is simply another demonstration of the fluidity of body. Though in my earlier years, I was often castigated and punished for my refusal to conform to predetermined gender roles and therapy for my lack of fit with prescribed gender roles was recommended, obviously I do not think that disagreement with conventional gender roles is a malady that needs to be cured.

Interestingly, Tibetan Vajrayana Buddhism expresses the fluidity of body in another way. As is well known, Vajrayana Buddhism is an exceedingly visual tradition, and visual representations of "enlightened body" are quite common. The *yidam*s, or "meditation deities," of Vajrayana Buddhism are such representations.[2] In some cases, the sex of these "deities" is quite obvious, but in other cases there are few, if any, masculine or feminine body markers. (The same is true for Hindu deities. I used to take great delight in holding up pictures of Hindu deities and asking my students what sex they were. With certain representations, I could trick the students almost 100 percent of the time.) Body is quite fluid. Recognition of the fluidity of body comes through in another way in Vajrayana Buddhism. There is no correlation at all between the sex of the meditator and the sex of the deity being meditated upon in the very common meditation practice of "self-visualization," in which the meditator visualizes him- or herself *as* the deity in question. Thus men routinely visualize themselves as female *yidam*s and vice versa.

Although people usually have clear knowledge of and bodily identification with their biological sex, the gender norms built on that biological sex can so easily seem so irrelevant because of the leading roles played by speech and mind in the experience of being human. When analyzing conduct, Buddhists always attribute the leading role to "mind" and recommend "mind training" to facilitate conduct more likely to result in contentment rather than misfortune. Furthermore, Buddhists have always claimed that mind is beyond gender. Buddhists also do not distinguish "male" speech from "female" speech, though some of the cultures in which Buddhism has become important do differentiate male and female speech. While body can be somewhat limiting and gender-specific, speech and mind are not. There are certain things that male bodies cannot do, and to a lesser extent, vice versa, but there is nothing that male speech and mind can do that female speech and mind cannot do, though socialization into gender roles can stunt the speech and mind capabilities of both men and women.

People easily identify primarily with speech and mind as the leading factors in human existence and thus easily envision themselves living out the speech and mind ideals of their culture and religion, only to become extremely frustrated when someone tells them that their body prohibits such a vision. This process can affect a boy who likes cooking as much as it affects a girl who likes woodworking, to use the stereotypical gender norms of my generation. Nor do I believe that such visions of unbounded speech and mind are limited to societies affected by European enlightenment proclamations of equality and individual choice. Buddhist literature is full of stories of girls who wanted to be yogis and monks, despite these usually being considered male roles. An underground stream of female resentment of male monopolies on privileged speech and mind disciplines is evident in most male-dominated societies.

If the situation outlined above were openly acknowledged, things could be relatively straightforward. Body does involve some limitations, but body is also most specifically involved in physiological reproduction. Thus, there is little reason for bodies not involved in physiological reproduction to be bound by any gender norms whatsoever. (The tendency of most cultures and religions to force bodies to reproduce is another matter that can only be addressed separately.) Speech and mind are unbounded, and therefore, gender norms are utterly irrelevant where they are concerned. But, obviously, such is not the situation for most people. Their speech and mind are utterly constrained by conventions dependent on their bodies, even though no sensible reason for doing so can be deduced. Most people, intuitively recognizing the unfettered nature of their speech and mind, do not completely conform to "appropriate" gender norms.

If it were widely recognized and admitted that speech and mind are irrationally constrained by gender norms simply because bodies are visibly different from one another, people might be able to negotiate successfully through the morass of gender expectations and know what applied to them and what did not. The real problem is a massive conspiracy of denial surrounding everything I have tried to clarify in the above paragraphs. It is the denial, rather than the straightforward situation outlined above, that led me to spend my life trying to unravel the mysteries of sex and gender, despite the fact that I am really interested in other issues that have little to do with sex and gender per se. (However, they do have to do with sex and gender because of unstated and unacknowledged assumptions about the artificial limits imposed by physiological sex.) It is also this denial about how sex and gender actually work that fatally confuses so many people on so many levels, thus making explicit commentary on sex and gender completely necessary.

This complex of denial is grounded in the doublespeak involved in telling people, implicitly more than explicitly, both that gender does not constrain them and that it does. For example, in my generation, girls were given the same education as boys, but expected not to do the same things with that education. I was socialized in an era when we were routinely told that the purpose of college education for women was to obtain an "Mrs." degree. We were taught that we could do anything we wanted to and anything that men could do, but we were then ridiculed if we actually aspired to follow our dreams if that dream happened to involve something usually done by men. We were taught equality, but punished if we expected equality. We were expected "naturally" to drop out of a track involved with education and a career fairly early in our lives to devote ourselves to taking care of men and children. Even if we did develop ways of supporting ourselves economically, it was supposed to be in a field that would easily allow us to drop out temporally or to move, so that we could meet the needs of men and children. We could have jobs, but not careers. Careers were too disruptive to men and children.

This doublespeak works because the messages that gender is irrelevant are explicit while the constraints imposed by gender are largely unconscious, maintained by a conspiracy of silence that is very powerful. Most people obeyed these unconscious injunctions without ever understanding them or being able to make a conscious decision about them. In some ways, societies in which girls and boys are socialized into very different tracks from infancy are more honest and less conspiratorial, even though Western feminists usually decry such practices.

People like me, who developed some awareness that there were constraining gender norms and railed against them, were told that we were mistaken, that gender norms did not exist, but we were also punished for not conforming to them. If we complained about the limitations imposed by the prison of gender roles, we were told that the playing field was level, but we were also told that these supposedly nonconstraining gender norms were "just the way things are." People became very exasperated with us if we questioned why girls could not become pastors or professors, for example, telling us that "men and women are different." We were told that there was something wrong with us for even thinking about such things and also something wrong with us for suggesting that we were being discriminated against in any way. Talk about doublespeak! Those socializing and training us were not even vaguely aware of the self-contradictory messages they were sending us, but we who had some awareness of what was being imposed upon us were reprimanded for having that awareness. The most effective tools of social control are those that are not even known to their perpetrators, which is why developing awareness is so critical.

"Men and women are different" is the slogan that was most often flung at me when I protested about all the gender norms constraining me, despite the proclamation that men and women were equal. But if it is so obvious that men and women are different, how can women so easily want to do things associated with the male gender role and vice versa? The slogan that men and women are different hides several important facts that intensify the doublespeak and denial surrounding gender.

As I have already indicated, men and women have bodies that are somewhat different, but human beings are also constituted by speech and mind, not only body, using a Buddhist analysis that holds much more widely, in my view. As I have already pointed out, speech and mind do not have any natural gender, only culturally imposed gender norms. If we are honest, I think it is rather obvious that in most cases gender roles function to make sure that reproduction happens and that women do most of the uninteresting, tedious, and repetitive labor that physiological reproduction demands from human beings. (I am not saying that *all* the labor involved in reproduction is uninteresting, tedious, and repetitious, only that conventional gender roles constrain women to do most of the labor that is uninteresting, tedious, and repetitious.)

Girls were not educated in many conventional societies, not because they have minds that cannot learn but so that their bodies can be available for reproduction. Women are excused from many religious and spiritual tasks, or even prohibited from participating in them, not because they have no interest in religion or spirituality, but because women's participation in these activities might make them less available for housework and child care, thus inconveniencing men who are pursuing religious and spiritual disciplines by demanding more involvement in housework and child care from men. (In some religious situations, this rationale for "excusing" women from religious and spiritual disciplines is openly stated.) But given even the slightest opening or opportunity, girls can become fascinated by the speech and mind disciplines that have characterized human culture for so long. Nothing is so heartbreaking or frustrating as to be told that, because one has a female body, those speech and mind disciplines are not going to be the major focus of one's life, especially if one has great aptitude for and fascination with those disciplines. I remember, with some pain even today, wondering why I had a high IQ and a great love of learning if I was not going to be allowed to use them because of my female body. It seemed like a cruel trick for a girl to be intelligent and curious, given conventional gender roles.

But it has to be that way, I was told. Men and women are different, even though they are equal and girls can go to school. Even today, not only in popular culture but in scholarly circles, male-female differences are asserted and debated. But I have always wondered, if these differences are so real and palpable, why don't I want what women are asserted to want? The last time I checked, I had a female body, but most of the things that are supposed to interest women do not interest me even though I have never been dissatisfied with my sex, but only with the gender role assigned to that sex, and am not lesbian. Thus, my sexual identity and orientation are clear and simple, even conventional, but that does not translate at all into a conventional gender identity.

To me, the question of whether women and men are the same or different makes as much sense as the question of whether women and women are the same or different. Is there something essential about being a woman? Is there a woman's nature? That would be tantamount to asserting that not only is there a female body, but also female speech and mind that are inherent, unalterable, not based on culture, and identical in all women but found in no men. Such an assertion seems absurd to me. I have never been able to understand an essentialist feminist position which claims that women are morally superior to men, inherently less violent, or more oriented to relationships. Those may be cogent generalizations, but the problem with even accurate generalizations is that they confine individuals in the prison of gender roles if they are taken very seriously. It is very easy for generalizations to skip from being reasonably accurate observations to becoming normative demands. "Most women want to have children; therefore, that must be what you want, and your life is going to be organized by that generalization, no matter what your own vision for your life may be." It is unbelievable how much of my life energy went into struggling against such gender essentialism.

It doesn't matter whether essentialist assumptions praise or blame any specific group. Negative generalizations about women are not cured by positing and promoting positive generalizations. Some women are as different from other women as any man and woman could be from each other. The true violence is forcing individual women or men to conform to essentialist gender norms, not making generalizations that may praise or blame any specific group of people. Maybe most women do want to have children, or are less violent than most men, or more oriented to relationships than most men. What does that say about me? Or about a man who is very interested in children and relationships, and not at all violent?

Because there is no real correlation between sex and gender, but only a forced, conventional correlation, I have great sympathy with two common contentions. Many have criticized the expectation of some Western feminists that women should identify first and foremost as (oppressed) women, and only secondarily with their culture or religion. Western feminists, very aware of the constraining and oppressive effects of gender expectations and very aware of how pervasive gender norms are in most traditional religions and cultures, expect that women everywhere would be outraged by male dominance and are puzzled that women often feel loyalty to the cultures and religions that seemingly oppress them. What has been forgotten is that gender norms have power mainly because for most people they operate unconsciously and seem "natural" rather than constructed. Thus, though gender may be the most dominant factor in people's lives, as observed by Western scholars, women easily identify more consciously with other aspects of their lives. To me, it seems quite reasonable that being Muslim or Buddhist, Asian or Middle Eastern, would seem to be more definitive to many people than being a woman or a man. Identity is complex and multifaceted. Even for me, having spent so much of my life thinking about the absurdities and constraints imposed by gender norms, being a Buddhist, being a scholar, and being immersed in issues having to do with religious diversity are at least as important as being a feminist woman. Only circumstances and necessity, not a primary identity as a woman or a feminist, forced me to think so much about sex and gender.

Paradoxically, I am also very sympathetic to a claim that is usually evaluated as antifeminist. Gender is actually irrelevant to anything important and does not deserve or need all the attention given to it in feminist circles. I would give almost anything just to forget the whole thing and live in a world unconstrained by gender norms, a world free of the prison of gender roles. But that is not possible in a world ruled by gender norms of which most people are unaware and oppressive gender constructions that people take to be "natural." So, in a way, I've been forced to spend my life on something that is irrelevant—gender! Why did I do it? Because of the denial surrounding gender. Everything is determined by gender, but there is total denial of that fact. That denial results in hostility to those who raise the issues. We are called dangerous troublemakers, and gender issues are declared irrelevant. It would be so simple for gender to be truly irrelevant, rather than being denied and ignored. But until gender is truly irrelevant, those of us who are aware of its imprisoning effects will have to continue to raise awareness about the suffering caused by the prison of gender roles.

SOLUTIONS TO THE GENDER WARS

Throughout the many years spent thinking about sex, gender, and religion, I have come to two main conclusions about how gender issues could be dealt with more cogently and with less pain. One of them applies more to my life as a scholar and dominated the earlier phases of my work as a feminist scholar. The second applies more to my work as a (Buddhist) critical and constructive thinker. The one is more concerned with how to do good scholarship, and the other has more to do with social and religious issues. The first gives us tools to deal with the glaring presence—though often overlooked—of gender norms, and the second deals with the fundamental irrelevance of gender, despite how much has been made of it. These two suggestions have dominated my methodological work for many years and are featured prominently in two of my major books, *Buddhism after Patriarchy* and *Feminism and Religion: An Introduction.* I have long referred to them as "feminism as academic method," better known as "women studies" in my view, and "feminism as social vision." These solutions are so breathtakingly simple that it is hard for me to imagine why there would be resistance to them, or why they would seem complicated. Some of the articles in which I developed these methodological arguments appear in section 2 of this volume, "Five Essays on Method."

As I have long argued, feminism both as academic method and as social vision, depends on seeing with blinding clarity that women are human beings, the slogan emblazoned on the T-shirt I referred to earlier: "Feminism is the radical proposition that women are human beings." Very early on, probably in 1971, I came up with this slogan as a response to exasperated and frustrated questioners who wanted to know what younger women were so upset about. They claimed to be happy under current gender roles and were very confused about the emerging second wave of feminism. The slogan may seem simpleminded and obvious. Of course women are human beings! But, as I often used to claim, if Martian scholars were to search our libraries, at least our libraries as they existed in the 1960s and 1970s, for materials about women's religious lives, they might well wonder whether the human species even included females because there was so little evidence of them in the literature. What literature did exist more easily supported the view that women were adjuncts and helpers (the biblical "helpmeet") to the real humans, but were not truly human beings in their own right. In most parts of the world even today, radical changes would be required if women were to be able to live up to the norm for human beings.

Feminism as Academic Method:
A Paradigm Shift in Models of Humanity

Opposition simply to *studying* women's lives, roles, and thinking is one of the most curious things to me in all the controversy surrounding feminism. Studying women's lives is, after all, very different from advocating for change in gender roles or elevating women's status. But in the late 1960s, when studies focusing specifically on women's religious lives began to emerge, established scholars were very threatened. They did not appreciate our contention that existing scholarship was inadequate and incomplete because it had neglected to study women's religious lives. But settling this issue should have been more a matter of simple observation than of argument. It is simply a fact that the existing literature in religious studies when I entered the field did not contain much information about what women had ever done or thought. They entered the pages of the books only when what they did or thought was of interest to men, and the rest of their lives, which in many cases encompassed most of their time and energy, was simply terra incognita, like spaces left blank on old maps simply because no one had ever thought to go there or had been able to get there.

   Thinking about why those spaces had been left blank and unexplored proved challenging when we took the search to more abstract and foundational levels. Why indeed? Usually I was told that women simply did not have roles in religion, so there couldn't be any data, and that lack of data was not due to inadequate scholarship. But that answer was absurd. Given the pervasiveness of gender roles and the extent to which men and women lead separate lives in many traditional societies, of course male scholars studying men were not going to report much about *women's* religious lives except for their occasional appearances in support roles. But what did women do and think during all that time when they were *not* supporting men and thus did not appear in descriptions of (men's) religions? If women truly were regarded as human beings rather than only as adjuncts to men, objects interesting to men, they would have been researched in their own right.

But obviously women had not been regarded as truly human, and this shattering discovery led to the call for a paradigm shift in models of humanity guiding research from androcentric models to inclusive models of humanity. Clearly, this was a major challenge to established methodologies and was sharply contested. When I made my first arguments about the need for this shift as a doctoral student in 1968, I was told in no uncertain terms that, as an intelligent person, I should understand that "the generic masculine covered and included the feminine, thereby making it unnecessary to focus specifically on the feminine." (That is nearly an exact quote from one of my mentors. His contention was traumatic to me and seared itself into my memory.) Of course, it is now widely conceded that the subject for Western scholarship until recently *was* males of an elite economic, racial, and cultural group, not people in general. People often credit poststructuralists and postcolonialists for making that attitude adjustment, but some feminists certainly made such claims very early. (Is this another example of the frequent phenomenon that an idea first put forward by a woman is not taken seriously until a man restates that same idea?)

Feminism as Social Vision:
Freedom from the Prison of Gender Roles

In my later work, a definition of the feminist goal as freedom from the prison of gender roles became more dominant. Though I cannot remember exactly when and how this definition took on so much importance to me, I believe that its emergence in my thinking had something to do with my increasing immersion in Buddhism, and I know that by the mid- to late 1980s this definition of feminism had become central to me. Often, I combined it with the claim that most of the unnecessary suffering in human life was due to the prison of gender roles.

One great virtue of this definition of feminism is that it gives up on the attempt to define what women's roles and status vis-à-vis men should be. It recognizes that when we try to prescribe norms and a way of life that should work for all men or all women, no matter how fair or just those standards may be, for some they will not fit well and will be a prison. The basic question is not whether men and women are similar or different, but whether all women are the same, whether any essential nature or traits can be ascribed to all women. I answer that question with a resounding "no," both on Buddhist grounds and on the basis of my own experience. I appreciate Buddhist thought so much for its thoroughgoing, completely deconstructive turn, something which it obviously discovered millennia before the Western version. I appreciate Buddhism for its unwillingness to put positive language on the deepest insights, for its reliance on silence and space where truth is concerned, for its trust in open-ended fluid states of mind, for its claim that the wiser we become, the less we need prescriptions and the less dogmatic we become. If only that open unboundedness were more prevalent in our discussions of social mores! Then there would be no need to try to devise a life plan that was appropriate for everyone. People who do not easily fit the usual gender norms and sexual orientations of their society could simply live lives more appropriate for them without so much struggle, strife, and suffering.

When I emphasize the suffering caused by the prison of gender roles, I am not only talking of suffering that results from manifestly unjust gender roles, such as those that privilege men or heterosexuals over women or homosexuals. I am not only talking about gender roles that prohibit girls from being educated or that force boys to become warriors. Very clearly, I am also not talking about the prison of gender roles as something that impacts only women and girls. Though men often seem to think that gender does not apply to them because they are just normal human beings, that whenever gender is being discussed, someone else is being talked about, men are imprisoned by gender roles as surely as women. It is only that they are usually much less aware of the prison and more resistant to recognizing that they are being held hostage to myriad expectations about how they should behave and feel.

What I am primarily talking about as the suffering involved in living in a prison of gender roles is the *lack of fit*, the fact that gender roles prescribe some abstract, impossible norm. Even people who have no major issues with their gender role struggle to embody it well enough to their critical eyes and to the critical eyes of their family and friends.

What about those of us who were called in different directions? Without that straitjacket of gender roles, people could simply have said to me, "So you don't want to have children; you want to read books and think. Go, and good luck!" Why did I have to be berated for not wanting to have children, to be told over and over that I was selfish, that girls shouldn't be so bookish because it was unattractive to men, and that I wouldn't be able to make a living reading books anyway? What about boys drawn primarily to art and music, or to child care and early childhood education? What possible benefit do gender roles provide? Wouldn't life be so much simpler and more pleasant if we simply did not attach expectations, assumptions, and projections to people based only on their bodies while totally ignoring their speech and minds?

There could be so much less defensiveness and struggle. For example, because the female gender role I was expected to assume is so distasteful to me, but the prison of gender roles is so strong, I have been forced to criticize the traditional female gender role to show why it's not what I want to do with my life. But then women who are more comfortable with that lifestyle feel threatened, when all I am doing is explaining why it feels so wrong for me and defending the dignity and compassionateness of my own values and choices. Why ever do we think there could be or should be a one-size-fits-all norm for all women and another for all men? Why assume that all girls like pink and all boys like blue? (Personally, I despise pink and like blue, but liking blue does not mean that I'd prefer to have a male body. It only means that I have a vision and a dream that does not involve conventional domesticity and child rearing.) Why should we continue to attempt to fine-tune a sex and gender system, trying to make it more fair, just, and equal? We just don't need those kinds of norms to function well as human beings. They have never helped us become better human beings and have only caused misery and confusion.

One may well wonder why gender roles are so persistent if they are so dysfunctional and hurt so much more than they help. One could provide answers from disciplines like sociology, anthropology, and psychology, and those explanations have some cogency. However, for me as a Buddhist, the rock bottom answer has to do with how Buddhist psychology explains the formation and maintenance of conventional ego. Buddhism has invested a great deal of intellectual and spiritual energy investigating how and why we suffer so much. The answer is that over a very long period of time, lifetimes even, we have misidentified who we are and have become intensely attached to that mistaken identity. Put very briefly, we mistakenly think we are somebody or something, an enduring, permanent, independent entity, whereas close deconstructive analysis clearly demonstrates that our lives are open-ended, interdependent fluidity. But to a well-established ego (in the Buddhist sense of ego), that's bad news, and it is resisted fiercely. What better place to anchor our desire to be an entity, to be somebody, than in a sexed body that is clearly distinctive and usually stays the same sex for an entire lifetime? Fastening a whole repertoire of gender roles onto that sexed body makes the self associated with it seem even more real and enduring. Buddhist analysis has shown that conventional mind often prefers a familiar situation that involves suffering to a more open-ended, free, and spacious, but unfamiliar, situation. The prison of gender roles is familiar; freedom from the prison of gender roles is formless and therefore much less tangible. Gender roles function very well to help a constructed ego feel that it is real.

The tragedy here is that though Buddhists have all the analytical tools needed to deconstruct conventional ego, including its gendered dimensions, traditional Buddhism has put all its energy into deconstructing ego while leaving gender largely intact. Most Buddhists know some of the arguments refuting the existence of a real, permanent self, but they never apply those same arguments to the gender associated with that self. It is very common for Buddhists to try to understand what it is like to defuse the delusion of being a permanent, abiding, independent entity, but those same Buddhists seem to assume they will still be gendered, even when they are no longer attached to an imaginary self. Instead, they tend to claim that they know that gender is *ultimately* irrelevant and the mind has no gender. Somehow, they make the illogical leap that, if they know that gender is ultimately irrelevant, then the *gender roles* so visible in Buddhist institutional life don't matter and don't need to be critiqued. Talk about doublespeak! Though Buddhism has the best tools I know of to deconstruct and dismantle attachment to gender roles, to demonstrate their dysfunctionality, and to demonstrate how they cause suffering, Buddhists have yet to apply those tools to their own literature and institutions in any consistent and thoroughgoing fashion. That is why there are such extensive Buddhist jewels on this *Garland of Feminist Reflections*.

HOW THIS GARLAND IS STRUNG

A garland is a string of jewels or flowers strung on a single thread and usually placed around one's neck, or the neck of an honored person or a deity. Garlands are highly valued and widely used in many Asian religions.

Given my long-term involvement with Buddhism, this analogy seems appropriate for the title of this collection of articles and essays, all strung on the thread of the feminist paradigm shift and the difference it has made regarding every topic I have ever studied.[3]

This garland is selected from among the one hundred fifty articles and essays I have written over the past thirty-plus years. Research that wound up in several of the earlier articles was actually begun in 1967, more than forty years ago. This garland also includes several very recently composed articles and essays. Thus, it literally encloses my entire lifework and includes examples from each of the diverse topics I have written about over the years. These topics are so diverse and different that it is unlikely that even people who have followed my work would be aware of all these articles and essays. Hence the analogy of a "garland" of feminist reflections. Each article, each bead on this garland, is quite distinctive, and like the flowers or jewels on some garlands, they look quite different. Yet they do constitute a single garland strung together on one thread. The subtle but profound shift of consciousness that results from the feminist paradigm shift is the thread that hangs these diverse subject materials together.

This sampling of my work is organized by topic, not chronologically. I have written on four major topics throughout my career—methodology and the feminist paradigm shift, applications of the feminist paradigm shift to various religious situations, feminist theology, and Buddhism, especially in relation to contemporary social issues, including gender. I have written about five religions or religious situations—Aboriginal Australia, Judaism, prepatriarchal religions in the ancient world, Hinduism, and Buddhism, though I have written far more about Buddhism than about any other religion. (I have also written some about Christianity and Islam in my survey *Feminism and Religion: An Introduction*.) Though this book is not arranged chronologically, each section is, and each begins with my earliest work on that topic. The chapters that begin each part were written in a very brief period of time, between 1975 and 1980.

Regarding each topic, I have selected what now seem to me to be the most pertinent essays, but I have also selected for variety, to show the wide range of topics I have written about. Because I have written so much on Buddhism, I had to be much more selective regarding that subject. I have not included any of my more general survey articles on gender and Buddhism except for the most recent ("Is the Glass Half-Empty or Half-Full? A Feminist Assessment of Buddhism at the

Beginning of the Twenty-first Century"). Instead, most of the articles in the section on Buddhism focus on what I have come to regard as the most important gender issue for Buddhists, the presence or absence of women teachers.

Except for correcting typographical errors and minor editing for clarification, with one exception, the articles and essays in this volume have not been revised. Revisions at this time would not be appropriate. The point is to present important examples of writing on these major topics, not to update articles that might be outdated by now in some ways. Cutting-edge articles cannot be expected to be timelessly accurate. The newness of their reflections and conclusion is sufficient and is why people continue to read "old" theory, even after new developments have occurred.

This garland of reflections begins with my earliest significant publication, "Androcentrism and Androgyny in the Methodology of History of Religions," written in 1975, and concludes with my most recent writings on gender and Buddhism. It has been an interesting and exciting ride through these thirty-plus years. People sometimes wonder when I'm really going to retire and spend more time in retreat. But I still have plans. Next? I already have an outline and two chapters of a book on a Buddhist approach to religious diversity, to be titled *Others, Identity, and Integrity: Surviving Religious Diversity.* If I live long enough, I have plans for another book on Buddhism and gender, to be titled *The Dharma of Gender,* and possibly even a history of Buddhism for Buddhist practitioners, if I get enough encouragement. Some of my Buddhist teachers want to me write a book on Buddhist teachings about the long-term usefulness of obstacles to mature spiritual development. This is certainly a subject I have a great deal of personal experience with, but I am not yet fully committed to that project.

CHAPTER I

How Did This Ever Happen to Me?

A Wisconsin Farm Girl Who Became a Buddhist
Theologian When She Grew Up

Given current conditions of backlash, I have sometimes commented that it is important for those of us who are old enough to remember why the second wave of feminism ever emerged to record our memories. Most people are astonished at how dismal things were only a few years ago, in the 1960s in the United States, when women could not establish credit in their own names and almost no women went into advanced training in any field.

Feminist reflections have always included the personal location of one's work as a matter of honesty. Claiming that one feels something to be true does not make it so, but it is also the case that no one does the work they end up doing or comes to the conclusions that they derive completely abstractly either. Personal experience is a factor in everyone's scholarly and theological work, period. "Objectivity" is better served by declaring one's perspectives as honestly and completely as one can, not by pretending that one has no standpoint. I am utterly clear that, for better or for worse, I would not have done the work I did, had I not been a woman who entered a male-dominated field, religious studies, in the 1960s. How I got to be one of the very few women who entered that field at that time is more of a mystery, as is how that woman ended up being a Buddhist theologian. Very few other women who entered the field at that time ended up as Buddhist theologians.

EARLY LIFE

I have written autobiographies before and have always included autobio-
graphical elements in my work when relevant, as I did in the introduction
to this volume.[1] There is always a principle of selectivity that goes into
writing a sketch of one's personal life. In this case, the principle is to try
to illuminate aspects of personal experience that may have led to my
doing the work that is collected here. However, when I reflect on my life,
it remains mysterious to me how I could ever have ended up as a leading
Buddhist feminist critical and constructive thinker, given where I started
out. Sometimes it seems to me that Indian notions of karma inherited
from previous lives work as well as any other hypothesis to explain how
one takes on certain elements of one's work and life. How else to explain
an immediate affinity for things Indian and Tibetan, even very early in my
life in northern Wisconsin, where those places were virtually unknown?
When I was about eight or nine, my parents went to visit friends in a
nearby town. I was supposed to play with their child, but I found some
cast-off books in the toy bin. Always hungry for books and never being
able to find ones I hadn't already read, I ignored my playmate, focusing
instead on the books. Among them was a half-intact geography book
which included a chapter on Tibet—certainly rare for an already cast off
book in northern Wisconsin in the 1950s. From reading this book, I
learned that Tibetans were dirty people who rarely bathed, but this supposed lack of cleanliness was explained by lack of water. I became indig-
nant saying, "That's not true. We're not dirty." I also remember somehow
understanding from AM radio news in 1959 that the Dalai Lama had fled
Tibet. Why did I search out books about India for high school book
reports in the 1950s, well before the countercultural Indian craze?

I suppose Western social science would say that as an alienated and
lonely, socially inept teenager, I was compensating for my social misery
by imaginatively identifying with places my peers would likely not ven-
ture. But sometimes it seems just as likely that karmic memories were
inserting themselves, given how many socially maladjusted teenagers
there are and how few of them gravitate to India or Tibet as a result, or
at least how few did in the 1950s in northern Wisconsin. Today, I still
live in Wisconsin, one hundred and fifty miles from where I was born
and grew up. It may seem that I have not moved very far, but internally
that is not the case.

I grew up in rural poverty, milking cows on a very marginal dairy
farm. Indoor plumbing, central heating, telephone, and television were

unknown luxuries. Nevertheless, that farm was imaginably beautiful and rich. I would not trade that rural childhood deeply immersed in nature for anything, despite its other travails. I have written about it elsewhere. The cultural environment was less rich. Neither of my parents went to high school, and education was not valued at all in my home. In another context, I have told the stories of how difficult it was for me to obtain books to read as a child.[2] In the 1940s and 1950s, northern Wisconsin was remote, culturally impoverished, and monolithic. I never saw a black person until I went to college in Milwaukee. As a child, I never left northern Wisconsin. My world literally consisted of an area of about fifty miles in any direction from the farm.

Religiously, that childhood consisted of indoctrination into an extremely rigid and literalist form of Lutheranism. I was taught that God put dinosaur bones into rocks to deceive later unbelieving scientists, who would reject the Bible and go to hell as a result. I was taught to laugh at and scorn all other religious beliefs and worldviews. The indoctrination was thoroughgoing, and I have reacted very negatively to it throughout my adult life. It was also intense enough that I later managed to pass several comprehensive exams at the University of Chicago mainly on what I had learned in that Lutheran day school. I also developed an intense appreciation for symbolism from being taught the meaning of tiles on the church ceiling, and an equally intense appreciation of sacred music from endless hours of singing in various choirs.

I suppose it is important to relate that in that rural environment I grew up very alone, as an only child whose overprotective mother would not allow me to have a bicycle or play with nearby children because she was afraid I might get hurt. In the redneck culture of northern Wisconsin in the 1950s, intelligence, especially in economically impoverished, not especially attractive girls, was more likely to result in social shunning than in friendliness or admiration. The combination of forced isolation and precociousness made for a miserable childhood and enduring social awkwardness which persists to this day, in some ways. I really had no friends except for my animals, who were very dear to me, but I had plenty of time and the incentive to speculate deeply. Very early on, I developed the habit of constant introspection, reflection, and imagination.

The loneliness of my early life was made up for in part by the joy I took in being out of doors much of the time, working hard with farm machinery and animals. Farmwork is physically demanding, and because there was only one man around, my father, my mother and I did a great deal of heavy work that women usually did not do in the 1950s. I suppose that experience had something to do with the disregard for gender roles that I developed early. I also never liked to play with dolls, preferring real and toy animals instead, and I always knew I did not want to have children even while I knew I would always have animals. Only during my four years of college and the first year of graduate school did I lack animal companionship. As soon as it was possible for me to have a cat of my own, I got one and am now surrounded by some rather wonderful and devoted felines.

Quite early on, my introspectiveness led me to resent what being female seemed to mean. So many times as a teenager wandering about in my wilderness, I exclaimed in misery to myself, "Why did I have to be a girl? Girls don't get to do anything interesting!" In the culture of the 1950s, that was an accurate observation. Females, at least as I was taught, had only one purpose in life: to get married and have children. My frustration with my expected role was not due to lack of experience with tasks defined as "female." Very early on, when I was about thirteen, I had to take over most of the housework because my mother was too immersed in the farmwork she preferred and thought more essential. I learned to sew very early, made all my own clothes for years, always cooked, and did all the other housework. I came to feel that I didn't want to look forward to a future as a housewife; I had done that already, and it was not enough to provide an interesting life.

I had also been taught male dominance and female inferiority by my religious teachers. Somehow, though, very early in my life, I had an experience that I think demonstrates that young children can be very good observers. My parents had hung a small framed picture of two children crossing a dangerous ravine on a rickety bridge, with an angel hovering in the background, protecting them. (This is quite a popular Protestant picture which one sometimes finds done up as garish velvet wall hangings. This was a small, tastefully framed picture.) One day I thought to myself, "Hum, God is male and so is Jesus. I wonder what that means about me, because I'm a girl." Then I looked at the picture and said, "But the angels are women! I guess that means I'm okay." That experience was strong enough that years later in confirmation class, when I was about twelve, I used that insight to object to what I was being taught about proper gender roles. "Christian women should be married if possible—not that single women can't do good work in the church, but it is better to be married. Women must submit to their husbands because men are superior to women. We know that because God is male and

Jesus was a man." I put up my hand. "But the angels are women," I said. The reply: "No, that's not correct. Artists don't paint angels correctly, so they look like women, but actually all the angels are men too."

I am very grateful that somehow, from some unknown source, one day I came up with the insight, "There's nothing wrong with me! There's nothing wrong with being a girl! It's the system! It's the system!" From then on I hated the system, but that was healthier than hating myself. However, it is very easy to remember how painful it was to grow up with such a self-image and with such religious doctrines, which helps explain my lifelong passion for finding freedom from the prison of gender roles and for helping others find that freedom. It probably also helps explain why my mature reflections on gender led me to conclude that the problem is the very existence of gender roles, rather than the inadequacy of any specific set of gender roles. (Incidentally, some years ago, in an antique store, I found a large version of the angel picture from my childhood. It now hangs in a hidden corner of my house.)

Other things were not going well in my religious indoctrination either. My habit of inquiry was strengthened by the fact that I became a philosophy major in college, with a passion for philosophy of religion and other ways of exploring religion. I had always been quite drawn to practical religious experience, and so my explorations were not completely theoretical. I became a member of the best Lutheran choir in Milwaukee, where I did my undergraduate degree, even though the church belonged to a forbidden, heretical version of Lutheranism, at least according to the very conservative church in which I had been brought up. (Lest one think that this church had been chosen by my parents for its doctrinal positions, let me make clear that was not the case. The church in which I grew up was the "German" Lutheran church in town. When I was a child in Rhinelander, there were three Lutheran churches within three blocks of each other—the German Lutheran church, the Norwegian Lutheran church, and the Swedish Lutheran church. Each belonged to a different Lutheran organization, but their ethnic identities, rather than any theological claims, were their primary markers. The German Lutheran church also happened to be extremely conservative, a member of what is still one of the most conservative religious organizations in North America—the Wisconsin Synod of the Lutheran church.)

To make matters worse as far as my religious indoctrination was going, I also began to attend the Reform Jewish synagogue across the street from the university. This was a rather radical move, given what I had been taught to believe about Jews, but I was exploring other religious options as well. I wasn't necessarily shopping; I was just exploring. Some years earlier, things had already come to quite a painful point. Disobeying orders, I had played the piano at my high school's baccalaureate service when I graduated from high school. We had always been taught that we should never engage in any interfaith activities (which included girl and boy scout programs) because we had been commanded not to be "unequally yoked together with unbelievers," which meant anybody who did not completely share the "one true faith" held only by Wisconsin Synod Lutherans. When I was hauled in to be reprimanded, I asked if it was not the case that everyone was striving for the same thing that we were striving for, using different language. I was told in no uncertain terms that my idea was wrong and that everyone else worshipped idols, false gods.

To make a long story short, at least for this context, soon after my mother died and while a senior in college, I was excommunicated for heresy at the advanced age of twenty-one. I had not yet done any of things I later did, which would definitely have severed my connection with the church of my youth. I was exploring, but because I was exploring I also refused to close my mind to what I was exploring and refused to affirm what I was told to affirm by an extremely authoritarian pastor. At that time, I wasn't denying any of those contentions; I was simply refusing to affirm them. The similarity to the positions I hold today, essentially Buddhist positions, is striking and uncanny. In any case, because of my refusal to agree with this pastor, I soon received a letter informing that I had "sold my soul for a mess of academic pottage" (a reference to the biblical story of Jacob and Esau) and that unless I "repented and apologized," I would face a very hot residence in the future. (Was he predicting global warming? Surely my religious ideas aren't that powerful.) I was also told, to quote the man, "I always knew I'd have trouble with you someday. You asked too many questions." These stories are indicative of a thread that is as strong in my life as the thread of feminism—the thread of seeking sane ways of understanding religious diversity, which is why I went into comparative studies in religion. This concern is represented by the twelfth bead on this "garland."

FORMATIVE EXPERIENCES IN GRADUATE SCHOOL

The threads of this narrative now bring me to the point of entering graduate school, which is a formative period for any scholar. I had decided I did not want to go on in philosophy because it seemed to be completely head-oriented, but I did want to pursue studying ultimate issues of meaning and relevance. Religious studies seemed the perfect field for that, even though the college professor who had paid the most attention to me, a woman professor of English, begged me not to go into the field of religion because, as she put it, "a woman can't make it in that field." Given what I have narrated above, it is not surprising that I had also decided it was meaningless and irrelevant to pursue only the answers to ultimate questions that had been proposed by culturally familiar religions. I wanted to study the world's religious options.

When I opted for the then-famous program in the History of Religions at the University of Chicago, I was not really aware of that program's reputation. I only knew that it seemed like a good program, and I was too poor to apply to multiple programs, so I applied only to the University of Chicago. When I think now of that risky behavior, I am impressed by two things. First, no one bothered to really mentor me about graduate school and career options. I was a girl and, therefore, was not expected to continue with any serious advanced training. I had been told not to expect to receive any prestigious fellowships, because I should understand that such money could not be wasted on a woman who would get married and have children instead of really pursuing an advanced degree and a career. (I did receive several prestigious fellowships as a graduate student.) Second, I was still very naive and really believed that intelligence and hard work mattered more than social class and party lines.

I was also extremely angry about options for women, but I tried hard to keep that under cover, because it was a deadly sin for women to be angry in those prefeminist days. Though I was very angry, I had not yet developed any interest at all in studying women and religion, nor had I really become angry about sexism in religion. Those concerns developed soon thereafter. I entered the Divinity School of the University of Chicago in 1965 at the age of twenty-two, intending to pursue a degree in what the university called the "history of religions." When I entered, the student body of the Divinity School consisted of about four hundred students, twelve of whom were women. Six of the twelve entered with me in 1965. At that time more women had PhDs in physics than in religious studies. The professors were overwhelmed that so many women wanted to study religion, worrying about what could be done with them all. In some cases, they changed the content of their lectures because of the presence of a single female (me) in their classrooms.

In graduate school, many of the concerns that would mark me for life came together, though I did not become personally interested in

Buddhism until somewhat later. How did I end up writing the first thesis in women's studies in religion in the country? First, I became painfully aware of male dominance in my newly chosen religion—Judaism. I had not yet converted to Judaism when I entered the Divinity School, though I was thinking seriously of converting if things went well after a trial period in a new setting. I did not think it was a good idea to make such a radical change based on an experience with a single Jewish congregation that happened to have a very charismatic and appealing rabbi. (Though I had had many disagreements with the pastor of my home church, after my comment about angels in confirmation class, the topic of gender did not come up again. I never went through a phase of trying to deal with Christianity as a feminist.) I became part of an extremely wonderful Jewish community at the University of Chicago Hillel Foundation and had many fruitful and rewarding discussions with people there. But I was still frustrated. I decided to write my required graduate school papers on women's religious lives in the area we were studying in that course, which turned out to be Aboriginal Australia, "to find out if things are as bad everywhere else as they are here." (This work began in early 1967.)

What I discovered was quite amazing to me. Western scholars had no interest at all in women's religious lives, but if they did talk about them, their theories did not match their field notes. Western scholars said that women had no religious lives to speak of, while their field notes reported a religious life that was different from that of men and practiced separately. This was when I first began to frame the thesis that Western scholars operated with an inadequate, androcentric model of humanity which could never guide research that would really illumine the human world, as opposed to men's lives in societies characterized by sexual segregation, though that thesis was not stated that clearly and succinctly in 1967. I also reported on a lot of fascinating information about women's religious lives that I had found in various sources, even that early. Mircea Eliade's response to that paper changed my life, drastically. He was very impressed with the paper and said, "You're going to do your dissertation on this material, aren't you?" My reply: "No. I want to do my dissertation on something important." Clearly, I had been socialized well enough into patriarchy to think women were less interesting and important than men, even though I was furious about that "fact." His reply to my rejection of his suggestion was very interesting. He said that I was seeing things in the data that he, as a man, would never have seen, and that it was very important that I should continue the work I was doing.

As a result of that conversation, I decided, for better or for worse, to continue my research into women's religious lives.

Was that a wise choice? I'll never know. What I do know is that it caused me endless grief in graduate school and later. The discoveries I was making were quite significant and came very early in the development of a concern that has been important in academic discourse for more than thirty years. I expected my mentors to be as excited as I was. Wasn't this what the intellectual life of research and scholarship was all about? Wrong again! My research proposal turned out to be extremely controversial, and I barely made it out of the University of Chicago with a degree because the study of women couldn't be "real scholarship." Perhaps I should have known that mere graduate students do not challenge established methodologies, but I was still naive. My research also elicited the comment, mentioned earlier, that "the generic masculine covers and includes the feminine, thereby making it unnecessary to focus specifically on women." In retrospect, I think that this experience soured me for life on academia. That men in such prestigious positions would react so defensively and with such little regard for the well-being of a student is still difficult for me to comprehend. As a result of my treatment as a graduate student, I have never contributed money to the University of Chicago, and I never will, though I still support the Hillel Foundation there years after becoming primarily involved with Buddhism.

These experiences again point to the question of gender essentialism. Could a man have figured out what I did? Is there anything essentially feminine that led to these questions, these concerns? I think not. I don't think my discoveries are located in my XX chromosome configuration but in the social conditions to which XX chromosome configurations are subjected. Being a woman entering the field at the time I did has colored my career and life immensely, because being a woman with some modicum of awareness who entered when I did meant that I was forced to think specifically about women and religion to survive. That's not what I intended or wanted to do, but what I ended up doing anyway, willy-nilly. What I really wanted to do was what led me into the field—to think about meaning and ultimate reality.

BECOMING BUDDHIST

As a convert to Judaism, my spirituality seemed settled. I had been utterly fascinated by what I had heard about "Vajrayana" in graduate school classes, but Vajrayana also seemed utterly inaccessible, even though I had read almost everything available in the late 1960s about "Vajrayana." I had a very satisfying experience with the Upstairs Minyan, a Jewish ritual community at the University of Chicago, and wrote some of the very early pieces in Jewish feminist theology (see chapter 10). But after I left Chicago and tried to mingle with more ordinary Jewish congregations, I quickly became disillusioned with them. Furthermore, after I moved to Eau Claire, Wisconsin, I began to discover, in the absence of a strong Jewish community, how communal Jewish life is. I was becoming tired of words as my spiritual medium and began to long for genuine silence. I was also finding it more and more difficult to take the notion of a personal God seriously. But, as I had spent a number of years moving into a Jewish identity, I spent a number of years moving on. I always emphasize when I talk about this chapter of my life that the time I spent deeply involved in Judaism was fulfilling and nurturing. I have no regrets about it.

I have told the story of how Buddhism imploded into my life before, but it bears repeating in this context. In 1973, when I was thirty, I moved to Eau Claire, where I have lived ever since, for my second full-time teaching position. After ten years in urban environments and the intellectual stimulation of the University of Chicago, I was concerned about moving to such a backwater, such a provincial place. (Eau Claire is no longer so provincial, but it was very different thirty-plus years ago.) I feared that I would be lonely and dissatisfied in this place, and for many, many years, I was. More was going on, however. I had just spent two years at an extremely frustrating teaching position in Florida, where I had been very badly treated. I was also in love, but my lover had been diagnosed a year earlier with an inoperable, terminal brain tumor, and I had just spent the Labor Day weekend seeing him for what I knew would be the last time. I was lonely, afraid, and miserable, as miserable as I have even been.

The new semester had just started, and I was teaching a survey course on Buddhism for the second time. I didn't understand Buddhism very well at that point, but I was trying hard to understand it better. It was the day for the lecture on the Four Noble Truths, which I was struggling to understand. I was walking toward my office on the sort of fall day that makes northern Wisconsin take one's breath away. I remember so plainly the blue sky and maple leaves beginning to turn, my overwhelming misery "inside," and the "outer" beauty. They seemed to be in such contrast. If only I could just drop the misery for one moment and experience only the beauty of the fall day, unimpeded! Something snapped.

I realized that I was so miserable only because I couldn't have what I wanted, and that was what was preventing me from enjoying the early fall day. I stopped and said to myself, "The Four Noble Truths are true. Our desires are the cause of our misery. If I didn't want something so fiercely, I would not be so miserable, and I could appreciate the beauty around me more fully."

That single moment is the clearest and most memorable experience of my entire life. It changed my life even more than had my conversation with Mircea Eliade on my paper about the role of women in aboriginal Australian religion. Though I did not realize it at the time, that moment also added another difficult dimension to my life as a scholar and an academic. I had always written from experience, not just from theory and information, which has always seemed to me to be necessary for scholarly integrity. I had already made the arguments for doing so as a scholar of comparative religions and as a feminist. I simply assumed that those arguments would transfer into the context of discourse on Buddhism, and I also assumed that feminist commentary on Buddhism would be welcomed, both by Buddhists and by scholars, given Buddhism's obvious gender problems. Wrong again! I must still have been naive and idealistic about both scholarly and religious institutions, despite all my experience to the contrary. When I began to write about Buddhism, an old prejudice that adherents of (Asian) religions could not possibly be accurate or trustworthy reporters on their own traditions was rampant, a prejudice to which I was often subjected. Additionally, nobody wanted to hear about gender issues in Buddhism, neither scholars of Buddhism, feminist scholars, nor Buddhists. Today, younger scholars are more interested in Buddhist critical and constructive thinking, whether feminist or otherwise. It is unfortunate that this change of heart was so little, so late.

Instantaneously with that insight into the truth of the Noble Truths, I said to myself that if the Four Noble Truths were true, that would include the fourth truth, the truth of the path of disciplined ethical conduct, meditation, and the pursuit of wisdom. Then and there, I realized that I needed to learn to meditate, though I put some academic qualifications around that decision at that time. Learning to meditate in northern Wisconsin in 1973 was not so easy, and it took some time before I actually accomplished that. However, I had studied Buddhism enough that I knew I wanted to practice in the Tibetan Vajrayana tradition. At the time, Chögyam Trungpa was big news, and a close graduate school colleague had already become his student, so it was easy enough to figure out where I should land. The practicality of finding my way there was more difficult. Besides, I still had a doctoral dissertation to finish, and I had never been to India. With those tasks accomplished, in 1977 I finally landed in Boulder, Colorado, then the capital of Trungpa's world, though I had begun to meditate under the direction of the graduate school friend some years earlier. I did not intend to "go for refuge" (the act of formally becoming Buddhist), because I didn't think I needed a third trip through a sexist religion, and I was very aware of Buddhist patriarchy. However, I fell hard for what we then called "the scene," and I did "go for refuge." So that meant I would have to write *Buddhism after Patriarchy,* and I knew that from day one of my life as a Buddhist.

Having made up my mind to take on Buddhism, I worked hard at my practice, and my progress through the required practices was quite rapid. Having so much academic knowledge before I ever began to practice meditation was also a tremendous advantage, and I always encourage my meditation students to learn a lot about Buddhist doctrine and history.

Buddhism has made the difference between life and death for me, I truly believe. I cannot imagine today how I would have survived everything I've been through were it not for the profundity of the Buddhist view and the effectiveness of its practices. Buddhist meditation practice had an early, and initially very frightening, impact on me. I had been extremely angry for years about sexism and patriarchy, and though I tried to keep it in check, that anger frequently found expression. After I began a serious meditation practice, I simply did not find that anger so accessible or attractive. Expressions of anger just didn't work or happen so much, which was frightening. In Buddhist terms, I was losing the ego I had developed as an angry feminist, and such loss, though positive, is also frightening. Strangely, I also found communication much easier. I became much clearer in my expressions, and people began to listen to me much more easily. This was a profoundly transformative experience that I have written about many times (see chapter 14).

LIFE TODAY

I still live in northern Wisconsin, and I love it now. My culture has now been made famous internationally by Garrison Keillor's radio program *A Prairie Home Companion.* I don't intend this as a commercial for his program, but I often tell people that I live in Lake Wobegon. It's easier than trying to explain why I still live in northern Wisconsin, given that

I could move somewhere else now that I have retired from academia. However, given that I was so unhappy in Eau Claire for so long, a legitimate question is, what happened?

It's hard to say exactly, but things have changed dramatically in the last ten years of my life. It is very difficult to disentangle all the threads, but three things seem predominant. I was offered and took early retirement from my academic position. After that, life in Eau Claire improved dramatically. I finally learned to be happy alone and gave up on seeking "Relationships." That led to a vast improvement in my quality of life. Finally, I also began working with a different Buddhist teacher, a young and thoroughly extraordinary Tibetan women, Venerable Jetsun Khandro Rinpoche, who seems to understand me better than anyone I have ever encountered except for an extraordinary psychotherapist I worked with here in Eau Claire. Nothing very dramatic ever happened. I just noticed that I felt much better, was much less discontented, and didn't always want things to be different, though it seemed nothing major had really changed in my life. I was still in Eau Claire, I still didn't have the kind of position I had always dreamed of, I still didn't have a relationship that was satisfactory in the way that we think relationships should be, nor was I a member of a community that delivered what we hope for.

But, in verbal terms, the word I found that seemed most accurate was "contentment." Eventually, I spoke with Khandro Rinpoche about this feeling, and she told me that contentment was the fruition of the journey. In the years since then, as I have learned more of the really profound levels of Buddhist teachings, I understand much more why this is so, and what it means. We really do create all our sufferings by wanting things to be different from what they are and by wanting things that we cannot have.

The Trials of Being an Academic

Though I love reflection, contemplation, and teaching, which seem to be some of the most meaningful and relevant things one can do with one's life, academia has been mainly disappointing to me, and I have no regrets to be much less involved with it. Some of this attitude is undoubtedly due to my disappointment that I never received a satisfying academic appointment in spite of my achievements. Actually, the dissatisfaction has much more to do with a lack of collegiality and appreciation at my institution than from its lack of prestige. I was the only woman, the only feminist, and the only person who cared about anything "non-Western" for most of my twenty-five years at the institution where I taught. I was also the only person in the department who was professionally active, who kept current in my field, or who published widely.

I was often told that students really didn't need to know about the so-called non-Western world, or that it was much more important for them to learn more about "their own" heritage than to learn anything about other cultures. I was frequently told that it was rather extreme of me to expect my students to call me "Dr." or "Ms." rather than "Miss" or "Mrs.," that such language made my students uncomfortable, causing them to drop my courses, which was bad for the department. I was told that success at writing and publishing only proved that I wasn't doing my "real" job at a teaching university. (I had plenty of students and most of the better students in the department took every class I taught.) If I ever talked about my work, I was told that I was "bragging again," so I learned to keep quiet about what I was doing.

What I missed most, though, being a reflective person who cares about communication, was students who really wanted to think about things, just as, when I had been a student, I keenly missed the presence of such fellow students, except during my years at the University of Chicago. I missed such students much more than I missed having graduate students. An appointment at a research university didn't matter much to me, but it would have been nice to teach at a liberal arts college where I would not have been confined to teaching "general studies" courses in a service department with few majors and minors. Regional state universities are, in many ways, vocational training institutions and do not really support or stimulate deep appreciation of reflective thinking in the humanities disciplines. It would have been wonderful to spend my teaching life at an institution where student evaluations were not mainly based on how easy the course was, but rather on how thought-provoking the course was. However, most students did not want their conventional thinking about either religious diversity or gender to be disturbed by a college professor. I often remarked that I didn't mind that students who came into my classroom were rather provincial in their thinking; I minded that they wanted to leave the class that way. Having come from the same utterly provincial culture in the same part of the country and having eagerly sought out much wider views, I did not have, and still do not have, much sympathy for such emotional and intellectual inertia.

The problems I experienced at my particular university are more generic, however, and seem to pervade academic culture. Having an alternative institutional world and reference point, the larger Buddhist *sangha,* which is not without its own discomforting, dysfunctional foibles, has given me some perspective on academia. I also trust impressions of outsiders about academic culture, and their impressions are often more critical than mine. Academia is extraordinarily competitive and uncompassionate. Criticism, not for the sake of making any overall improvements, but only to further one's own position and agenda, is the norm. Everyone tries to tear down and discredit anyone who has any credibility, mistakenly thinking that such a wholly negative outlook furthers knowledge and understanding, but failing to realize that the fresh insights of later generations depend on the work of those who have gone before. Even more sadly, what were once fresh insights harden into doctrinaire positions with their own arcane jargon and established orthodoxies. The feminist movement, as well as other expansive movements in the new scholarship of the 1970s, turned into a race to claim the status of "most victimized of all," what I call the "victimer than thou" mentality. People then think that such history justifies their holding a grudge against the world.

Buddhist psychology is familiar with the mind-set that dominates academia; it is called the "*asura* realm," one of six modes of "rebirth" that prevail in our world system.[3] Though it is difficult to find an English equivalent for this term, many translate it as the "jealous god" realm, which means that it is occupied by beings who are actually quite well off but who nevertheless eagerly discredit and fight with anyone and everyone. In academia, part of that jealous fighting includes the hostility toward genuinely creative and insightful thinking that seems so curious, given what the academic claims to be about and which I first encountered as a graduate student. I have long thought that the way Buddhist psychology describes the "jealous god" realm is a perfect description of the competitive, cold, and uncollegial environment that characterizes academia.

I still wonder if I could somehow have made years as a professor in Eau Claire into a happier lot, and I am sure that if I had been more spiritually mature, I could have been more contented and less unhappy. Nevertheless, my contentment would not have actually undone the inadequacies of academia or my specific situation. In my view, one of the great difficulties of spiritual and intellectual life is being able to call a spade a spade, in the popular phrase, without resenting it for being a spade. A discovery of spiritual contentment should not make us deaf and dumb to the inadequacies still around us and within us. I now understand much more fully than I did in those years why Buddhism consistently claims that we can never find happiness in something else, somewhere else, outside ourselves. Maintaining a critical stance without being miserable and unhappy because of one's keen, accurate analyses is a great challenge. No wonder Buddhism claims that realizing the inseparability of wisdom and compassion is a supremely difficult and supremely essential task.

Nevertheless, despite finding academia frustrating in many ways, I am grateful that I managed to maintain an academic career despite all the odds against a woman of my generation. I can think of no other situation that would have allowed me to accomplish what I know is the purpose of my life, making the intellectual and spiritual contributions that I have, especially writing *Buddhism after Patriarchy*. In 2005, I was invited to contribute a paper to a celebratory conference in Korea. While I was there, a Korean nun to whom I had never been introduced, approached me, took off her wrist *mala,* and put it around my wrist. I have never taken it off. This wordless tribute is more telling than a prestigious academic position or the feedback of American students that my courses made them think too much.

Transcending the Need for "Relationships"

Regarding relationships and community, my thinking has changed more drastically than about any other topic. Much of my adult life was characterized by excruciating loneliness, longing for a satisfying relationship, and for membership in a supportive, workable community. I have written a great deal about these topics over the years.[4] I wouldn't exactly retract those statements. I'm sure that those who have satisfying relationships or membership in supportive communities do benefit greatly, but these things simply were not in the cards for me. Basically, over the years, I kissed a lot of frogs, and for the most part, they remained frogs. I never found what I thought I wanted and needed, at least not for very long at any one time.

However beneficial it is to be in a long-term relationship that works or in a supporting community, *needing* such things, which I certainly did for many years, is another matter. Such *need* only increases misery. It is another case of assuming that one's happiness is dependent on something else, somewhere else, on something one does not have, which only increases one's misery. One may indeed live in less than ideal circumstances, at least as many people conceive of ideal circumstances. But resentment, self-pity, and longing regarding those conditions only increase one's misery without improving the situation in any way.

When I began serious study with my current major teacher, Jetsun Khandro Rinpoche, in 1998, I was still quite miserable about my social situation. In those days, she frequently taught that, while on the one hand one's true family is one's *vajra sangha,* not one's biological family, she also taught that, on the other hand, one should be content with one's situation, whatever it is, whether one is in a relationship or alone, and that it doesn't really matter what that situation is. She also taught that one of the most difficult things to learn, and also one of the most important, is how to be happy alone. I vividly remember complaining to myself, "How can she say that when she has such a close relationship with her sister!" The two of them were virtually inseparable, and she also had a strong relationship with her natal family and her *sangha* of nuns. How could she say that I should be able to be contented with my life as it was, a life without a satisfying relationship!

Things changed only very slowly. My last relationship had broken up not long before I began to study with Khandro Rinpoche. I still had my antennae out and thought that I wanted to find a new relationship. But after a while, I began to notice that, without all the drama and trauma of a relationship, I was actually becoming less miserable. The turning point was one day when I reflected that while I might be happier if I was in a good relationship, the chances for that to happen were actually quite low and I was quite a bit happier than I would have been in a stressful relationship. I don't remember exactly when that happened, but I have a visceral memory of that insight. I pulled in my antennae and started moving as far as possible away from the bouquet tossing at weddings. It was around 2003 that I really made peace with being alone and told Khandro Rinpoche, "You said one of the hardest and most important things to learn is how to be happy alone. Well, I'm there! I have absolutely no interest in another relationship." She clapped her hands, laughing with happiness. I think that was the only time she has had that particular response to something I have said. By that time, I had also realized that my future did not hold membership in the kind of local community I had dreamed about for so long.

I must acknowledge two relationships that were different. Enough of the story of the first, the lover with the inoperable brain tumor, has already been told. It ended with the insight that basic Buddhist teachings actually made profound existential sense. The second was a very happy but very brief relationship with a colleague at UW, Eau Claire, a man some years my senior. He died the day I was finishing *Buddhism after Patriarchy,* and the book is dedicated to him. During the few years of that relationship, I could feel the toxins resulting from having experienced quite a bit of emotional abuse leaving my system, and I could feel healing taking place within the experience of being appreciated and valued for being who I am. This relationship had a life span of only about three years. I learned a great deal in the process of grieving after his death,[5] and I recovered quite well eventually, but thanks, I think, only to Buddhist practice. Earlier, I somehow railed against the Buddhist advice not to get completely attached in relationships because all meetings end in parting. That seemed to me to be unfair. Now nothing seems more reasonable.

Today, I live alone in Eau Claire, in an old house in which I have lived since 1977 and have renovated extensively, with my cats, many houseplants, and extensive gardens. I am much more contented than I have ever been before, which does not mean there are not frustrating days, but they are simply part of the whole mosaic. However, I somehow seem to have more friends than when I was so desperately lonely and in search of relationships. For example, my neighbor sometimes gives insulin to my diabetic cat, and I sometimes walk her dog.

Actually, such a life is not very different from my teenage fantasy of what life would be like, except that, as a country girl, I always imagined living in a more remote location. I spent a lot of time alone growing up, and while I was often bored because books were so hard to come by, I was seldom lonely. Rather, because I was teased and shunned a lot, I preferred to be in my own world. Being an intelligent, not-too-attractive girl in the boondocks is rather difficult. I did not date at all in high school and very little in college, nor was I really interested in dating for a long time. I have often wondered if I might have easily moved into a celibate and solitary lifestyle if I had lived in a society that promoted and tolerated a diversity of lifestyles, rather than relentlessly pressuring everyone into the two-by-two situation of being in a couple. It now seems to me that skipping all the anxiety and drama of always looking for a relationship that would work and would last could have made life a lot simpler and more enjoyable. Of course, I was the one who believed that I needed a "relationship" to complete my life and continued to act on that belief again and again.

Working with Jetsun Khandro Rinpoche

The third component of my life in the last ten years involves my relationship with Jetsun Khandro Rinpoche. Many of the stories about my relationship with her are told in part 5, so I will not focus on them now. But from my first meeting with her in 1995, she seemed to understand me and what I was trying to do in my work more than anyone else ever had. I already had a long-standing involvement in the Shambhala community, which had been founded by Chögyam Trungpa, and I had taught within it for many years. In 1998, I began to attend Khandro Rinpoche's two-week advanced retreat every year and even spent some time in India at her nunnery and at Mindrolling Monastery, her late father's monastery. In 2005, when Jetsun Khandro Rinpoche first appointed *lopons,* or *acharyas* (senior teachers) within her community, I was one of the six who were selected. In that position, I have been able to fulfill my heart's desire to teach fully and completely, incorporating all the perspectives on knowledge that I have collected through scholarship and Buddhist practice. I also still teach within the Shambhala *sangha* from time to time when I am invited.

As a *lopon,* I have teaching responsibilities at programs and retreats held at Lotus Garden, Khandro Rinpoche's North American center in Virginia. I also lead several retreats a year in the Midwest for students of Khandro Rinpoche. My niche, however, is teaching a sequence of courses on the history of Buddhism at the *shedra,* or scholastic studies program, which takes place each spring at Lotus Garden. For years I had nurtured the dream of teaching a rigorous course on Buddhist history for Buddhist practitioners, a course that would combine all the tools of the academic study of religion with all the tools available to dharma practitioners. This course would go into much more depth than the one-semester survey course on Buddhism which was the most advanced course on Buddhism I had been able to teach at the university. Western converts to Buddhism tend to know very little about Buddhist history and almost nothing about schools of Buddhism other than their own. This course would be nonsectarian, unlike most of what little training in Buddhist history convert Buddhists usually have acquired. Using academic tools, it would teach people the value of both legend and history, and more important, how not to confuse them.

I tried for a long time to get the Shambhala community to sponsor this course as a month-long study program at one of their retreat centers, but there was no interest. I also tried to convince the Minneapolis *sanghas* to combine forces and offer the program as a sequence of courses with weeknight lectures. But if one center sponsored a course, almost no one from any other center attended, and people were not interested in overall Buddhist history; they only wanted to study "their" history. I taught several five-week course segments, but my dream was not coming true at all.

In one of my letters to Khandro Rinpoche, I described my project to her, and a few weeks later in India, I asked her opinion of the project. "I like it," she replied. "Should we do it at Lotus Garden?" I ventured. "Yes," she replied. Later that evening, I approached her again. "Before we teach that history of Buddhism course at Lotus Garden, I want to tell you that most Tibetans would find much of what I will teach quite heretical." She threw her head back in one of her most characteristic gestures, laughing uproariously. "That's good for us! It makes us think!" she replied. It took a few years for things to come together. At the 2006 *shedra,* we finalized arrangements. She asked me what I needed, and I replied that I wanted five two-hour slots and that these classes not be pushed into lunch hour or some other unworkable slot, as was happening with one of the enrichment classes at the 2006 *shedra*. She said not to worry. In May 2007, I became the first Westerner to have a major teaching role in a program taught under her auspices. I taught the most in-depth history of early Indian Buddhism it has ever been my luxury and pleasure to teach, using all the tools of academic and dharmic methods of teaching and understanding at my disposal. It was extremely successful, and Khandro Rinpoche was really happy with the result. The enterprise is to be continued, for at least another five or six years before we repeat the sequence.

CONCLUSION: THE UTILITY OF OBSTACLES?

Much Buddhist practical advice counsels people to appreciate the obstacles they encounter in their lives because obstacles that are dealt with well deepen a person in ways that would not otherwise be possible. In other words, obstacles are teachers, to be learned from, not rejected and reviled. Yet, while one is experiencing obstacles, advice to appreciate those obstacles does not seem very helpful. When I was actively dealing with loneliness, professional frustration, and the death of those close to me, I wanted to hit anyone who told me to appreciate those obstacles as teachers. Now I am trying to figure out how to be more effective in talking with people whose obstacles are very active, for I do realize that I could not have accomplished what I have accomplished without at least some of the obstacles I have faced.

As I reflect on my life, the most useless obstacle I faced is being in so many situations in which relevant others would have preferred that I be more conventional and less thoughtful, that my vision would be much smaller. My mother would certainly have preferred a less intelligent child who wanted to stay on the farm to milk cows. The University of Chicago would certainly have preferred that I not discover the androcentrism of conventional scholarship as a graduate student. The University of Wisconsin, Eau Claire, would certainly have preferred that I be an ordinary professor who did not continue with scholarly activities or develop an international reputation. (Professors in my department got tenure and promotions without publishing even so much as a book review.) And I suspect that the Shambhala community would have preferred that such a well-known feminist critic of Buddhism not be from their ranks. It is still hard to make sense of this obstacle. Why would people and institutions prefer conventionality to achievement of something noteworthy and meaningful?

Not being able to make use of and contribute one's gifts and talents is truly painful, and it is still difficult to make sense of such an obstacle. However, for many years I have studied spiritual teachings which claim that one's concern should be doing what is appropriate, without concern for the immediate outcomes or results. I have always been inspired and impressed by such teachings, but learning to be less ambitious and more content with what transpires has not been easy. No wonder the Tibetan Buddhist tradition, with its well-honed psychological wisdom, regards concern with fame or negative reputation, praise or blame, as among the most seductive barriers to true spiritual development. It is also an obstacle that is wholly internal and self-made; no amount of external approval would really satisfy a need for more praise and fame. Therefore, it can only be overcome through true confidence and contentment.

Traditional Buddhism does regard being a woman as an obstacle, usually an obstacle that cannot be overcome, at least in this lifetime. Much of my work has been about defusing that belief, showing its utter incompatibility with the most basic Buddhist teachings. As for myself, I had ceased hating my female body long before I became a Buddhist, though anger over what is done to women became less intense only after considerable meditation practice began to teach me that anger solves nothing while making the angry person even more miserable. I do not speculate on how life might have been different if I had not been a woman, though it is completely clear that my career would have been totally different had I been a man doing creative scholarship on something men care about. Nevertheless, such speculation is totally beside the point. In any case, whether or not being a woman is an obstacle, I am satisfied with what I have done with a female rebirth in this lifetime. I was both lucky and perseverant. I did manage to avoid the conventional female gender role that I dreaded so much as a child and have helped many others to have more self-determination as well. I can't think of anything better to do with a precious human birth.

PART TWO

Five Essays on Method

I HAVE WRITTEN MANY ARTICLES on various issues in the methodology of religious studies during the nearly forty years of my career to date. What some might regard as an undue emphasis on methodological issues accords well with both my training and my inclinations. I was trained at the University of Chicago in the late 1960s, when the doctoral program in the history of religions emphasized method and theory more than linguistic and historical studies in one's area of specialization. The program emphasized that while it is important to have information at one's disposal, it is crucial to know how to think about that information.

As narrated in chapter 1, my early attempts to study women and religions only fueled this emphasis on method and on issues of how to organize and think about the data with which one was familiar. Why had such an obvious subject matter as the religious lives and thoughts of women been completely omitted from scholarly accounts of virtually all societies studied by historians of religions? That question dominated my earliest work and led to my earliest methodological thesis—that previous work had been characterized by a flawed and inadequate model of humanity, which I and many other young scholars concerned with similar questions called the "androcentric," or "one-sexed" model of humanity.

My attempts to discern a methodology that would allow and require adequate study of women also led to concern with a "meta" level of method, with concern about the often unconscious presuppositions that underlie a chosen or a conventional and accepted methodology. I have claimed for many years that these presuppositions are extremely powerful determinates of what is seen or not seen, reported or not reported, as relevant data for the study of religion. Therefore, I have argued, it is necessary to admit that there is no neutral "no place" from which to view religious phenomena and report on them objectively, though many scholars dominant when I entered the field appeared to have such an agenda. Later, my Buddhist training intensified the awareness I had already gained from my independent methodological explorations. Our own projections can deeply color what we see. Therefore, it is as necessary to investigate our own presuppositions as it is to investigate the data we wish to understand. This level of methodological inquiry is much less likely to be explored, and reflection upon it is resisted, often quite fiercely and vigorously.

Methodological studies also deal with the nature of religion, though they deal less with the validity of religion as a human enterprise and its relevance in contemporary life, which are usually considered to be more theological or normative questions. As already narrated, I entered the field of religious studies more to explore existential concerns in broadly comparative and cross-cultural contexts than to acquire information about other historical and cultural situations, though such information is necessary for my work. I did not want to be limited to culturally familiar situations in my scholarly work, but I also did not want to be limited to completely descriptive, historical scholarship. In the late 1960s, when I was a graduate student, such concerns were completely off-limits to students in comparative and cross-cultural studies of religion, and a very strict division of labor between descriptive and normative studies prevailed. Those of us who wanted to study the religious dimensions of unfamiliar cultures were strictly limited to descriptive accounts of those cultures, preferably to the study of their texts rather than studying living people. Any concern with the meaning, value, or relevance of any of the phenomena we were studying quickly led to being labeled "crypto-theologians," a label meant to discredit and denigrate our work.

Though prevailing scholars fiercely denied the subjectivity of their own work, I had already clearly seen the subjective dimensions of conventional scholarship so evident in its prevailing androcentrism. The unwillingness of established scholars to admit their own androcentrism and own up to its inadequacies instilled in me a thoroughgoing mistrust of prevailing scholarship.[1] Thus, though the professional costs were high, I was determined to follow my own insights and frequently crossed the line between descriptive and normative concerns in my work, always being careful to make clear to readers what were my standpoints for the inquiries I was conducting and the conclusions I was reaching.

In addition to exploring methodologies that could take better account of the data about women's religious lives and thoughts, I became interested and involved in what is usually called feminist theology. I became interested, normatively, in what would make women's lives better religiously and what would make their traditions less misogynist. I also became interested in exploring what was often called the "insider-outsider" issue, especially after I began to do critical-constructive work concerning the Buddhist tradition. The issues of whether so-called insiders could do adequate scholarship on their own tradition and whether "insiders" might not bring a dimension of understanding to accounts of their own tradition that would be difficult for an "outsider" to replicate became dominant. I was also interested in the question of whether ideas and symbols from culturally distant religious traditions might hold some meaning and relevance for scholars and critical-constructive thinkers like myself, a question and concern that goes back to my original interest in the field of cross-cultural, comparative studies in religion. Additionally, I became quite concerned about the propriety and ethics of such cross-cultural evaluations. Finally, and most of all, I became concerned with questions of how our exploding knowledge about the world's various religions could contribute to a theory or theology of religions that could foster peaceful coexistence and mutual acceptance in the religiously plural world, rather than the rabidly exclusivist and missionary theologies that continue to dominate, especially among some monotheisms.

Thus my interests in "method and theory" in which I had been so thoroughly trained in graduate school have expanded well beyond the question of whether phenomenological or reductionist methods best explain the data of other religions, times, and places. That was the only allowed methodological question then, and not too surprisingly, at the University of Chicago we were taught that phenomenology was far superior to reductionism because religion was a sui generis phenomenon requiring its own explanatory framework which could not be completely encompassed by the social sciences. Nevertheless, personal interest in any of the phenomena we were studying was off limits, as were any "theological" interests. Obviously, such a stance involved its own orthodoxy, a point I discuss in chapter 4.

In part 2 I have gathered five of what I consider to be my most innovative writings on method. All of them have either been out of print for some time or were published in sources that are difficult to find. Chapter 2, "Androcentrism and Androgyny in the Methodology of History of Religions," which was written in 1975, draws upon the conclusions I reached in my doctoral dissertation, "Exclusion and Participation: The Role of Women in Aboriginal Australian Religions." In the late 1960s and early 1970s I had spent many, many hours trying to figure out why accounts of women's religious lives in the sources that were available then seemed so inadequate and incomplete. The main interests of scholars seemed to be about detailing a perceived inferiority of women, whether or not their field notes backed up that perception, and explaining why women deserved their inferior status, which meant that they were excluded from all the interesting and important dimensions of all religious traditions. With very few exceptions, no one was interested in what women themselves might have thought or experienced. This state of scholarship was irritating and frustrating to me, and I knew there had to be more adequate ways to present women's religious lives and roles. However, I found no help in the prevailing literature or from my mentors.

My first clue that something was amiss in the scholarship came in 1967, when my research for a paper on the role of women in Aboriginal Australian religions made it clear to me that field reports often did not match dominant theoretical conclusions. Theoretical conclusions focused on a dualism between "sacred" and "profane," which paralleled a "male-female" dichotomy. This conclusion could be maintained because women were almost always excluded from very elaborate and culturally important rituals which were performed by men alone, but the conclusion also ignored what Aboriginal men themselves said about women and about why they did not perform their rituals in the presence of women. It seemed that the sacredness attributed to men and the profane nature attributed to women were more in the heads of Western theoreticians than in the data reported by fieldworkers. After much difficulty, it finally dawned on me that women's religious lives, as well as the relations between women and men, could be more fruitfully explored as involving *patterns of exclusion and participation* than as hierarchical discussions of male sacredness and female profaneness. The primary issue was finding tools to describe women's lives and thoughts, but all that androcentric scholars seemed interested in was their status vis-à-vis men, which they always evaluated as inferior to men. My explorations of the role of women in Aboriginal Australian religions proceeded much more smoothly after that discovery. Chapter 2 summarizes those findings.

However helpful it may have been to drop concern with hierarchical evaluations of women's status and simply explore data about their lives and thoughts, the problem of why prevailing methodologies fostered such inattention to and negative views about women still remained. I continued to explore that problem with dogged persistence. Finally, it occurred to me that scholars simply assumed that men were the normal and interesting human beings, which is why they always focused on men in their research and theory. If men alone were at the center of their field of vision, the only place for women would be on the periphery.

Scholars were interested in women only as women appeared to the men they were studying, an angle of vision that grew out of the marginal status of women in their own worlds and consciousnesses. Men took themselves to be subjects and women only to be objects. (Remember, this was the reign of the generic masculine, when it was claimed that "man" included women, even though women were excluded from most of the things men did.) In my doctoral work, I named the prevailing attitude the "androcentric model of humanity" and its alternative an "androgynous model of humanity" and first published those reflections in the article included here as chapter 2.[2]

Chapters 3, 4, 5, and 6 were all written some twenty-five years later, early in the twenty-first century, and in various ways reflect my dissatisfaction with what had happened with feminist scholarship and methodological studies in the intervening years. During those years, I had worked out many of the implications of my early methodological thinking, including the important distinction between feminism as academic method, or women/gender studies on the one hand, and feminism as social vision and social criticism on the other hand, which were briefly reviewed in the introduction to this volume. I had also worked out my two primary definitions of feminism—the paradigm shift involved in recognizing that women are human beings and the social vision of freedom from the prison of gender roles, both of which are also outlined in the introduction. These conclusions have been published in my two best-known books, *Buddhism after Patriarchy* and *Feminism and Religion*. Therefore, these conclusions are readily available, which is why they are not reproduced here.[3]

Chapter 3, "Where Have We Been? Where Do We Need to Go?" might be considered the culmination of my work on the methodology of women's studies in religion. It reflects my growing concern that women's studies is becoming an isolated discipline unable to integrate itself into and affect the rest of the academy and suggests that women's studies is now well enough established to become more integrated into gender studies.

Chapters 4 and 5 reflect my concerns with religious studies methodology in general. "The Place of the Personal and the Subjective in Religious Studies" deals with what I came to regard as an unavoidable subjective dimension in religious studies. By that I mean nothing more than that there is no "neutral no place" where a scholar may stand and from which religions may be viewed "objectively." I regard making peace with such subjectivity, learning how to deal with it honestly, and then using it productively in commentary on religion and religious studies as an enduring and valuable legacy of my early struggles with androcentric scholarship.

Chapter 5, "Methodology: Tool or Trap?" which was written for an international conference on methodology, challenges the tendency of scholars to follow what I call "academic fashions," by which I mean that established methodologies tend not to be examined very reflectively but only imitated. Continued marginalization of feminist and women's studies methodology is partly due to the fact that it is less "established" than other methodologies. The main point of the chapter, however, is not to argue in favor of feminist methodologies. The main point is that unless care is exercised, methodologies stop being tools and become traps which limit further understanding of religion. I use the emergence of feminist methods and resistance to those methods precisely to make the point that a method can easily become a trap. I demonstrate why religions and cultures which have gender roles strongly in place simply cannot be studied adequately with an androcentric methodology, and then delineate many of the subjective and unconscious reasons why some scholars seem to be unable to make the paradigm shift to inclusive models of humanity despite their cogency and relevance for good scholarship.

At the end of the chapter, I make a suggestion about another assumption that may well undergird much contemporary scholarship about religious studies, especially in its phenomenological and reductionist modes. I suggest that many current discussions of method in religious studies still make certain assumptions about what religions are claiming and that those assumptions may well reflect monotheistic and theistic perspectives. In this suggestion I wanted to test whether, after all my discussion of methodology as a potential trap, the scholars present at the conference would even consider the possible cogency of my assertion about an assumption underlying much scholarship in religious studies. I was disappointed but not surprised that all the discussion was about the pros and cons of feminist methodology, which was not the main substance of my presentation. The suggestion that methodology can be a trap as well as a tool was not discussed by the respondents, nor was my assertion about a potentially problematic assumption underlying much of religious studies. It was as if that portion of the presentation had been omitted entirely.[4]

Chapter 6, "What Went Wrong? Feminism and Freedom from the Prison of Gender Roles," is quite different from the preceding chapters. It is not an argument about scholarly methods in religious studies but grows out of my work on feminism as social vision, especially my concern with feminism as freedom from the prison of gender roles. This chapter reflects my concern with feminism's slide into an ideology of gender essentialism as well as with its lack of a sufficiently radical critique of conventional, prevailing gender roles. This chapter is my most complete statement of the social dimensions of freedom from the prison of gender roles.

CHAPTER 2

Androcentrism and Androgyny in the Methodology of History of Religions

The questions that a feminist scholar asks of her discipline when she is a historian of religions must be understood within the context of the paradigm shift that feminist thought requires of all disciplines in the humanities and social sciences. That basic paradigm shift is the transition from an androcentric methodology to an androgynous methodology. The resulting transformation of the history of religions would be quite subtle and overwhelming, though not total. The unconscious androcentric presuppositions undergirding almost all work done to date in the history of religions cause serious deficiencies, especially at the primary level of data-perception and gathering, and this deficiency in turn generates serious deficiencies at the level of model-building and theorizing whenever any hint of sexuality or sexual imagery is present in the data being analyzed. However, the most abstract level of history of religions theory—regarding questions such as the nature and scope of religion itself—is not so vulnerable and inadequate.

The scope and the limitations of the feminist critique and reformulation of history of religions methodology will be dealt with as answers to two frequent, somewhat defensive questions asked by those who want history of religions methodology to be adequate, but also wish to assert that the feminist critiques that can be leveled at other disciplines in religious studies do not apply to history of religions. The first question is, "Yes, but we investigate religious situations in which women are scarcely involved and work with texts that reflect that androcentrism, so what can we possibly do?" Those who ask this question believe that if there is any androcentrism in the history of religions, it resides in the data themselves, not in the methodology of the discipline, which is free of any distortion or bias toward androcentrism. The second question is, "Yes, but even if the feminist critique has some validity, aren't these concerns peripheral and trivial compared to questions like discerning an adequate model of religion, comprehending myth, or understanding Buddhist philosophy?" Those who ask this question do not wish to be bothered with the feminist critique themselves and wish to dismiss or denigrate those who are. They wish to assert that they are already dealing with the central questions in history of religions, without ever having thought about androcentrism and androgyny.

Do most of the books written about history of religions and non-Western religions talk only about men and their religious lives simply because that accurately represents the religions being studied? If there is male-centered perspective in the history of religions, is it the unavoidable result of the materials being studied and not part of the outlook of the scholars? The feminist critique could not be so easily dismissed even if the religions studied by a historian of religions were indeed androcentric. The question of whether or not the religious ideas and practices investigated by the historian of religions are part of an androcentric worldview is irrelevant from a methodological point of view because even a highly male-dominant and male-centered set of rituals and images could not be adequately or fully understood if only data about men are reported and analyzed. The real question is whether the investigator is androcentric in outlook and thus more interested in or liable to study men and their involvement in the religious symbol system, while overlooking data about the female half of the religious community. Furthermore, though the investigated religions may well be at least somewhat androcentric, I suspect most of them would appear less androcentric if we stopped projecting our own androcentrism onto them. Every religious system and set of data that I have investigated thoroughly has turned out to have been seriously misunderstood by historians of religions because of an unconscious androcentric bias and not to be nearly so male-dominated and male-centered as it is generally portrayed in the scholarly literature. I cannot overemphasize that statement: the real issue is whether or not the historian of religions has an androcentric set of suppositions, not whether the systems the historian investigates are male-centered.

Thus far, I have made explicit my conviction that the conventional program and methodology of history of religions, rather than, or perhaps, in addition to, the data being discussed, reflect an intensely androcentric worldview and that the average historian of religions is intensely and unconsciously androcentric in outlook. What precisely do I mean by this statement? The literature defining and demonstrating androcentrism is already large, so all that is needed is a brief summary of the three central characteristics of an androcentric outlook, followed by an equally brief demonstration of their scope in basic dimensions of the methodology of history of religions.

First, in androcentric thinking, the male norm and the human norm are collapsed and become identical. That is to say, it is assumed that one standard and one norm really are applied to all humans, both male and female. Therefore, secondly, because the male norm and the human norm are collapsed, it is assumed that the generic masculine habit of thought, language, and research is adequate. To study males is to study humanity. No special attention to women is required, because they are assumed to be fully covered by the generic masculine. Third, and most important, when women, per se, are considered, after it becomes obvious that there is sex role differentiation in every religion and that, therefore, women are not adequately discussed in research, language, and thought couched in the generic masculine, women are discussed as an *object* exterior to "mankind," needing to be explained and fitted into one's worldview, having the same ontological and epistemological status as trees, unicorns, deities, or any other object that must be discussed to make experience intelligible. Women are there in the world, but they are discussed as an "other"[1] to the human subject attempting to understand "his" world (generic masculine deliberate), as a problem to be solved, but not as a co-subject in a mutual attempt to understand human sexual differentiation and all its manifestations.

If all the above statements are the case, then it should be no surprise that one of the primary constructs in the history of religions, *homo religiosus,* really turns out to be *vir religiosus,* who relates to woman as a symbol, not a human co-subject. He constructs a religious universe in which she functions as something exterior to "mankind" (generic masculine used deliberately), as a symbol of good or of evil, as a deity or a demon, as an object to be excluded or included in ritual, as a being whose ontological status can be debated. But *homo religiosus* as constructed by the history of religions does not include women as religious subjects, as constructors of religious symbol systems and as participants in a religious universe of discourse. History of religions really only deals with women and feminine imagery *as they are thought about by* the males being investigated, whether they are the males in a specific religious situation or in the abstract model, *homo religiosus.* Because the discipline of history of religions is concerned with discovering and understanding humans as religious beings, the androcentric limitations of the construct *homo religiosus,* religious humankind, constitute a very severe liability indeed.

Once one has become fully aware of androcentrism, the habits of thought compacted into the previous paragraphs are glaringly, frustratingly omnipresent, in every book, almost in every line. They account for the fact that the usual method of discussing women is either total silence about women and sex role differentiation or a special chapter or footnote. They also account for the fact that we *never* find discussions in which *full* information about women and the feminine in a religious context is presented naturally and completely, with the matter-of-factness that information about men is presented. Nor do we find discussion in which that *full* information is interwoven with the other data and integrated into the entire presentation. These habits of thought also explain why even the most sympathetic outsiders expect discussions of women and religion either to be about men's views of women, the restrictions imposed on women, what they are allowed to do, and so on, or to be about female symbolism, deities, mythic characters, and the like. They do not think of the possibility that the discussions might be about women's religious lives and roles, their appropriations of the culture's symbol system, their deviations and independence from it. Even less likely is the expectation that the study of topics such as "men's views of women" or "the female deity" might yield different results if the student began with less androcentric presuppositions.

Actually the three central propositions that characterize the general ideology of androcentrism contain an interior contradiction that makes androcentrism glaringly inappropriate as a mind-set for cross-cultural or historical research. The first two elements of androcentrism, when combined, proclaim that the generic masculine is adequate to illumine the human—that *homo religiosus* is genuinely *homo religiosus,* not just *vir religiosus.* But those two propositions hide what the third covertly recognizes—that this is not the case, that woman-the-object is essentially not encompassed by *homo religiosus.* She is different and is instead an object of contemplation and symbolization by *vir religiosus.* So we are left with a situation in which sex role differentiation is assumed to be part of the human condition, and women are assumed to be different from men, but because of the authority of the generic masculine, we have no conceptual tools for rigorously dealing with the sex role differentiation that is so pervasive in all religious symbol and ritual systems and, therefore, no knowledge about women.

Thus, we paint ourselves into a corner with the androcentric habit of thought. The generic masculine would work only for religions in which there is no sex role differentiation, but there is no such religion, not even our own, to say nothing of the religious situations usually investigated by historians of religion. However, the authority of the generic masculine is great. In that conflict between the authority of the generic masculine and the reality of sex role differentiation, our knowledge about and understanding of women is crushed. Nor can the problem be solved by expanding our knowledge about woman-the-object. Making sure that a footnote or a chapter about women and religion is tacked on to the rest of the book or curriculum simply is not intellectually satisfying, rigorous, or adequate, given the pervasiveness of sex role differentiation. That would only perpetuate the woman-as-object syndrome, the attempt to define woman's place in man's world, in a slightly less androcentric fashion. Instead, we must find other methods, other models of humanity, that require us to have *full knowledge about women thoroughly integrated into* our discussions of the human, if we want to contend that we are doing adequate scholarship. Nor is this paradigm shift of relevance only to a few female scholars. It affects everyone trying to think about the human phenomenon. I might add in passing that the failure of conventional methodologies even to raise these issues, let alone to deal with them, is at the same time most condemning and most confirming of our own androcentrism

Therefore, instead of patching up the androcentric habit of thought, I would argue that we should abandon forthwith all three components of androcentrism and substitute an alternative outlook. I must emphasize once more that I am discussing an internal change in our own outlook, which is prerequisite even to understanding religion fully and which has nothing to do with whether or not the religions being studied are androcentric. Even an androcentric religion cannot be understood if the scholar is androcentric in outlook and, therefore, does not or cannot provide clear and complete knowledge and understanding of women's involvement in the religious situation.

I choose the word *androgyny* for the alternative method and model of humanity because even the simplest meaning of the term—"both male and female"—involves the negation of all three components of androcentrism. We no longer collapse the male norm and the human norm. Because that is no longer done, the generic masculine habit of language, thought, and research is no longer adequate. Then the whole "woman-as-object" syndrome also collapses. Simply put, there is a fundamental reorientation of consciousness to the deeply internalized realization that, however similar or different men and women may be in any religious situation, however dominant one sex or the other may be, they both represent modes of the human. Therefore, information about and understanding of both must be a part of the data that go into creating a human perspective on a human world, a model of religion, or an analysis of any specific religious situation. All this represents a profound and subtle shift in basic thought patterns, for the thought patterns of woman-as-object and "man" as sole representative of the human are deeply ingrained in our intellectual heritage. We are advocating a basic paradigm shift from models of humanity and modes of research and thought that perceive males at the center and females on the edges to modes that perceive both females and males at the center and reflect the essential "femaleness-maleness" of androgynous humanity.

Thus far, androgyny has been discussed very abstractly. This abstract level of definition *is* also most basic. It *is* more difficult to suggest more concrete and specific guidelines for an androgynous methodology, because as each historian of religions internalizes the basic paradigm shift from androcentrism to androgyny, each will see new ways in which the model of religion, as well as the theories and monographs dominant in the specialization, is skewed by androcentrism and will have numerous concrete suggestions for deriving an androgynous understanding and ordering of the data. Therefore, the specific suggestions I conclude this section with should be taken, not as foolproof guidelines, but as the formulations I have derived thus far in my attempts to do more adequate scholarship in several areas within history of religions. I might also say in passing that the amount of data not perceived by androcentric scholarship *is* astounding and that the hypotheses used to understand and order the perceived data simply are manifestly inadequate after one leaves behind the androcentric model of humanity. I cannot overemphasize how subtly different the entire discipline of history of religions looks after an androgynous perspective is internalized.

I would like to suggest that both the ritual dimension of religion, that is, the religious life of humankind, and the symbolic dimension of religion, that is, the mythic prototypes and constructs of the Ultimate by means of which religious humankind understands itself, need to be reinvestigated from an androgynous perspective.

First, I would like to suggest two guidelines for research into the ritual dimension of religion that yield a more adequate and whole portrait of and theories about ritual. These two suggestions are the result of my attempt to find androgynous descriptive and theoretical handles on the role of women in Aboriginal Australian religions, and I am convinced that they would illumine most other religious situations as well.

The first suggestion is exceedingly simple and I think exceedingly basic, because so much of the passage from androcentrism to androgyny simply involves new ways of organizing material and of relating data and ideas to one another. I suggest that women's religious lives and roles should be investigated and understood as a *pattern of exclusion and participation.* This methodological-organizational formula meets several very important criteria. It is reversible; that is, we could investigate men and religion as a pattern of exclusion and participation, and therefore it is nonhierarchical, treating males and females coequally as modes of the human, whichever sex is dominant. In addition, instead of ignoring or suppressing sex role differentiation, it deals head-on with this important facet of all religious situations. It allows us to discuss all aspects of women's religious roles and lives in a sexually differentiated religious situation and *requires* consideration of significant data that are glossed over in androcentric, hierarchical considerations of women and religion. Implicit in this methodological-organizational framework is the demand to study not just the *exclusion of* women (which turns out to be much more complex than androcentric scholars imagine), but also *exclusion by* women—that whole dimension of any religious situation exhibiting significant sexual differentiation that will be known *only* to women. This framework is also conducive to a more sensitive and subtle understanding of *coparticipation* than is provided by hierarchical, androcentric presuppositions.

The data and interpretations that arise when sexual differentiation is acknowledged and studied as a pattern of exclusion and participation rather than ignored give rise to the second important guideline for androgynous study of the ritual dimension of religion. When the patterns of exclusion and participation are analyzed, they reveal that male and female modes of being in a situation of sexual differentiation *hide a pattern of overarching and parallel experiences and expressions of sacredness.* To understand the total pattern of exclusion and participation, both modifiers of "sacredness" must be understood and recognized and their relationship with one another carefully delineated. On the one hand, both men and women participate in the sacred cosmos and are sacred; in that sense, there is overarching sacrality. However, at the same time the *expression* of that sacredness usually occurs by means of parallel, separate rituals for males and females because it is felt that to have one set of rituals for both men and women or to allow men to observe or participate in the women's spiritual universe, or vice versa, is dangerous and inappropriate. This dual recognition is fundamental, for without it one cannot understand the complexity and ambiguity of women's role in most religious situations. At the most generalized and abstract level, both males and females have access to the same experiences and expressions of sacredness. However, in the most concrete, everyday, and visible dimensions of the religious situation, that overarching sacredness is reached and expressed by differing, parallel, and mutually exclusive modes of religious experience and expression. This facet of women and religion in sexually differentiated religious situations has been almost totally overlooked. Instead, scholars have noticed only the mutual antagonism of male and female approaches to the sacred and have misinterpreted these different avenues to the sacred as a male monopoly of religion and the sacred.

Finally, I would like to suggest that, although throughout this chapter I have stressed the religious life and criticized the history of religions for insufficient and androcentric attention to the role of women in religion, the study of the symbols and constructs of the Ultimate used by religious humankind are almost as inadequate, for precisely the same reasons, as are the studies of the religious life of humankind. This suggestion grows out of an incomplete, continuing study of Hindu concepts of deity which makes me ever more dissatisfied with standard presentations of Indian concepts of deity, because androcentric presuppositions obscure what is clearly present in the iconography and even the texts relating to Indian concepts of deity.

Basically, androcentric presuppositions have led most scholars to unconsciously view feminine symbols and constructs of the Ultimate as secondary, unusual, and aberrant. As a result, goddesses and other feminine symbols, like women, receive a chapter, usually short and at the end of the book, in which consideration of them is *tacked on* rather than *integrated* into a full presentation of the symbols and constructs of the Ultimate. That, I am convinced, is a subtly but fundamentally wrong model of deity for most religious situations. Instead, I suggest that we should not be surprised by a fundamental bisexuality or androgyny in theistic imagery, but rather should be surprised when it is lacking. As humanity is male and female, whatever hierarchical relations between men and women may be, so in most cases will anthropomorphic symbolisms be fundamentally female-and-male, whichever is dominant. Furthermore, I suggest that the female dimensions of deity-images are too fundamental to be appended, androcentric-wise, to the central and normal subject matter—male images of deity. A more integrated, androgynous model of deity *is* much more in order. Such *is* certainly the case with Indian images of deity and probably also with many other theistic systems. Only an androcentric model of humanity could have made us so insensitive to this fundamentally bisexual imagery and then led us to present the minuscule portion of female imagery that was perceived as an appendage to discussions of the male images of deity.

Answering the first of the skeptical, defensive "Yes, but . . ." questions with which historians of religion often respond to the feminist critique of the discipline and its methodology has taken us deep into a discussion of the nature of androcentric thinking, its scope within the discipline, and the inherent unfeasibility of androcentrism as a mind-set conducive to good cross-cultural research and theorizing. Trying to answer this question has also led us into a discussion of corrective measures for history of religions methodology. It seems completely clear that we cannot weasel out of feminist criticisms of history of religions methodology by appealing to the supposed androcentrism of the religious systems studied by historians of religion.

Now, in conclusion, what of the second "Yes, but . . ." question? "Yes, but isn't all this peripheral compared to other issues in the history of religions?" I understand the question, but the wrong word is chosen. These issues are not peripheral. They are terribly central. But they are also *preliminary*. They are not the only program that I, or any historian of religions, would want to investigate for my entire scholarly career. However, despite their preliminary nature, they are also absolutely central. Therefore, I can't get out of this corner, called "women and religion," that I've been backed into until the discipline reforms itself so that we always deal with women and religion whenever we discuss religion. We should not really need to spend time and scholarly energy discussing something as completely preliminary as the inadequacy of androcentrism for a cross-cultural and historical discipline like the history of religions, nor should we have to discuss whether we need to know and understand women and religion as well as we understand men and religion ever to understand *homo religiosus*. It would be advantageous to the discipline simply to accept the feminist critique and to make the requisite corrections in methodology and research programs.

Then we could get on with doing history of religions instead of arguing about preliminaries. For "women and religion" is by no means the only or even the central issue for the history of religions. But until an adequate solution to that problem is integrated into the discipline, no other subject matter can be dealt with adequately, because all our theories and models are based on the data of religions, and so far we have been blind to much of the data and have looked at the rest of it with very skewed perceptions and presuppositions.

CHAPTER 3

Where Have We Been?
Where Do We Need to Go?

*Key Questions for Women Studies
in Religion and Feminist Theology*

As someone who helped found the disciplines of women studies in religion and feminist theology and as someone who has written a great deal on these topics, I have a long vantage point from which to view our concerns. In this chapter, I seek more to review the essentials of our disciplines than to blaze new methodological trails. That is a task for younger scholars who have the freshness that I had in 1967 when I wrote my first paper on women and religion, which was then unexplored and novel territory that quickly became controversial.[1] I suggest that it is instructive to ascertain what we have clearly established as scholars of women studies and as feminist theologians, what has been suggested but is not yet firmly in place, and what needs to be integrated into our scholarly and theological agendas. I will be as concerned about how best to maintain and advance our agendas, given the politics of academia, as I will be about purely scholarly concerns.

WHAT WE HAVE ESTABLISHED:
A PARADIGM SHIFT IN MODELS OF HUMANITY

In my view, the single most important accomplishment of women studies and the feminist movement has been to change the model of humanity with which many people and many scholars operate. There is no question that I was socialized, both as a human being and as a scholar, to think with an androcentric model of humanity. Widespread use of the term *androcentric* is itself a product of the conceptual revolution initiated by women studies.[2] Before that time, the term had been rarely used, because it was not understood that there was any other way to conceptualize humanity or that we all operated with a model of humanity that put men in the center of attention as normal and normative human beings and women on the periphery as a "special case" and a bit abnormal. Such a mode of language and scholarship and such a model of humanity were normal and without alternatives. Only when we began to ask why women so rarely appeared on the pages of the books we read, even in descriptive accounts of religion, did we begin to figure out that the model of humanity we had imbibed from our culture made women invisible or that there were alternatives to that model of humanity.

I will never forget how hard and long I struggled as a graduate student to figure out why all the scholarship on women and religion seemed so inadequate and unbalanced until one day when I realized the problem was that whenever women were studied, a rare occurrence, they were studied as objects in an androcentric universe. I also realized that we would never get anywhere in understanding *women* until we changed that basic methodological assumption. These things were already quite clear to me in 1968, when I took my doctoral prelims.

The distinction between androcentric models of humanity and what I called "androgynous models of humanity" for many years is clear and explicit in my doctoral dissertation, most of which was written in 1974,[3] and it is very explicit in one of my early publications, written in 1975 and finally published in 1977.[4] In that work, I suggested that most topics in the field of religious studies could benefit from the application of an androgynous model of humanity.

The relative success of this conceptual revolution can be measured by the facts that the generic masculine has largely gone out of style, even in many popular media, and that many general accounts of religion, such as introductory textbooks, are gender-balanced. Of course, there are holdouts, such as conservative religious groups who refuse to change their liturgies to gender-inclusive language, but it is a significant victory that most academic journals now demand nonsexist language, that textbooks publishers solicit gender-inclusive manuscripts, and that daily newspapers avoid the generic masculine. In my view, these changes in more popular and more widely accessible venues are more important and more significant than the rather considerable body of women studies scholarship that has accumulated in the last thirty years. Such changes indicate real changes in cultural consciousness, whereas scholarly literature usually reaches a far smaller audience. I do not think we can say too often or too clearly that this fundamental shift of consciousness is the most basic and fundamental point of women studies and feminist theology.

However, a major problem remains. We have definitely succeeded in highlighting women's lives and concerns and in making women much more vividly present than they were before the advent of women studies. Unfortunately, we often end up preaching to the choir. Courses, talks, and books with the words *women studies* or *feminism* in the title, of which there are now many, are usually attended or read almost exclusively by women. As a result, women are put in the odd and uncomfortable position of carrying the whole burden of human genderedness by ourselves, thus freeing men to go about business as usual, unencumbered by gender issues and gender concerns, as unknowledgeable as ever about the content of women studies.

Men often do not regard the term *gender* as something that applies to them; they regard it as applying mainly or exclusively to women. Thus, the presence of women studies and feminism, by themselves, do not solve the problem of androcentrism. Women now are regarded as truly human rather than something on the periphery of humanity, but men still don't regard themselves as gendered beings, just like women in that regard, and they tend to regard any topic dealing with women as irrelevant to them, despite the fact that most men live with women and all men live among women. The paradigm shift from androcentric to gender-neutral and gender-inclusive models of humanity is still incomplete in that women have taken it more to heart than have men.

In some ways, the existence of various programs devoted to the study of "minorities"—women, blacks, native Americans, gay and lesbian people—is an important development, given that all these perspectives were almost completely ignored in the scholarship that dominated the academic world several decades ago. But the existence of these programs and disciplines, taught mainly by members of these groups for members of these groups, also leaves the dominant group free to continue on its course, its consciousness unchanged by the information conveyed in books written by and classes taught by members of the "minority" groups. Therefore, intellectually and ideologically, the problem of human genderedness and other human diversities is not solved by developing specialized disciplines, taught by and for the various "minorities," that can then be ignored by the dominant groups.

For these reasons, I have severely restricted my acceptance of speaking engagements on "women and Buddhism," "Buddhism and feminism," or even "Buddhism and gender." Instead, I offer to speak on "Buddhism and social justice" and use gender issues as an example of social justice. I find that my audiences are no longer mainly made up of women, which is what I want, given that many women are well educated on gender issues while most men are not. I am really tired of gender issues being isolated from other social justice issues and considered a special case, which is what often happens when the focus is on women, and I am really tired of women studies and feminist theology being marginalized as special interests.[5]

At this point, both because of the success of women studies in illuminating women's lives and because of the peripheral role women studies still plays in the academy, I suggest that the time is ripe to regard our main enterprise as gender studies, with women studies as a subdiscipline within gender studies, rather than an independent discipline. I think there was a time when women's religious lives were so unknown and unresearched that focusing on women, almost exclusively and to the exclusion of men, was warranted. I also think that there was a time when gender studies would have overwhelmed women studies if we had tried to move toward a greater emphasis on gender studies. But I do not think that is the case anymore. Furthermore, intellectually, the main issue always was gender and its unacknowledged role in human affairs, not women. Because gender was not acknowledged and recognized as a fact present in all human societies, women were ignored. Focusing on women corrects part of the problem, but it does not correct the failure to integrate knowledge about women into knowledge about humanity, which is what a complete paradigm shift in our models of humanity would require.

I make this suggestion for both intellectual and strategic reasons. I believe we will be more successful at achieving major goals of women studies and feminist theology in the long run if we conceptualize our work as part of the project of gender studies. We want what we have discovered to become general knowledge so that it can have society-wide impact. We cannot achieve that goal by remaining an enclave that attracts mainly women. Men need to think about gender and become more familiar with their own genderedness, as well as with the content of women studies and feminist theology. The project of gender studies, with women studies as one component of the field, is more likely to achieve these goals than is a continued emphasis on women studies in isolation. We need to do whatever it takes to undermine the assumption that *gender* is a women's issue, is another term that can be used interchangeably with *women*. Until then, the paradigm shift in models of humanity that is our most basic agenda will still be incomplete.

AGENDAS IN THE PRESENT:
UNDERSTANDING THE DISTINCTION BETWEEN
WOMEN STUDIES AND FEMINIST THEOLOGY

In the foregoing section of this chapter, I have repeatedly used the phrase "women studies in religion and feminist theology." I am not repeating myself or trying to increase the word count of this chapter in order to meet the editor's guidelines! I think of "women studies in religion" and "feminist theology" as two distinct academic enterprises that should not be confused or conflated, though they are related. The relationship between these two subdisciplines duplicates the relationship between religious studies and theology, between the descriptive and the normative tasks in the discussion of religion, a topic over which too much ink has been spilled. I have contributed to that deluge of ink largely to argue that the same scholar can participate in both religious studies and theology without confusion or self-deception.[6] I have also argued that there can be no hard and fast division between these two disciplines, because the scholar's standpoint always affects the selection of subject material and findings, at least to some extent, and because there is no "neutral no place" from which the scholar can observe and report on religion.[7]

In my view, the distinction between the normative and the descriptive aspects of discussions about religion is, unfortunately, drawn too tightly and too sharply concerning the links between religious studies and theology, while the distinctions between women studies in religion and feminist theology are drawn in an overly lax manner and the two are often confused. Simply studying women's religious lives is often regarded as a feminist project rather than a necessary and ideological neutral (though not methodologically neutral) component of religious studies. Blurring this distinction often weakens the case for women studies while doing little to promote the cause of feminism.

Put briefly, women studies is essentially an academic method that has to do with including all the relevant data, while feminism or feminist theology is a social vision that critiques and reconstructs one's own religion, culture, or academic environment. One is descriptive and the other is normative. Both of them grew out of what is usually called "the second wave of feminism" and its attendant paradigm shift in models of humanity. But if there is any place in religious studies where the distinction between descriptive and normative needs to be understood and honored, it is in matters dealing with women and religion.[8]

Paradoxically, the *connection* between women studies in religion and feminist theology makes this distinction crucial. The agenda simply to *study* women's religious lives, to insist that information about women is crucial to any account of any religions, still engenders hostility and dismissal from some who regard the *study* of women and religion as a political rather than an intellectual enterprise. But the study of women's religious lives is not, by itself, a feminist project, because it does not entail making judgments about the information that is discovered in one's scholarship. It only entails the judgment that, because women are human beings, one cannot study any religious situation adequately if one neglects or refuses to collect information about women. After the emergence of the discipline of women studies in religion, it is inexcusable for any scholar to be hostile to that endeavor, given that we now have countless demonstrations of how seriously one can misunderstand a religion if one does not notice its women.[9]

I would contend that it is strategically advantageous to be able to claim that a scholar's personal adoption of a feminist lifestyle and belief system is completely irrelevant to whether or not he needs to pay attention to women studies in religion in his descriptive scholarship. Though women as subject matter may have initially been discovered by feminists, the data concerning women as subject matter is relevant to *all* scholars, not to feminists alone. We cannot make that point too often or too forcefully. Therefore, it is crucial to distinguish carefully between those aspects of our work that fall within the domain of women studies in religion and those that fall within the domain of feminist critique and reconstruction of our traditions—feminist theology.

The distinction between women studies and a feminist critique is crucial for another reason that is more relevant to those of us who work with topics concerning women and religion than for others in the field. Many of us who do scholarship regarding women studies in religion are also feminists, but as scholars we have to be careful not to project our feminist values onto the religious and cultural situations of other times and places. These are complex issues, and most of us have undoubtedly experienced gratitude that we do not live in some of the times and places in which we study women's religious lives. Nevertheless, it is anachronistic to criticize ancient Israelite culture, for example, for not meeting our expectations regarding equitable relations between the sexes. It is even more problematic, especially in impersonal and public contexts, to preach to people of cultures and religions not our own about what their standards for relations between women and men should be. Such practices easily become naive and arrogant. Given that we share the world with those who practice contemporary religions and live in cultures that we, as feminists, may find difficult, I regard the proper division of labor between women studies in religion and feminist critiques to be especially crucial, especially in cross-cultural studies. Western feminists have already done enough damage rushing to criticize cultural situations they do not understand well.

For this reason, I have long advocated thorough descriptive study, seeking to understand a religious doctrine or practice as insiders would understand and justify it, as a prerequisite to making any normative comments about that doctrine or practice. Quick condemnation of unfamiliar beliefs and practices is one of the great pitfalls of cross-cultural studies. The point of such study is not to feel smug and superior. The ground rules of cross-cultural studies require suspension of judgment at first, until one is thoroughly familiar with the situation being studied. One must first understand why such doctrines and practices exist and what purposes they serve according to the viewpoint of those who hold those doctrines and follow those practices. Empathy is the most critical tool for engaging in cross-cultural studies in ways that do not create further mutual entrenchment and scorn. It must be applied in all cases, even the most unsavory, before any normative comments would be appropriate.

If one does not jump to conclusions about how certain religious or cultural phenomena are experienced by projecting from one's own values, but takes more time to reflect on the practice, some surprising conclusions may result. Some practices that seem undesirable may turn out not to be as completely disadvantageous to women as they might at first appear to be. Arranged marriages, polygyny, and modest dress codes can seem advantageous to the many women who live with these practices, even though they would drive many Western women, both feminist and nonfeminist, mad. But these women's explanations and justifications have cogency, and understanding them is certainly part of the task of women studies in religion.

However, certain religious doctrines and practices are difficult to explain even after employing considerable empathy. If one chooses to continue one's reflections into the realm of evaluation and normative comments, certain precautions should be taken. First of all, it should be made clear that one is switching hats, from being a women studies scholar to being a feminist theologian or ethicist. As I have argued many times, I do not agree that it is impossible for one person to fill both roles, but it is important not to confuse them in one's own mind or in one's work. Second, it is far easier and more straightforward to make normative claims about a tradition or culture in which one participates than about another tradition or culture. Nevertheless, on ethical grounds, feminists and others sometimes do experience an imperative to speak out against certain practices, common in a culture other than their own, that cause great human suffering. There is no alternative but to acquiesce to complete relativism, a moral position that is never adequate.

The major question, then, becomes one of what Buddhists would call "skillful means." What actions or statements would actually alleviate the situation about which I am concerned, as opposed to simply allowing me to feel self-righteous and relieved that I have made a statement? In particular, cross-cultural denunciations from first world countries and former colonists probably only entrench the situation further. Then resisting changes in women's situations becomes part of national pride and resistance to Westernization. It is also important to avoid inflammatory rhetoric and language. It is less divisive to talk about traditional African genital operations than to talk about African genital mutilation, for example, and probably more effective. One must also evaluate whether quiet support, both emotional and financial, of indigenous women who are fighting for change in their own cultures might not be the most effective action we could take.

In the context of one's own culture or religion, the situation is much more straightforward. Insiders to a tradition certainly are appropriate spokespeople for that tradition and architects of its future. As such, they cannot be faulted for not having the appropriate credentials for evaluating the tradition. Some of the most creative, interesting, and exciting work that has been done on women and religion, or on religious thought in general for that matter, involves the critiques and reconstructions of religious traditions done by feminist commentators and theologians, most of them women.

The obstacles a feminist theologian is more likely to face have to do with the arguments between theology and religious studies on the part of those involved professionally in the study of religion. Normative work is not considered to be "scholarship" by many in the field of religious studies. I am reminded of the remark that came back to me regarding an early article I wrote on Hindu goddesses as a resource for Western attempts to reimage the deity as female: "It's a very interesting article, but *that* is not scholarship."[10] It seems that if one thinks about and thinks with certain data, rather than only reporting on them, one crosses over a certain line between "scholarship" and "speculation" which makes one suspect and untrustworthy as a scholar in the evaluations of some. Another problem facing those who do normative work is that, except at seminaries, finding employment can be difficult. And seminaries may well be reluctant to hire feminist theologians and almost always refuse to hire non-Christian theologians, whether feminist or not.

Here, too, a clear distinction between women studies in religion and feminist theology may help. Many of us who have done feminist theology also do purely descriptive work which we regard as a necessary foundation for feminist commentary. One can hardly do good normative work if one is not thoroughly informed about the tradition one is critiquing and reconstructing. To do normative, evaluative work without that basis would be sheer speculation, but such exercises do not usually characterize the work of academic scholars who also do academic theology. When attempts are made to undercut and dismiss our work because of its normative dimensions, we can reply not only by arguing for the dignity, necessity, and inevitability of a normative dimension in scholarly work. We can also rightly point to the fact that we have thoroughly researched women's religious lives, experiences, and thought, using the standard methodologies employed by religious studies to engage in women studies in religion.

WHERE SHOULD WE GO?
EMERGING ISSUES IN WOMEN STUDIES
IN RELIGION AND IN FEMINIST THEOLOGY

The dominant issue for women studies in religion and for feminist theology is, in my view, the extent to which the whole field of women and religion has become identified with and collapsed into Christian feminist theology. There are two components to this problem. One is the extent to which scholars, especially those who primarily study a non-Western religion, no longer identify with academic groups and publications that specialize in women and religion, even though these scholars may well study women and religion extensively. The other is the extent to which feminist theology is assumed to be *Christian* feminist theology, which mirrors and parallels the way theology and *Christian* theology are confused in the academy at large. One would think that only Christians carry on normative discussions, to observe the configuration of many forums for the study and discussion of religion.

The frustration this situation can lead to is evident in the comment of a colleague, who is a Buddhist and scholar of Buddhism, in her response to a recent roundtable discussion which I wrote on this topic: "I have participated for many years in the same groups and gatherings Rita mentions. Like Rita, I have drifted away from feminist theology activities because I find little of interest going on there, despite the fact that I consider my work to fall, in some sense, under that rubric. I can confirm Rita's experience of passive exclusion from these groups, manifested in their offering little of interest to feminist scholars involved in non-Western, and especially in non-Christian religions."[11] Equally telling is a comment by the editors of the recently published volume *Is There a Future for Feminist Theology?* "Although we have included diversity in terms of theoretical and methodological issues, what this volume lacks . . . is any dialogue with non-Western contexts. This lack of ongoing engagement by feminist theology, and gender theory itself, with experience outside Western culture artificially limits the issues of gender and religion. From our perspective, this is the major task for the next millennium. The traditional dichotomy between East and West, a meta-narrative of a past age, needs to be dissolved to allow the vast plurality of global experience to take center stage."[12]

Thus, at least in the North American world with which I am most familiar, the movement to study and discuss women and religion, broadly conceived, has been collapsed, for the most part, into feminist theology, and feminist theology has become almost exclusively Christian feminist theology. Those scholars who focus on descriptive accounts of women and religion, especially in the rich fields of Asian and Middle Eastern religions, no longer find relevant scholarly forums for their area studies in the fields of women and religion or religion and gender and have abandoned primary identification with those fields.

Unfortunately, at the same time, most of the scholars and theologians who continue to think of themselves as involved in the field of gender and religion usually are not conversant with the scholarship produced by these experts on non-Western and nonmonotheistic religions, which weakens their work. When the agenda is specifically feminist theology, rather than women studies in religion, this narrow focus intensifies and creates even more problems. As I have already indicated, many theologians, feminist or otherwise, assume that the theological arena is, by definition, Christian. They do not study or refer to scholarship about non-Christian traditions, such as Hinduism or Islam, even if it is on a topic about which they are concerned, such as imagery for the deity. Nor are they familiar with the theological work of their colleagues in other traditions.

I have long lamented these Eurocentric and Christian-centered biases in feminist theology and, to a lesser extent, among those who identify as scholars of gender and religion.[13] (There is plenty of good scholarship on gender and religion in non-Western contexts; it just isn't being taken seriously by many Western theoreticians of gender and religion.) Given the paradigm shift in models of humanity from less inclusive to more inclusive models of humanity that was both the inspiration and the primary achievement of the movement to study women and religion seriously, these Eurocentric and Christian-centered tendencies are highly problematic and disappointing. For a movement that based its raison d'être on the need to include those who had formerly been excluded—women—to limit its discussions to European or North American women and Christian women is inexcusable.

Thus, feminist theology, especially, needs to redirect itself. It needs to return to its original vision of inclusivity, with the understanding that inclusivity goes beyond Christianity or Europe and its cultural derivatives. That is to say, an emphasis on diversity, which is already quite common in the feminist theology movement, must include concern with religious diversity if its alleged concern with diversity is to mean anything. Promoting intra-Christian diversity does not lead to attention to religious diversity and does not provide policies and stances that would be inviting to people of non-Christian religions. Nor is it adequate to consider that one's efforts to be religiously diverse have been successful if there is some token inclusion of Judaism and Goddess-worshipping members of the feminist spirituality movement while Buddhists, Muslims, Hindus, and members of the various small-scale traditions and ethnic traditions are ignored, find nothing of interest in feminist theological forums, and feel excluded. Failing that, the movement needs to stop calling itself "the feminist theology movement" and start labeling itself honestly as the "*Christian* feminist theology movement." It would be difficult to overestimate how irritating I find it to read of yet another book or conference on "feminist theology" that clearly is concerned only with Christian feminist theology.[14]

I would also like to see more communication between those interested in descriptive accounts of women's religious lives, especially in non-Western religions, and those interested in theoretical issues surrounding gender and feminist theology. In particular, I would like to see forums devoted to discussing gender and religion or feminist theology explicitly invite specialists on women and gender in non-Western contexts to their meetings, because now there is little to suggest to an expert on Hindu women's rituals, for example, that she or he might want to read a paper at the Women and Religion section of the American Academy of Religion, for example. Such exchanges would be mutually beneficial, but they would be especially helpful in overcoming the parochialism concerning gender and religion, women and religion, and feminist theology that can plague English-speaking discussions of these topics.

CONCLUSION

Though in a certain sense, I have discussed the past, present, and future of our endeavors as scholars of women studies or gender studies and as feminist theologians, I have had more to say, in each case, about future directions than about present accomplishments. Concerning our most significant achievement, the paradigm shift in models of humanity, I suggest that we solidify that achievement by taking the next logical step and make our major focus *gender* and religion, seeing women studies in religion as one aspect of that larger project. We should also do everything we can to insist that these materials be included in "general" textbooks and courses, rather than limited to contexts for gender studies or women studies.

To safeguard women studies and gender studies from politically and ideologically motivated attacks, I suggest that we clearly differentiate women studies or gender studies from feminist theology, that we clearly differentiate our descriptive work from our normative work, even though they are intertwined. Others may disagree with us about the validity or results of feminist theology, but there can be no grounds for disagreeing with the need for gender studies and women studies as academic disciplines.

Finally, to achieve "truth in advertising," we need either to label what many now call "feminist theology" as "Christian feminist theology" or to foster religious diversity in our discussions of feminist theology. Clearly, I prefer the latter option. As part of that endeavor, I also would suggest that we put more effort in bringing together scholars of women and gender in non-Western contexts with those who study gender and religion or do feminist theology in Western contexts.

CHAPTER 4

The Place of the Personal and the Subjective in Religious Studies

Religious Studies is the academic discipline devoted to studying and commenting upon the extremely diverse religious beliefs and behaviors found in all cultures around the globe, in all periods of human history. Nevertheless, studying or teaching religion in the college or university is also a very politically sensitive enterprise because everyone has personal opinions, often very strong personal opinions, about religion. Because of the intensely personal, often passionate attitudes people have about religion, calls for neutrality and objectivity can be very strong in this field, and expressing one's own personal interest in or subjective views about religion can be dangerous to one's career (unless one expresses critical, antireligious sentiments). How did this situation develop?

The European enlightenment brought about great changes in how religion was understood, which made possible the eventual emergence of the discipline of religious studies. Rather than being part of a communal ethos, religion came to be viewed as a personal belief system to be studied because of personal religious commitments (or rejected because of personal conclusions—something not really possible in premodern Europe or any other traditional culture). This, in turn, caused changes in how religion was studied, as Christian theology fell from its position as "queen of the sciences" in medieval universities to become a much less prestigious and much less common pursuit. These changes in perspective, though very briefly sketched here, largely explain how studying religion was viewed until relatively recently (the 1950s or

1960s) in the United States, which will be my primary reference point in this discussion.

Until the 1950s and 1960s, most study of religion was done at private colleges and universities, which often had some Christian denominational affiliation. Studying "religion" really meant studying Christianity. The religious studies requirement common in the graduation requirements of these colleges and universities was defended as a strategy for strengthening the religious affiliations and commitments fostered earlier by churches. All this is in accord with the European enlightenment notion of religion as a personal, private matter, not a public ethos. Meanwhile, in the United States, large public universities not connected in any way with any religious denomination became increasingly important as more and more people received their educations in such institutions rather than in private colleges and universities. And it seemed self-evident to most people that religion could not and should not be taught in any way at such institutions. This too is completely in accord with the European enlightenment notion of religion as a personal not a public affair. Most also assumed that to study a religion is synonymous with advocating for that religion. (This has, in fact, been the dominant mode in traditional forms of religion worldwide.) Clearly, if advocacy for a religion were the only method and motive for studying it, public universities devoted to educating people from very diverse backgrounds could not afford the divisiveness that religion would have brought to the curriculum.

As an example, when I was an undergraduate at a public university, my formal major was philosophy, despite my interest in religious studies. I was told that to teach about religion in such an institution would violate the separation of church and state and was both impossible and nonsensical. (I did manage nevertheless to study a good bit of what today could easily be taught in any religious studies department.) Eight years after my graduation, I returned to teach religious studies at a different campus of that same university system. But I returned to teach world religions, not only Christianity. Clearly, something major had changed in the meantime in that particular university system. This change was repeated at countless other institutions, both private and public. Private institutions, which had always taught "religion," now routinely teach world religions, not just Christianity, and the study of religion is no longer so frequently viewed as a way to further inculcate the training of a confirmation class. Public universities now routinely include a department of religious studies. It is assumed by all that this department will teach about all religions, not just Christianity, and it is crucial to such institutions that the teaching of religion not be a front for evangelizing for that religion. What had happened to promote these drastic changes? In answering that question, we will also discover why calls for neutrality and objectivity are so strong in religious studies and why expressing personal interests and subjective views about religion can be so dangerous.

Beginning in the late nineteenth century, a new discipline had developed, primarily in European universities. Its German title, *religionswissenschaft,* the scientific study of religion, says best what this discipline wanted to accomplish. The transformations regarding the study of religion in universities and colleges in the United States, both public and private, that I just described were largely due to the influence of this European model of how religion should be studied. So it is important to discuss why this new discipline developed and its methods and ideals.

This new field developed in large part because, in the late nineteenth century, so much new information was being discovered about religion, and because this newly discovered information dealt with a multitude of religions, not just Christianity. Whole dead religions of the ancient world came to light again, largely through exploration and archeology in the Middle East. These discoveries forced new critical historical scholarship about the Bible. At the same time, the wealth of Indian religions and the religious universes of China and Japan were being studied in depth. Finally, early anthropologists brought home a veritable cornucopia of religious beliefs, practices, and artifacts that seemed thoroughly exotic and fascinating to Europeans. All these discoveries dramatically changed how Christianity was studied and definitively undercut any Christian claims about its uniqueness and superiority. Suddenly, there was much more to religion than just Christianity, on the one hand, and "heathenism" on the other. More and more, Christianity came to be seen as another religion among many religions, not as "Religion." This change is a conceptual revolution still contested by many conservative Christians.

For *religionswissenschaft,* religion is global in scope and Christianity holds no privileged position among religions. Such theological and subjective judgments about the *value* of any religion were simply inadmissible, impossible for the *scientific* study of religion. Thus, we see the source of the fact that the study of religion is now practiced, in both public and private colleges and universities, as the *comparative* study of religion, inevitably cross-cultural and global in scope. But we also see the source of the difficulty with expressing any personal or subjective views about religion in the discipline of religious studies.

The proponents of *religionswissenschaft* claimed that they were scientists, not philosophers or theologians, which made their method of studying religion academically rigorous and appropriate in the modern university. To study religion "scientifically" meant to them that they were simply observing religion "objectively," without adding or subtracting anything, just as a scientist observes nature objectively, without any personal interest in or bias about what is being observed. Like many nineteenth-century scholars, they really did believe in such objectivity, in being so able to divest oneself of one's cultural baggage that it disappeared completely. If one can't attain that ideal 100 percent, one should at least keep trying. This was not a situation that created much room for talking about the personal and the subjective in religious studies. Instead, it created a lot of what I call "science envy." Claims about the possibility of such objectivity still seem self-evident and unproblematic to many contemporary scholars of religion. The strictest proponents of *religionswissenschaft* also claimed that theirs is the *only* legitimate method for studying religion, at least in the academy. Academic studies of religion must not be tainted with anything personal or subjective, evaluative or normative, because such comments would not involve knowledge, but only opinion. This claim also contributes to the "science envy" so apparent in some aspects of religious studies and is also still held by many scholars of religion. But the weakness, indeed the untenability, of these two claims is the wedge that reintroduces the possibility of academically respectable expressions of personal interest and subjective judgments about religions into our discipline. The necessarily and inherently comparative character of our discipline, however, is uncontestable.

The historical narrative outlined above has led to the current tangled situation in the field of religious studies. Theology, understood broadly as the actual claims about the nature of reality made by religions, has of course not gone away, and people still do take religions to be personally relevant. If one is going to study a religion, then one cannot avoid studying its theology. It is impossible to teach a course on world religions without teaching about myriad truth claims made by religions. How do you do so within the value system of *religionswissenschaft?* The solution was to have outsiders to the various religions teach those religions. That was thought to be much safer, since outsiders would be "neutral" and "objective" about a religious system, whereas insiders, it was claimed, could not be objective and might describe the religion positively and persuasively. For Hinduism and Buddhism, that solution was easily applied.

Until very recently, these religions were most often studied and taught by Westerners who were not themselves Hindus or Buddhists. But it is much harder to have Judaism and Christianity taught by genuine outsiders. It seems that not enough Asian non-Christians were interested in or allowed to receive the training required to teach Judaism or Christianity in Western universities. So Judaism and Christianity have been taught by nominal Jews and Christians who were expected to do historical scholarship and to be disinterested in the religion itself.

In general, it was thought to be safer to entrust the study of religion to atheists and unbelievers, who were thought to be more objective and neutral. (That atheism or unbelief is itself a religious position was ignored or not recognized by these advocates of neutrality.) The strange effect of this logic is that "objectivity" and neutrality actually mean *caring against religion rather than caring for religion,* because complete indifference to the claims made by religions is impossible.[1] But one set of reactions—caring against—is promoted as preferable to the other set of reactions—caring for, as if caring against religion were more neutral, more objective. It's a very strange situation when one of the best ways to further claims to academic rigor is to say one has no *personal* interest in what one spends one's life studying, without getting paid a whole lot for it!

But what about someone who is actually interested in religious truth claims and practices the spiritual disciplines recommended in some of these teachings? Under the claims of orthodox science of religion, such a person *could not* be a good scholar, because such a scholar is not "neutral" vis-à-vis religion. This has led to a lot of hypocrisy, as some scholars actually *do* practice the religion they study, but secretly. This conundrum has been particularly difficult in one of the areas in which I have done much of my work—Buddhist studies. I was one of the first "out" Buddhist scholars of religion and have done a lot of Buddhist feminist reconstructive work for which I am well known.[2] A friend of mine was interviewing a young graduate student on the job market sometime in the late 1990s. She asked the graduate student about her approach to the study of religion. When my friend heard the replies, she said, "Oh, it sounds as if you've been influenced by Rita Gross." The graduate student reacted quite defensively. "Not me. Her practice of Buddhism obscures her ability to understand it." This strange comment typifies the absurdities to which extreme claims for "objectivity" in religious studies can take one. I would reply that my practice of Buddhism has certainly *changed* my understanding of Buddhism, but not so as to make Buddhism more *obscure,* either to me or to those to whom I explain it.

According to some in religious studies, the way out of this illogical impasse is to admit the impossibility of complete objectivity and neutrality and the inevitability of a subjective and personal element, not only in the study of religion, but in all studies. Open admission of the obvious, that our personal interests and standpoints *do* influence our choices of subject matter, the data we see, and the conclusions we derive, does not turn us into unbalanced fanatical zealots and proselytizers. Nor does it mean we become sloppy scholars; good rules of argument and good use of evidence remain important. But we do become more honest—and more humble, which, though usually considered a virtue, is not a virtue to which scholars are often prone.

As teachers, we should always make it clear that teaching *about* religion is not the same as giving *religious instruction* in the classroom. We do not, and never should, give religious instruction in our university classrooms, though we can let our students know that we have interests and preferences regarding religion, for which we can make sound arguments. For example, it would be very difficult for me to teach religious studies without my feminist stance coming through clearly. But none of my exams or essay assignments require a feminist stance on the part of the student, though they may well be required to demonstrate that they understand the arguments made by feminists in religion. Much as in teaching evolution, still a touchy topic in some universities, we require students to learn the arguments, and we test them on how well they understand the arguments regarding a certain position, but we don't test their personal beliefs.

Actually, the issue of the personal and the subjective plays out differently in the two major subdivisions within religious studies. The first of these is the descriptive study of religion, devoted to historical and anthropological interests (which describes *what is* concerning religious beliefs and behaviors). The second is the normative, or constructive study of religion, devoted to theology and ethics (which studies claims about the nature of reality and what *should be* regarding religious beliefs and behaviors and often enters the debates concerning what *should be* ethically). Religious studies journals and departments argue endlessly about the relationship between these two wings of the discipline. Some claim that they are completely distinct and separate; some scholars who take this position often also argue that religious studies should consist *only* of descriptive enterprises, that any normative or constructive concerns are invalid and inappropriate. Not surprisingly, scholars in this camp also argue most vociferously that objectivity and neutrality are possible and desirable. Others, myself included, see inevitable links between descriptive and normative studies in religion, arguing that part of the job description of a scholar of religious studies includes evaluating religious phenomena and discussing what religious beliefs and behaviors are more likely to promote human and planetary well-being.[3] Needless to say, those of us who take this position regarding the field of religious studies are not so afraid of or worried about the personal and the subjective in religious studies, because we claim that they are impossible to avoid, even in descriptive dimensions of the field.

The case for admitting the subjective and personal in the descriptive wing of religious studies turns on claims that scholars inevitably bring their own outlook, experience, training, life situation, and values into the study, making complete objectivity and neutrality impossible. One cannot get completely outside one's skin and one's culture to observe religion from some neutral nowhere, reporting *what is* completely separate from one's own observational viewpoint. That being the case, claims to pure objectivity only obscure the dense interplay between "what is" and "what I see" in descriptions of religious phenomena, making "what is" less, not more evident. Scholars are not merely blank receptive mirrors on which can be inscribed the data of the religious situation they are studying. They also project onto the data from their subjectivity. The more adamant the claims that this process is not occurring, the more the data are actually skewed and obscured. The only correctives are self-consciousness and self-awareness, and the modesty to admit that one may not be seeing *everything*. Then what one does see and report on will be much more accurate.

In my view, the claim that descriptive studies in religion could be completely objective was completely discredited by women studies scholarship in religion. Women studies scholarship has demonstrated, beyond any doubt, that who the scholar is determines, in part, what the scholar sees. Before the second wave of feminism, the study of religion was almost exclusively in the hands of men—and what they saw was the religious activities and thinking of other men. When I entered graduate school in religious studies in 1965, there were only twelve women in a student body of over four hundred at the University of Chicago Divinity School, and people were worried that so many women (six in the entering class) were pursuing graduate studies in religion. Not surprisingly, given this situation, we students were taught *only* about what men did and thought religiously. Women were, literally, invisible to these male scholars. If they ever studied anything about women, it was not what women themselves thought or did, but what men thought about and did with women. So even when peripherally studying women, they were still really studying men, while also claiming to be doing objective and value-free scholarship. These male scholars were quite unaware of their androcentrism, of the way they projected onto the data their own deeply held viewpoint that men are more interesting, important, and *normal* than women. They simply did not notice that half the participants of any religion would be women and that often cultural norms dictated that women's religious lives would be considerably different from men's. This failure to study women, when infrequently pointed out, was excused by the claim that women were subservient and secondary in most religious situations. Somehow, in their minds, women's subservience meant that a complete and accurate portrayal of the religion they were studying could be obtained even while ignoring women.

The claims to objective, value-free scholarship turned into ridicule of the first feminist scholars, who pointed out that androcentric scholarship provided an incomplete, skewed, and inaccurate portrait of the religion being studied. Ridicule turned into resistance to feminists' demonstrations that studying women's religious lives changed the reported portrait considerably. That resistance generated negative consequences for these feminist scholars, who were often denied good jobs and career advancement by androcentric scholars who discredited their work, often claiming that it lacked "objectivity" or was "biased" because it focused on women. All these value judgments made by androcentric scholars because of their androcentric outlook and values would have been less problematic if they had been able to admit that they simply regarded men as more interesting, important, and normal than women and, therefore, focused their attentions on men. But that seemingly obvious fact was adamantly denied. *Obvious selection of data based on one's own values and interests combined with the illusion of objectivity is an especially pernicious and dangerous combination.*

Feminist scholarship in religion has demonstrated far more than that who a scholar is often greatly influences what a scholar sees and what that scholar finds interesting and important. Feminist scholarship has also demonstrated that including women in the data has a greater impact on our understanding of religions than simply providing add-on information. As I wrote when discussing this point in my book *Feminism and Religion: An Introduction,* "Feminist scholars often discover that information about women simply cannot be added onto the picture scholars already have. *In almost all cases, they discover that they have to repaint the whole picture,* which . . . is much more troublesome . . . than merely filling in some details in a blank corner of the canvas."[4] This is the case not only in religious studies but in virtually all disciplines. Feminist scholars, who were propelled into the study of women by our own personal experiences as women in male-dominated fields and confess our personal standpoints and interests, have produced scholarship that has considerably changed the whole academy in the last twenty-five years.[5]

The field of religious studies has only reluctantly accepted feminist scholars' demonstrations that the standpoint and interests of the scholar affect scholarship. But more recently, another perspective demonstrating the same claim has become quite popular, especially in comparative studies of South Asian religions, Hinduism in particular. This is the postcolonial critique, which claims that the common portrait of Hinduism found in virtually every world religions textbook, as well as in much of the advanced scholarship about Hinduism, exists much more in the minds of Western (male) observers of Hinduism than in the lives of the vast majority of ordinary Hindus.

This Western version of Hinduism, it is claimed, was actually the product of one male educated elite (Western) talking to another educated male elite (Hindu). It focused on ancient texts (the *Vedas* and *Upanishads*) that are barely known by the vast majority of Hindus but which are important to this small male elite with classical educations.[6] It ignores the fact that much Hindu religiosity is focused on rituals rather than texts and that for most Hindus, taking *darshan* (auspicious seeing) of an icon or a teacher is far more important than reading or hearing a text. But, given that Western religions are text-based, Western observers were far more likely to notice textual dimensions of Hinduism, even if they are a minor strand in the whole fabric of Hinduism. Because the ancient texts favored by Western scholars, the *Upanishads* in particular, teach a highly abstract monistic philosophy in which deity is nonexistent or unimportant, generations of Western undergraduates in world religions courses have learned that Hinduism is a monistic philosophy. But the vast majority of Hindus worship the various deities of the Hindu pantheon with ecstatic fervor unrivaled in any other religion. If the deities of Hinduism are discussed, one would gain the impression that male deities are the popular norm and goddesses represent a minor strand of Hindu theism. But, if anything, various versions of the Goddess are the dominant deity of Hinduism. (It has been particularly hard for Western scholars of religion to notice that male monotheism is a peculiarly Western phenomenon unknown in all other religious contexts.) Finally, because women were rigorously excluded from text-based dimensions of Hinduism, the religious lives of women were completely ignored. One easily gained the impression that women simply did not participate in the Hindu religion, whereas women carry on richly developed religious lives on their own, separate from male religious specialists and men in general.[7] (On this point, the postcolonial and feminist critiques converge.)

But why did early Western observers of Hinduism see a monistic, text-based, male-dominant religion when India presents so much and such overwhelming evidence of ritual, mythology, icon-veneration, ecstatic devotionalism, and women's independent religious lives, even in spite of the views of India's educated male elite? Why was it so convenient to have one male elite talk to another male elite while ignoring the everyday Hinduisms that teemed all around them? The postcolonial analyst claims that the conventional Western portrait of Hinduism served the colonial powers very well. For this portrait of Hinduism also included a thesis about Hindu development; the Hinduism of the *Veda*s and *Upanishad*s was said to represent "true Hinduism," while contemporary popular Hinduisms, with their wildly exuberant mythology, rituals, and visual imagery, were a degeneration. Hinduism had fallen on hard times throughout its long history and needed help to revert to its former rational monism. Enter the colonialists and their missionary friends, who were only too glad to criticize contemporary popular Hinduism and offer to replace it with something they deemed more worthy. Thus, the colonial rulers of India gained some moral legitimacy for their occupation of India because of what scholars told them about the development and current status of Hinduism.

Based on my own knowledge of and experience with Hinduism, I would agree that there is no question that the standard portrayal of Hinduism found in Western textbooks bears almost no resemblance to the Hinduism one commonly encounters in India. Clearly, the philosophical and textual preferences of early Western observers of Hinduism were projected onto Hinduism itself, obscuring the myriad phenomena that did not fit into that model of religion. As with androcentric scholars, their ideology that scholarship should be objective and neutral did not protect these scholars from their own subjectivity. To later generations of scholars or scholars from another culture or scholars with a different set of experiences, their subjectivity is glaringly obvious, just as the androcentric subjectivity of the male scholars who dominated religious studies until recently is very obvious to feminist scholars.

The subjectivity of these scholars itself is not so much of a problem, because of its inevitability. The damage is done by denial of one's own subjectivity, of one's own standpoint. As we have seen in both examples of unacknowledged subjectivity on the part of the scholar, this denial is especially problematic when the power of the scholar as male or as colonial undercuts and dismisses other subjectivities. Thus, the justification for seeking or claiming objectivity—that it would produce more accurate descriptive scholarship than scholarship which openly admitted its subjective and personal elements—turns out to be quite misleading and very oppressive. When *we*—whatever subjectivity that might be—insist that our subjectivity is normative and neutral, all that results is the constriction of knowledge and oppression of other subjectivities—not objectivity.

But if objectivity and neutrality are impossible simply because there is no neutral "nowhere" from which to conduct one's observations, and because personal experiences of gender, class, race, culture, and education inevitably affect what one sees, does that mean we have permission simply to let go of our critical faculties and see whatever we would like to see? Commentaries from oppressed groups often fall prey to this tendency, as can readily be seen in some fanciful feminist reconstructions of the ancient past.[8] But, obviously, I am not suggesting that because our personal subjectivity inevitably influences what we are interested in and what we see, we can, therefore, ignore research and critical thinking. If anything, because our critical thinking tells us that personal subjectivity always affects scholarship, we should engage in more self-correction and greater modesty. We do not claim that *we feminist scholars,* for example, now have *the* complete accurate picture, but only that our subjective urgency to know about women's religious lives and to understand women better has *improved* our understanding of religion in general, has made it *more* accurate and complete than was possible when all the scholars wore androcentric-colored glasses. Therefore, we should welcome a variety of standpoints and perspectives on our subject matter because such variety will bring us a fuller, richer picture than any single angle of vision. Finally, while scholars who long for neutrality and objectivity might regard the inevitable subjectivity of scholarship as a handicap, we can celebrate the creativity that can result when we speak genuinely out of our subjectivity.

Constructive or normative studies in religion have a somewhat different perspective on the place of the personal and subjective in scholarship. On the one hand, by definition, constructive studies evaluate religious phenomena and recommend some alternatives over others. Therefore, they do not claim to be an objective description of *what is* but a prescription for *what should be*. As such, the critical thinking of the scholar is paramount in constructive studies in religion. But, on the other hand, constructive theology often expresses significant reluctance to openly admit the importance of personal experience in forming one's theological outlook. Instead, the conventional tendency has been to presume that pure reason, devoid of the influence of one's own life experiences, is the prime mover in theological thinking. In fact, conventionally, the dominant opinion has been that one should rise above and ignore personal, idiosyncratic experience when thinking normatively and should try to achieve a "universal" perspective instead. Additionally, theologies often make the claim that their content is not even a human construction at all, but that "divine revelation" is the ultimate source of the basic ideas and norms of theology. Therefore, it is sometimes argued that such theological givens are unalterable by humans. Clearly, if that were the case, personal experience would be irrelevant to theology. Thus, despite the fact that constructive studies in religion do not claim to be objective and neutral descriptions, nevertheless, they have almost as must difficulty admitting the legitimacy of the genuinely personal and subjective as do descriptive studies.

As in descriptive studies in religion, the first major inroads into the hegemony of impersonal, "universal" norms in theology were made by feminists, by those of us who were "outsiders" to the supposedly universal presuppositions of theology. As outsiders, as people who were different, we clearly saw how limited the "universal" presuppositions of theology were, how much they depended on projections of gender onto conceptualizations of ultimate reality, and how much those projections served the interests and needs of those who had controlled the theologizing process. Paralleling early insights in descriptive studies in religion, much of the early insistence that theology cannot help being personal and subjective was the result of seeing clearly just how androcentric the conventional, supposedly "universal" theological norms and constructs actually are. Also paralleling conclusions reached by feminist scholars of descriptive studies in religion, feminist theologians claim that since we cannot avoid subjective elements in our theologizing, we might as well openly admit our guiding experiences and perspectives and use them to further our creative insights. Therefore, feminist theology is unapologetically personal and subjective; in fact, it glories in the openly personal and subjective, combined with rigorous critical think-ing. Feminist theology is considerably more open and up-front in its declarations about the centrality of the personal and subjective in theol-ogy than are most feminist scholars who focus on descriptive studies in religion. With this agenda clearly stated, feminist theology has become a major player, especially in Christian and Jewish circles, though it is much less developed in other major world religions.

Noticing how androcentric conventional "universal" theology actu-ally is, feminist theologians have taken as their first principle the claim that all religious thought is grounded in and derives from human experi-ence. The words and concepts of religion do not come from extra-human divine sources but from the familiar features of our ordinary human lives. For example, only a society that included the institution of king-ship would conceptualize deity as a king, lord, or ruler. Likewise, only a society that prizes the patrilineal relationship between father and son above all other relationships would imagine deity in terms of a father-son relationship. And, regarding one of the topics most explored by feminist theology, only a society that regards men as more important, interesting, and *normal* than women would evaluate an anthropomorphic male deity as acceptable and commonplace while evaluating female anthropomor-phic deities as abhorrent and abnormal. Theology is thus always extremely subjective, though that reality is often hidden and denied.

Based on this first principle, feminist theology takes as its second principle the claim that valid theology would reflect and be based on all humans' experiences, not those of a small and limited group of humans. Thus, the express purpose of feminist theology is to reflect on the received norms and insights of the tradition in the light of women's expe-riences, rejecting and recasting as necessary. In this task, there is no apology for open inclusion of the personal and subjective. In fact, auto-biographical elements are quite common in feminist theology, as femi-nist theologians explore and explain how their formative experiences helped shape their theological outlooks. The common justification for such personal disclosure is that it makes clear and unambiguous what is obscured and hidden in theology without personal disclosure.

Since the rise of feminist theology, many other subjectivities have given themselves permission to speak openly and have taken up the task of articulating their perspectives theologically. Race, class, culture, and sexual orientation are now commonly explored as significant factors that shape one's theology. Even white male heterosexual theologians, who used to think of themselves as so generic, so much the universal norm that admitting their subjectivity was unnecessary, are beginning to explore and express the impact of their personal experiences on their theologies. The result of this celebration of subjectivity in theology is that many more points of view are now expressed, read, and commented upon than in earlier, more monolithic times. This can only represent an improvement in theological discourse, as well as an improvement in our recognition and appreciation of human diversity.

Needless to say, just as in descriptive studies, acknowledging the subjective and personal factors in theologizing does not lead to wanton, self-indulgent, narcissistic self-expression. Theological thinking is always a process of interaction between the received tradition and the reflecting theologian. That process requires deep knowledge of the tradition and keenly critical thinking. These are clearly present in all the new theologies. What is different with the new "subjective" theologies of identity—feminist, womanist, black, Asian, Asian American, Latina, gay, lesbian—is the sheer *variety* of viewpoints from which theologizing is done and the honesty and openness with which the subjective and the personal in theology is disclosed.

Unfortunately, in North America the situation I am describing for normative studies pertains almost exclusively to those who do constructive work out of a Jewish or a Christian perspective. The academy has learned how to accommodate Jews and Christians who think normatively, but because of the confusion regarding the relationship between teaching or studying a religion and practicing a religion discussed at the beginning of this chapter, the bias remains that all religions except Judaism and Christianity should be approached only descriptively, preferably by outsiders. In other words, the legitimacy of the *constructive*, or *normative* study of religion is denied for any religions except Judaism and Christianity. For complex reasons, in the cases of Confucianism, Taoism, and Islam, many East Asians and many Muslims do, in fact, research and teach these religions, making the prohibition against the personal and the subjective in the study of these religions less stringent. But the "native speakers" of these traditions rarely do genuinely constructive theology; they study the received theological tradition instead. Thus, the issue I am addressing, that of the difficulties faced by those of us with normative interests in religions other than Christianity and Judaism, is not corrected by the ease with which native East Asian and Muslim scholars are admitted to the academy.

As a result, "other" religions, especially Hinduism and Buddhism, are usually taught and researched only descriptively, as if they were archaic museum pieces foreign to North Americans and irrelevant to the modern world. Unlike Judaism or Christianity, they are not taught or studied as living wisdom traditions that are still developing in response to modernity or as possible gold mines of inspiration for *us* for dealing with contemporary crises. This is an unfortunate and artificial situation. There is no cogent reason why the Asian and indigenous wisdom traditions should be so circumscribed in religious studies, or why they should be approached so differently from Judaism and Christianity.

Unfortunately, a scholar who takes a constructive approach to Buddhism or Hinduism is in great jeopardy. In fact, nowhere is expression of the subjective and the personal in religious studies so repressed and so dangerous to one's career as it is for those of us with constructive interests in Buddhism and Hinduism. There are few places to publish research on such topics because of the editorial policies of journals and publishers. A track record of such constructive work in Buddhism or Hinduism means that one is perceived as fitting nowhere—neither in positions devoted to Asian religions, which are reserved for translators and historians, not constructive thinkers, nor in positions devoted to theology and constructive studies in religions, which, almost by definition, are reserved for Christians, or more rarely for Jews.

This final barrier to admitting that personal and subjective elements are an inevitable and legitimate dimension of religious studies has yet to be overcome. Those involved in descriptive studies of religion are admitting, somewhat reluctantly, that who the scholar is influences what the scholar sees and what conclusions are drawn. Jewish and Christian constructive thinkers have learned how to do theology without the kind of exclusive advocacy that is so inappropriate for the academy. They have also become much more comfortable admitting the personal sources of their theologies, and the academy has learned how to find a place for such thinkers. But what about scholars with constructive interests in religions other than Judaism or Christianity, especially those with normative interests in Buddhism and Hinduism?

In conclusion, I have argued throughout this chapter that subjective and personal elements in the study of religion are inevitable. Therefore, it does no good to advocate the impossible goals of neutrality and objectivity. Scholarship will be much more adequate if we properly understand the role of the personal and the subjective in religious studies. But, especially because of the power of religion in human life and the dangers of religious advocacy, accommodating the influence of the personal and the subjective is probably more sensitive and delicate in religious studies than in many other disciplines.

I believe that several guidelines are essential to accommodating inevitable personal and subjective influences in religious studies without allowing them to degenerate into advocacy and dogmatism. The first of these guidelines is always to maintain a comparative dimension in religious studies. The founder of the discipline of the academic study of religion, Max Müller, is famous for his slogan "To know one religion is to know none."[9] He is certainly correct. And the more we delve into personal interests in religion, the more necessary it is to maintain the perspective and the corrective provided by the "comparative mirror,"[10] whether we are doing descriptive or normative scholarship. When we are genuinely, wholeheartedly comparative in our study of religion, it is virtually impossible to become intolerant, narrow advocates for our subjectively generated approaches to religion and our personal agendas with religion. When we are genuinely, wholeheartedly comparative in our studies of religion, we cannot help but see that there are a multiplicity of other possible ways than our own to think, to live, and to practice religion.

Second, I would argue that the study of religion is vastly improved by admitting the validity of diverse methods and encouraging all of them. This position is greatly preferable to the methodological straitjacket found especially in some descriptive approaches to religion. For example, in the field of Buddhist studies, translation and historical studies are often considered to be the only legitimate methods with which to study Buddhism. The study of contemporary Buddhism, or understandings of Buddhism that include personal experience of the Buddhist lifestyle, are simply not admitted into the academic arena. In other cases, there might be promotion of deconstruction, for example, to the denigration of all other theological methods. Or in feminist theology, one often encounters the bias that only post-Christian feminist spirituality is genuinely feminist, that feminists who remain within the framework of a traditional religion have simply been co-opted by patriarchy. But the study of religion requires translators, historians, fieldworkers, constructive thinkers, insiders, and outsiders. Some of these methods give freer rein to the subjective and personal than do others. But the field is richer and our understanding of religion deeper if, as professional students of religion, we encourage methodological flexibility and variety. Those who are less prone to using methods that encourage subjective, personal explorations of religion will rein in those of us who are more prone to personal and subjective explorations of religion if we slip into inappropriate advocacy in our personal commentaries on religion. Conversely, when those who are less prone to take account of the fact that religion is existentially relevant make sweeping claims for their methods, those of us who revel in the subjective significance of religions can tweak them into realizing that without people who practice religion and care about it, they would have nothing to study; there would be no religions. Finally, no matter what methods we prefer or what religions we study, we should always know who we are and who we are not, and be completely candid about it. We should not pretend to an objectivity and a neutrality that are impossible, nor to a universalism that is arrogant.

CHAPTER 5

Methodology: Tool or Trap?

Comments from a Feminist Perspective

Questions as to how best to study religion and to understand religion have fascinated me from early in my studies of religion. In this chapter, I want to reflect on questions about how scholars construct, accept, and reject methodologies, more than to argue for or against any specific methodology. I agree with scholars of religion who take methodology very seriously. Whether one is deeply self-reflective about or largely unconscious of one's methodological assumptions, those assumptions determine what data one sees and how one organizes those data. Methodologies should be tools that improve our studies of religion, but they often become traps that curtail our ability to take in previously unseen data or more deeply examine the assumptions underlying our methodologies.

In this chapter, I will recount the development of feminist methodology in religious studies and resistance to that development as a case study about how scholars deal with new methodological developments. The point of this case study is not to argue for the superiority of feminist methods in religious studies over conventional methods, but to demonstrate how easily received methodologies become traps that silence critical thinking. Using that case study as example, at the end of this chapter, I will suggest other underlying methodological assumptions, akin to androcentric assumptions, that may well deeply affect scholars' conclusions about religion.

GENDER STUDIES IN RELIGION AS CASE STUDY:
THE PERSONAL NARRATIVE

Like many in the study of religion, I was first drawn to this field as a quest for personal understanding of how life and the world work. That motive continues to fuel my study of religion. Today, I am especially concerned with questions about the purpose of the study of religion in a religiously plural world.[1]

However, along the way, very early along the way, I was forced by circumstances to deal with another methodological issue which has taken up a great deal of thought and energy in my career. Two facts puzzled and irritated me. Religions routinely said terrible things about women and discriminated severely against them, at least in the textual and public dimensions of religions almost always studied by scholars of religion in prefeminist days, but other than that, women and gender were largely ignored by scholars of religion. In addition, those who studied religion were almost universally men.[2] These facts did not seem noteworthy to my male colleagues, and I suppose the fact that I am a woman is responsible for my being unable to ignore them as easily as they did. I would prefer to live in a world in which these facts were not so, because that would make feminist concerns unnecessary, but I do not live in such a world. That women usually raised the issue of the need to study women, and men often resisted that study and punished those who insisted on its importance, was my first introduction to an important conclusion I have reached about method in the study of religion. There is no neutral "no place" from which one can objectively study religion.

In addition to the more abstract issues that usually dominate discussions of methodology in religious studies, I want to emphasize a dimension that is often overlooked. Personal histories and experiences have a role in determining what subject matter and methodologies are "chosen" by every scholar. We cannot stand outside time and space to choose, unaffected by our life circumstances, what subject matter and methodology we deign to take up. The fact that I would be forever excluded from the class of "men" in a world made up largely of men who were comfortable ignoring the real religious lives of women in their scholarship and not reflecting critically on the demeaning things said about women in the traditions they studied launched me professionally in a direction I would never have chosen had I not inherited these scholarly norms.

Admitting and reflecting upon how our life situations affect scholarship does not mean, as someone wrote in an article attacking my work, that such reflection is license to randomly conclude whatever one wants to conclude.[3] Scholarly standards of research and argumentation still hold; they simply are applied to a wider field of vision. It is not the case that androcentric scholars who had always ignored gender in their work were objective, whereas I and other feminist scholars were partisan in challenging their work. *Objectivity* and *neutrality* often mean nothing more profound than following the conventions one has inherited. "We" are always tangled up with our methods, whether we want to believe that or not, whether or not we approve of that entanglement. Denying this entanglement does not undo it. That is why methodological reflection is always foundational to our work as scholars of religion and why that work is never completed. But methodological reflection "facing outward," asking how best to look at data, is not enough. Self-conscious, introspective methodological reflection looking inward, asking why I choose certain subjects and methods over others, is also necessary.

I want to focus on methodological issues regarding gender and religion, not so much to review the arguments themselves, which are reasonably well known by now, but to focus more on why scholars initially proposed, and then accepted or rejected, arguments about doing serious scholarship on gender and religion. Thus, scholars who ignore gender in their analyses and scholars who insist on including gender in their analyses are my primary "data," rather than any specific set of gender practices. While I could argue that scholarship which takes gender into account is "better" than scholarship which does not, in this context I am more interested in the scholars themselves. Scholarship about women and gender, feminist analyses of religion, and the sheer presence of women scholars in the field have all been resisted, sometimes quite fiercely, by established scholars in religious studies. Those who have ignored gender in their scholarship fared much better by every measure of academic success than those who pointed out the importance of gender analysis. Most of the scholars who steered the field of religious studies in the direction of taking gender seriously have never held prestigious or influential academic positions, even though their work is widely used by professors in such departments and, according to a relatively recent report on religious studies training in the United States, the major new development in the field in the last thirty years has been the development of women studies and feminism.[4]

The earliest feminist analyses of religion were made in the late 1960s, and some of the classical essays had already been published by the mid-1970s. By the early 1980s there was no excuse for any scholar of religion not to be familiar with women studies and feminism.[5] Early feminist scholarship in religion was provocative and original. One could easily make the case that, though we haven't gotten the credit (or the blame) for it, feminism presented the first postmodern analyses, in that we argued very strongly that the social and cultural contexts of the researcher *do* matter. From the beginning we understood that gender mattered to us in ways that it doesn't seem to matter to male scholars, both because the gender norms of our own cultural world affected us very negatively and because, as women, we identified with the women researched by scholars of religion and shuddered in a way that men did not shudder when men (or women) were the research subject. People are quite invested in their gender identities; scholars of religion are no exception, and that investment does seem to affect scholarship.

Before continuing this critical investigation of method, I want to clarify my use of the terms *feminism, women studies,* and *gender studies,* because I think that confusion about these crucial terms is often at the heart of opposition to "feminism." Thus far, in keeping with much current usage, I have used the term *feminism* as something of a generic term. But this usage conflates anything concerning "gender" with "feminism," which I contend is a mistake. "Women studies" and "gender studies" are fundamentally *descriptive* disciplines; their content is the myriad practices concerning gender difference found in most religious contexts. They do nothing more. By themselves, such disciplines do not make any evaluation of practices surrounding gender discovered by scholars of religion. By contrast, *critical evaluations* of ways gender is marked and how such gender differentiation affects people's lives is the work of *feminism.*[6] In other words, describing what religions do with gender is the work of women studies or gender studies; expressing dissatisfaction with or approval of what is found or suggesting alternative gender arrangements is the work of feminism. I insist on this distinction because it makes clear that women studies or gender studies are the work of all scholars of religions, not just those who consider themselves feminists.

By honoring this distinction, gender studies can be depoliticized, can be taken from the arena of the contentious and perhaps personally threatening realm of gender politics and placed in the realm of "information," part of what we need to know about to fully grasp a specific religious context. The more we remember and honor this distinction, the more we separate information about gender practices from personal beliefs about gender, the less excuse there is for ignoring gender in our theoretical and descriptive work. This distinction is especially critical for those who consider themselves scholars of religion, not theologians.

I would be the first to concede that this distinction is often not honored by many who call themselves feminists, which in my view considerably muddies the water.

Concerning "gender studies" and "women studies," I have recently advocated that the time is ripe for "women studies" to be seen as part of "gender studies" and for gender studies to become a much more serious dimension of religious studies than it is currently.[7] I make this claim because it seems to me to be more accurate to regard gender, not women, as the main topic requiring investigation. More important, I make this claim because when we focus on "women studies" alone, it is too easy for men to ignore their own genderedness, to conflate women with gender, and to continue to be oblivious of the need to include gender in their research agendas. Because of our situation in a historically male-dominated society, women can never really forget about gender; men should be in the same position of never really being able to forget gender, given that they are as gendered as we are. It is time for women to stop having to carry the whole burden of human genderedness.

GENDER STUDIES AND RECEIVED METHODOLOGIES

To scholars who were already established when the first gender studies in religion critiques emerged, the subject being studied was assumed to be a man or the male members of the community, though this assumption was implicit rather than explicit. To established scholars of that time, it did not seem necessary or even possible to study the religious lives and thoughts of women. No one declared that they had no interest in what women might be doing or thinking, but the result would not have been different if they had made such a declaration. Scholars did not especially set out self-consciously to study *only* men and religion; they simply did not perceive women as subject matter, mainly because of the androcentric model of humanity that guided their research.[8] Nevertheless, that unconscious model was deeply embedded in scholars' worldviews, patterns of awareness, and consciousnesses; it was a fixed ideological trap rather than an open-ended guideline concerning how to do research on religion and think about religion.

When questioned as to why there was not more information about women in their accounts, these scholars usually answered that there was nothing to study—that women were not interested or involved in religion. One of the more vicious jabs that some colleagues inflicted upon those of us who taught courses on "women and religion" went something like

"How are you going to make a whole course out of *that?*" Others complained that when a course on women and religion was introduced, there needed to be a balancing course on men and religion. That there already were many courses on men and religion was the standard retort to this complaint. However, the source of both this conclusion and this taunt is not in the subject matter but in the minds and values of the scholars.

This is equally the case for the most famous phenomenological descriptions of religion and for varied "reductionistic" explanations of religion. Both operated with an enlightenment idea of a generic, universal subject, a subject who would reach the same conclusions and behave the same way because of universally valid laws that reason discovered. But that subject was also always a male, which is why feminists called this construct the "androcentric" model of humanity.

One of the most famous "universal" generic models, prevalent in religious studies when early feminist criticisms of methodology were first being proposed, was Mircea Eliade's *homo religiosus*. In Eliade's model of religion and in his methods for studying religion, there simply was no place for women as religious subjects to be studied as religious human beings in their own right. A glance at the table of contents of his famous handbook *Patterns in Comparative Religion* shows this very clearly. "Woman" (not "women") appears as one of the hierophanies experienced by *homo religiosus,* alongside the sky, the sun, the moon, water, stones, the earth, and so on.[9]

Eliade's only other significant discussions of women or gender occurs in his work on initiation, in which he solves the problem of sex segregation in initiation rituals by proposing that men's initiations are cultural events, whereas women's initiations occur in the realm of nature rather than culture because they are triggered by natural events such as menstruation or childbirth.[10] That women's ritualization of these "natural" events is a cultural phenomenon was not noticed, nor was it noticed that physical maturation of boys, which prompted their initiations, was a "natural" event. Instead, women are noticed only when they deviate from patterns that have come to be expected as normal for men, and it is women's "deviance," not patterns of male behavior, that require explanation. There is no hint of recognition that gender plays a significant role in determining how one will experience a religious phenomenon in Eliade's work.

Being more empirical and less based on abstract models than phenomenological accounts of religion, one might expect that various "reductionistic" explanations of religion would be more aware of the significance of gender in religious practice. However, by and large, the same androcentrism prevails. In account after account, gender is not noticed or theorized as a significant category, and for the most part, all we learn about women is how they appear to men or how they affect men's lives. They enter the picture for certain purposes on certain occasions but disappear most of the time. What are the women doing when they're not interacting with men, which can be most of the time in many settings? What do women think about their lives? For the most part, these are nonquestions in older explanations of religion.

Upon reflection it is also clear that the androcentric results obtained by most prefeminist scholarship are not the fault of either the phenomenological method or the explanatory method. There is no reason either method must be used in an androcentric manner or could not be employed to study women as subjects in their own right, making their thoughts, activities, and relationships with men, their communities, and the world the focus of one's research. So something other than the data actually present in religions and the standard research methods for looking at data "out there" is responsible for both the prevailing androcentrism of most scholarship and the widespread unwillingness to consider the merits of gender studies and critical feminist analyses of religion and religions.

It is not completely surprising that such models of humanity were once commonplace; scholars make mistakes and academic fashions come and go. Much more surprising is the fact that, once the androcentric inadequacy of such a model of humanity and the scholarship based on it was pointed out, those who suffered were those who had pointed out the problems in established methodology, not those who continued to do scholarship as if these discoveries had never been made.

WHY GENDER STUDIES ARE NECESSARY

What is the case for "gender" being an important category in religious studies? Abstract methodological and theoretical discussions about the nature of religion and how best to study it are so interesting and satisfying. Why do these pesky feminists always have to bring up such an unpleasant and contested topic? For scholars of religion, as opposed to theologians, the answer should be simple. Religions, our subject matter, *do* pay a great deal of attention to gender. In fact, in most religious contexts, gender probably affects a person's options and possibilities, as well as the quality of life, more than any other aspect of the religion. Only a methodology that excluded significant segments of the population from its database could be blind to something that makes so much difference in so many lives. A religious context that does not pay significant attention to gender, that is genuinely gender-neutral and gender-inclusive, is far rarer than a religious context in which multiple gender norms, restrictions, and privileges come into play. Furthermore, most religious situations that are primarily gender-neutral and gender-inclusive are also modern and have been influenced by the second wave of feminism, if not its first wave. Therefore, "traditional" religious situations, less influenced by modernity but typically more preferred by scholars of religion, by definition, require attention to gender.

It is hard to understand how we would get accurate descriptions of religious situations in which, for the subjects of our inquiry, participants in religions, gender determines a great deal, while scholars also ignore or suppress the data about gender. How could theory built on such descriptions accurately tell us much about religion? If religions place a great emphasis on gender—and in both their practices and their theories they do—then the study of religions would also need to take gender into account. By taking gender into account, I mean presenting both accurate and complete descriptions of gender practices and norms in a religious setting, and some theoretical account for why gender is constructed as it is, both in specific contexts and in meta-theory or methodology.

Nevertheless, one of the reasons gender may be ignored by many scholars is that many religious practices surrounding gender seem very unpleasant, even to nonfeminist scholars. They can make female scholars angry or frustrated and male scholars uncomfortable, perhaps as much in anticipation of the reactions of women in their own group— scholars of religion—as due to any personal feelings of anxiety or grief occasioned by these gender practices. However, that religious gender practices may be unsavory is not a good excuse for ignoring them. Scholars of religion do not expect religions to always have positive or beneficial effects for those who participate in them.

THE POLITICS OF ANDROCENTRISM

Early feminist scholars encountered ideological and political resistance to their new scholarship more than methodological challenges. Because one cannot make a good *methodological* argument against what early feminist scholars of religion wanted to do, their scholarship could be rejected only by relying on the ideological and political subtext of an already established method. Mutual entrenchment rather than mutual enlightenment followed, so that today we are in the unworkable situation that gender is most frequently studied by women while many men go about their studies as if feminist scholarship had never occurred and pretend that gender does not pertain to them or their subject material. How easily methodology slides from being a tool to being a trap.

Why would so many scholars unreflectively retain the androcentric model of humanity? Many reasons can be given. In addition to being part of a deeply held, but largely unconscious worldview that saw men as normal human beings and women as deviations from that norm, the androcentric model of humanity had significant personal implications for many scholars of religion. Early feminist scholarship challenged *who* should be allowed to study religion, which some experienced as a professional threat. But many already established scholars felt a deeper threat. Their model of humanity also contained an implicit political code concerning how women and men should interact, and that code dictated male agency and female passivity. If women's religious lives, including women's agency, became a legitimate topic of scholarship, and women engaged professionally in the study of religion, what would that mean for the personal life of the already established (male) scholar, especially concerning his relationships with women?

I will also propose a much more radical hypothesis that will return to play a large part in the conclusion of this chapter. My hypothesis is that, though many scholars thought that their basic assumptions about the world were derived from the European enlightenment and that they were rejecting older religious models of the world, they actually adopted a great deal more from Christian-based models of the world than they realized, including the androcentrism and misogyny of the older religions they claimed to reject. The androcentrism they uncritically retained is much more in keeping with the values of misogynist monotheistic religions than with the core values of the European enlightenment (though it is important to remember that even thinkers of the European enlightenment did not always transcend their androcentrism). As someone who has trained seriously in a spiritual alternative to Christianity for about half my life, I am constantly amazed by how much, including the androcentric model of humanity, many scholars of religion owe to Christian outlooks even while they vigorously protest that they are uninfluenced by such outlooks. We will return to this rather unusual hypothesis in the conclusion of this chapter.

Clearly, this is an instance of methodology becoming a trap rather than a tool. The dimension of methodological inquiry that is introspective and asks, "Why am *I* interested in or resistant to these data and conclusions?" was insufficiently employed. Any historian analyzing early feminist critiques of religious studies methodology will not fail to notice that those critiquing androcentric research methods were women and those replying that critique was unnecessary were men. The gender politics of that situation are quite obvious. In those days before postmodernism, it would have been academic suicide to suggest that gender politics had something to do with the unwillingness of our mentors, all of whom happened to be men, to acknowledge that religious studies had used thoroughly androcentric methods and that androcentrism was inadequate and problematic. Even if postmodernism had already come onto the scene, such discussions would have been dangerous because we were all graduate students and young scholars standing up against established scholars as best we could, knowing that our academic futures were on the line.

With these comments we have crossed a line that scholars do not like to cross—a line that separates abstract reasoning from personal self-interest and defensiveness. Countless times I have heard colleagues, almost always male, speak disparagingly and derisively of women studies and feminism. Popular culture commonly blames feminism for everything from a shortage of nurses in North America to economic downturns. It is difficult, if not impossible, to distinguish cheap, belittling humor from hostility in these comments or to find any substantive arguments in them. It is equally difficult to defend oneself from these "below the belt" nonarguments.

In academia, one still hears doubts about whether women studies or gender studies really are legitimate and serious academic enterprises, which are then used to justify not promoting or hiring those who practice them and discouraging graduate students from studying women or gender until they are more "established." All these hesitations turn on unwillingness to regard women as fully within the human realm, whether as subjects in the religions one researches or as colleagues in one's discipline. Equally important is the point already made in this chapter and in chapter 3, that many men seem to regard women studies or gender studies as irrelevant to them. Gender strikes many men as someone else's issue, as foreign to their interests and the "real" subject matter of the discipline because they have the impression that *gender* does not really apply to men, who are somehow seen as "normal" rather than gender-specific. Men seem to prefer to see themselves as generic human beings rather than as males and to see women as limited by their gender. If that were the case, one could question whether studying gender could be anything more than a potentially interesting footnote. But maleness is just as much a specific condition as femaleness. It is not normal to be male and aberrant to be female, despite the legacy of generations of androcentric scholarship and patriarchal theology.

One also hears more emotional reasons for dismissing gender studies or distancing oneself from it. It is commonly assumed that "male bashing" is a staple of gender studies. "I just don't want to deal with a bunch of angry women complaining about what men have done to women!" is a common reaction. However, many female scholars who study gender and religion are not especially angry, and I have also discovered, as a woman with some scholarly standing, that it is not possible to be mild enough to pacify all men. Behaviors and speech patterns that would be accepted without comment if practiced by men often are evaluated as "strident" when practiced by a woman. As for the "male bashing" content of gender studies, much of the data about relations between the sexes throughout history, especially in religion, is not edifying or uplifting. However, those of us who study gender did not invent these data; we simply notice them, bringing into view what others might prefer to pass over. Ignoring and refusing to see certain data do not dispose of them.

In view of these realities about the politics of studying gender, which are rarely discussed in an academic forum, it is worthwhile to ask questions about reflexivity in the study of gender. Will women study different things from men and will they see the same data differently? These questions need to be answered differently, depending on context. If we could work in a genuinely gender-free, gender-neutral, and gender-inclusive academic environment, I seriously doubt that women and men would pick sex-specific subject matter or see the same data differently. For them to do so would require sex-specific traits that were essential— something found in the minds of all men but no women and vice versa. There is little reason to believe in gender essentialism, however.

But in a highly charged academic environment, such as the one I worked in early in my career, it is not surprising that women and men might see things differently. Furthermore, in such an environment, it is crucial that personal preferences and habitual thought patterns be openly admitted and investigated, even though scholars often like to hide behind a mask of neutrality that they do not actually possess. There is no question that my being female in the highly sexist environment of the field of religious studies and University of Chicago Divinity School steered me in the direction of women studies, against my will and better judgment. My sex was assaulted and denigrated from all sides. Most of the literature I was assigned to read declared that women were inferior to men in one way or another, and every religion I studied seemed to be completely male-dominated, to have no place for women, to exclude women from everything interesting and important. The professors didn't see this as a problem and thought that they were completely fair and neutral. Inwardly I seethed daily, but I did not dare express any of my feelings because it was unacceptable for women to be angry about sexism.

When I first began to study women specifically, I discovered the shock of my life. Much of the denigration of women present in the literature I read was the result, not of the religions being studied, but of androcentrism on the part of scholars. It was (male) scholars who thought men were the only interesting and worthwhile members of the religion or culture under discussion, not the members of that religion! While there is a great deal of male dominance in many religious contexts, studying that religion using an androcentric model of humanity seriously distorts that religion, something that I have discovered time after time in every religious context that I have investigated somewhat seriously. I had been upset that religions seemed to denigrate women so much, but I became much more upset that scholars were so completely androcentric in their methodology and, worse yet, that they didn't even realize there was a problem with regarding men as the normal human beings and women as a deviation from that norm. Nor did they wish to have their androcentrism pointed out to them.

In such circumstances, it is not surprising that I, a woman, sometimes saw things in the materials I was studying that men who had studied them many times did not see. As already narrated in chapter 1, I was initially pushed in the direction of studying women and religion because one of my doctoral advisers, Mircea Eliade, told me I was seeing things about Australian Aboriginal religion that he not seen and he attributed my seeing to my gender. I have no idea whether he attributed my ability to see to gender essentialism or to historical conditions, though I attribute it to historical conditions. If I hadn't been a woman working in such an androcentric, male-dominated environment, I doubt I would ever have focused so much of my scholarly career on gender studies.

Much later, another notable example of my seeing things differently occurred. It was reported to me that a well-known Buddhologist said about my book *Buddhism after Patriarchy,* "Her interpretations of these texts are obviously correct. We've all read these texts many times. How come we never saw what she's seen?" I guess it just didn't occur to (male) scholars working with an androcentric model of humanity that the texts could be interpreted in less patriarchal ways.

What does all this mean for scholars and scholarship? Do we now assume that women have some special ability that most men don't have? Do we cultivate women scholars to peer into the hidden corners that men can't see? For the most part, I don't think so. The only situation I can think of in which being female would be a necessary part of the job description would be doing fieldwork in cultural contexts with a high degree of sexual segregation. In comparative studies in religion, that would be a fairly common situation, justifying a continuing stream of women scholars on practical grounds alone. We need women scholars to go places where men are not allowed, just as we need the reverse. Of course, I also want to see women in the field of religious studies, as a matter of fairness and equity.

I think it was much easier for women to see through the mistakes of androcentrism, given the historical circumstances in which those critiques were first made. But I believe it would be a serious mistake to develop an ideology that claims men think men's thoughts and women think women's thoughts. I don't want gender studies to become a women's specialty while men go about their scholarship as if gender didn't exist. If that is not to happen, all scholars need to be introspective and self-conscious about their methodological choices, exploring not just the methodology but their reasons for preferring this method to that method, this subject matter to that subject matter. Without such introspection, methodology easily slips from tool to trap.

WHAT IS METHODOLOGY FOR?

I have set this exploration of the necessity of gender studies in the larger context of discussing how scholars of religion should approach questions of method altogether, trying to demonstrate that methodological rigidity and certainty are usually an impediment rather than an aid to scholarship. The assumptions and methods we bring to the study of religion so deeply affect the results of our research that they need first-order critical reflection.

What is methodology for? Clearly, it is not an end in itself. A method should help us understand religion or some religious phenomenon accurately. Therefore, methodologies should be worn very lightly. If another method is proposed that better explains the material being discussed, switch; don't fight! Besides, any good scholar will probably use several different methodologies, depending on what is being explained and the audience to whom the comments are directed. I write and speak to a number of different audiences about a number of rather different topics, and my comments and tactics are always material- and audience-specific. Phenomenological methods work somewhat well to explain how a religious phenomenon feels to an insider, though there are limits to what can be done by a scholar *imagining* what it would feel like to be an insider. But the phenomenological method is terrible at ascertaining histories that could be accepted by a critically trained historian, would not uncover oppressive aspects of the religion under discussion, and cannot take into account many of the economic, social, and psychological factors that help explain religious phenomena. Nevertheless, an explanation of religion that has no place for empathetic description of the religion's claims and worldview is simply short-changing those who want to understand the religion. Part of understanding a religion includes understanding the cogency it holds for its followers. This aspect of understanding religion is especially important to the humanistic and liberative mission of those of us who teach religion widely in a public context.

The most critical and liberating thing to be said about methodology is that it is a tool. Therefore, it should suit the task at hand. Sometimes we need a hammer, and sometimes we need a screwdriver. Flexibility and an open-ended, somewhat skeptical attitude toward methodological absolutism serve the scholar well. Unfortunately, methodology often seems to become a trap instead. People become fixated on the virtues of a specific method and can no longer see that it does not work well for all purposes. Methodological orthodoxies develop, and orthodoxy is usually lethal to productive inquiry.[11]

Methodology often turns from tool to trap because aspects of a scholar's personal interest and identity become tangled up with supposedly neutral scholarly methods. This is especially likely to happen if one isn't even aware that such entanglement is occurring. If one looks closely at methodological arguments, one can see that often they become ideological or political statements as well. Arguments over method often contain a covert theory or philosophy of religion. Beliefs about religion are at stake, no matter how neutral their proponents claim to be. And beliefs about religion bear a striking resemblance to religious beliefs. They are held to be overarching and irrefutable explanations, which means that they function as "theologies" in the worldviews of scholars of religion, even though those scholars may eschew theology in its more literal and traditional sense. Such doctrinal adherence to an already accepted methodology is usually what bars further advances in the field.

WIDER IMPLICATIONS ABOUT METHODOLOGY

The critical lesson in the above narrative is that methodologies need to be worn lightly and shed easily. They should be tools, not ideologies, so that when materials turn up that simply can't be dealt with using old methodologies, the old ones should not be clung to. Better to let familiar androcentric research methods and models of humanity go than to continue to have no theoretical or methodological tools for handling data about women as human beings in their own right who are more than objects that appear in men's universes. We have also learned that scholars need to be introspective regarding their methodological choices. Personal self-interest probably had something to do with established scholars' resistance to something as eminently sensible as early feminists' interest in what religion means to women, how women are affected by religion, and what women do and believe religiously.

As I survey the world of religious studies, I am struck by how little of the general principles articulated above have been taken in by scholars of religion. Gender studies and feminist thought in religion may have some standing in religious studies today, but generally, scholars still hold whatever methodology they favor with the same tenacity as before, and while it is now more common for theologians to openly state their working basis, those in the academic study of religion usually do not.

When I read anthologies on method, I am struck by the dogmatism that often prevails. Most people who argue about methodology seem to have strong opinions about religion, its source, and its value for human life. They have beliefs about religion which look suspiciously like religious beliefs. They adamantly claim that religion should be studied *sui generis!* Others yell as loudly that religion should be reduced to economic, social, and psychological causes. Some claim that religion cannot be studied adequately by insiders or believers, and others that scholars must submit their conclusions to the evaluation of the people being represented. What amuses me about these debates, besides the seriousness with which people take these positions, is that all these positions have some merit and are useful in some scholarly contexts. Why are we so interested in finding the "one true faith"?

My facetious use of the phrase "one truth faith" points to what I think is the problem underlying many of these debates. Earlier I suggested that scholars of religion were not as liberated from Christian understandings and had not adopted the values of the European enlightenment as much as they thought they had. I used as evidence their retention of the androcentric model of humanity, which has much more in common with classical theism than with the European enlightenment.

I now argue that most of the methodological arguments current today likewise depend much more on Christian models than their advocates realize. In one way or another, all these arguments depend on a model of religion which posits that religions claim to have a transcendent source. But what if religions don't claim to have a transcendent source? Christianity and other monotheisms claim that religion comes from a transcendent source, and most scholars of religion have accepted that as a fundamental claim made by *all* religions, which then colors their other conclusions about religion. But Buddhism doesn't claim to have a transcendent source, and Taoism and Confucianism probably don't either. So what would happen if a religion that didn't posit transcendent, nonhistorical entities as its source were the model against which scholars spun their theories and methodologies? Would arguments about religion's uniqueness versus the need to explain religion as the product of mundane causes be so divisive? Would insiders and outsiders come up with such different versions of the same material?

I contend that much current methodological discussion is still trying to prove that religion couldn't have validity because it could not be a transhistorical phenomenon with a transcendent source. But what if some religions aren't claiming to be transcendent phenomena? What if the model of religion that has prevailed in Western academic studies of religion from the beginnings of that discipline is partial, incomplete, and inaccurate for some religions? Androcentric methods couldn't see women properly. Models of religion that assume religions claim transcendence as their basis may well be just as incomplete. And just as women were basically invisible in androcentric methods, and thus could not be conceptualized as anything except objects in men's universes, so religions that do not base themselves on claims of transcendence may be beneath the radar of theories of religion that presume monotheistic religions are typical for religion.

Clearly, in this context, I cannot really make the above argument in anything approaching an adequate fashion. I am more interested in reactions to the suggestion than anything else at this point. Is the reaction out-and-out rejection because the suggestion sounds outlandish, just as it seemed extreme to call for the study of gender and women some thirty years ago? Or is the reaction one of loose, relaxed curiosity that neither accepts nor rejects the proposal? One reaction indicates still using methodology as a covert belief system about religion, using methodology as a trap rather than a tool. The other indicates some awareness that methodologies fit best when they are loose-fitting and easy to remove. They work better as tools because then they can serve the purpose of exploring hidden corners and new options in the study of religion. What else would they be good for?

If I were to follow my other main recommendation for the use of methodology, I would need to ask why I might come up with these ideas and find them more than random thoughts not worth pursuing. Anyone analyzing my work would probably say, "Oh, that's because she's been a Buddhist practitioner for thirty years and has let it influence her scholarship." According to conventional views about method in the study of religion, it's okay to let the ideas and values of the European enlightenment influence one's scholarship, but any other influence is "prejudicial." Such a judgment would give other scholars license to dismiss my suggestions without examining them, just as in an earlier time the calls to study women as subjects in their own right were simply dismissed without being examined.

But, quite frankly, one effect of many years of Buddhist practice on my worldview is that I am much less ideological, that I trust theory much less, and the more rigidly the theory is held, the less I trust it. Such intellectual flexibility and nondogmatism is not especially an attitude I try to maintain; it is simply almost as natural to me as breathing. And I would argue, that such flexibility of mind offers scholars a great deal and helps the advancement of knowledge and understanding more than its opposite. This recommendation should not be dismissed because the person making the argument is a Buddhist scholar-practitioner. Scholars of religion who operate with a Buddhist outlook are not taken especially seriously in the academic study of religion, precisely because of who we are. But then, not too long ago women and others who wanted to look directly into religions' norms and practices surrounding gender were equally suspect.

CHAPTER 6

What Went Wrong?

*Feminism and Freedom from the Prison
of Gender Roles*

In his novel *The Town Beyond the Wall,* Elie Wiesel tells the story of a time when God and humans changed places, and the human, now God, refused to revert to the original order. But after infinite amounts of time, "The past for one, and the present for the other, were too heavy to be borne." He continues: "As the liberation of the one was bound to the liberation of the other, they renewed the dialogue whose echoes come to us in the night, charged with hatred, with remorse, and most of all with infinite yearning."[1]

After thirty years of feminism, I look at the society in which I live. What has gone wrong? I ask myself. Though I wouldn't want to return to the situation women were placed in before this current feminist movement, it also is clear to me that many conditions of our lives have gotten worse, not better, since the onset of feminism. After thirty years of feminism, the culture is much speedier, much more materialistic, competitive, and aggressive. More people work longer hours in more isolating and alienating conditions, and friendship has become a major casualty of our lifestyle; no one has time for it. Women participate in this mad materialistic dash completely, fully. Women can do anything men can do. We can earn high salaries, work sixty or eighty hours a week, fly military airplanes, fight in the army with men. Sometimes it seems that all feminism has gotten us is that now women can be "men" too, can do just about everything that was once defined as the male gender role. But what about the virtues that go with what was once defined as the female gender role? Who takes care of them? Instead of freedom from the prison of gender roles, we have gained freedom from both the virtues and the defects of the female gender role while we—both women and men as well as the entire culture—have become ever more enamored of the male gender role—and a fairly unsatisfying version of that role.

One day some years ago, as I contemplated my frustration with this situation, the phrase "the liberation of the one is bound to the liberation of the other" seared itself into my consciousness. It expresses very beautifully a Mahayana understanding of emptiness and interdependence. The whole Bodhisattva path is built on the insight that if any one person is not free, then no one is free, that individual liberation is impossible. Either women and men are both free of the prison of gender roles or neither is free. That realization is followed by the recognition that dialogue, however painful it may be, is the only way out.

I now use the word *feminism* less and less, not because I have given up on its ideals, but because at present it seems better to use other words to convey its message. Nevertheless, my definition of feminism has remained the same for many years—"freedom from the prison of gender roles." I contend that most of the unnecessary suffering in human life, the suffering due to clinging, aggression, and bewilderment rather to birth, aging, sickness, and death, is due to the prison of gender roles, which is why we need freedom from that prison, not new or reformed gender roles. Clearly, my proposed definition of feminism is gender-neutral and pertains to men as much as it does to women, but that vision has not been pursued in the same way by men as it has by women. Therefore, since liberation for all has not been achieved, liberation is quite limited. It is time to renew, or perhaps to start, a real dialogue about the prison of gender roles in which we discuss the reality that *both* the male and female gender roles are imprisoning and ask what we can do to free ourselves as a culture from an obsolete and dysfunctional definition of the male gender role that has become dangerous to human survival even as it has become more entrenched as a cultural ideal for both men and women.

However, I most adamantly am not advocating that the human variety which expresses itself in varying and multiple concepts of masculine and feminine gender be replaced by a monolithic unisexual human norm. That would also be a prison. By themselves, images of masculinity and femininity are not imprisoning; they are useful cultural constructs with which to discuss human options and possibilities. For example, in Tibetan Vajrayana Buddhism, compassion is said to be "masculine" while wisdom is "feminine." These are culturally arbitrary associations; many in our culture would expect the opposite assignment. Their purpose is to talk about equally important, yet significantly different human ideals, not to talk about women and men. These associations do not lead to the ludicrous claim that only men can be compassionate and only women can be wise; in fact the ideal person would manifest both wisdom and compassion, the goal of much Vajrayana practice. What imprisons is the insistence that men must and should be only masculine while women must and should be only feminine, not the existence of gender symbolism. Especially imprisoning is a situation in which both sexes are confined by gender norms that are a caricature of human wholeness and prohibit mental-spiritual health and well-being, gender roles that promote mutual incompetence between women and men, as is the case with the traditional gender roles of our culture.

While extended discussion of conventional gender roles is impossible here, some generalizations help frame the discussion. Most introductory anthropology texts, especially older ones which more unconsciously reveal conventional gender expectations, would see the core of the female gender role as nurturing and the core of the male gender role as protecting or defending. The task of providing should not be limited to one sex, because familiar patterns of the male "breadwinner" only hold in wage labor situations in which home and workplace are distinct and separate. However, for many North Americans, "providing" was seen as a male task. Another valid generalization is that women often operate in a more limited private realm, whereas public affairs, especially politics and public dimensions of religion, are in the hands of men. Going along with these tasks are stereotypical psychological traits which can be described positively or negatively, depending on the whims of those making the comments. The female gender role promotes competence in relationship skills, but cultural incompetence was also a norm for women. The male gender role promotes physical prowess and cultural competence, but male achievement usually has more to do with bravado than with sensitivity.

Part of the blame for what has happened regarding gender, despite thirty years of feminism, lies with some of the rhetoric employed by the women's movement. A common way of stating what that movement is about is the call for women to be able to do whatever men can do or the claim that women are equally competent with men at most or all tasks or the push for women to have the same rights that men enjoy. But notice—that kind of rhetoric assumes that what men do and the way they are is the ideal and the norm toward which women should strive or which they should be allowed to attain.

It is easy to understand why this style of analysis dominated early feminist writing if one has had personal experience of being socialized to the conventional female gender role in the 1950s and early 1960s. Given the current tendency to dismiss feminism, those of us who are old enough to remember why feminism developed in the first place should write about our experiences of the mind-numbing cultural irrelevance which girls were expected to embrace in the 1950s, a time when it was a tragedy if a girl needed to wear glasses because that marked her as too bookish, and possibly too independent in mind and spirit, to be attractive to men, when it was assumed that women's main reason for going to college was to obtain that all-important "Mrs." degree. We need to remember how many of the "happy homemakers" of the 1950s were so unhappy that they were maintained on Valium; no one realized they had good and ample reasons to be unhappy. These are degraded circumstances in which to grow up and to live. In that environment, it is completely understandable that early feminist thought developed as it did. Nevertheless, this style of feminist rhetoric is just as androcentric as the male dominant laws and norms against which it is rebelling, with the result that women are freed from the female gender role to take up the male gender role. But no one talks about the virtues of the female gender role or the down side, the destructive aspects, of the male gender role.

When I ask my students about the negative side of the traditional female gender role, they come up with a long list. Feminism has thoroughly critiqued the traditional female gender role, and as someone who avoided that role at all costs, I share that critique. However, the problems with the traditional female gender role are not the tasks assigned to it, which must be done, or the psychological traits associated with it, which are emotionally healthy, but the rigid way in which these tasks and traits were assigned to women alone, at the same time as women were confined only to those tasks and traits. Especially destructive of women's well-being was the demand that women should carry out their tasks and exhibit feminine traits in the private sphere alone, thus condemning us to cultural irrelevance and incompetence. Part of that package included the demand that women would expend their nurturing skills and energies in a nuclear family which they cared for emotionally and physically almost without male help, which isolated us and trivialized our competence.

Often my students can articulate much of this critique, but when I ask them about the downside of the male gender role, they draw a complete blank—silence. This silence masks three deeply rooted problems in our cultural psyche. One is lack of awareness that gender is a *human* phenomenon, not something that pertains to women alone. The second is a deeply rooted cultural preference for maleness over femaleness, probably due in part to religious symbol systems that contain deeply misogynist elements and personify the most valued and ultimate symbols as masculine. The third is that, in the absence of discussions of gender as something that pertains to men, not just women, a dangerous and destructive version of the male gender role is emulated not only by men but also by women, even as it damages those who accept its hegemony.

One of the reasons I have become increasingly reluctant to give talks on women, feminism, or gender is men's long-standing refusal to recognize that these topics concern them and are relevant to them. As a result, the audience for such talks is usually about half the size it should be and consists mainly of women. But women really don't need to talk and think a lot about gender at this point in time. Many women have already done their homework on gender issues; it is men who need to catch up. With individual exceptions, men as a group have refused to take up their end of the issue of human genderedness, leaving it entirely up to women and continuing to foster the illusion that women are gendered but men are not. "Gender? Oh, you must be talking about someone else; I'm just a normal human being," seems to be the most common reaction by men to the topic of gender. I think it unlikely that we will get any further in finding freedom from the prison of gender roles until men begin to acknowledge and take seriously their own genderedness.

When this begins to happen, issues of gender oppression and gender justice can take their rightful place among other major social issues, such as the need to stem consumption and growth, to promote economic and racial justice, and to promote concern for the environment. Now, usually gender issues are placed somewhere else in the program, not regarded as significant enough to be billed alongside other major social issues. For example, recent books on various engaged Buddhist movements do not include chapters on Buddhist women's movements, though virtually every other topic in which Buddhist activists are engaged is covered. The books and chapters on gender and Buddhism are put into another category—a major conceptual mistake, in my view. Such practices perpetuate the tendency of men not to want to talk about gender, to regard themselves as unencumbered by gender, unlike women.

I would argue as strongly as I can that these presuppositions and reactions about human genderedness are rooted in a deep cultural preference for the cultural construct of maleness over the cultural construct of femaleness, which is why women want to act like men, but men don't want to act like women. It is so much more acceptable for a woman to take on "masculine" traits and tasks than for a man to take on "feminine" tasks and traits. Surely that prejudice exposes deep cultural misogyny. Nothing more cogently demonstrates the pervasiveness of these patterns than the fact that women now wear trousers everywhere with impunity while men never even think about the convenience and comfort of wearing skirts in certain situations. Forget about the fact that men have worn skirts in many cultures historically, or that famous male religious leaders still wear skirts. Skirts (assuming that they are long and full) simply are more comfortable for some activities, including most seated activities, than are pants, and they are infinitely cooler. Think of the energy wasted on extra air-conditioning that could be saved! But, when I point out how this fear of and distaste for things female inhibits and limits men, the response is usually that I'm crazy to suggest that men might take up the practice of wearing skirts.

In my own classes, once in a great while, an unconventional and usually gay man might wear a skirt to my class on women and religion for one evening. In North America, the only situation in which I have seen men regularly wearing skirts is at Tassajara Zen Monastery during the summer tourist season. There students work in torrid conditions without air-conditioning, taking care of tourists who flock to the mountain retreat to partake of its sulfur hot springs. In return, they earn credits to participate in the practice periods that occur during the winter season. These young men frequently wear skirts. They are proud that they are so sensible, proud of their deviance from conventional cultural norms, proud that they had already thought to engage in this gender-bending practice before I mentioned my usual proof that men are much more stuck in the prison of gender roles than are women, and that maleness is far more acceptable culturally than is femaleness. (Paradoxically, these two seemingly opposite realities go together.) Imagine my surprise and delight when, while watching coverage of the Samoan color guard engaging in the last lowering of the colors for the last millennium, I witnessed an army in skirts. At first glance, I saw only dark legs below light skirts and immediately thought that there must be women in this color party. Close up footage made it quite clear that these skirt-wearing, gun-toting soldiers were men.

The issue of who gets to wear skirts, by itself, is somewhat facetious. The larger point is that we have no dearth of women taking on male traits in our time. But there has been no corresponding eagerness on the part of men to escape the prison of the male gender role and take on some healthier and more sane human traits that have stereotypically been associated with women. Not only do men not usually wear skirts; they also rarely take paternity leave or work professionally with young children, and they often are not as comfortable with or competent in the vital human tasks of relating and nurturing. Herein, I would suggest, lies much of the malaise of our times. But when I suggest that the greatest need vis-à-vis gender issues is for men to become more feminine, most men look radically uncomfortable. I see their eyes shifting about, looking above my head and behind my back, looking for an "exit" sign. Failing to find it, they look as if they may become sick in the very near future. What is it that makes men so uncomfortable with their own unacknowledged and unsought femininity? Why is it such an insult to a man to be labeled "feminine" while the reverse is rarely true? Can the cause be anything other than a deeply entrenched cultural prejudice for masculinity and against femininity? For women to gain their human rights will not, by itself, undo this deep and destructive prejudice. Instead, as women have freed themselves from the prison of the female gender role and taken up many tasks and traits traditionally associated with men, so men need to free themselves from the prison of the male gender role and take up tasks and traits traditionally associated with women. In fact, it could be claimed that women have successfully integrated masculinity into their personas and lifestyles; it is men who are trailing behind in their self-inflicted prison of fear and avoidance of anything feminine in themselves.

When we come finally to examine this masculinity that men so jealously guard from the taint of femininity and the male gender role that women so eagerly seek and imitate, what do we find? Granted, they confer independence and privilege, qualities that women want as much as men. But the rest of it? The violence and competitiveness that are so prevalent in many contemporary images of masculinity, especially in media and popular culture, are decidedly unattractive and destructive, both for individuals and for society. Even if we look past the Rambo images so popular in movies and comic books as merely psychological release rather than role models for men, we mainly see images of successful businessmen and politicians—and that success demands extreme competitiveness and hyperactivity (an extremely long workweek with little attention to friends and family). As Allen Ginsberg once said to me, "Being a man in this culture means needing to have it up all the time." What men, and those who aspire to the male gender role, take on is astounding; what we, as a culture do to men and to surrogate men, is inhumane, though no more inhumane than what was done to women under the gender conventions that held before feminism. Men have relatively few role models of men who are both gentle and competent, not because such men do not exist but because they are not idealized in our speedy, competitive, hypermasculine culture—a culture that focuses upon and instead idealizes the most problematic aspects of the male gender role. Why not have men like the Dalai Lama, Martin Luther King, or Gandhi as male culture heroes and icons of highly accomplished masculinity, rather than athletes, lawyers, businessmen, and generals?

Lest I be accused of simply overdrawing this stark portrait of the male gender role, I have gathered items from popular media that were not intended to discuss gender, but which reveal gender stereotypes quite well. A *Newsweek* article about a successful investment banker who suddenly left his position spells out the competitiveness and lack of concern for relationship skills that are the norm for men: "In the macho arena where Lee thrived, he knew that talking about family values could brand him at best a wimp and at worst a liar. 'In the power alleys of Wall Street and the East Coast, it's not manly to admit that work/family is an issue,' Lee shrugs. 'In fact, the manly thing to say is "I don't have a life and I'm proud of it."'"[2] The local newspaper runs frequent columns in which high school students review movies. Comments about the movie *Gladiator* by a young man and a young woman spell out the male love affair with violence. The young woman wrote that the movie did not appeal to her, because it was about three things: "Violence, violence, and more violence." She goes on: "Perhaps I didn't like 'Gladiator' because I'm a girl. I suppose that is why my male colleague could not find anything wrong with 'Gladiator' and was astonished that I thought otherwise." She points out that the movie's elaborate killings generated the most audience approval, expressed in the form of "excited bellows." "This was especially true with the men seated behind me exclaiming with laughter every time a gladiator was sliced in two or dismembered."[3]

When I ask my students to think about the disadvantages of the traditional male gender role, a few people sometimes mention their typical inability to be involved with young children and their frequent difficulty with feelings and emotions. Almost no one mentions the expectation for men to be soldiers, probably the stereotypical male work throughout much of recent history, as a negative aspect of the male gender role. Yet most defenders of rigid and strictly segregated gender roles posit both the necessity of military activity and the need for men to take charge of this activity. Men need to be aggressive and territorial because defense (offense) is assigned to men for biological reasons. And that is the end of the story, many claim. Yet the logic defies me. "From what am I, a woman, being defended that requires such destructive traits to be socialized into men?" I must ask. Ninety-nine percent of the time, the answer comes down to "Other men!" whatever other verbal sleights of hand may attempt to disguise this reality. What a waste of human ability! Channeling the toughness required for military success into economic or legal competitiveness and victory does little to alleviate the damage done, both to individuals and to society, when toughness and winning are all that matter.

We should also note that this version of male gender role, focusing on military prowess, physical superiority, and beating everyone else is actually neither very Christian nor very Buddhist (nor, for that matter, in accord with the values of most other great religions). The spiritually mature practitioner of any tradition would rarely, if ever, be described in such terms. (This is not to suggest that the traditional female gender role is any closer to the traditions' ideals, as is sometimes argued by those who explain women's exclusion from many religious practices by saying that women in their traditional submissive and passive roles already embody religious ideals.)

One of the greatest problems in proceeding further in dealing with these issues is that critiquing cultural ideals of masculinity or the stereotypical male gender role is culturally unacceptable. The excesses of gender feminists, with their notions of female superiority, have contributed to this situation, but men have also become quite defensive about feminism's legitimate complaints concerning male gender privilege. In such an environment, discussions about what's wrong ethically and psychologically with the stereotypical behaviors of those who take on the male gender role, whether they are men or women, are likely to be evaluated as "men-bashing" or as blaming men for everything that's wrong with human civilization. But to understand my arguments, it is critical to distinguish between *men* and *masculinity* or the *male gender role*. I am talking about cultural definitions of masculinity and about what men do with their maleness, not *men* per se. It is quite possible to be horrified about cultural constructs of the male gender role without being against men, hating men, or blaming them for all human woes.

Men in general, though not every individual, could perhaps be criticized for being too addicted to cultural definitions of masculinity and for lacking a critical perspective about those definitions. That is vastly different from criticizing men for being men, from men-bashing.

Whether or not individual men manifest these traits, many of the traits associated with men or socialized into men are just plain stupid, as are many of the traits of the conventional female gender role, of course. It is stupid not to ask for directions when lost, and it is stupid to be reluctant to go to a doctor. It is stupid and self-destructive to thrive on violence, and it is stupid and self-destructive to work such long hours that one does not know one's children. It is stupid and self-destructive to refuse to become relationally competent. Yet criticizing these tendencies is culturally taboo, because criticizing the expectations placed on men or others who fill the conventional male gender role is confused with being anti-men. But such stances are actually radically pro-men. Such expectations should not be placed on people because they happen to be men. Nor does requiring those qualities in women who want to be free of the liabilities of the traditional female gender role address the fundamental problems surrounding gender in our time and place.

Another way of talking about the cultural malaise in a situation in which everyone tries to emulate the conventional male gender role is to point to a dearth of "feminine" energy and skills, especially those having to do with caretaking. No one wants to take the time to nurture and befriend anyone—children, other adults, community life, civic projects. The arts and humanities, which nurture an interesting and meaningful human life, go unsupported while fields that enhance "technology," economics, or militarism flourish.

If the problem is too much "masculine" energy and not enough "feminine" energy, the solution is not to pull women out of the classrooms, courtrooms, boardrooms, and other places where "public" work is done to send them back to the private world of nurseries and kitchens, as many who decry what feminism has done to the culture suggest. That would only put us deeper into the prison of gender roles, not free us from excessive pursuit of the male gender role. If anything, rather than confining the nurturing and relationship skills associated with the female gender role to the private sphere, we need to infuse the public arena with these skills and see both men and women exhibiting them.

What would it take for that to happen? I suggest that only a massive defection from the conventional male gender role *by men,* parallel to women's defection from the conventional female gender role over the last thirty years, will bring us a more humane society. I do not believe that women can do much more to solve the cultural malaise surrounding gender. Many women have become much more androgynous, in the sense of combining positive elements of both the male and the female gender roles, than have most men. I suggest that much of our continuing discontent over gender stems from the fact that most men have not taken their own genderedness seriously, have not taken seriously the project of attaining freedom from the prison of gender roles, and have not become more feminine in the same way as women have become more masculine. "The liberation of the one is bound to the liberation of the other."

As I have already indicated, most men look for an escape route or look as if they will become ill when I make the suggestions that men need to own their genderedness, look into the negativities of the conventional male gender role, and take on certain "feminine" traits and tasks. Rather quickly an appeal is made to "hardwiring" and the Y chromosome. Competitiveness, aggression, and lack of relationship skills are all built in to the Y chromosome, I am told. We know that higher levels of testosterone *do* make *people,* not just men, more prone to aggression. But the words "more prone" indicate a high level of cultural complicity. The Buddhist distinction between innate and acquired afflictive emotions (*klesha*s) would be useful here. Men, on average, probably do have more innate aggressiveness than do most women. But both men and women will be more tolerant of aggression and competitiveness in a culture that values these traits over gentleness and friendliness, and both women and men will pursue them. The "hardwiring" argument is often a handy excuse for not doing the psychological and spiritual hard work that genuine growth and change require, especially if that growth contradicts socialization and cultural values. But it should not take too much thought to realize that *Gladiator*-type violence is not conducive to a peaceful, nonviolent society. I find it difficult to believe that young men are condemned to relish such violence by virtue of their Y chromosome rather than by virtue of a culture that tolerates violence and rewards competitiveness. Nor do I think it is too much to expect of men that they would turn their backs on such violence, as well as on the lifestyle of "not having a life and being proud of it." The more stereotypically "feminine" reactions to both of these examples are simply more humane and more sane. There is no good reason for men to shun them because they are culturally associated with "femininity."

I have a friend, who happens to be a man, with whom I regularly walk. We have spent many walks talking about gender. We also talk about emotional maturity. One day, he said to me, "You know, Rita, most men eventually do make it to emotional maturity, but, damn it, it takes most of us twenty years longer than it takes most women. Why is that?" The only reply that makes sense to me is, "Because men can get away with delayed emotional maturity." Having employment and girl-friends does not seem to be connected with emotional maturity for men, and so men have little incentive to develop themselves emotionally until their own pain brings them to a breaking point. This is one of the many disadvantages of the conventional male gender role.

In suggesting that men need to defect from the conventional male gender role and become more "feminine," I realize that I am suggest-ing a cultural tectonic plate shift. But I am not suggesting something impossible. We know that because of the way women have defected from the traditional female gender role in the last thirty years. It is often said that our culture does not support men making the kinds of changes for which I am calling, but our culture did not support the changes women were making in the early days of the current feminist movement either. We made those changes anyway. Women's lives have changed radically in the last thirty years. Even religiously conservative women now espouse beliefs that were once considered radical: that women should work outside the home if they want to; that women should be able to have any job for which they are qualified, including supervising men; that women should have equal pay for equal work; that there is no problem with women making more money than their hus-bands. I certainly would be the last person to contend that men are inca-pable of doing what women have done. Certainly men can do everything that women can in the realms of culture, psychology, and spirituality. Women have critiqued and transcended conventional gender expectations. Surely men can do the same!

As always, vision is easier than practicality. It is easy to imagine what could happen if society were to defect from its current version of the male gender role; it is more difficult to figure out what practices would encourage that defection. Furthermore, I believe that men are the only ones who can do much of that work. For women to try to coach men too much in this undertaking would be arrogant and inappropriate. All they should need from us is some cultural analysis, a challenge, and encouragement, as well as emotional support. As with every significant cultural revolution, this tectonic cultural plate shift would happen only because of deep internal psychological, moral, and spiritual changes, individual by individual.

But one suggestion may be appropriate. Just as women studies and women's groups worked so well for women, men studies and men's groups, both of which are already somewhat developed, should work for men. Just as women often complained, when the general masculine was the norm, that we couldn't tell when we were included as humans and when we were excluded as women, I believe confusion between maleness and the human norm has limited men from understanding their experiences *specifically as men*. Rather than being suspicious of men's studies and men's groups, I would suggest that women should encourage them, *so long as it is clear* that such activities do not replace or substitute for women studies and women's groups and their purpose is not to blame women, especially mothers, for whatever problems men encounter. We have reached a stage where three closely interrelated but distinctive disciplines are needed—men studies, women studies, and gender studies. That development would help us find something closer to true "freedom from the prison of gender roles." That is only one suggestion. Many others are needed. But given that "the liberation of the one is bound to the liberation of the other," I call for us to "renew the dialogue whose echoes come to us in the night, charged with hatred, with remorse, and most of all with infinite yearning."[4]

PART THREE

Theory Applied

Three Tests

CHAPTERS 7, 8, AND 9 ARE somewhat technical discussions of three very different topics, all resulting from the paradigm shift in models of humanity initiated by feminist scholarship. Thus, they could be seen as test cases, or applications of the effectiveness of that paradigm shift. They demonstrate that what one sees can change when one's model of humanity changes. More important, they demonstrate that changes in *how* one organizes or puts together the data follow from internalizing that paradigm shift. Both demonstrations are equally important. Sometimes, the androcentric model of humanity makes it difficult to see certain data, as demonstrated especially by the chapters on Aboriginal Australia and the prepatriarchal hypothesis. Looking through a different lens, scholars actually *see* materials that were invisible to them earlier. In other cases, it is not so much that newly seen data emerge when we use gender-neutral and gender-inclusive models of humanity as that familiar materials *look* very different when they are organized by scholars who are not guided by an androcentric model of humanity.[1] This is the case with my proposed revised model of the Hindu pantheon.

Chapters 7, 8, and 9 are more scholarly than many others in this collection, and a great deal of information about very different sets of data is presented in them. The main purpose of including these chapters here is not, however, to present information, but to demonstrate that there is little, if any, completely neutral information, which is why the lens we use as we craft our scholarship and understand our worlds matters a great deal. I will try to demonstrate, minimally, that how things look *changes* when models of humanity change. I would also argue, of course, that gender-inclusive models of humanity produce *better* scholarship than do androcentric models of humanity. That conclusion would involve a philosophical argument that I will forgo in this context. My hope for the reader of these chapters is not especially that a great deal of information is remembered but that one follows the arguments and learns about the *process* of reasoning about data, about how they are gathered and about how they are organized.

If one were to study my resume of twenty-plus pages even superficially, two articles on women in Aboriginal Australian religions might raise questions. Why, in the midst of so much writing on South Asian religion, method, and theory, and feminist theology, these two articles? Because, as I narrated in chapter 1, I accidentally wrote a dissertation on the roles of women in Aboriginal Australian religion, despite my intended and actual area of specialization—South Asian religions—and my investment in the study of Sanskrit. As narrated in that chapter, this "accident" was due to Mircea Eliade's encouragement. His original idea was that I should write a large comparative thesis that would include my already-established specialization in South Asian religions. This was the kind of project that was dear to his heart, and to the outlook of the History of Religions program at the University of Chicago at that time, but it was a life project, not a realistic PhD dissertation. Nevertheless I was encouraged to go forward with the larger project, until politics in the department changed. The research on Aboriginal religions was already complete. It was quite substantial and was deemed a realistic project for which to receive a PhD. I did what most new PhDs do and published a few articles based on my dissertation. Unlike most new PhDs, I then returned to what had always been my major interest—South Asian religions, but with a focus that had been radically altered by the "feminist" questions that had led to my "accidental" dissertation.

The major results and implications of that dissertation were and will always be in its methodology. Chapter 7, "Menstruation and Childbirth as Ritual and Religious Experience among Native Australians," based on research done many years ago, is included here primarily as a methodological demonstration. It is historically important as a condensation of one of the first book-length demonstrations of what happens when one reexamines a set of data using gender-inclusive rather than androcentric models of humanity. It is also historically important because the example of this research led directly to the publication of *Unspoken Worlds: Women's Religions Lives,* a book that is still in print (in its third edition) and that greatly influenced the rising generation of scholars in graduate studies in religion in the 1980s.[2] It has been the concluding chapter of that book in all three of its editions.

The genesis of Chapter 8, "Toward a New Model of the Hindu Pantheon: A Report on Twenty-Some Years of Feminist Reflection," is sufficiently explained in its introductory pages and need not be reiterated here. As I completed minor editing to prepare it for publication in this volume, I reaffirmed both the methodology and the conclusions I reached regarding a new model of the Hindu pantheon. The review of the literature is now dated, of course, but the way it critiques so many presentations of the Hindu pantheon still holds. The most important section of the chapter by far is the final one, "Gender and Number in a Polycentric Symbol System." As I reread that section for the first time in a number of years and edited it, I found my arguments quite convincing, even though I really don't feel much ownership of work I did some years ago. In addition to being another example of the implications of gender-inclusive models of humanity, this chapter also demonstrates a broadly comparative approach, which I think has much to recommend it. This is not an appropriate context in which to make an extended argument in favor of such broadly comparative methods. I would say only that, just as the academic study of religion has a place for specialists, so it needs a place for generalists and comparativists. The two kinds of scholarship are mutually enriching and supportive.

Chapter 9, "The Prepatriarchal Hypothesis: An Assessment," is a complex chapter that is part of my book *Feminism and Religion: An Introduction*. It requires close and attentive reading. I have included it here primarily to demonstrate that allegiance to feminism is not an intellectually easy task. What I called the prepatriarchal hypothesis is not as popular at this writing (2008) as it was when I did this analysis. When I wrote the article, many people were ideologically and passionately committed to either supporting or rejecting this hypothesis, and it was almost an article of faith for many feminists. I took on a close analysis of the hypothesis to demonstrate how someone committed to *scholarly* feminism could be loyal both to feminist visions of the world and to scholarly norms and standards. It was not an easy task.

A brief explanation may be helpful. Throughout the chapter, I refer to an "accurate past" and a "usable past" and the distinctions between them. Conventional historians would argue that there is no such thing as a "usable" past, but feminist historians introduced the distinction early in their work, in part because the records of the past we had inherited seemed so dismal and depressing by feminist standards.[3] Gradually, but very early in feminist scholarship, people began to discover historical materials that had been largely buried under the remembered past generally passed down to us as "accurate" history but that were much more inspiring to those interested in feminist and gender-inclusive understandings of humanity. As a result, we began to claim that there were some "usable" records in the past, by which we meant historically accurate though largely forgotten records.

We also began to realize that male-dominated religious communities maintained themselves partly by which parts of their pasts they chose to memorialize and idealize, and which parts they chose to "forget." Professional historians also began to realize that all histories are, by definition, selective records. Feminists added the insight that who gets to do the selecting makes a great deal of difference in what is remembered. Therefore, feminists in various religious communities, especially Christianity and Judaism, began to reread their historical records, while feminist theologians more oriented to goddesses initiated research into other histories relevant to the development of European culture. (I did much the same kind of research into Buddhist history in *Buddhism after Patriarchy*.) We discovered that there was much, much more to every past than we had been taught in graduate school and began to hypothesize that there might really be some "usable" models in the past. That would mean we did not necessarily have to start over at a ground zero.

For many, a veritable treasure trove seemed to have been unearthed by certain archeological discoveries that became well known by the late 1980s and early 1990s. It was claimed that a "golden age," when women were free and equal and goddesses were revered by all, had been found in places such as Old Europe, Chatal Huyuk, Crete, and other places well-known to historians of the ancient world. Others were aghast at these claims and said that while it might be fun to think about such a "golden age," ideas about it were largely fiction. Feminists had been fooled by a fable common to oppressed peoples. They "find" a past before their oppressors had come into power, when the oppressed had been equal or dominant.

A great deal is at stake in sorting out the accurate parts of this story, the usable parts, and the clearly mistaken parts. Essentially, what is at stake is a claim about whether male dominance is biologically inevitable for humans beings. If that were the case, there would be no point to feminism. Or are there accurate and usable elements somewhere in the records we have of the vast human past? I claim in this article that patriarchy is indeed a historical invention due to causes and conditions, not an inevitable necessity. However, I also claim that most feminists' stories of how patriarchy was invented are not especially accurate and that the models they find in the past "golden age" are not nearly as useful today as is claimed by many feminists. It's a complicated analysis.

Menstruation and Childbirth as Ritual and Religious Experience among Native Australians

The subjects of this chapter are menstruation and childbirth as they figure in the religious lives of both Australian Aboriginal women and men. In the religious lives of women, these biological experiences are the occasion of significant rituals. In the religious lives of men, who of course cannot experience them directly, they are often ritually imitated. The significance of menstruation and childbirth in both women's and men's religious lives has not been especially noted or studied by most scholars of Aboriginal traditions. I believe that this oversight is a result of the fact that Aboriginal religions have usually been studied by male anthropologists from a strictly male point of view.

A few comments on Australian Aboriginal culture and on scholarship about it are crucial preliminaries to our discussion. The Aboriginal peoples of Australia are a hunting-and-gathering society whose material culture is exceedingly simple. Yet their social organization and worldview are so complex that they have long fascinated anthropologists and historians of religion.

Two noticeable features of Aboriginal religion have been the basis of all theories about the role of women in it. The first is the extreme sexual differentiation that characterizes religious life in Aboriginal Australia. Women are almost completely excluded from the men's rituals; and—although this aspect has been much less noticed—men are also completely excluded from women's rituals. Second, the most obvious, elaborate, and time-consuming dimension of Aboriginal religion is represented by those men's rituals from which women are so rigidly excluded. These rituals alone are also the basis of most theories about Aboriginal religion, because male anthropologists found them more interesting and easier to study than the women's rites. This situation led to the classic interpretation of sexual dichotomy in Aboriginal religion: "Masculinity is inextricably interwoven with ritual cleanness and femininity is equally intertwined with the concept of uncleanness, the former being the sacred principle and the latter the profane. This sexual dichotomy and its correlation with the Murngin beliefs of what are the sacred and profane elements of the group, are again connected with a further principle of human relations, namely, that of super-ordination and subordination."[1]

This idea of women's "profaneness" led many scholars to downplay the religious significance of women's rituals. It has been argued that women's religious life is so different from men's as to be unworthy of the label "religious" and that menstrual taboos and childbirth seclusions are imposed on women by men who abhor and fear these physiological events. Women's ceremonies are said to be uninteresting and insignificant in comparison to men's rituals: "Aboriginal women have ceremonies of their own, some commemorating their 'femaleness,' some with highly erotic content, but little is known of these except that they seem to be a pale imitation of masculine ceremonies and they play little part in tribal life."[2]

In all these statements one theme predominates—the attempt to differentiate women's ceremonies from men's ceremonies and, in differentiating them, to indicate that women's ceremonies are inferior in scope, intensity, and religious significance. However, I would contend that, although women's ceremonies are indeed different from men's, if we explore those differences, rather than assuming that difference implies inferiority, other interpretations are possible. What is most significant about women's ceremonies is that, *by being different from men's ceremonies and by focusing on women's unique experience,* they perform the same function for women that the men's rituals perform for men. The women's unique experiences are religious experiences and become rituals; they are symbols and metaphors through which women express and attain their adult status as sacred beings within the Aboriginal community. Just as the men's ceremonies indicate the sacred status and potential of men, so the women's ceremonies indicate the sacred status and potential of women and not some opposite, "profane" condition.

The basic reason for my interpretation can be stated rather succinctly. The experiences and rituals of menstruation and childbirth are laden with clues and characteristics that, were they found in connection with anything else, would be automatically referred to as "sacred" or "religiously significant." *All* attitudes and behaviors that are correctly deemed clues to the sacredness of the male mode and of men's rituals are also found in connection with women's ceremonies; but, when observed in connection with women's ceremonies, their existence and significance have not been noted.

First, the exclusiveness and secrecy surrounding women's rituals are significant because, in Aboriginal religion, both are indications of sacredness. Second, the ideological underpinnings of women's and men's ceremonies are identical. Both women's and men's ceremonies were instituted in mythic times by the totemic ancestors, and both confer great potency on those who perform them. The basic ritual patterns are identical, in general as well as in specific detail. Most important is the basic initiatory structure of withdrawal, seclusion, and return, thought of as death and rebirth, which is found in women's ceremonies to the same extent as it is found in men's. Finally, neither men nor women achieve full initiation and sacred status until old age. All these parallel attitudes are important because they indicate a parallel (not identical) access to sacrality. The women's *different* religious life has the *same* outcome as the men's—membership in the sacred community, not exclusion from it.

Although girls undergo some prepuberty rituals, the first occurrence of menstruation is the most significant event in a woman's ritual progression from the relatively insignificant status, religiously speaking, of being a child to the religiously significant status of being a woman. The reason for it lies in the significance of menstruation itself. "Because menstruation was introduced by mythical characters—as, so to speak, a rite performed more or less automatically by women (although imitated artificially, in various regions, by men)—it has mythical sanction: it is . . . not a mundane or ordinary state of affairs. . . . Menstrual blood is "sacred," declared to be so by the mythical Sisters themselves."[3]

The details of first-menstruation rituals vary considerably, but the pattern is always the same. The girl is secluded by the other women of the group. During the seclusion men are avoided, and various ritual practices are followed. After the seclusion, the girl's return to the group involves a celebration and recognition of new status.

The parallels between these rituals and male initiations are obvious. Not only the general pattern but also innumerable details of ritual behavior are identical. Also, before contact with missionaries, the attainment of womanhood probably involved much more elaborate rituals.[4] If this is true, the parallels would be even stronger, since the relative simplicity of girls' initiations often results in the interpretation that they have less religious significance than the more elaborate boys' ceremonies.

If the *one* existing early account of girls' initiations is accurate, it is clear that, indeed, girls' menstruation ceremonies were quite lengthy and elaborate in earlier times.[5] According to that account, an old woman took the girl out of the camp into the bush. They made a shade, and the old woman built a fire and performed the smoking ritual for the girl. She made the girl sit over a hole in the ground and told her that she was now a woman. In two months "you go and claim your husband," she said. After a two-month seclusion, they moved their camp closer to the main group. The girl was decorated and painted. "To show that the occasion was a sacred one, a sprig of Dahl tree was placed through the hole in the septum of the nose," the account continues. Carrying smoking twigs, the girl walked toward the main camp, following the old woman's instructions. When the women saw her coming, they sang to her. Her betrothed sat with his back to her. She walked up to him, shook him, and ran away, pelted with twigs and sticks by the women. For another month she camped with the old woman, moving even closer to the main camp. A few weeks later she camped just outside the main camp and then moved to the opposite side of her betrothed's fire. Finally, the couple slept on the same side of the fire.

Unfortunately, even this account cannot answer one of the most important questions that arise in connection with menstruation as an initiation into a woman's mode of sacred being. We know nothing of the spiritual teachings that may have been imparted during the seclusion, which, if this one early reporter was correct, was quite lengthy. It seems unimaginable that during a three-month seclusion secret instruction and initiation into women's modes of being did not occur. Nor can anyone claim that, if such teaching had occurred, we would know about it. So far as I can tell, none of the early fieldworkers in Australia who produced the standard descriptions of men's ceremonies actually saw a woman's menstruation ceremony. The instruction in mythic and cultural knowledge, if it occurred, would strengthen even further the interpretation that men's and women's ceremonies are different but parallel ways of achieving the same results. Many of those who focus only on the differences between women's and men's ceremonies and see men's ceremonies as having deeper religious significance than women's ceremonies also contend that men's rituals are somehow concerned with cultural and spiritual matters, whereas women's rituals are merely biologically oriented ceremonies.

Because menstruation is so significant, subsequent monthly periods are also ritualized to some degree. These ritual practices usually include seclusion or avoidance of men as well as some dietary restrictions. Even today, when seclusion is impractical, some care is taken to ritualize menstrual periods. However, while menstrual blood is to be avoided by men, it is considered valuable to women so long as they observe the rituals correctly. For example, "At each menstruation until she is fully developed a young girl receives some of her own menstrual blood, which is rubbed upon her shoulders by the older women. When she is mature, she may perform this duty for younger girls."[6]

Those who have tried to see women as "profane" vis-à-vis the "sacrality" of men have generally supposed that men have imposed menstrual taboos on women because they find this aspect of womanhood the most "profane" of all. However, this interpretation does not seem to point to the true reason why men avoid menstrual blood. Menstrual blood is powerful and magical; therefore, it must be handled carefully and circumspectly, but it is not shameful or unclean. A menstruating woman is taboo, but she is not impure. This realization is extremely important for an adequate interpretation of the role that menstruation plays in women's and men's religious lives.

Childbirth functions as a religious resource for women in much the same way. Pregnancy and childbirth are mythically grounded; female totemic ancestors underwent those experiences themselves and provide the models for women today. In the relatively informal age-grading system that applies to native Australian women, pregnancy and childbirth mark another transition and another level of attainment. Childbirth ritual is secret. Children, younger women, and men are prohibited from the place where birth is occurring just as rigorously as the uninitiated are prohibited from the place where male sacred rituals are culminating. This prohibition is very widely reported. Even in those cases in which a medicine man attends some stages of labor, no man is permitted to see the actual birth.

Fortunately, the literature concerning childbirth rituals is richer than that dealing with menstruation rituals. Phyllis Kaberry and Ursula McConnel have both provided extensive descriptions, based on their field experience, of aboriginal childbirth ceremonies.

Phyllis Kaberry's lengthy description is invaluable for its insights into the religious significance of these practices:

The old women and those who had children went apart with a pregnant woman and danced around her . . . songs were sung. The old women examined her and then would sing. The women said it would make birth easier and charm the pelvis and the genital organs. . . .

As the moment of birth approached the pregnant woman left the camp with her mother and an old female relative, one of whom would act as midwife. During labor, songs were sung to facilitate delivery and prevent haemorrhage, the umbilical cord was cut and the placenta was buried secretly. . . . Mother and child were secluded from the men for about five days.

This ritual is characterized by features which would seem to be typical of that associated with most of the physiological crises of the individual: (1) The observance of food taboos at this time by the mother on behalf of the child; (2) the spells and rites to safeguard them both during parturition; (3) the remedial use of smoked conkaberry bushes; (4) the belief that the blood from the female genitals is dangerous to the men; hence the secret burial of the placenta and the refusal of the women to discuss it in the presence of the men. (5) Finally, the segregation of the woman—a prohibition that is paralleled by the seclusion of a girl at her first menstruation and introcision, and by isolation of a boy after circumcision and subincision. These two factors are so closely interlocked that they can scarcely be considered apart. On the one hand, the child itself may sicken if the placenta is found by the men or if the cord is lost; on the other hand, both mother *and* child, whether the latter is a boy or a girl, may be harmed if they have contact with the men until four or five days afterwards.

Now although the men know some of the details of childbirth, such as the severing of the umbilical cord by the female relative . . . still they are ignorant of those songs which are sacred . . . songs which for all their simplicity are fraught with the power that they possess by virtue of their supernatural origin. . . . Their efficacy is attributed to the fact that they are *narungatlij*, that they were first uttered by the female totemic ancestors. They have the same sanctions as the increase ceremonies, . . . subincision and circumcision. . . .

The whole of the ritual surrounding pregnancy, parturition, and lactation . . . has its sacred and esoteric aspects, which are the most vital aspects to the women, and which are associated specifically with female functions. They are believed to be a spiritual or supernatural guarantee from the Totemic Ancestors that a woman will be able to surmount the dangers of childbirth.[7]

Ursula McConnel's materials are quite similar to Kaberry's. There are myths, known only to women, about the first birth. The myth that prescribes seclusion for the mother serves as a model that women still follow today. The women also have myths that establish the ritual method for extracting the placenta and naming the child. The two events occur simultaneously. The midwife tugs gently at the cord while reciting possible names for the baby. When she says the correct name, the placenta is expelled. It is then buried, and men are forbidden to go near that spot. The myths prescribe a seclusion of two weeks to a month following the birth, during which time no man, including the father, can see the mother or the baby. When the mother's afterbirth blood ceases, both mother and baby are painted for the presentation ritual, which also follows a mythic model. The painting takes place inside a shelter that is taboo to men. Then, followed by very old female relatives, the mother walks toward the father, who is seated on the ground waiting for her, and circles him twice. Then she kneels in front of him and hands him the baby.[8]

Finally, mythology also dictates certain ritual practices for the father. Among the Munkan, he must observe dietary restrictions. In other groups, he and other male relatives must remain silent from the time a woman enters her childbirth seclusion until the baby is born. Such rituals of support by men parallel some of the things women do for men during men's rituals. Women may observe dietary restrictions, silence, or other limitations for their male relatives while they are being initiated. Such parallel support rituals further strengthen the interpretation that the native Australian men's and women's ceremonies are different but parallel ways of achieving the same "sacred" status and are not indications of men's "sacredness" and women's "profaneness."

Having demonstrated the religious significance of menstruation and childbirth for women, let us now discuss these events as symbols in the religious lives of men, for, as I said earlier, these events also play a central role in the men's ceremonies. Such a role indicates that not only do women have their parallel access to "sacred" status, but men themselves see women as "sacred," in another complementary, although ambiguous, mode of sacrality.

The best-known fact about the role of women in Aboriginal religion is their exclusion from the men's ceremonies. Many subtleties of that exclusion are not so well known. It is true that sexually mature women—those who menstruate and give birth—are rigorously excluded; however, in some rare cases *older women* past menopause are initiated into the men's rituals.[9] Furthermore, outside the men's ritual context, women are not generally avoided unless they are going through menstruation or childbirth. When these subtle aspects of women's exclusion have been noted at all, they have been interpreted as evidence that menstruation and childbirth are considered as negative symbols and as part of the justification for excluding women from men's ceremonies. However, the avoidance of women's blood in both menstruation and childbirth is part of a very complex ritual and mythical pattern in which these same events also serve as potent and important metaphors in the religious lives of men.

Let us consider the men's myths first. The northern Australian epic of the Djanggawul brother and his two sisters illustrates one kind of response to women's physiological events.[10] The sisters are perpetually pregnant and giving birth. During these childbearing activities, the women are not kept separate from the man. Instead, the brother often helps his two sisters as they deliver their children. Although this myth dwells extensively on childbirth, there is no implication of danger and no ambiguity. It is also interesting that menstruation is not mentioned at all. Equally important is the fact that at this mythical time, the sisters still carry the sacred emblems and perform the tribal ceremonies. Later, things change. The brother steals the religious paraphernalia and rituals from the women as part of a series of events that mark the transition from mythic to postmythic conditions. Only when the women perform the tribal rituals do the men participate in childbirth. Thus it seems that what was mythically an undifferentiated complementarity became in postmythic times two mutually exclusive, but still complementary, spheres.

The mythology of the Wawalik sisters, also from the north, contains other themes that can help us understand the men's attitude toward women. Few statements illustrate more clearly the ambivalent fascination with childbirth, menstruation, and women's blood than the central parts of this narrative. The two sisters are traveling. The elder is pregnant, and after she has her baby, they take to the road again while the afterbirth blood is still flowing. They camp near a sacred well, and the python dwelling in the well is attracted by the smell of the blood. The snake causes a great storm as it emerges from the well, intent on swallowing the sisters. The younger one dances and is able to keep the python away, but she tires and asks the older sister to dance. She, however, cannot keep the snake away because the odor of her blood attracts it. Finally the intense dancing causes the younger sister to begin menstruating. At this point she, too, cannot fight the snake, and they are all swallowed by it. The sisters later revealed these events to the men in dreams, and such events represent the mythic basis of the men's ritual cycle.[11] Clearly the women and their blood are quite potent. Although the older sister's "mistake" of traveling too soon after delivery had "negative" results, because that "mistake" is a mythic model often ritually repeated by the men, one cannot say that the menstruation, childbirth, and the attendant blood are evil, profane, or unclean but only that they are potent, fascinating, and ambiguous in their potential.

The men's rituals are even more interesting than their myths. It seems that, in addition to the avoidance of women coupled with a sort of fascination with women and women's biological functions, the complex of men's religion also involves ritual duplication of childbirth and menstruation. The women serve as models for men and their rituals, a point that has been made by prominent anthropologists and students of Aboriginal culture: "Many of the rites which men carry out themselves, away from women, imitate, symbolically, physiological functions peculiar to women. The idea is that these are natural to women, but where men are concerned, they must be reproduced in ritual form."[12]

It is difficult to imagine an initiation that does not involve rebirth symbolism. Therefore, in an abstract way, any initiation is a kind of duplication of birth. It should also be noted that duplication of birth occurs in almost every religio-cultural context, not just among the Australian Aboriginal population. The ways birth is duplicated in ritual are quite varied; overall, however, the duplication of the birth process on the part of the Aboriginal men is self-conscious and graphic.

A man's initiation, marked by circumcision, signifies death to the world of women and children and rebirth into the male world. But the circumcisers behave like male mothers, and the novices are thought of as their infants. Before the circumcision, but after the boys have been taken from their mothers, they are sometimes carried about by their fathers in the same way women carry babies. After the operation, the pattern continues. The initiators imitate women in childbirth to the extent that sometimes "the old men build a stone fire and the men inhale the smoke and squat over the fire to allow the smoke to enter their anuses." The explanation given is that "'this is like the Wawalik women did when that baby was born.'"[13] (Women who have just given birth go through this purification rite today.)

Novices and initiators are both secluded from women—a practice that parallels women's seclusion from men at childbirth and menstruation. The newly circumcised boys learn from men how to behave in their new role, just as babies learn from women. The novices learn a totemic language unknown to women, which parallels their learning to talk when they were babies. Finally the boys are ceremonially exhibited as new beings by the men who have transformed them and seen them through rebirth, just as a baby is shown after its mother comes out of seclusion, or just as a girl is exhibited after her first menstrual seclusion. No wonder circumcision "is said to symbolize the severing of the novice's . . . umbilical cord."[14]

Although usually not so graphic and explicit as in Aboriginal religion, the equation of birth and initiation is relatively common in religions around the world. However, male duplication of menstruation is much less common. In Aboriginal Australia, men's menstruation is less widespread than men's childbirth but still occurs over a wide enough area to be germane to this analysis. Two methods are used to produce male menstruation. Subincision is an operation in which the underside of the penis is repeatedly cut until it is grooved from root to tip. The initial operation is far less significant than the subsequent reopenings of the wound, which can be done periodically, yielding large quantities of blood. The large amounts of blood are used as body decoration and as glue for attaching down and feathers to the body, thereby transforming the man into a totemic Dream-time ancestor.

M. F. Ashley-Montague contends that subincision is also considered valuable because it allows men to menstruate, thereby getting rid of a collection of "bad blood" that results from sexual activity or dangerous tasks. Women lose this "bad blood" naturally, but men must take direct action to obtain the same result.[15]

Several authors who have written on the subject have made a further interesting observation concerning subincision. Not only does the male organ now produce blood periodically; the operation transforms the penis so that it looks much more like the vulva.[16] Thus the man can be said to symbolically possess the female, as well as the male, sex organs.

Other groups that do not practice subincision also imitate menstruation. Among some groups blood obtained from piercing the upper arm is used for the same purposes and interpreted in the same manner as subincision blood.

> The blood that runs from an incision and with which the dancers paint themselves and their emblems is something more than a man's blood—it is the menses of the old Wawalik women. I was told during a ceremony: "that blood we put all over those men is all the same as the blood that came from that old woman's vagina. It isn't blood any more because it has been sung over and made strong. The hole in the man's arm isn't that hole any more. It is all the same as the vagina of that old woman that had blood coming out of it. . . . When a man has got blood on him, he is all the same as those two old women when they had blood."[17]

Thus, the men's secret ritual life has a double-edged quality. Men are introduced to a world that is closed to women, but myth and ritual proclaim that, nevertheless, this world is the province of women in important ways. Achieving the sacred status of maleness occurs through mythic

and ritual appropriation and imitation of the female mode of being—
even though women are avoided. Then, once men are inside the realm of
male sacrality—having made the transition by ritual imitation of childbirth and menstruation—the secrets that are now revealed to them can
include myths about female totemic ancestors, rituals reenacting their
adventures, and designs and emblems representing them. At a certain
point, in some groups the male initiate learns of mythic times when men
knew nothing about the sacred. One day, he is told, the man reversed
that situation and stole religion from the women. The men's myth states
that when the Djanggawul sisters discovered what had happened, they
said, "We know everything. We have really lost nothing, for we remember it all, and we can let them have that small part. For aren't we still
sacred, even if we have lost the bags? Haven't we still our uteri?"[18]

Contemporary aboriginal people seem to agree with that mythic
statement.

> But we really have been stealing what belongs to them [the women], for it is
> mostly all women's business; and since it concerns them, it belongs to them.
> Men have nothing to do really, except copulate, it belongs to the women. All
> that belonging to those Wauwalek, the baby, the blood, the yelling, their
> dancing, all that concerns the women; but every time we have to trick them.
> Women can't see what men are doing, although it really is their own business,
> but we can see their side. This is because all the Dreaming business came out
> of women—everything; only men take "picture" for that Julunggul. In the
> beginning we had nothing because men had nothing because men had been
> doing nothing; we took these things from the women.[19]

One could hardly find a more decisive statement that women's unique
experiences are potent metaphors in the men's religious lives. Such a
conclusion can be stated also in another form: it seems clear that
women's experiences provide men as well as women with access to the
sacred. By duplicating menstruation and childbirth and by identifying
men's blood with women's blood, men transcend the ordinary and
become "sacred." They become the mythic models themselves.

Thus I would argue that, when one carefully analyzes all the relevant
data—the myths and rituals of the secret male sacred life and not just
men's ritual avoidance of women—a different interpretation of the relationship between the men's sacred life and exclusion of women must
emerge. Men's avoidance of women is only part of the total picture. It is
one element of an ambiguous, ambivalent reaction to an incredibly
potent and significant presence. Therefore, the exclusion of women is
part of a typical avoidance/attraction pattern relating to that which is
perceived as sacred and should not be interpreted as indicating religious

irrelevance or lack of value. Insofar as the term *sacred* is relevant, there is every reason to use it in interpreting men's ritual responses to women.

It therefore seems clear that women, women's blood, menstruation, and childbirth are religiously significant for both female and male Aboriginals. For women, their biology is one of the major foci of their religious lives, providing them with a unique set of ceremonies, parallel to the men's, that allow them to express their "sacred" status. Menstruation and childbirth, rather than being disqualifiers for significant religious involvement (although they are disqualifiers for involvement in men's cults), are avenues to, and vehicles for, significant religious experiences and expression. In the men's religious rituals and experiences, women's biological functions, far from being irrelevant or antireligious, are utilized as a root metaphor by men seeking to experience and express their own parallel and complementary "sacred" status.

What kind of conclusions can we draw from this chapter? First, we can suspect that most of the world's women have found some kind of significant religious expression, although the presuppositions of Western scholarship have sometimes prevented us from seeing this. Second, we can also suspect that the relationship between men and women in religious life, as in everyday life, is far more complex than most scholars have so far imagined. What becomes of classic patterns of male domination, for example, when they are counterbalanced by awe of women's sacral power? Third, just as we have found that women's religious lives cannot be understood without some reference to the religious worlds of men, so it now seems clear that the reverse is also true.

These conclusions result from the initial impulse to understand women's religious lives more accurately and fully. Thus, they underscore what is perhaps the most radical, and yet commonsensical, conclusion of all. If we seek to understand the whole of religious experience, we must study women as thoroughly and empathically as we have thus far studied men. This conclusion is radical because it involves a basic reorientation of scholarly vision. It is commonsensical and obvious because it is hard to imagine that people could actually have claimed to study something "human" without recognizing that women must be as much a focus of study as men.

Recognizing how much new scholarship has been done on Aboriginal women's religious lives since my very early explorations, I have appended a bibliography including that recent scholarship, as well as some of the older studies relevant to this article.

CHAPTER 8

Toward a New Model of the Hindu Pantheon

A Report on Twenty-Some Years of Feminist Reflection

One of my favorite unfinished and unpublished manuscripts is titled "The Significance of Gender in the Hindu Pantheon." This chapter represents my return to that manuscript, which has spent more than fifteen years in my to-do pile. Both manuscript and chapter circle around my dissatisfaction with the model of the Hindu pantheon found in most textbooks. My dissatisfaction applies equally to the chapter on Hinduism found in world religions textbooks and to textbooks designed for a first course on Hinduism. Having taught introductory courses on Hinduism many, many times, and as a feminist scholar on the lookout, I found the standard description of the Hindu pantheon as consisting of Vishnu, Shiva, and Devi to be incredibly androcentric—and I still do. But now, I have other reservations as well.

The literature on Hinduism which introduced me to that religion routinely presented a model of the Hindu pantheon that is still very much with us, especially in textbooks used by those who will most likely never again study Hinduism. That model tells students that there are three major Hindu deities—Vishnu, Shiva, and the Goddess, always presented in that order, and almost always with fewer words devoted to the deities further down on the list. My early objections remain. This model gives the impression that male deities are more important and more popular than female deities. It also often gives the impression that male deities are normal and understandable while goddesses are odd and exotic. And, finally, the two male deities stand out as distinct personalities, while the female deities, who also have distinctive mythologies and iconographies, are lumped together under the generic title "Devi" or "the great goddess." That portrait is incredibly androcentric.

Hinduism is the only major contemporary world religion in which goddess worship is prominent and normal. In such a religion, it does not seem likely that the female deities would be regarded as an add-on or an afterthought. It is also unlikely that the numerous and varied goddesses would be so generic and so undifferentiated that they could accurately be lumped together under one label. It has long seemed to me that something must be askew in this stereotypical textbook model of the Hindu pantheon.

However, this androcentric interpretation of information from another culture cannot be attributed solely to the androcentric mind-set of Western scholars, as was the case with much of the earlier literature on primal traditions such as Aboriginal Australia.[1] Western scholars could, with some justification, claim that they were merely reporting faithfully what Hindu informants and texts told them. Many Hindus share the perception that there are three major sects of devotional Hinduism—Vaishanvite, Shavaite, and Shakta, the latter often being lumped with Tantric sects and presented as exotic and foreign, even to Hindus. Rather than an imposition of Western androcentrism on the information, we seem here to have mutually cooperating androcentrisms—Hindu and Western.

In such a case, some might argue that, while feminists may not like androcentric models, if they accurately reflect a religion's own self-declared theology, Western feminist scholars are not in a good position to attempt to discredit that model or to configure the data with a less androcentric model of the Hindu pantheon.

Against this argument one could make two counterarguments. First, Western scholars do not simply uncritically accept Hindu claims about Hindu phenomena which do not so closely match Western values. For example, Western scholars of Hinduism do not generally present the Hindu caste system as an inevitable social ideal even when they try to explain it empathetically. And Hindu claims about Hindu origins and history are not taken any more seriously than are the claims put forth by any other sacred history, Western included. So there must be another explanation for Western scholars' uncritical acceptance of the Hindu model of the pantheon as consisting of Vishnu, Shiva, and the Goddess. I would suggest that androcentric Western scholars didn't see anything unusual or questionable about Hindu androcentric interpretations of the Hindu pantheon because they accord so well with Western preconceptions about deity. In the West, it has been many hundreds of years since female deities have been a normal part of the religious imagination. It might not be too surprising that prefeminist Western scholars of Hinduism so uncritically accepted the model of the Hindu pantheon that they found in the literate, elite level of the tradition.

If the Hindu pantheon were approached as critically as are Hindu explanations of the caste system or Hindu versions of Indian history, something else might emerge. We might discover that, though Hindu androcentric interpretations of Hinduism are common, they do not reflect Hindu practice any more accurately than Western androcentric interpretations reflect Western practices. Hindus include many passionate goddess worshippers, despite the more well-known male deities. It has been slowly dawning on Western scholars and observers of Hinduism, ever since the beginnings of current Western feminist scholarship, that Hindu goddesses simply are not a poor third in comparison with the male deities in the affections of Hindu people or in the frequency with which they are worshipped. Nor are they all faceless, identical versions of a generic goddess, any more than the male deities are a generic god. Somehow, this theological point gets lost when discussing the anthropomorphic deities; Vishnu and Shiva are never lumped together as a generic god, while very diverse goddesses are frequently reduced to a generic goddess. It would be more accurate to point out that in some versions of Hindu theology, *both* gods and goddesses are declared to be nothing more than diverse names for an underlying reality.

It is also becoming clearer that the goddesses could be overlooked and reduced to a generic goddess because Western scholarship concurred with a certain segment of Hinduism in its preference for texts and elites. Those Hindus who put forth the androcentric model of the Hindu pantheon are an elite and a minority themselves, not necessarily sympathetic to the religious practices of nonelite Hindus. And, given the tremendous bias of Western religions in favor of texts, it is understandable that Western scholars regarded texts, rather than icons and rituals, as the carriers of the normative Hindu tradition. Thus androcentrism, together with a text-elite bias against popular religion, powerfully combine to justify a model of the Hindu pantheon that seriously obscures its goddesses.

By now, I think that the situation I have outlined above would be generally agreed upon by specialists in Hindu studies. But somehow, that understanding has not yet made its way into literature about Hinduism intended for introductory courses and general audiences, nor are these conclusions often made explicit, even in scholarly books on Hindu deities. I think that this neglect is largely due to the casual attitude on the part of the academy toward the correctives offered by feminist scholarship in all fields.

In the remainder of this chapter, I will turn my attention to the deconstructive task of a preliminary review of three classes of literature that discuss Hindu deities and then to the reconstructive task of asking whether any more adequate model of the Hindu pantheon can be found.

THE RECEIVED PORTRAIT

I am particularly concerned about the impressions conveyed in textbooks intended for use in world religions classes, because in so many cases, the only information about Hinduism that people will ever learn comes from these textbooks. I am sure many would share my evaluation that the chapters on Indian religions, especially Hinduism, are often the most challenging and least adequate in such textbooks, which usually are not written by scholars with significant South Asian training.

At this time, I have not been able to systematically survey all the major textbook choices on this point; instead I will review two recent choices in our department for the world religions textbook. Theodore Ludwig's text, *The Sacred Paths: Understanding the World's Religions,* with which I am generally quite satisfied, follows exactly the model that I have outlined above, with all its drawbacks. (Vishnu gets two columns, Shiva a column and a half, and "the great goddess" barely a column. The information is presented in the stereotypical order.) The new choice, William A. Young's *The World's Religions: Worldviews and Contemporary Issues,* with which I am less satisfied in general, is slightly more adequate on this score. Instead of focusing on Vishnu, Shiva, and Devi, Young claims he will focus on "gods and their accompanying goddesses." (p. 112) That description is somewhat androcentric, although it is also *one* among other accurate characterizations of Hindu gods and goddesses. Much more problematic is the fact that Young doesn't really follow through on presenting this model. The only goddess described individually is Kali. The consorts of the Trimurti (Brahma, Vishnu, and Shiva, the so-called Hindu trinity) are named but not described, while each god in the Trimurti, even the largely extinct Brahma, receives at least a paragraph of description. Durga, Radha, and Sita (all of whom are important goddesses) are not even mentioned, though Krishna, Rama, and Ganesh (male deities who are no more important) are described to some extent. Seemingly, Young recognized that the stereotypical androcentric presentations of the Hindu pantheon were inadequate, but he was unable to provide a more adequate alternative.

Given these stereotypical portrayals, unless the professor supplements the textbook, and most will not, many students may not even recognize and most probably will not remember that the major theistic alternative to monotheism among world religions views goddesses as normal and important to religious life. To some, this may seem insignificant, but to someone who recognizes how critical introducing the divine feminine into religious discourse is for the development of postpatriarchal Western religions, such omissions and distortions are painful.

Another class of literature involves books designed to introduce students to Hinduism in a more in-depth fashion in a semester-long course. In 1980, I surveyed some of the options most widely used at the time: Zaehner's *Hinduism*, Troy Wilson Organ's *Hinduism*, Hopkin's very widely used *The Hindu Religious Tradition*, and also the older classics, Basham's *The Wonder That Was India*, Zimmer's *Myths and Symbols in Indian Art and Civilization*, Danielou's *Hindu Polytheism*, even Eliot's three-volume *Hinduism and Buddhism*. That literature more than warranted my description of the standard androcentric model of the Hindu pantheon presented earlier.

What has happened in the few surveys of Hinduism that have been issued in the intervening years? By and large, though the "Vishnu, Shiva, Devi" model hovers in the background, it is put forth much less forcefully. Goddesses are much more frequently discussed, not only in special sections devoted to them but in the overall narrative about Hinduism in general. Both of these tendencies lean toward less androcentric organizations of the Hindu pantheon. But, in many cases, the question of how the Hindu pantheon hangs together at all is also avoided. As a result, nonspecialists consulting these books to gain some general overview of Hindu theism might come away with no clear impression about the relationships and interactions between the many gods and goddesses.

To illustrate these generalizations, I will point to two newer surveys of Hinduism, one by David Kinsley and the other by David Knipe, each part of an important series of textbooks on major world religions, and I will also mention Klaus Klostermaier's large work *A Survey of Hinduism*.

David Kinsley is well known for his work on Hindu goddesses, so one would expect his textbook not to be androcentric but to highlight information on goddesses. In the first edition of his text, one of two examples given of worship in the Hindu tradition was a description of "common worship of the Goddess" (pp. 123–8). The second edition added a chapter called "Sacred Female Imagery and Women's Religious Experience in Hinduism," which in my view actually makes the book more, not less, androcentric. I have never been convinced that the way to overcome androcentric interpretations is to add a separate chapter on goddesses and women. Information about goddesses and women should not be an "add-on," but an integral part of our understanding of the overall situation. When discussing the pantheon, Kinsley only mentions the common "Vishnu, Shiva, Devi" model a few times in passing, so briefly that someone who does not know its prominence in earlier literature would not realize that this is one of the most prevalent conventional models of the Hindu pantheon. He also does not attempt to solve the problem of how better to picture the pantheon as a whole, nor is it easy to discern the nature of Hindu deities or their role in Hindu religious life from this book alone.

David Knipe's book does not turn on the "Vishnu, Shiva, Devi" model either, though, like Kinsley, Knipe makes oblique references to it. For the most part, when gods enter the narrative about Hinduism, so do goddesses, though Vishnu and Shiva are named while the phrase "regional and pan-Indian goddesses" most commonly denotes the presence of goddesses in his narrative. The commendable feature of this technique is that gods and goddesses are discussed together as deities in theistic and devotional Hinduism, rather than artificially separated by gender, as they are in most other accounts. Knipe's book, like Kinsley's, seems to be suspicious of the familiar "Vishnu, Shiva, Devi" model but unwilling to offer an alternative. It is also difficult to obtain a clear picture of the Hindu deities or their role in Hindu religious life from this book alone.

Klaus Klostermaier's book, in contrast, relies rather heavily on the more familiar model of the Hindu pantheon. A chapter titled "The Many Gods and the One God of Hinduism" surveys Shiva, Vishnu, and Shakti (in that order) and is followed by five chapters on the path of devotion (*bhaktimarga*). The initial chapter on *bhaktimarga* explains that Hindus generally understand that the many gods and goddesses somehow merge into unity without conflict, and also explains the theory of devotion. The next three chapters are devoted to Vishnu, Shiva, and

Devi, in that order. (The fifth chapter on *bhaktimarga* is concerned with the Tamil gods.) However, despite the conventional organization, Klostermaier's discussions of goddesses display none of the diminutive, trivializing tendencies found in many works that use that model. The goddess is not the last deity discussed; all the chapters are of equal length; information about goddesses is not confined only to the chapter on the goddess. And, given that this is a very large book, there is, in fact, a great deal of information about goddesses in this book. Additionally, this book gives the reader more coherent and graspable picture of the whole pantheon and of Hindu theism in general.

Finally, a complete survey of the literature would consider the pros and cons of the many new books specifically on Hindu goddesses, but such a survey is far beyond the scope of this chapter. Probably the single biggest difference between literature on Hindu theism before and after the rise of feminist scholarship is the large number of books on Hindu goddesses published since 1980.[2] Surely the size of that list is directly dependent on the rise of feminist scholarship. But these works are specialized and focused on a single deity or on a small social group; they are not attempts to rethink our model of the Hindu pantheon, nor should they be, since that is not the task taken up by their authors. However, they provide all the evidence we need to make the case that a more adequate model of the Hindu pantheon would not consign the goddesses to a rank of poor third or lump them all together as a generic goddess.

Throwing out the androcentric "Vishnu, Shiva, Devi" model is much easier than coming up with a replacement that would deal differently with gender within the Hindu pantheon. I am convinced that overcoming the androcentric "Vishnu, Shiva, Devi" model is intimately connected with the problem of how better to understand the relationship between plurality and nonduality in Hinduism.

GENDER AND NUMBER IN A POLYCENTRIC SYMBOL SYSTEM

"Gender" and "number" are both critical categories in Hinduism, and both are handled far differently in Hinduism than in monotheism. A more adequate model of the Hindu pantheon must deal differently with both. Though I am willing to hazard some suggestions about an alternative model, I think it is important to concede first that the very idea of a model of the Hindu pantheon, even the idea that there is a *pantheon,* an organized collection of all the gods of Hindu polytheism, is somewhat artificial. Though we know that Hinduism is not a systematic, organized, coherent whole, we keep expecting it to be so, by analogy with other major world religions or ancient polytheisms, frozen in place at one moment in their development.

I am becoming ever more convinced of the thesis put forth by Nancy Falk and others that Hinduism is not one the oldest world religions, but one of the newest, being forged in recent and contemporary times, though certain strands of Hinduism, usually not too important for most people's religious lives, do date back thousands of years. Therefore, one should not expect a coherent Hindu pantheon or theology, any more than one would expect a unified North American Indian theology or a unified Aboriginal Australian pantheon. Instead, we have many local versions of a religious worldview, and all the versions bear a cousinly resemblance to one another, but trying to impose a superstructure on the local variants is both impossible and something only outsiders would want to do. Nevertheless, in all these cases, under modern influences, coherent, unified theologies and pantheons are emerging.

If correct, this insight also means that when using the comparative mirror to look for relevant comparable religious phenomena, care is required.[3] The least relevant comparative model is Western monotheism, but whether consciously or unconsciously, it has been the model most frequently used by Western scholars of Hinduism. Given its intense fixation on the superiority of the number "one," monotheism provides no relevant models for thinking about a polycentric worldview. Westerners, from Max Müller with his henotheism to many current commentators have been mystified as to how multiple personifications of the Ultimate could be mutually tolerated.[4] There has always been an attempt, both on the part of some Western scholars and some Hindu apologists, to see Hinduism as essentially monotheistic. I have always seen this trend as a concession to monotheism that does disservice to Hinduism, the only polytheism ever to successfully withstand many centuries of monotheistic onslaught. Rather than cosmetically redoing this robust polytheism as monotheism in disguise, I think we should be actively inquiring into the dynamics of polytheistic imagination.

In addition, monotheism provides no help at all in thinking about how female deities fit into a pantheon, because monotheism is actually *male* monotheism. Probably one of the reasons why Hindu goddesses came in as a poor third in so many textbook portrayals of them is because the monotheists who wrote the textbooks found female deities even stranger than a plurality of deities and actually barely saw those deities when they looked at Hinduism.

Even among other polytheisms, it is hard to find an analogy for Hindu polytheism, largely, I think, because India has defied political unification and thus avoided religious unification. Other major examples of polytheism, such as Greek and Shinto polytheism, present much more highly organized pantheons largely because a winning tribe benignly imposed its version of a pantheon of familiar gods onto the rest of the population and that pantheon became frozen in time. Therefore, perhaps the continually shifting Egyptian or Mesopotamian pantheons would be more relevant comparative models. But they are also difficult to use as models because they are so remote historically that one cannot really live within their worlds conceptually or imaginatively, as one can with Hindu polytheism. These polytheisms lost out to monotheism many centuries ago without leaving much trace in the contemporary world, which is not at all the case with Hindu polytheism.

If we are left without useful models in the comparative mirror for understanding the Hindu pantheon, I would suggest that at least Hinduism be approached from the angle of vision presented by religions like the primal traditions or Shinto, rather than monotheism. The current tendency prevalent among authors of textbooks on world religions to isolate "the sacred" as the lowest common denominator of religious experience is, in my view, completely on target. Without question, the most obvious examples of "the sacred" as the primary building block of religion are found in the primal traditions and Shinto. The effectiveness with which Hinduism could be interpreted by using this model of religion is underestimated because of tendencies to approach Hinduism doctrinally, relying mainly on Hindu literary sources and monotheistic religions.

If we must approach Hinduism doctrinally, then I would suggest that the doctrinal system most commonly put forth as the dominant Hindu religious outlook is simply a philosophical rendition of the primal worldview of all-pervading sacredness. *Brahman nirguna* (the unqualified absolute), commonly presented as the substratum into and out of which all diverse phenomena (*brahman saguna*) merge and arise, is like the all-pervading sacredness of primal traditions. Immanent nondualism, so commonly presented as the dominant Hindu doctrine, is, I would suggest, simply a philosophical and abstract reading of the sense of all-pervading sacred presence.

If that is correct, then the many deities of Hindu polytheism are simply crystallizations—high points of energy—in the generally sacred phenomenal world. As such, they are more similar to the *kami* of Shinto tradition or the energies of the four directions in North American Indian religions than to the deity of monotheism. In these cases, the emphasis is on sacredness, with the anthropomorphic personifications of sacredness being less central. But, on the other hand, though Hindu deities may well be understood as such high points of sacredness, they are unusually vivid and long-lasting crystallizations. They have very strong and distinctive personalities and devotees who are oriented primarily to one among the many deities, making them somewhat more like the deity of monotheism than like the deities and spirits of indigenous traditions, who are more amorphous and interchangeable.

At this point, we outsiders again encounter headlong the puzzle of Hindu polytheism. I am convinced that it is mistake to simply merge all the Hindu deities into an underlying substratum, as if that substratum were the only important phenomenon, but I am equally convinced that arranging the Hindu deities into a neat pantheon or hierarchy in which maleness predominates is also inaccurate.

Working with people who had never before encountered the Hindu tradition has convinced me that the first requirement for a more accurate model of the Hindu pantheon is to overcome the Western bias for oneness over plurality.[5] My students almost universally felt that Hindu polytheism might be tolerable so long as Hindus understand that some underlying unity is more important and more basic. Using my hands to demonstrate, I suggested that *both* the unity *and* the plurality are equally important. Unity is not the upper hand lying over the lower hand representing plurality; both hands are upraised, at the same height, parallel to each other.[6]

However, the problem remains. If we can somehow come to realize that plurality is not inferior to unity, how can the plurality of the Hindu pantheon be organized in a manner that does not cater to androcentrisms? I am convinced that models of the Hindu pantheon are necessary pedagogically, especially for new students, because a *model* will inform the student in ways that mere descriptions of the many Hindu deities will not.

The foremost requirement for a nonandrocentric model of Hindu plurality is that the primary fault line of Hindu plurality be correctly located. The familiar "Vishnu, Shiva, Devi" model incorrectly locates that fault line in gender. It suggests that the plurality of the Hindu deities is most adequately described by appealing to the gender of the deities— two guys and a girl! But gender simply is not the major fault line in the plurality of Hindu deities and therefore should not be used as the major organizational principle in the model of the pantheon. Using gender as the primary fault line within the Hindu pantheon does not work, because female dimensions of deity are important in both Vaishnavite and Shaivite systems (usually thought of as "male" deities), and male dimensions of deity are usually found in Shakta systems (which are usually thought of as "female" deities).

Those who describe themselves as primarily oriented to one of the major male deities readily emphasize the importance of female deities in their system, and those who are primarily oriented to a female deity usually include some male figures within their system. The question is not whether Hindus venerate goddesses—virtually all Hindus venerate goddesses. The questions is which goddesses different Hindus venerate, which clearly indicates that the fault line around which Hindu polytheism organizes is *not* gender. Therefore, the "two guys and a girl" model is out.

We need a different fault line along which to organize the Hindu pantheon. I suggest using the fault line that has proved to be so successful in other attempts to understand Hinduism in ways that outsiders can comprehend and that is also at least somewhat accurate—the *moksha-dharma* tension and synthesis. *Moksha* connotes release from cyclic existence and conventional patterns of behavior, while *dharma* (for Hindus but not Buddhists) connotes the importance of upholding those conventional norms. In terms of Western logic, these goals are mutually exclusive, but one of the defining traits of the Hindu tradition is that it affirms both of these paradoxical goals rather than coming down on one side or the other of that dichotomy.

Thus, I suggest that discussions of the Hindu pantheon as a whole, *especially in introductory contexts,* be organized around a dyadic *"moksha-dharma"* model, rather than around the triadic "Vishnu, Shiva, Devi" model for several reasons. First, the *moksha-dharma* model builds upon one of the most illuminating models of Hinduism as a whole. Second, it is not hierarchical, either regarding number or gender. Oneness is not privileged over plurality, and maleness is not privileged over femaleness. Third, it is not androcentric and does not give the impression that male deities are more normal and important than female deities.

Such overviews of the Hindu pantheon would explain very explicitly that the Hindu pantheon as a whole, like Hinduism in general, affirms both *dharma* and *moksha.* Some deities tend to emphasize *dharma* more than *moksha,* and others reverse that emphasis, but all deities actually emphasize both in the long term. Only the more relative and obvious emphases differ. That is to say, the pantheon as a whole and all the deities within it are involved both in giving life and in giving death, in some way or another. The cyclic interdependence of life and death is integral to the Hindu understanding of our lot, and each deity within the pantheon speaks to the whole of existence.

The emphasis differs, depending on whether a specific deity patronizes *moksha* or *dharma* more, but Vishnu is not only The Preserver and Shiva is not only The Destroyer. The deities who patronize *dharma*— Vishnu (m.), Laksmi (f.), Krishna (m.), Radha (f.), Rama (m.), Sita (f.), Sarasvati (f.)—also patronize *moksha* in subterranean ways. And the deities who patronize *moksha*—Shiva (m.), Kali (f.), Durga (f.)—also have a major concern with the continuity of *dharma*. By making it very clear that no deity is only a destroyer and no deity is only a preserver, but that all deities manifest a symbolism of the coincidence of opposites in every detail of their mythology and iconography, we could easily present a much more vivid and accurate portrait of deities like Vishnu and Shiva. These deities often seem, inaccurately, to be quite flat and unidimensional in their standard textbook portrayal, and unless the professor is careful, some students also project a moral "good-bad" hierarchy and dualism onto the Hindu deities.

To return to gender and the Hindu pantheon, whether a deity tends to emphasize *moksha* or *dharma*, that deity is not ultimately singlesexed. As in the human realm, so in mythology. Female and male deities are interdependent, and dominance flutters back and forth between them. One could also make a strong argument that the predominant divine image in Hinduism is not of a singe deity with a clear-cut gender, but of an androgynous deity (a deity who is both male and female), often pictured as a couple and less often as a hermaphrodite. Thus the primary deities are a Preserver who also destroys and a Destroyer who also preserves, sometimes seen as a couple, sometimes as a male, and sometimes as a female. But in all cases, the primary division is not along gender lines. Both genders are prominently found on both sides of the *moksha-dharma* fault line.

Regarding dominance, sometimes the male seems more dominant, sometimes the female, and sometimes genuine mutuality is portrayed. But, clearly, Hindu goddesses do not bear out many stereotypes about goddesses. They are almost never portrayed as child rearers, nor are they merely wives or adjuncts of the male deities, though sometimes they bear that identity. The fact that Hindu goddesses do not bear out these stereotypes is more easily demonstrated using this dyadic model than using the "Vishnu, Shiva, Devi" model. Yes, Laksmi is Vishnu's wife and is often portrayed as submissive to him. But she is also an important deity in her own right, often portrayed without her consort. Sita is almost the paragon of the Total Woman who lives through her husband. But Kali dances upon Shiva's prone body—to his delight in iconography, though not always in texts. Durga and Sarasvati function almost independently of any males. The relationships between the male and the female aspects of deity are not at all monolithic, and this important information is easily communicated to beginning students through this dyadic model of the pantheon.

Only one safeguard needs to be emphasized. Unless it is very clearly seen that neither major deity is fundamentally single-sexed, blatant androcentrism would again distort one's overall view of the Hindu pantheon. But clearly such a leap would take a great deal of selective vision. It is impossible for anyone with his or her eyes open to look at Hinduism and not see goddesses everywhere.

It must also be conceded that this suggested dyadic model is still only a model and thus inadequate to fully grasp the kaleidoscopic diversity of Hinduism. But, especially in introductory contexts, we need models. The primary virtue of this abstracted model is that it more closely adheres to prominent fault lines in the Hindu tradition. Just as important, this model does not artificially divide the Hindu pantheon into two guys and a girl who are somehow analogous to the deity of monotheism. It recognizes that both female and male personifications of the sacred are equally concerned with both *moksha* and *dharma*.

CHAPTER 9

The Prepatriarchal Hypothesis

An Assessment

The prepatriarchal hypothesis is both a popular sacred history—the sacred history of the feminist spirituality movement—and a scholarly hypothesis which argues that "the creation of patriarchy" is a historical event occurring in the relatively recent past due to certain causes and conditions.[1] Many scholars and popularizers also speculate about what religion and society were like in the prepatriarchal world, frequently portraying it as a "feminist utopia."

Located at the interstices of several disciplines, including prehistory, archeology, anthropology, mythology, history, and the comparative study of religions, as well as being of considerable importance to feminist discourse, the prepatriarchal hypothesis has generated a great deal of controversy not only with nonfeminists, but also *within* the ranks of feminist thought and scholarship. Because the scholarship on which this hypothesis is based is quite technical and difficult, and because of the passion with which feminists argue for and against this hypothesis, one can feel as if one is walking through a minefield when attempting to survey these materials.

What is at stake in the validity of this hypothesis? Why does it raise so much passion and controversy among feminists? Insofar as communities constitute themselves on the basis of their remembered past, many feminists think that a great deal is at stake in determining that patriarchy is a relatively recent historical development. It would be far easier to claim the seeming inevitability of patriarchy and the futility of feminist efforts if one could demonstrate with reasonable certainty that "it's always been that way." If patriarchy extends infinitely back into the human past, it is easier to argue that male dominance is somehow written in human genetic material rather than produced as a result of certain historical causes and conditions. It is no accident that new forms of biological determinism, such as sociobiology, became popular soon after the current wave of feminist thinking became established. Nor is it accidental that extreme claims for an evolutionary and genetic basis for male dominance, such as Lionel Tiger's *Men in Groups,* or diatribes about the biological dangers of egalitarian social arrangements, such as George Gilder's *Sexual Suicide,* became popular at the same time.[2] Arguments based on biology or nature often seem stronger than claims about the cultural nature of patriarchy and claims that the future is open-ended, not determined by the past. Therefore, both feminists and antifeminists rely heavily on arguments about the nature of the first human societies.

Finding an accurate passage between advocates and critics of the prepatriarchal hypothesis in not simple. As guidelines, I first suggest that we emphasize the conclusions of prehistorians, archaeologists, anthropologists, and historians who are both informed by feminist values and conversant with relevant scholarly literature. The most vehement advocates and attackers of the prepatriarchal hypothesis often treat this material lightly in their writings. Additionally, some detractors of this hypothesis tend to argue as if casting doubt on a single aspect of the hypothesis invalidates the entire hypothesis, a conclusion that is not warranted. Another tactic taken by some detractors is to argue against popular rather than scholarly versions of the prepatriarchal hypothesis. Obviously the cogency of the prepatriarchal hypothesis should not be argued on the basis of the popular literature that fills the women's spirituality sections of some feminist bookstores. Finally, and most important, the most adequate negotiation though these questions, I suggest, will involve evaluating the various components of the prepatriarchal hypothesis separately, rather than trying to reject or justify the whole complex.

I suggest separately analyzing three components of the prepatriarchal hypothesis. First, is it reasonable to conclude that patriarchy arose relatively recently in human history, due to certain causes and conditions? Second, does the thesis of a prepatriarchal "golden age" for women hold up? Finally, what are the most cogent explanations for the emergence of patriarchy in human history?

IS PATRIARCHY ORIGINAL?

The question of a prepatriarchal hypothesis is greatly simplified and clarified by placing equal emphasis on both words. The word *hypothesis* concedes that this account of early society is a probable reconstruction from limited information, rather than an incontrovertible fact. Like all hypotheses, it is subject to continual revision and possible replacement if a more cogent explanation is developed. More important, the modest term *prepatriarchal* simply indicates that it is extremely unlikely that patriarchy prevailed in the earliest human societies. Patriarchy requires the kind of social stratification and social complexity that develop with high population density and urbanization—not the conditions of early human societies.

However, beyond suggesting that patriarchy could not have been the earliest form of human society, this phrasing does not attempt to describe in any detail what the earliest forms of human society were like. Specifically, the prepatriarchal hypothesis, at least in any form that has scholarly reputability, does not assert or assume a prior *matriarchy*. As Riane Eisler notes, people stuck in dualistic, either-or thinking often assume that "if it isn't patriarchy, it must be matriarchy,"[3] an assumption made by Johann Jakob Bachofen as well as by many popular writers. Why a feminist would want to claim this misnomer is somewhat unclear, since little is to be gained by reversing patriarchy into a matriarchy, whether past or future. One can be sympathetic with the impatience of some scholars who don't want to devote further serious attention to a thesis which is sometimes so badly stated by some of its most adamant defenders.

By far the most skeptical critics of any version of the prepatriarchal hypothesis are those trained in the history of religions and the study of classical civilizations. Because the societies studied by these scholars have been patriarchal for so long and because these societies have become so dominant over so much of the globe, classicists and historians of religion often find the hypothesis of nonpatriarchal social organization unbelievable. For example, David Kinsley's major reason for rejecting the prepatriarchal hypothesis is "the few examples we have of cultures in which men do not dominate women. The tendency toward male dominance is strong in both historical cultures and in non-literate cultures."[4]

But both anthropologists and archaeologists trying to reconstruct the earliest foraging and horticultural societies simply do not agree with the conclusion of universal male dominance any longer. As Peggy Reeves

Sanday says in her major study of the origins of male dominance, "Male dominance is not an inherent quality of human sex-role plans. In fact, the argument suggests that male dominance is a response to pressures that are most likely to have been present relatively late in human history.[5]

If one thinks about the requirements for human survival guided by the androgynous rather than the androcentric model of humanity, it is difficult to imagine that humanity could have survived if early humans had insisted on wasting female productivity and intelligence in the way that patriarchal societies have always done. It is no longer supposed that earliest human foragers could have depended solely on men for their food supply, or that men alone were responsible for the discovery of tools, the development of language, or other crucial advances made by early humans. All cogent reconstructions of early foraging life posit an interdependence and complementarity between women and men, rather than male dominance and patriarchy. Nothing in the material conditions of early human life would suggest that male dominance would have been adaptive or likely.

Furthermore, even though sex roles are often strong in contemporary foraging societies, male dominance is rare. The sexes are seen as complementary and of equal importance.[6] While everyone recognizes that the ethnographic present cannot establish an archeological past, and that reconstructions of prehistory will probably always remain *hypothetical,* the notion of a strongly male-dominant, patriarchal foraging past seems to be an especially unlikely hypothesis. Of course, the unlikelihood of patriarchy in the Paleolithic does not establish the existence of either female dominance or equality either.[7] But only extremists leap from the unlikelihood of Paleolithic patriarchy to certainly about a Paleolithic feminist utopia.

Much the same "middle path" reconstruction of early Neolithic societies, which were horticultural (using the hoe) rather than agricultural (using the plow), is suggested by many anthropologists and archaeologists. In early settled food-growing communities, women and men remained interdependent and complementary. Again there is nothing to suggest that male dominance was practical or adaptive. And, again, contemporary or recent horticultural societies do not always exhibit strong male dominance and patriarchy, though some do. Some of the more recent societies most noted because women have considerable autonomy and power, such as the Iroquois and the West African kingdoms, are horticultural.[8] In fact, even many nonfeminist scholars have seen Neolithic horticulture as a period in which women enjoyed higher status and more autonomy than they typically did later. What changes in feminist commentaries on the Neolithic is to regard this situation as an ideal rather than an aberration.

Therefore, without inventing a fanciful past, it is reasonable to conclude that an accurately reconstructed early history of humanity is empowering and useful. "It hasn't always been that way." It is reasonable to conclude that foraging and early horticultural societies were not patriarchal. As we shall see, we may not be able to establish any adequate models for the postpatriarchal future in the prepatriarchal past. Nevertheless, knowledge of the prepatriarchal past alters our perceptions and assumptions greatly to realize that it makes no sense to claim that male dominance stretches as far back into the past as we can see. At the conclusion of her book *Women in Prehistory,* which no one could fault for lack of caution in its interpretations, Margaret Ehrenberg states the case well: "Although the social status of women has long been inferior to that of men, it must also be remembered that the foraging societies of the Paleolithic and Mesolithic spanned an immense period, many hundred times longer than the mere 12,000 years or so from the Neolithic to the present, and that many of the world's people continued to be foragers long after farming had been discovered in the Near East. So, throughout human history, the great majority of women who have ever lived had far more status than recently, and probably had equality with men."[9]

INTERPRETING PREPATRIARCHAL EVIDENCE

The weak link in many versions of the prepatriarchal hypothesis is, in my view, the attempted reconstruction of prepatriarchal religion and society. That patriarchy arose in history due to certain causes and conditions seems to me to be as incontrovertible as any historical hypothesis ever can be. Nevertheless, there is no easy passage, and probably no passage at all, from establishing the cogency of the thesis that patriarchy is a late development to establishing the kind of prepatriarchal feminist utopia claimed by the most ardent advocates of the prepatriarchal hypothesis.

Societies that are especially interesting to advocates of the prepatriarchal "golden age" include Paleolithic foraging societies, Catal Huyuk, Old Europe, ancient Megalithic cultures, and Crete, perhaps their favorite society. These feminists usually invoke the numerous and powerful goddesses of antiquity as models for contemporary women, reconstructing a detailed and elaborate myth and ritual complex surrounding these goddesses. They posit an era of peace, prosperity, stability, and egalitarian social arrangements that prevailed far and wide for a long period of time before being destroyed violently and relatively quickly by patriarchal and pastoral nomads, including the precursors of both the Indo-Aryans and the Semites. In this prepatriarchal world, women enjoyed autonomy, power, and respect under the aegis of the Goddess, who was universally revered by all members of society and was the embodiment and source of life, death, and renewal. Gradually, as societies became more male-dominant, both women and the Goddess lost their power, autonomy, and dignity, a process that culminated in the eclipse of the Goddess represented by the Hebrew Bible and the thinking of classical Greece.

Such a hypothesis has always enjoyed some currency, going back at least to the theories of Bachofen.[10] Early in the second women's movement, the thesis was again taken up by feminists, who unfortunately had little scholarly training in any of the disciplines at the nexus of this complex hypothesis. The most notable and influential of these writers were Elizabeth Gould Davis and Merlin Stone.[11] Anne Barstow contributed an influential and extremely balanced article on the prehistoric society of Catal Huyuk, one of the most famous Neolithic sites cited in contemporary discussions.[12] And the well-established archeologist Marija Gimbutas, whose interpretations of the culture of Old Europe pioneered a new chapter in prehistory, has taken up this reconstruction with passion and conviction.[13] Elinor Gadon and the team of Anne Baring and Jules Cashford have written engaging and complete histories of the various ancient goddesses, from the Paleolithic to medieval veneration of the Virgin Mary.[14] Relying on the archeological work done by Gimbutas and others, Carol Christ has made the prepatriarchal hypothesis central to her goddess thea-logy.[15] The most visionary and poetic reconstruction, which connects the prepatriarchal past with an unfinished but absolutely essential evolutionary transformation still awaiting completion, is Riane Eisler's *The Chalice and the Blade*.[16] Pulling together a great deal of information from prehistory through classical biblical and Greek materials, as well as discussing what is needed in the present to allow the survival of the species, she contrasts the values of the chalice with those of the blade. The chalice represents a "gylanic," peaceful, and egalitarian value system prevalent in the prepatriarchal world, while the blade represents the androcratic values of the "dominator" societies that overthrew and partially, but never completely, destroyed the gylanic values of prepatriarchal societies of empowered women, peaceful men, and strong goddesses. Clearly, remembering such a past could be empowering and useful in today's world.

Why, then, would some *feminists,* not merely antifeminists, be extremely skeptical of the prepatriarchal hypothesis? The answer is twofold. Some feminists object that such "spiritual" issues are largely irrelevant to contemporary women, citing the oft-quoted truism that goddesses frequently coexist with male dominance and cannot be correlated with high status or autonomy for women. Many such feminists feel that economic, political, and social issues are of far higher priority and that antiquity holds few models in this regard. They also feel that goddess worship in the *present* does little to alleviate women's real problems. Other feminists are not especially opposed to goddess worship for contemporary women and agree that the ancient world included many powerful and impressive goddesses. But these feminists are skeptical of the scholarship that has reconstructed a *utopian* or a *female-dominated past* based on the existence of these goddesses. Many argue that extreme caution is required when interpreting material artifacts and that one cannot easily deduce ideology or social structure from them. The ease with which Gimbutas, Gadon, and Baring and Cashford, for example, deduce extremely detailed myths and rituals from limited and opaque material artifacts is the weak link, in my view, for such reconstructions are easily subject to projection and wishful thinking.

Such disclaimers about the prepatriarchal hypothesis seem to be especially numerous among academically trained scholars of religion who are otherwise interested in or sympathetic to feminism, such as David Kinsley, Katherine Young, and Joan B. Townsend.[17] All three of them have voiced sharply worded critiques of these reconstructions of the prepatriarchal period. Young and Townsend express the opinion that the feminist reconstruction of the prepatriarchal past "puts forth as *historical fact* the myth of a golden age of the past to give ego reinforcement, to weld a bond among women in order to create a unified force, and to provide women with historical precedent for their aspirations."[18] In other words, that remembered past, however *useful* it might be, is not *accurate* and is therefore unacceptable. Rosemary Ruether has also been a longtime critic of the prepatriarchal hypothesis. Her argument, most fully developed in her book *God and Gaia,* seems to be that she finds the claims for the innocence or goodness of prepatriarchal societies untenable, because such claims link failure and greed with patriarchy and men, instead of with human beings, both female and male.[19]

What is at issue in these debates? What are the weak links, and which links hold? That many female forms are found in the archeological record of prehistoric and protohistoric societies is uncontested. It is equally uncontested that early mythological literature tells of many important and powerful goddesses. However, these facts do not prove that women were equal, in the modern sense of the term, which seems quite unlikely, or that they lived lives with which modern women could be satisfied, or that the numerous female figures that have been discovered can easily be interpreted as Mother Goddesses. When interpreting these numerous female forms, it is much safer to note their presence and to hypothesize that they indicate appreciation of female sacredness, rather than to speculate in great detail about their theology or to try to determine whether they are goddesses or priestesses. One can have sympathy with critics who weary of the certainty with which Eisler and Gimbutas sometimes retell the myths and restage the rituals of prepatriarchal societies. However, skepticism about some of the details of some interpretations and reconstructions should not lead one to dismiss the thesis that patriarchy arose relatively late in human history.

Though it may not be possible to demonstrate what prepatriarchal societies were like in detail, or to interpret their symbol and myth systems with the certainty that some believers in the prepatriarchal hypothesis would advocate, nevertheless it seems reasonable to conclude, simply because patriarchy had not yet evolved, that women were less dominated than in later societies and that female sacredness was more commonly venerated than in later societies. It would seem quite likely that women's relationships with men were more satisfactory, by feminist standards of assessment, than they became in male-dominated societies. It also seems extremely likely that female sacrality, whether human or divine, was a commonplace of religious ideology for both women and men. These modest, and to my mind, relatively certain conclusions, are both accurate and useful. One does not need the extremes of either those who reconstruct details of a prepatriarchal feminist utopia or those who reject the prepatriarchal hypothesis entirely.

Several other theses central to many standard feminist reconstructions of prepatriarchal societies and religions deserve individual commentary. Feminists often argue that these prepatriarchal societies were both egalitarian and peaceful. They link these desirable (by feminist standards) conditions with the respect accorded to women and to the appreciation of females, whether divine or human, as sacred.

Predictably, the critics attack both of these conclusions. Townsend argues that many bodies buried in supposedly peaceful Catal Huyuk show evidence of severe blows to the head, and Young argues that private property, which undercuts egalitarianism, could have begun in the Neolithic period.[20] But the descriptions of the town plans, the houses themselves, and the art of Neolithic Europe, which occur in source after source, support the conclusion that these societies were relatively peaceful and egalitarian, *especially when compared with later societies.* To say that these societies were peaceful is to say that they did not expend major resources, human or material, on organized, large-scale warfare. It does not mean that individual feuds, resulting in severe head wounds, would never occur. It is important to recognize that feuding and private fights, which seem impossible to avoid in human society, are completely different from diverting major resources and human energy into defensive or offensive warfare. This is a critical distinction. It is naive to attribute the human tendency to aggressive behavior to patriarchal social arrangements. Patriarchy may encourage such tendencies, but it does not create them. On the other hand, the nonmilitary prepatriarchal societies give evidence to something that is critically important. *Human beings can live together and deal with their aggressions without resorting to large scale, organized warfare as a major preoccupation and use of resources.* Even a nonfeminist historian, Thornkild Jacobsen, locates the beginning of warfare, *as a major threat,* in the third millennium BCE, but not earlier, when, in his view, famine was a much more severe threat.[21] And early private property was not sufficient to result in the great inequities of wealth and poverty characteristic of later societies, as is clear from descriptions of town plans and houses.

However, it may not be possible to establish that this peaceful, egalitarian lifestyle was *caused* by the relatively high status of women combined with veneration of female sacrality, as is so often claimed by feminist advocates of the prepatriarchal hypothesis. On the one hand, material conditions of life do argue for the likelihood of relative peace and egalitarianism and against large-scale warfare and significant hierarchy in early foraging and horticultural societies. It can also be argued that women had relatively higher status in these societies than in later patriarchal societies. But, on the other hand, *once large-scale warfare and significant social hierarchies become part of human society, women and goddesses readily support and patronize both.* This embarrassing fact argues against the conclusion that earlier societies were relatively peaceful *because* women insist upon peace. Women's preferences for or against hierarchy and warfare do not seem to be the driving causal link in the whole sequence of developments. It seems, rather, that certain technological complexities, once unleashed, are hard to restrain from bringing hierarchy and violence in their wake, a topic to which we must now turn our attention.

THE CREATION OF PATRIARCHY

With the transition from horticulture to intensive agriculture, which began somewhere in the fertile crescent after 5,000 BCE, male dominance first becomes clear-cut and obvious, both in the archeological record and in contemporary societies studied by anthropologists. This transition is explained quite differently by the most strident advocates of the prepatriarchal hypothesis and by less ideological scholars. Somewhat caricaturing the most ideological feminist explanations for the demise of peaceful Neolithic societies, it is claimed that men, seemingly by nature more prone to violence and less moral than women, took over by force of their superior physical strength and began their reign of terror and dominance. While invasion from nomadic warriors is one factor in the decline of some prepatriarchal societies, this explanation begs the obvious questions. *Where did these men come from and why did they turn to warfare, violence, and domination?* Furthermore, this explanation depends on an essentialist understanding of male and female natures as static, unaffected by varying cultural and material circumstances. Ultimately, this explanation is quite discouraging regarding the possibilities for postpatriarchal society. Locating the cause of the transition from prepatriarchy to patriarchy in morality rather than in material and technological changes strikes me as counterproductive—a hypothesis of last resort if one wishes to work for the demise of patriarchy. This explanation pits women against men morally and seems to conclude that men have no choice but to be violent and immoral. If this is so, then it will probably be impossible to eradicate patriarchy.

If, on the other hand, patriarchy is the result of certain causes and conditions, then, when those causes and conditions are removed, patriarchy can die a natural death. Therefore, it is important to look behind the immediate cause of the decline of many prepatriarchal societies—conquest by patriarchal outsiders—to the more basic causes that led to the development of warrior, male-dominated societies in the first place. At the other end of a spectrum of explanations for the rise of patriarchy is an explanation that looks at changing technologies rather than morality.

Patriarchy emerged because, for the first time, the *material conditions* of life promote male dominance. Newer technologies, involving the plow and draft animals, complex irrigation systems, and a new emphasis on labor-intensive grain crops favored men as the primary producers, while women were reduced to the role of processing agricultural produce. Labor-intensive agriculture increased reproductive demands at the same time as an increased food supply permitted higher rates of fertility. Women began to have more babies, and populations increased greatly. Specialization and social stratification became possible. Resources became scarcer and competition for them increased, making organized, communal violence (warfare) attractive and seemingly advantageous. Specialization also made increasing amounts of private property possible at the same time as there was increased competition for scarcer resources, thereby also increasing the attraction of warfare. All these factors are essential in the transition from a kin-based society to the process of early state formation. And, to some extent at least, these processes seem to have been replicated in other parts of the world that went through the same transitions.

Thus a complex web of technological, social, and material changes, rather than a change in morality or religious symbols, made dominance and hierarchy, including male dominance over women, possible for the first time in human history, relatively late in human history. The highly respected historian Gerda Lerner arrives at this conclusion, as do many anthropologists and archaeologists.[22] Thus, we have established the first claim about patriarchy again, on different grounds. The part of the prepatriarchal hypothesis which claims that patriarchy, as we have experienced patriarchy in most or all societies since the Bronze Age, is the product of historical causes and conditions, rather than a timeless human condition or the result of male moral depravity, seems as incontrovertible as any historical hypothesis ever can be.

When asking about the creation of patriarchy, it is also important to discuss how important warfare and invasion were in the demise of prepatriarchal societies. While evidence seems quite clear that Old Europe and the Mediterranean regions were, in fact, overrun by patriarchal outsiders who violently and quickly destroyed peaceful, matrifocal Neolithic villages, it seems equally clear that in the Ancient Near East, in Mesopotamia, among others, *internal* developments toward social hierarchy, including male dominance, preceded large-scale warfare as major threat and preoccupation.[23] Thus, ultimately warfare is an *effect* rather than the *cause* of the end of prepatriarchal society, though some individual prepatriarchal societies were destroyed by outsiders who had already become patriarchal warriors. We should probably look to increased population pressures and competition for scarce resources as the *causes* that made warfare an attractive option in the first place— a lesson that is certainly important in contemporary times as well.

Finally, we can return to the link between symbols of sacred females and the emerging patriarchal order. It seems quite unlikely that the new emphasis on warfare and male dominance occurred because patriarchal ideology or symbolism replaced symbolism and ideology that empha- size women and feminine sacrality. If anything, the reverse occurred. With growing male dominance brought about by technological and cultural changes, religious symbolism gradually became more male- dominant—the next phase of the story to be discussed. Material or tech- nological changes and changes in symbolism or religious and social ideology are always closely bound up with each other. In this case, it does not seem cogent to give religious symbols the role of causal agent in these massive changes.

However, given the link between religious symbols and social forms, the feminist advocates of the prepatriarchal hypothesis are also right when they claim that the patriarchal ideologies, symbol systems, and social systems that now rule the planet could never produce a return to peace and egalitarianism. The technological possibility or necessity of peace and egalitarianism will require postpatriarchal symbols and ide- ologies as well. And postpatriarchal symbols and ideologies will resem- ble prepatriarchal symbols of female sacrality and egalitarian gender relationships more than they will resemble patriarchal symbols and gender relationships.

SOME CONCLUDING COMMENTS
ON THE PREPATRIARCHAL HYPOTHESIS

Several weaknesses are endemic to the prepatriarchal hypothesis as usu- ally presented in feminist literature. One is its obvious Eurocentric bias, and the other is its unilinear model of cultural evolution. The prepatri- archal hypothesis explains *Western* patriarchy, not other forms of male dominance. And it seems to assume that patriarchy emerged *once,* in Western antiquity. Both of these omissions need to be addressed.

Very little research has been done concerning the cultural and religious development from prepatriarchy into patriarchy in other parts of the world. Though the case has not been made very thoroughly for India, well-known and easily accessible archeological and historical data would appear to warrant extending the hypothesis to include India. However, even though Indian male dominance could possibly be explained through the same waves of cultural contact and invasions that explain Western patriarchy, East Asia does not participate in those historical processes. East Asian patriarchy requires a separate explanation, which has not been made to any great extent. In a noteworthy exception, Robert Ellwood has argued that "in early Japan we have a narrative which, taken at face value, seems to show patriarchal revolution in full spate."[24] Probably Asia has been overlooked simply because so few feminists and feminist scholars are well trained in cross-cultural studies. This limitation is not as serious as one might at first suspect, because it is difficult to imagine that foraging or horticultural societies were vastly different in other parts of the world than they were in Europe and the Middle East. While the locus chosen to argue out this hypothesis reflects an obvious and unfortunate Eurocentric bias, this bias does not invalidate the hypothesis.

The unilinear model of evolution into patriarchy is a more serious problem, for it assumes that all societies go, lockstep, through the same historical processes. This was a popular hypothesis in nineteenth- and early twentieth-century anthropology, but it has not been taken seriously for many years. The work of Peggy Reeves Sanday in *Female Power and Male Dominance* offers a major corrective concerning theories of the origins of male dominance. Rather than isolating single or even multiple chains of cause and effect leading to male dominance, she locates patterns of cultural forms that tend to be found with male dominance and with female power. Chief among her findings is that it is possible to talk of female power and male-female equality when women have economic and political decision-making powers, which they do in about 32 percent of societies studied. Only 28 percent of the societies in her large sample are clearly male-dominated. The remaining 40 percent are neither clearly egalitarian nor male-dominated, but fall between those opposites.[25]

Sanday studies many factors that play into the level of male dominance in a society. If the environment is beneficent, then women and men tend to work together, men spend time with young children, and people develop what she calls an "inner orientation," including a symbol system that features female creative beings. Such societies are not usually male-dominant. By contrast, if the environment is harsher and providing basic necessities produces stress, or if livelihood centers around large animals or migration, people develop an "outer orientation," in which the creative powers are male. Male dominance is likely in these societies, in part because men and women do not work together and men spend little time with children. But these lines of explanation are not neat and unilinear. Though, in some cases, one can "establish a causal relationship between depleting resources, cultural disruption, migration, and the oppression of women," male domination of women, when it occurs, "is a complex question, for which no one answer suffices."[26] In the long run, her less than neat, nonlinear discussion of female power and male dominance is more satisfying than even the refinements of the prepatriarchal hypothesis that do no more than explain the emergence of patriarchy in Western antiquity. Her findings are recommended not only to historians who want to explain the rise of patriarchy, but also to ethicists and theologians seeking the postpatriarchal future of religion.

Finally, we must return to the question of prepatriarchal religion and society as an accurate and usable past. That it is accurate to speak of prepatriarchal pasts is, by now, as well established as is possible. But what is the contemporary usability of these pasts? I would suggest that prepatriarchal pasts provide proof of the possibility of a postpatriarchal future, but are not a model for it. We need to recognize, as does Barstow,[27] the limitations of the usefulness of the prepatriarchal past. While it is useful to know that patriarchy has not always been women's lot, modern women should find the forms and symbols of ancient religion only of limited utility in constructing postpatriarchal religion.

Most interpreters of these female forms and symbols stress their fertility and maternity, by no means a sufficient meaning for female sacrality in today's religious universe. While valorizing motherhood is an important issue in contemporary feminist religious reconstruction, not privileging that symbol is absolutely vital, even mandatory, for human survival. Considering that increased maternity, resulting in increased population density and competition for scarce resources, is probably one of the causes of patriarchy, feminists should be loathe to enshrine physical reproduction as the primary symbol of female sacredness. Because human population growth threatens to stress the environment immeasurably in the very near future, if not already doing so, and since environmental stress is one of the root causes of male domination, feminism needs to sanctify images of women and goddesses that would reverse and undercut excessive physiological reproduction. Such models are not in abundance in the prepatriarchal world, at least as interpreted by many of its advocates.

It is futile to look for the birth of human aggression, or whatever else we may see as the genesis of human misery, in the birth of patriarchy. Patriarchy adds its own special and unnecessary dimensions to human misery, to grasping and the resultant suffering, but it is naive and unhelpful to locate the origins of grasping and aggression, tendencies basic to being human, in the origins of patriarchy. They will continue to challenge us even in postpatriarchal forms of religion and society. To regard "the fall" as a historical, preventable event rather than an ahistorical mythic event, which is what happens when the origins of patriarchy are equated with the origin of evil and suffering, is an uncritical appropriation of one of patriarchal religions' most destructive tenets. Furthermore, this version of "the fall" turns on an essentialist theory of male and female natures, of moral women and immoral men, that gives little hope for a post-patriarchal future.

Nevertheless, it is equally important to recognize the profound usefulness of this material. "It hasn't always been that way." Men have not always dominated women. Additionally, while recognizing the contemporary limitations of images specific to the Paleolithic and Neolithic, it is important to recognize that the *example* of images of female sacredness is useful and empowering to Western women, so long denied this simple and almost universal affirmation.

PART FOUR

Feminist Theology

THE VERY FIRST PAPER I WROTE after I finished the final draft of my Ph.D thesis in 1974 was an essay I called "Female God Language in a Jewish Context," and that essay eventually became what is reprinted here as chapter 10, "Steps toward Feminine Imagery of Deity in Jewish Theology." If I had been following scholarly conventions, I would never have written that essay. Technically speaking, it was completely outside my supposed field of specialization, and in those days such indiscretions were quite dangerous. But I followed my inclinations. I don't remember for sure if there was a publication in the works at the time, but I believe that probably someone was trying to put together a collection of essays on Jewish feminism. There was already a nascent Jewish feminist movement in which I had been involved, and I was somewhat well known in it. In any case, the essay was published in an alternative Jewish magazine in 1976 and included in the landmark anthology *Womanspirit Rising,* published in 1979. I wrote the essay because I had been seriously involved in Jewish practice and thought during my graduate school years and had already thought a great deal about women and Judaism. By the time I wrote that essay, I had come to believe that, ultimately, there was a connection between the prohibition on female names and images of deity in Judaism and women's exclusion from significant participation in Jewish public religious life.

The conclusion that feminine names and imagery of deity are crucial to women's well-being has remained one of my core convictions and has informed much of my later work in one way or another. In 1974, however, the furthest I could get was what then seemed to be a daring suggestion—using the feminine gender instead of the masculine gender for the pronouns used in Jewish prayer to address deity. I well remember feeling as if my mind simply hit a wall when I tried to imagine anything more concrete or vivid than the simple pronoun *you* in the feminine gender. The theological arguments I have continued to use about the inability of positive language to describe Reality at any level were already well developed in 1974, but I could get nowhere regarding imagery at that time. Within a few years, however, I became convinced of the centrality of feminine imagery of deity. A key experience involved witnessing a local woman respond to a speaker who had used a feminine pronoun for deity in a panel discussion on women's ordination. The woman proclaimed, her voice dripping with self-hatred and scorn, "How dare you refer to our Lord and savior as a *woman!*" About the same time, I recovered my memory of the story about angels as women, recounted in chapter 1.

I realized that there might be some clues about viable feminine imagery of deity in the Hindu goddesses whom I had studied so much and for whom I felt a great of abstract reverence. I thought they were magnificent, though I had no personal relationship with them. By 1978, I had published my long article "Hindu Female Deities as a Resource in the Contemporary Rediscovery of the Goddess" and put together a slide show about Hindu goddesses which I showed very widely.[1] That article is, in some ways, the missing bead in this garland, but it *is* long and it is very difficult to communicate those insights about female images of divine without the visual dimension provided by the slides. It is not very interesting and, more important, it is not very instructive to read long descriptions of iconography without any reference to the visual dimension. Suffice it to say that I proposed a base image of divine androgyny, by which I meant that deity is both female and male, and five additional images built on that base. Those five images, discussed in chapter 10, are goddesses who patronize both life and death, goddesses who are strong protectors, goddesses as mothers, goddesses as patrons of culture, and goddesses who are sexual and give positive value to sexuality. Simply listed, they do not sound very profound, but with fuller explanations and the visual dimension added, there is much more to them.

I added a long role reversal to chapter 10, which sounds as if I might be caricaturing something in the nineteenth century or earlier. Most younger people reading it today might well not believe I could be writing from experience. But I am. This is an accurate caricature of conditions in the late 1970s and early 1980s. Every bizarre explanation of sexual difference and female dominance used in this role-reversal fantasy to caricature male-dominant religious practices had been patronizingly presented to me in all seriousness by religious and Jewish authorities. As testament to the effectiveness of gender role-reversal fantasies in general, I have heard, but cannot verify firsthand, that in the early 1990s some Tibetan nuns staged a very similar (Buddhist) role-reversal fantasy in the presence of the Dalai Lama: all the Dalai Lamas had always been women, most monks and teachers were women, and so forth. I was told that it was very effective, that the Dalai Lama got the point, and has been increasingly supportive of feminist and women's issues in Buddhism. The role-reversal fantasy in chapter 10 actually made it into the prayer book of one group of Jewish synagogues, the Reform Synagogues of Great Britain, as an additional reading.[2] In that and other Jewish prayer books, the linguistic changes suggested by myself in this article, and by others as well, have been adopted to some extent.

Chapter 11, "Is the (Hindu) Goddess a Feminist?" was written in 1994, well after the period in which I did most of my work with Hindu goddesses as a resource for Western theologians. It serves as a summary of the issues that developed out of such discussions about South Asian goddesses and feminism, as a corrective to several common misunderstandings of the claims I had made, and as a response to some of the common objections to linking South Asian goddesses and feminism.

Chapter 12, "Life-Giving Images in Vajrayana Buddhist Ritual," is my own contribution, working as an insider and a Buddhist critical and constructive thinker, to solving problems that can arise regarding a common traditional religious image in Tibetan Vajrayana Buddhism. As is well known, explicit though discreet sexual imagery is widespread in Tibetan Buddhism. In the context of Vajrayana Buddhism, these images are not really about sex but are symbols for significant ethical and philosophical claims. However, this imagery arouses too much prurient, voyeuristic interest in the West, where this symbol is almost always misinterpreted. It is also deeply perplexing to other Buddhists. Thus, on the one hand, as an insider to this tradition, I am compelled to demystify and explain this imagery. On the other hand, as a feminist, I have my own issues, not with the basic image of a copulating couple, but with its specific execution, with choices made by artists long ago which are now so common that challenging them presents enormous difficulties. As I challenge the specific execution of this image, but not its underlying form and meaning, this chapter becomes one of the most idiosyncratic of those included in this volume.

Chapter 13, "Feminist Theology as Theology of Religions," takes on a different but related issue. It seemed to me that what I sometimes call the "feminist establishment" in religious studies had become increasingly Christian and that there was little place anymore for non-Christians in the ranks of feminist theologians or in the women and religion section of the American Academy of Religion. A movement which I had helped to found no longer seemed to have a place for me at the table, in part because interest in "women and religion" had largely come to mean interest in "women and Christianity." Furthermore, these Christian feminist theologians seemed to have no interest at all in non-Christian religions. This chapter expresses my frustration with that situation. It also takes up at some length a more important issue: the reasons why there must be interaction among the world's religions today and the ethics and methodology of such cross-cultural interchange and learning. Thus, this chapter is almost the only evidence in this volume of another of my major life pursuits in addition to feminist reflection. Interreligious dialogue, interreligious exchange, and theology of religions have also been important foci for me. They are of increasing importance to me today.

Each of the concluding chapters in parts 2, 3, and 4 contains a critique of tendencies that had become common in the broad feminist movement by the late 1980s and early 1990s. Part 5 *begins* with a Buddhist critique of one common feature of feminism. Though I have made many feminist critiques of Buddhism, on the whole, probably for me, Buddhism has transformed feminism more than the other way around. Feminism is, of course, a multifaceted movement, and no single definition really applies to more developed feminist thought. Nevertheless, my work does include frustration with what seems to me to have become common feminist emphases as feminism lost the spark of its initial inspiration and became more established. Or perhaps these "critiques" represent nothing more profound than inevitable internal disagreements within a large movement.

CHAPTER 10

Steps toward Feminine Imagery in Jewish Theology

The most profound, intriguing, and inviting of all Jewish theologies—the *Kabbalah*—teaches us that *galut*—exile—is the fundamental reality and pain of present existence. It teaches that one of the causes of *galut* is the alienation of the masculine from the feminine in God, the alienation of God and the *Shekhinah*. But it also teaches, especially in its Lurianic phases, that each of us can effect the turning of *galut* by dedicating all our efforts to the reunification of God and the *Shekhinah*. Now that the masculine and feminine have been torn asunder and the feminine dismembered and banished, both from the discourse about divinity and from the human community, such a *tikkun* (reparation) is obligatory, is a *mitzvah*. When the masculine and feminine aspects of God have been reunited and the female half of humanity has been returned from exile, we will begin to have our *tikkun*. The world will be repaired.

I can no longer remember the first time I imagined a *berakhah* in the female grammatical form. I do remember the first time I heard it voiced aloud communally, years after having first experienced participation in my own right in the Jewish ritual covenant community. It was as appropriate and natural as any Jewish expression—and less problematic and alienating than many. In fact, the potential for meaning and identification experienced by saying "God-She" convinced me that it must be so. Since then, I have been using female pronouns for God relatively frequently in various contexts—teaching, reflection, private religious expression. As the linguistic forms and the sound of the words become less exotic, it no longer seems daring or unconventional to speak of God in such a manner. Instead, it seems appropriate, natural, what one would expect, the way things would be except for a massive skewing and programming of religious consciousness. It also frees us from alienation, anger, pain, and sorrow over the exclusion of women from the religious and spiritual dimensions of being Jewish in a way that is unsurpassed.

It is time, therefore, to move beyond the image of God the Father to a more complete set of images of God. To do so requires some clarity about what is at stake in the use of the image of "God the Father." The most crucial points, I believe, are thorough awareness of the inherent limitations of any theological or religious language, combined with some awareness of the inevitability of anthropomorphic images in the Jewish religious enterprise.

Before anything else can be properly discussed, one must understand the inevitable limitations of all religious language. *All* expressions used in the religious enterprise are, in the long run, analogous and metaphorical. Every statement contains a bracketed "as if" or "as it were." Statements about God should not be taken literally. They do not exhaust the possibilities at all. Rather, they are the most adequate expressions available within current idioms—linguistic conventions that function as tools, used to point to that which transcends language. Therefore they contain no inherent finality or unalterable relevance and convey no ultimate truth.

To ignore this limitation by fixating on one set of ideas and thinking that a real correspondence exists between these images of God and God is to be unrealistic, self-aggrandizing, and fundamentally idolatrous. Nevertheless, because expression and communication are inevitable, images and concepts of the Ultimate are also inevitable. Therefore, the limitations of language present no problem—if one is willing to remember those limits whenever one is tempted to literalize and absolutize one's language.[1] The only problem is that temptation. It is clear that the tendency to absolutize some manners of speaking about God has been very strong throughout the history of the Jewish tradition. Specifically, masculine pronouns are always used for God by traditionalists and even by atheists and philosophical critics of anthropomorphism. Closely linked to the masculine pronouns, especially in the imagination of traditionalists, is a whole array of masculine images—father, king, judge, warrior. At the same time, an automatic and very strong prejudice against using feminine pronouns and images exists, not only in the minds of

traditionalists, but also in the minds of atheists and philosophical critics of anthropomorphism, who usually justify that response by appealing to the inherent limitations of language. They contend that their
automatic use of male pronouns and images as well as their out-of-hand
rejection of female images and pronouns doesn't mean anything.
Certainly it does not mean, they contend, that they think of God as
male. "That God is exalted above all sexuality is part of *His* transcendence," one commonly hears. However, if one insists that one must use
the pronoun "His" in the preceding sentence and that the pronoun
"Her" is improper, the claim that gender-specific images are not part of
one's image of God becomes self-contradictory and a bit ridiculous.
Likewise, the claim that one is not absolutizing one's image of God
becomes untenable. What *is* going on?

I suspect that those who become entangled in such absolutizing of
masculine pronouns and imagery genuinely do believe in and are trying
to express the concept of a God who transcends sexuality. At the same
time, however, they wish to retain the concept of a personal God—a theistic rather than a nontheistic Ultimate, because the concept of a personal Ultimate is at the living heart of the Jewish symbol system. The
whole *siddur,* most of *halakhnh* and *aggadah,* in short, almost everything
that makes the Jewish religious enterprise distinctively *Jewish* becomes
nonsensical without the metaphor of a divine Person in a covenant relationship of mutual responsibility and love with human persons.

However, the metaphor of a gender-free person is impossible. Persons
are male or female. A person without gender defies the imagination; few
people can imagine a concrete specific person without also imagining
some female or male characteristics.

Equally, no set of religious images has ever talked of a personal
Ultimate without the use of masculine or feminine imagery or both.
Theistic religions, including Judaism, have always had to make peace
with anthropomorphism, which necessarily includes making peace with
genderized language about deity. Unless Jewish theology *and practice*
take a 180-degree turn from the metaphor of relationship with a personal deity to the metaphor of a nonpersonal Ultimate, to which one
could scarcely *daven* and which would be unlikely to give *mitzvot,* they
too will have to continue to utilize anthropomorphisms, all of which are
always problematic and inaccurate nonliteral manners of speaking.

Why, then, the knee-jerk refusal to speak to God-She? To answer this
question, we must move from the level of abstract theological analysis to
the level of more empirical study of religion. Historical and cross-cultural

studies of religion demonstrate a great deal about how religious metaphors function in religious communities. Though language about God cannot really tell us about God, because of the limitations of language and the nature of God, it can tell us a great deal about those who create and use the God-language. The metaphors and concepts used to communicate about the inherently translinguistic Ultimate must come from somewhere; furthermore, it is impossible to avoid the recognition that these metaphors and analogies bear strong resemblance to basic human experience, especially valued aspects of human experience and aspiration.

What, then, of the common Jewish usage of "God-He" and shock at the idea that Jews might *daven* to God-She? I contend that this shock mirrors and legitimizes the profoundly androcentric character of Jewish society, especially "spiritual Judaism" or the religious dimensions of being Jewish. It expresses a profound and long-standing alienation between women or femaleness and the central values of Jewish religious tradition—an alienation that I believe stretches to the origins of our tradition. That usage and the alienation it reflects is also the most basic explanation for the traditional exclusion of women from almost all of the most meaningful and most normative dimensions of Judaism—its covenanted, "religious," and "spiritual" aspects.[2]

Courageous honesty is required to acknowledge the exclusion of women from the most meaningful and important aspects of Jewish living. Perhaps it is more difficult yet to realize the extent to which that painful exclusion is bound up with traditional Jewish ways of speaking about the Ultimate as a male person but not as a female person. Role-reversal fantasy may be the most potent way of driving home both points, because in role-reversal fantasies what is normally done to females becomes intolerable, simply because it is being done to males instead.[3] Therefore, I ask you to imagine the following situation:

> The male Jew grows up securely knowing his place in the community. Some day he will be a father in Israel, enabling his wife to fulfill her *mitzvah* of reproduction, making himself available for her sexually by maintaining the laws of purity, surrounding his body and its strange, periodic, regular secretions and no less scrupulously maintaining the ritual purity of the food eaten in his home. Most important of all, he will pass on the faith of the mothers, at least until his daughters are five or six and start religious school. What more could any man want? Especially when he knows that God Herself intended this role for him, this special role which wins him a weekly moment's notice and praise: "A virile husband, who can find him? He is far more precious than wealth, for he busies himself making wealth for his wife. She is praised in councils of the leaders for such a husband."

He does not envy the world of women, the world of synagogue and school, for he has never really been taught about it. "It is better for Torah to be burned than to be entrusted to a man," he has been told; and "She who teaches her son Torah teaches him lewdness." Besides, "men are light-headed." So only the women learn. Every morning they wrap themselves in those mysterious wonderful prayer shawls. They look so comforting and so private, as if one could sense more strongly the love and warmth of God-Mother. But they are feminine garments, he has been told, even though there are no laws actually prohibiting men from wearing them. He would lose his masculinity and women would be de-feminized if he started *davening* in a *tallit*, assuming he *davens* at all, which no one has ever seemed that concerned about. As for *tifillin*, don't even think of that. The synagogue, with its beautiful haunting rituals and melodies, further justifies this division of labor between women and men, spiritual and physical. The preciousness of being Jewish is especially clear to him when he watches the Torah scrolls being taken out and seven women being called to read Torah. Perhaps the highest moment comes as he watches the women undressing and dressing the Torah scroll, that supreme masculine symbol that contains the essence of the Jewish faith. From behind the high curtains you can almost see what's going on in most synagogues, even though it's very far from the reader's stand and often very difficult to hear the reader above the din of gossiping men's voices. But it *must* be that way. Think how disruptive it would be if men ritually took part in the synagogue *davening*. Why, the women might even be distracted by the presence of sex objects erupting into their world of spirituality. To protect the women's concentration at prayer, it is necessary to separate the men and put them out of the way.

If there are vague feelings of discontent, the very words of Torah hasten to quench them. After all, God is always referred to as "She," even though everyone says that doesn't mean we should think of God in a sexual sense, since God is beyond all human qualities. But language is limited and we use the most honorific terms for God, despite their obvious limitations. All the prophets were women—except for a few that nobody talks about much; and God *chose* Sarah, our Mother. and the promise descended through the line of her daughters. The covenant is addressed to the *b'not Rahel v'Leah*, which means the *daughters*, not the *children*, of Rahel and Leah. And finally, God will send Her *goelet*, and She will end the suffering of the daughters of Rahel and Leah—we pray in those terms all the time— *Berukhah at ha-shem, elohenu malkat haolam elohai Sarah, elohai Rivkah, elohai Rahel v'Leah ha-elah ha-gedolah, ha-giborah, v'ha-norah. Elah elyonah, gomelet hasidim tovim, vkonah et ha-kol, v'zoheret hasdei imahot u'meve'ah goelet livnot bnotehen l'ma'an shema b'ahavah.*[4] When God gave Her Torah to Her daughters through Miriam, She said to the women, "Do not go near a man," before the theophany . . . just as men shouldn't intrude into the women's spiritual universe today.

Besides, the outside world also reinforces this natural division of labor. All important positions in education and business are filled by women. Rarely, one sees a male professor, and then his voice sounds funny—too low. Recently they hired a male to be a newscaster, and a lot of people thought that was noteworthy and strange. There has never been a male president of the United States either, though the last president got a lot of publicity by appointing two men—an unheard-of number—to her cabinet.

When we try to explain all of this, it is obvious. Whether or not people believe in God-Mother anymore, it is clear that this division of labor is grounded in nature itself, and we religious Jews know that God Herself intended things this way. Why, any discontented male is denying his true vocation bestowed on him by the Creator Herself. No one is wise enough to know why God made female reproductive organs compact and internal so that woman is physically free to move about unencumbered and take her natural place of leadership in the world of womankind. Or why She made male organs external and exposed so that man would demand sheltering and protection from the outside in order that he may be kept for reproducing the race. The very vulnerability of the penis is a paradigm of all vulnerable things in need of protection and explains why men are naturally more nurturing than women. Surely this is why God Herself made men that way. And if men, dismissed from the time-bound *mitzvot* because of their heavy involvement in nurturing roles that come to them naturally, ever feel deprived, they should only remember that God is already close to men and that they, naturally, without benefit of the covenant, do God's will and are close to God. That is why She gave the covenant through women instead.

Furthermore, men don't need those *mitzvot*, which seem to be the core of Judaism, because what they do is create for women a sense of rhythms and cycles and flow. Women can't do that without ritual, but men already experience that in the periodic, mysterious risings and failings of their bodies, imitated by the tides and many other natural phenomena. . . . Surely we don't want to disrupt all these harmonies and balances created by God Herself in Her Wisdom.

Theological analysis of the nature of God-language, combined with some understanding of the social origins and ramifications of specific images of deity, are my major arguments for abandoning forthwith traditional modes of religious expression that utilize masculine imagery of deity while refusing to use feminine imagery of deity. The social destructiveness of the exclusively masculine style of religious expression, so evident in the role-reversal fantasy, is of more concern to me than are its theological inadequacies. It would seem that the Jewish sense of justice would demand that such inhumane practices be transformed.

Frequently those who realize the inappropriateness of the exclusively masculine language and imagery of traditional Jewish religious expressions want to opt for a style of language that speaks of the Ultimate as "neither male nor female." At a certain level of philosophic analysis that is, of course, a viable and perhaps even a more adequate concept than the theistic and therefore inherently anthropomorphic imagery of a personal God in covenanted relationships. I will concede to them the use of female pronouns and imagery of deity, but obviously only in return for an equal ban on all masculine pronouns and images of deity—given that their case is that God should be imaged as *neither male nor female*. I await their *siddur* in English, let alone in Hebrew.

It seems much more feasible *and traditional* to take some steps toward feminine imagery of deity in Jewish theology. The first step is theologically relatively simple and unproblematic, though emotionally profound. It requires only that female language, especially pronouns, be used of deity in *all* the familiar contexts. It seems to me that for every assertion one wishes to make of God, one must be willing to say that it characterizes God-She as well as God-He. In other words, the familiar *ha-kadosh barukh hu* is also *ha-kedoshah berukhah hee* and *always has been*. Only the poverty of our religious imagination and the repressiveness of our social forms prevented this realization. Everything that has ever been said or that we still want to say of *ha-kadosh barukh hu* can also be said of *ha-kedoshah berukhah hee* and, conversely, "God-She" is appropriately used in every context in which any reference to God occurs. That is to say, wherever the symbol or metaphor "God" is still relevant in any way, we must imagine "God-She" and speak to Her.

That first step must be experienced to understand its subtle but over-whelming and profound effect However, the pronouns begin to blossom into full-blown images, which is another and much more revolutionary step, whether the images are female versions of traditional male images of God or whether they have little precedent in Jewish tradition. That development of full-blown female imagery of deity is difficult and revolutionary because it goes beyond traditional Jewish sources, both in expression and for inspiration. Immediately, the problem of locating appropriate resources for developing feminine imagery of deity is more pressing than the problem of expressing those images in Jewish modes. Psalms, prayers, and *midrashim* will follow once the imagery really takes hold in the imagination.

Two major reservoirs for developing feminine imagery of God exist. First, it is important to highlight the rather considerable amount of feminine imagery of deity that has already developed throughout the history of Jewish tradition. Few Jews really take the time to put all the scattered feminine imagery together and thus to acknowledge that this combined resource has already made inroads into the assumption that "God-He" is proper while "God-She" is improper.

Nevertheless, that resource by itself is probably not enough. It is too embedded in patriarchal contexts. Almost without exception, traditional

Jewish usage speaks of some variant of "God and *his Shekhinah*." Seeing feminine imagery of God as some sort of attachment to or appendage of the more familiar male images of God would only compound the currant inadequacies. Something like the coequal balance of the attributes of justice and mercy is a much better model for the relationship between the attributes of femininity and masculinity in deity.

Because both the coequal balance of maleness and femaleness in metaphors about God and a full-blown feminine imagery of God go beyond Jewish resources, these developments, though desirable, are difficult. When I first began to think about these necessary outgrowths of saying "*ha-kedoshah berukhah hee,*" my mind simply stopped as if it had encountered an impenetrable veil. Fortunately, however, I am by training and conviction a student of the cross-cultural comparative study of religion, and my exposure to feminine imagery of deity in other religious contexts proved to be a godsend, so to speak. Religious-symbol systems that have not been so wary of feminine imagery of deity are the second great source of inspiration in developing feminine imagery of deity.

People often seem more upset by my suggestion that religious insights and images important for Jews can be found outside Jewish tradition than they are by the clear imperative to develop female imagery of God. That attitude seems very strange to me, given that it would require some sort of antiseptic barrier between what Jews think and what other people are thinking. Such conditions have never prevailed, and many elements of the worldview of most contemporary religious Jews depend significantly on the thought of non-Jews. Furthermore, I am not advocating mindless borrowing or wholesale syncretism. I have in mind something more like the creation of a Jewish version of insights gleaned from relevant religious-symbol systems.

Years of living with both the lack of Jewish female imagery of God and with knowledge about non-Jewish Goddesses have led me to envision five basic images that need translation into Jewish media.[5] I am sure that they are not the only relevant images and that the resources I have drawn upon are not the only relevant ones. However, they are offered as a starting point. It is especially important to note both their continuity with traditional Jewish concepts about God and the subtle ways they go beyond and enrich traditional Jewish theology.

The most significant of these five images involves a combination of symbols that is usually called "the coincidence of opposites" or "ambiguity symbolism." This image of the Goddess is very close to many Jewish insights about God Who creates both light and darkness, Who has both the attribute of justice and the attribute of mercy, but it also develops these Jewish insights in significant ways. The images of the divine feminine who contains all opposites and manifests the coincidence of those opposites have more ability to communicate acceptance of limits and finitude than anything in Jewish resources. The basic message is the coincidence and relativity of "positive" and "negative," "good" and "bad," "creation" and "destruction." The Goddess gives and She takes away, not out of transcendent power but because that is the way things are. She patronizes both birth and death, and neither is desired or undesirable. Both are part of the order of existence. Birth without death would be a monstrosity—a cancer. What is born must die, and what dies nourishes life in some form or other. Two things should be especially noted. In this symbolism, the deity does not stand outside and above this round but rather *is* the round. Second, limits, end points, and death are not punishments dealt by an external, transcendent deity, but simply part of reality and, thus, neither positive nor negative. The deity who is the eternal round of growth and decay, birth and death, increase and decrease, encourages in the worshipper an attitude of receptivity to the given rather than willful attempts to remake the given.

Within this matrix, four additional images of the Goddess find expression in my vision. Some of them are most significant for their power to break stereotypes of the feminine; others are significant for the insights about deity they contain.

It is important to discuss the need for images of Goddess as an extremely capable and strong figure—one worthy of trust and able to aid. This kind of image, which runs counter to popular expectations, is found in every example of imagery of the divine feminine in world religions. It undercuts the objection I sometimes hear that the deity can only be imaged as male because God must be strong and trustworthy, and female imagery cannot invoke those responses. Goddess can be fully as strong, even as omnipotent as God. Thus the image of Goddess breaks the stereotype of feminine weakness, which is important for women. Secondly, there is no hint that this strength and capability is at the expense of the femaleness of Goddess. In fact, if anything, the images and stories of the hero Goddess exaggerate her female characteristics and her beauty. Thus another stereotype is broken—that strength and femininity or beauty are incompatible, especially in women.

The next two images of Goddess that I envision as part of feminine imagery of the divine within Jewish theology are somewhat interdependent and need to be discussed together because in combination they also break many stereotypes. Images of God the Mother are inevitable and to be expected. It is important to immediately join that image with the image of Goddess equally involved with culture in all its aspects.

One of the strangest and most inexplicable features of Judaism to me is that while images of parenting are so central, "God the Mother" brings a shudder to people who daily use metaphors of God the Father. How can that be? How can God be a parent but not a Mother? How can the Creator and Caretaker of the world be devoid of femaleness? Nothing seems more obvious than the fact that our current imagery of the Father without the Mother is a bit one-sided and unbalanced, to say the least.

On the other hand, it is equally important to point out that God the Mother is not just a mother and nothing else. That when most people do image a female deity they talk only of some sort of "fertility Goddess" and nothing else reflects the way we think of women today: they are mothers and nothing else. Goddess as patron of culture breaks the stereotype that the feminine and women are involved mainly with nature and reproduction, while culture and the spirit are male and masculine pursuits. Instead, we would need Goddess involved in the broad range of valued Jewish traits and activities, from defense, study, and livelihood to nurturance and housekeeping, without regard for whether men or women are expected to perform these tasks in society. Especially noteworthy would be images of Goddess as giver of wisdom and as patron of scholarship and learning, as teacher and meditator. These are already found to some extent in traditional Judaism but need to be emphasized much more.

The last image I will discuss is as significant as the first, and often even more disturbing. Once we begin to speak of deity in both female and male terms, sexuality reemerges as a significant metaphor for imaging both intradivine relating and the divine-human relationship. This is sometimes disturbing because people imagine that the traditional images of deity, God the Father, the God of our fathers, is a nonsexual symbol. We have already seen how impossible it is to have a concept of a theistic, personal, anthropomorphic Ultimate that is also exalted above all sexuality. In fact, God has been exalted above female sexuality only. This results in the destruction of the personhood of those who are not made specifically in the image of what is taken to be Divine Personhood. God the Father is not a gender-free image of God, and thus it deeply undercuts the personhood of Jewish women.

Using sexuality as a religious metaphor will add a great deal to the texture of Jewish religious expression. To see part of its enriching effect, it is necessary to ask why there has been some reluctance to use sexuality as a religious symbol in Jewish tradition, though that reluctance is not omnipresent, as we can see in segments of Kabbalistic imagery. The rejection of sexuality as an acceptable religious symbol is, I believe, closely connected with fear and rejection of our embodied condition, particularly the female body. Because we are embarrassed by our own sexuality, we reject it as a suitable symbol for the deity, while those aspects of ourselves that are not embarrassing to us—honor, fidelity, justice, military prowess, the ability to arrange our societies hierarchically, with rulers and ruled—become symbols of deity. But why should sexuality be so problematic? Why are all the images that promote hierarchy and violence not embarrassing?

The answer brings us back to the first image I discussed, the "coincidence of opposites," and indeed there is a strong correlation between the occurrence of a coincidence of opposites and the use of sexual symbolism in world religions. Sexuality is strongly connected with the experience of limits and with the kind of transcendence that the coincidence-of-opposites symbolism teaches us. Sexuality limits us to being one sex or the other, and sexuality is closely connected with the limitations of our birth and death. If we did not die, we would not need to be sexed. Rebellion against the closed round of our natural existence and our attempts to identify with a nontemporal principle transcending that closed round necessarily deny any ultimate significance to the primary method of continuity within that round—sexuality. When sexuality loses its significance as a sign of the Ways Things Are, one can pretend that women/Goddess don't exist significantly (or that men/God don't exist significantly, I suppose—though it didn't happen that way). Thus, one has lost, all at once, the symbolism of the coincidence of opposites in the great round of birth and death, the realism of sexuality as a primary metaphor for expressing our deepest insights about reality, and Goddess Herself. Yet I think they all return together. This combination also brings with it a different kind of transcendence, the kind of transcendence that comes with discovering the meaning available *within* the circle of existence. Reconciliation—with ourselves, our bodies, our limits—is the gift of Goddess.

My remarks on the imagery of Goddess, which I think takes us far beyond the simple insertion of female pronouns into familiar contexts, seem to have stressed two points over and over. One is that we need Goddess because She breaks stereotypes of the feminine, thus freeing women from the limitations of that stereotype. Women can be strong *and* beautiful, feminine *and* wise teachers, mothers *and* participants in culture. If Goddess provided that much, it would have been enough. But it seems that She brings much more. Dimensions of deity that have been lost or severely attenuated during the long centuries when we spoke of God as if God were only a male are restored. They seem to have to do with acceptance and immanence, with nature and the cyclic round. Metaphors of enclosure, inner spaces, and curved lines seem to predominate. What a relief from the partial truth of intervention and transcendence; of history and linear time; of going forth, exposure, and straight lines! For insights that are true but incomplete, when elevated into the totality of truth, become false and dangerous. Goddess completes the image of God and brings wholeness. One begins to sense that God, as well as Woman, has been imprisoned in patriarchal imageries.[6] That discovery is at once scary, painful, and exhilarating.

CHAPTER 11

Is the (Hindu) Goddess a Feminist?

Is the Goddess a feminist? That's a good question. In my view, the only possible answer is, "It depends." Initially, I want to suggest that it depends on two things. It depends on how the term *feminist* is defined. And it depends on who the Goddesses' devotees are.

Depending on how the term *feminist* is defined, various Hindu and Buddhist goddesses could be shown to be either feminists or nonfeminists in their traditional manifestations. But, in the long run, if the Goddesses' devotees are feminists, then the Goddesses will either come to be seen as feminists or be abandoned by their feminist devotees. And if the Goddesses' devotees are antifeminist or nonfeminist, then the Goddess will not be a feminist, whatever her appearance to outsiders who might find her appearance inspiring to their own feminism. Thus, the answer to this question lies, not in the imagery and mythology of the Goddess per se, but in a complex and subtle interaction between the Goddess and her devotees. I make these correlations between Goddesses and devotees because, as historians of religions, we know that, in the long run, Gods and Goddesses are created by devotees, though in the short run, any individual is formed in part by the images of Gods and Goddesses imbibed from the culture. As historians of religion, we know that divine imagery is not arbitrarily given by something outside human cultural creativity, and we know that divine imagery always bears some relationship to human culture, though that relationship is not as simple as the direct mirroring some expect.

Nevertheless, despite my emphasis on definitions, answering this question is not merely a matter of clever definitions. Important issues are at stake in the question of whether or not the Goddess is a feminist.

Definitions of feminism turn on the point that, according to feminism, women are human beings in their own right. This contrasts with androcentric scholarship and patriarchal social forms, in which males are the only genuinely human subjects. In patriarchal societies, women are controlled by men and, at least theoretically, do not have self-determination. In androcentric scholarship, women are classified, analyzed, and, in general talked *about* as if they had no consciousness, no sense of self, and no ability to name reality. Thus, despite the many varieties of feminism and the many arguments within feminist theory, I am suggesting that feminism focuses on the *humanity* of women and searches for that which promotes and recognizes their humanity, though there is significant disagreement over what women need and want as human beings. Nevertheless, to focus on their humanity rather than to legislate *for* them and to theorize *about* them, as if women are no more human than the phenomenal world or the deities, is a massive conceptual leap from the way most of us were taught to think about women by our culture and by our academic mentors.

Because Hindu society is at least nominally patriarchal and because much Hindu religious thought is androcentric, it would seem, at least superficially, that Hindu Goddesses have not done a good job of promoting the humanity of Hindu women. This could mean that the Goddesses are not feminists but are the creation of patriarchal males and serve their needs. Some would even argue that the Goddesses function to help maintain patriarchy by feeding women contrasting divine images of decent Goddesses who are submissively married versus frighteningly out of control, unmarried Goddesses. The message would be clear to women. Because independence makes females bloodthirsty and dangerous, women would imitate Sita rather than Kali, which indeed seems to be the case when one studies Hindu society anthropologically. Hindu women indeed *do* have a divine role model, unlike Christian, Jewish, and other monotheistic women, but it is easily arguable that the divine role model does not promote the kind of lifestyle choices for women that feminists want. Many Hindu women would respond that they don't *want* those choices and take great comfort in having a divine role model with whom they can identify and who validates them. But, superficially at least, such a situation is *not* what Western feminists want from Goddesses.

Indeed, many Christian feminists do not regard reimaging the divine as feminine as the central agenda for Christian feminism, precisely because, according to them, Goddesses are not usually good for women. They make this assertion about the ancient near Eastern Goddesses, whom other feminists regard as providing evidence that women do need the Goddess. Such "Goddess feminists" claim that women's status was higher in early Goddess-worshipping societies of the ancient near East than in later Judaism and Christianity. But their Christian critics hotly dispute this claim, regarding with skepticism the notion that there is any real correlation between Goddesses and women's well-being.

Certainly, looked at superficially, the evidence presented by world religions, including the Hindu Goddesses who are our primary focus here, do not present a strong case that the Goddesses have been very good feminists. However, it is possible that there are subtle interactions between Goddesses and their devotees which would make the question of whether the (Hindu) Goddess is a feminist much more complex. I will outline several possibilities.

WESTERNERS (AND OTHERS) INSPIRED BY THE (HINDU) GODDESS

On the other hand, Western feminists, myself included, have been attracted to some Hindu Goddesses as intensely liberating. The traditional imagery of the Indian Goddesses, abstracted from the Hindu social context and considered in the context of what some Western feminists want, is compelling, provocative, and inspiring. Her ferocity is not at all frightening but is a model for strength and autonomy. Many other dimensions of the symbolism of Hindu Goddesses are also provocative and inspiring. I have long claimed that Western feminists could learn a great deal about the Goddess from contemplating her various Indian forms.[1] For us, the Goddess is a feminist because she promotes our humanity in powerful ways.

A Different Kind of Feminist Service Provided by Hindu Goddesses

But how can the same Goddesses serve patriarchy in one case and promote women's humanity in another? Obviously everything depends on what the devotees make of the Goddess, on how the devotees interpret her myths and images. The Goddess herself is neither feminist nor non-feminist, since she does not exist as an independent autonomous entity, but only in relationship with those who know her, revere her, and follow her bidding—as they understand it.

Because the Goddess is neither feminist nor nonfeminist apart from her devotees, it is most effective not to ask the question of whether the Goddess is a feminist in the abstract, but to look into specific situations. Therefore, I will focus on two separate areas of inquiry. First, I will ask whether the Goddess is really as much a patron of patriarchy in the Hindu context as is often supposed. Then I will turn again, in more depth, to the question of what is going on when Western feminists use the Hindu Goddess as a model for their feminist reflections.

It is intriguing to ask to what extent the Hindu Goddesses have actually served the interests of patriarchy in India. Perhaps they have served instead, or additionally, to affirm the humanity of women but in ways that Western feminists are ill prepared to notice or appreciate. Western feminists tend to evaluate women's status and well-being in terms of women's autonomy and self-determination. They tend to look at law, politics, and economics as the factors that determine how well off women are. But in societies where individualism is less pronounced and much less valued, very few people, male or female, have much autonomy. And the Hindu Goddesses have given Hindu women neither autonomy nor the legal, economic, or political status that most Western women find essential.

But Hindu Goddesses can promote the humanity of Hindu women by providing the psychological well-being that positive female imagery brings. Against some Western feminists, I have long argued that the first function of Goddesses is not to provide equal rights or high status, but to provide psychological comfort, and that nothing is more basic to psychological comfort than the presence of positive female imagery at the heart of a valued symbol system. The sheer contrast between Hindu polytheism, with its numerous Goddesses, and Western monotheism, with its long struggle to exterminate the Goddess, is overwhelming. What could possibly be a clearer indicator of the humanity of women than the visual presence of numerous divine females in a variety of roles and poses? And what can more effectively undercut the humanity of women than to regard femaleness as unworthy to symbolize the sacred? I always remember the question and the comment of a Hindu friend who, on our strolls through the Delhi suburb in which she lived, asked me things she didn't understand about America. "Is it really true that there people don't regard God as female?" "Yes," I had to reply. Her quick response: "What does that say about what they think of women?" (This event occurred in 1976.)

In this way, even a Goddess like Sita, who certainly would not be the *ishta* (chosen personal deity) of any Western feminist, may well promote the humanity of Hindu women by providing a relevant and comforting model of wifehood. It is not difficult to imagine or to understand that the life of a Hindu wife would be even bleaker without the example of her divine counterpart and role model. The fact that Western feminists do not approve of the way Sita promotes women's humanity does not mean that Sita has been a negative factor for Hindu women. Rather, given their life situation, Hindu women probably are better off with Sita than without her, just as the Moroccan women Fatima Mernissi writes about are better off with their refuge in the saints' sanctuaries than they would be without them.[2] Or to use an example closer to home, even though most feminists do not find Mary an acceptable female image, nevertheless, Mary has been comforting to women who had few other solaces in their lives. In our zeal to promote the kind of human life we Western feminists value, we should not overlook or deny the ways things we do not want for ourselves can comfort women whose lives are very different from our own.

In addition, some Hindu Goddesses provide something that is unavailable in the West's repertoire of images—strong-willed, creative, and powerful females who are auspicious and beneficent. For, clearly, it was a misperception on the part of earlier Western scholars of Hinduism to interpret the strong Goddesses as feared, negative entities. That is not the dominant Hindu response to them, though in some contexts they are feared. Furthermore, these images are appreciated by men as well as by women. Because both men and women are used to and comfortable with divine images of female strength and power, powerful women should be less frightening than they are to Westerners. It is worth noting that it would be difficult for an American woman to attain the political position of Indira Gandhi, no matter whose relative she might be. Though powerful Hindu women may, at present, be few and far between, nevertheless, they are not without divine counterparts, who should make them more acceptable and familiar. In some instances the Goddesses clearly promote the humanity of women by encouraging men's approval of strong, empowered females. I once was quite struck by a male guide telling, with great enthusiasm, the story of a virgin Goddess of south India who had killed her would-be rapist. He clearly identified with the female and had no sympathy for the violent male.

In this context, one may well question the pervasiveness of patriarchy in Hinduism. Hindu society is patriarchal, at least in what it tells itself and what it says about itself when asked. Though the preference for males and male control is clearly real in many instances, nevertheless,

Hindu communities yield interesting results when they are analyzed in terms of the distinction between authority, which is held by men, and power, which both men and women wield.[3] Some Hindu patriarchy may be what anthropologists call "mythical male dominance," rather than the literal male dominance the Laws of Manu prescribe.[4] Studies such as those done by Susan Wadley indicate that women do what they can to take control of situations that are important to them, often with a Goddess as their patron.[5]

Hindu Feminists and Hindu Goddesses?

These are some possible ways the Goddess may promote the humanity of Hindu female devotees who are not especially feminist, at least as Westerners usually define that term. In addition, in the present and future, Hindu devotees of these Hindu Goddesses may well become more frequently and more overtly feminist, though in Hindu not Western terms. Then the Hindu Goddesses will easily and naturally become feminists, though some, such as Kali and Durga, seem more attuned to the role than do others, such as Sita and Lakshmi. Because deity is so naturally seen as female in Hinduism, to see the deity as *feminist,* not merely *feminine,* would in fact, be less revolutionary than are some feminist interpretations of monotheism, especially those claiming that deity must be envisioned as both female and male. Some Hindus who are also familiar with Western feminist theology are beginning to write of a Hindu Goddess who is overtly a feminist.[6] Expansions and elaborations of such discussions will be intensely interesting, and some of us are very curious to see what will be forthcoming. Such discussions, however, simply cannot be done by outsiders, no matter how knowledgeable and sympathetic we may be.

THE POLITICS OF THINKING ABOUT HINDU GODDESSES

Hindu (and Buddhist) Goddesses represent the largest extant collection of living Goddesses on the planet. For that reason alone, I have long advocated that their imagery, symbolism, and mythology be carefully considered as a resource for the contemporary rediscovery of my Goddess, to quote the title of my own article on that topic.[7] Western feminist theologians who think that feminine names and imagery of deity are crucial for future well-being of both humanity and the planet are rather bereft of resources, after all. Where to turn for inspiration? To turn to contemporary Hindu (and Buddhist) Goddesses for inspiration make as much sense, if not more, than looking to ancient Goddesses who have not had living devotees for millennia. And it is very difficult to invent the wheel, whole cloth, out of one's own experience.

Of course, such a project, like any other, involves problems and difficulties. Two different sets of issues emerge when one tries to rediscover the Goddess with the help of Hindu (and Buddhist) Goddesses. In my view, the first set of issues requires serious concern, while the second set of issues is spurious, the product of questionable motivations.

What happens when Western feminist theologians look to Hindu or Buddhist Goddesses for inspiration? This project is essentially a kind of translation project. Clearly, it does not involve the literal translation of a text from one language to another. Nevertheless, translation is involved, in that meaning is transferred from one context to another. A cultural commentator, familiar with both Hindu Goddesses and Western theological contexts, suggests that the symbolism, imagery, and mythology of Hindu Goddesses might help us think through certain issues, problems, or lacks in Western religious discourse. Or, put another way, the cultural commentator, familiar with both contexts, might be inspired by specific symbolisms found in connection with Hindu or Buddhist Goddesses to construct or intuit certain interpretations that would be helpful to Western religions.

However, it must always be remembered that such discussions are *not* about the meanings the Goddess has had in traditional Hindu contexts, but about how her imagery, contemplated in a certain way, can empower and inspire us in our quest for the Goddess, who now is the Goddess whom we envision, *owing something to her Hindu models, but not the Hindu Goddess*. Some people have missed this subtlety and have assumed that I was talking about Hindu Goddesses as perceived by Hindus. I have always been clear, however, that I am not talking about what Hindu Goddesses mean to Hindus, but what *we* might learn from those images.

Others have misread me in a different way, claiming that I advocated that Christians and Jews simply worship Hindu Goddesses and then decried that as "appropriation." But such appropriation is abhorrent to me. Furthermore, it is impossible for non-Hindus to worship Hindu Goddesses, and it would be totally inappropriate for Jews and Christians to try to do so. Because I advocate *learning from* Hindu Goddesses, not simply taking them whole cloth from their own contexts, simply stealing them from the spiritual supermarket while shopping for the "good parts," it is simply a cheap shot to call the complex learning I have advocated "appropriation." It would make as much sense to call how Mahatma Gandhi and Thich Nhat Hanh have been influenced by the story of Jesus and the Gospels "appropriation."

Still others have claimed that since Hindu women do not seem to experience the kind of liberation I am talking about, the Goddess does not provide it and I have misunderstood the Hindu Goddesses. But I have never claimed that I was doing anthropological fieldwork on Hindu Goddesses. I have been quite clear in stating that I have, for the most part, discussed Hindu Goddesses as a *resource* in the contemporary rediscovery of the Goddess.

The more spurious set of objections to using Hindu and Buddhist Goddesses as resources for the contemporary rediscovery of the Goddess involves a claim that one cannot or should not use materials from other cultures to think with, to imagine with, to be inspired by. This objection travels in two directions.

On the one hand, many from Western religions simply dismiss non-Western religions as having no theological relevance for them. Such people may be willing, at best, to study non-Western religions as information. But they cannot imagine taking such religious ideas or images seriously into their own thinking, whether because of attitudes of cultural superiority or because they feel it is just too much work to learn any non-Western religion well enough to be able to use it as a theological resource. I remember well the incredulous hostility that sometimes occurred when I showed slides of Hindu Goddess imagery to Jewish audiences as I discussed the theological meanings these images might hold for female god-language in a Jewish context.[8]

There are also pressures from the opposite direction, often linked with postcolonialism. Some contend that it is improper for Westerners to be inspired by ideas and images from the religions of formerly colonized people or to translate them into their own theological repertoire. To me, as someone who has spent more years as a practicing Buddhist than following any Western ideology or religion, this is a very strange claim indeed. One might as well claim that Africans, Chinese, or Indians should not adopt anything from Christianity or convert to Christianity because it is the religion of their former colonizers. In my own experience, I have usually observed this judgment coming from Westerners, not Asians, from people who know little about Asian religions, and from a certain kind of politically correct liberal who is trying to score political-academic capital against other scholars.

I am not claiming that inappropriate borrowing, even "appropria-tion," does not occur. The superficial shopping in the great spiritual supermarket that characterizes some commercial cross-cultural transla-tion is inappropriate. That such shopping occurs should not be used to condemn the translations of serious religious scholars who put in years-long apprenticeships before they attempt to suggest in what senses the Hindu (or Buddhist) Goddesses might be a resource in the contempo-rary rediscovery of the Goddess.[9]

Finally, in conclusion, it seems to me that both (or all) versions of a claim that cross-cultural learning should not occur depend on a false notion of cultures as hermetically sealed units isolated from one another and developing internally, without significant influence from "outside," wherever that might be. If such has ever been the case, it certainly is not the case now in a global village linked by multifarious webs of commu-nication. Cultures are influencing each other willy-nilly anyway, so there should be no problem with self-conscious, deliberate, and educated mutual transformation.

CHAPTER 12

Life-Giving Images in Vajrayana Buddhist Ritual

To discuss women changing ritual and ritual changing women, I will return to a problem that has haunted me for years. This issue concerns the visual forms that are central to Vajrayana Buddhist *sadhana* meditation-rituals. First, some words about ritual in Buddhism and about which rituals I could comment on as a woman insider discussing how women might change these rituals and be changed by them. As a historian of religions, I am sensitive to the centrality of ritual in religion and in no way sympathetic to the usual Western rationalist disregard for ritual. Nevertheless, both as a religious studies scholar and as a Buddhist, I must begin by saying that ritual is not as central to Buddhism as it is to most other religions, though many colorful rituals have developed in all traditional forms of Buddhism. Any coffee table picture book on Buddhism will quickly dispel the misimpression of many Westerners that Buddhists meditate but do not practice rituals. In fact, the relationship between meditation and ritual itself becomes an interesting question, especially for the Tibetan Vajrayana *sadhana*s I will be focusing on.

However, from my perspective as a Western feminist Buddhist, many Asian traditional rituals are not the appropriate focus for my discussion of how women might transform Buddhist ritual. That is an arena for Asian Buddhist women and feminists. I will confine myself to rituals that I know well and firsthand—rituals in which I have participated for many years. These rituals are definitely Asian; they are practiced in the same way in Tibetan communities as among Western convert communities, except that we Westerners usually perform them in English.

The question of whether meditation is a ritual is very interesting. Meditation per se, by which I mean the silent focus upon the breath that most people think of as meditation, is not exactly a ritual. Nevertheless, to the observer, and even to the practitioner, it has some kinship with ritual. One observes people in a very specific posture, often in very precise spatial arrangements vis-à-vis each other and a shrine. Sometimes meditators engage in verbal utterances and predetermined, very precise movements. From the outsider's point of view, such behavior might well look like ritual, although meditation would be an unusually boring ritual to watch. From the insider's point of view, however, what counts is the mental state of one-pointed concentration, the calm, abiding, and clear awareness that ideally accompany the verbal utterances and the movements.

This emphasis on the mental state of the meditator is what makes meditation only akin to ritual, rather than just another ritual. In ritual, the major emphasis is on the correct performance of the movements, not on the mental state of the ritual performers, even though an important side effect of ritual is social and individual transformation of consciousness.[1] Several classical ritual settings will demonstrate this claim. For example, in a traditional Jewish synagogue, it only matters that the service is proceeding correctly; individuals often come and go as they need to and converse with each other during nonessential parts of the service. (In fact, in some situations, women, who previously did not read Hebrew and couldn't participate in the service fluently, often spent the majority of the time chatting when they infrequently attended synagogue services.) In Vedic-inspired dimensions of Hinduism, correct performance is paramount and, again, individuals may come and go, so long as the ritual goes on. Most decisively, one of the many controversies in early Christianity concerned whether the state of mind of the officiating priest determined the efficacy of the Mass. The winners were those who claimed that it did not, so long as the Mass was correctly celebrated.

I am most familiar with Buddhist meditation and ritual in the Vajrayana traditions associated with Tibet. In Vajrayana Buddhism, there are two types of meditation—formless and with form. Formless meditation is the silent focus on the breath discussed above and found in all forms of Buddhism. Meditation "with form," which is much less well known to the general public, means that not only the mental stability of the meditator is emphasized. This meditation involves many *forms*—liturgies, visualizations, hand gestures—which means that meditations with form are much more akin to ritual, both to the observer and to the participant. In Tibetan Buddhist *sadhana*s, liturgies or services, the participants may chant for long periods of time, doing complex hand gestures, sometimes with and sometimes without ritual implements and musical instruments. An elaborate, precisely arranged shrine is integral to the *sadhana,* and during more complex versions of the *sadhana,* such as feast practice, a ritual leader manipulates various objects on the shrine. Sometimes even dress is ritually controlled, as in the four karmas fire *puja,* in which participants all dress in the color appropriate for the section of the *mandala* and the Buddha family to which that day's meditation is dedicated.

Clearly, such behavior looks like ritual and is interesting enough to observe that commercial videotapes of some *sadhana*s are available. However, such videos always pare the ritual down to the more colorful moments because it is unlikely anyone not participating would be willing to watch such a video for many hours. In addition, a video can capture only the outer form of this ritual. The *visualizations* that accompany the words of the chant, the meanings of each detail of the visualization, and the meanings of the ritual gestures are essential to the ritual. Without knowledge of the visualizations, one cannot understand much about the words and the gestures. (To compensate for this lack, some videos and books try to portray the visualization as a picture, somewhat like the captions in a comic book, above the meditator's head.)

*Sadhana*s thus include both elements essential to ritual and elements essential to meditation, as more usually understood. There is an immense emphasis on correct performance of the many details, including invisible ones—the visualizations and the meaning of the details. But unlike a ritual in which the main concern is correct performance, in *sadhana* practice, equal emphasis is focused on the stabile mental state of the participants. In that sense, it is *meditation* just as much as the better-known formless, silent forms of meditation. In addition, except for an initiated participant, it is quite difficult to understand a *sadhana* accurately, even if one has the *sadhana* text in one's hands. This point is very important for later analyses in this chapter. These rituals are said to be self-secret, that is, incomprehensible apart from the oral instructions given by the initiating guru and one's own practice of those oral instructions. I have found this to be the case time and again.

We can now discuss the pith of what I have to say about women transforming ritual and ritual transforming women in the context of Vajrayana *sadhana*s. I want to discuss what is at the same time one of the most public, one of the most esoteric, and one of the most basic aspects of *sadhana* ritual, the icons of the *yidam*s (meditation deities, or anthropomorphic representations of one's own innate enlightenment) that are the main focus of *sadhana* ritual. I want to focus on these images for many reasons. Not the least is because such a focus is in continuity with my long-standing concern with liberating and gender-balanced images of deity, previously discussed in my work of female god-language in a Jewish context and on Hindu female deities as a resource for the contemporary rediscovery of the Goddess.[2] In this case, I am working completely as an insider within one tradition, and I am not talking about "introducing" female imagery. There is no lack of positive female symbolism in Vajrayana iconography. Nevertheless, there is a major problem in this iconography which has troubled me as a feminist for many years and which will be very difficult to resolve satisfactorily.

First, however, some basic information about this iconography is necessary. As mentioned before, the meditator visualizes a *yidam*, or so-called meditation deity, throughout much of a *sadhana* ritual. As an aid to forming and stabilizing the visualization, two-dimensional and three-dimensional icons of the *yidam* that is the focus of the *sadhana* are usually hung above the shrine or placed on it. Though these icons are painted or cast as ritual tools, not as art objects, are supposed to be used only in a sacred manner and cannot be accurately understood apart from the oral commentaries, nevertheless, outsiders to the world of Tibetan ritual are quite familiar with these icons. Countless art books and some museum exhibits have made them easily available to those who will never use them in their intended ritual context or even read any of the vast literature about their symbolism. Because many of them are quite provocative and seem to be highly sexual, these icons have provided endless entertainment and titillation for outsiders, much of it rather ill informed.

When one looks at these icons, regular patterns quickly emerge. The *yidam*s are humanlike in shape, though they may have multiple heads, eyes, arms, and, more rarely, legs. They are painted in vivid colors (usually blue, red, green, yellow, black, or white). They routinely appear in both sexes. Typically, they sit, in meditation posture or in the relaxed teaching posture (with one leg drawn up and the other extended), or they dance. Rarely do they simply stand still. Their hands hold ritual implements or form *mudra*s (hand gestures). They are bejeweled and richly garbed with scarves, crowns, and skirts, though they are also usually seminude to the waist, whether male or female. Their demeanor is classified into three types—peaceful, semiwrathful, and wrathful. Obviously, the peaceful *yidam*s smile calmly, while the wrathful *yidam*s generally look like someone you would not want to meet alone at night (or during the day with your friends, for that matter) unless you knew the password. Both female and male *yidam*s appear as both peaceful and wrathful. Either the male or the female *yidam*s may appear independently, or they may appear together. When they appear together, they usually appear as a couple in sexual union, the famous *yabyum* (father-mother) icon. Not surprisingly, given what I have said about *sadhana* practice, every detail means something, and those meanings are communicated in the *sadhana* text itself and in the oral commentaries, both of which are restricted to initiated practitioners.

Because all these icons are quite available publicly and because I am personally immersed in the symbolism and the practice of some of the well-known *yidam*s, I will discuss the possibilities and the problems presented by these ritual icons for a Buddhist feminist seriously concerned with how these meditation-rituals might transform and be transformed by women. By "personal immersion," I mean that I live every day surrounded by the icons in my own collection. All my work is done with their presence, with them in view. I also mean that I have done many, many hours of formal *sadhana* practice, both alone and in groups, dedicated to various *yidam*s, female, male, peaceful, wrathful, *yab-yum*. I have a long-standing and deep appreciation of the Indian understanding that revelation occurs as readily through the sense of sight as through the sense of hearing, that pictures and statues are no less (and no more) reliable than books and words to act as media for communicating the incommunicable Beyond at the heart of all religions.[3] Hence I have no sympathy for the monotheistic command not to make "graven images" and its frequent diatribes against "idols" when understood as pictures and statues of the divine. Given this orientation, I have found immense comfort in these Buddhist icons, which have been literally life-giving, but as a feminist, I have also found significant problems with some of them.

In terms of life-giving comfort, I especially want to briefly mention my acquaintance with Vajrayogini, who was the first *yidam* whose *sadhana* I practiced—many, many, many times. She was and is of great comfort. (I use the past tense because her *sadhana* is no longer a main practice that I do regularly.) In fact, she has been perhaps the most comforting of all, not only because she was the first *yidam* whose *sadhana* I was allowed to practice, but also because, as a longtime critic of male monotheism and a longtime advocate of use of Indian imagery of female deities to reimagine Western religions, I was more than ready for a spiritual discipline in which the imagery of a strong, fiery, fierce, beautiful female was so predominant.[4] This practice is especially empowering because, like all more advanced *sadhana* practices, it involves self-visualization of one's self *as* the deity. Therefore, she is no imagined external presence but my own body and mind.[5]

Since the days when Vajrayogini was my main *yidam* practice, I have worked a great deal with *sadhana*s involving a *yab-yum* deity. (Note the language which came very naturally to me—a father-mother *deity* in the singular number. I think this says a great deal about how the icon actually functions and means, no matter how it looks.) I was curious, of course, to begin such practices, but also quite apprehensive, based on how the icon looks and my feminist values.

Because the icon is publicly available while texts and oral commentaries that might clarify certain issues are not, let me first focus on the icon. Whether in its two or three-dimensional form, the icon presents her back and his front to the viewer. She is often significantly smaller and often has fewer arms. Sometimes, when she is not a distinctively different color from him, she is barely distinguishable in the tangle of arms, faces, and bodies. So that one can see her face, especially in *thangka*s, her head is flung back and twisted in an impossible pose that some of us have begun to call "the broken neck" syndrome. In a three-dimensional form, her representation may be essentially unfinished, with stubby little legs that look like vestigial limbs. (They were not intended to be seen.)

I have never met an outsider to Vajrayana Buddhism with any sensibilities about gender equity and equality who did not assume that this icon is essentially a male icon that makes a very androcentric and male-dominant statement about the relationship between men and women. This icon has long been interpreted as a statement that he is the real focus of the portrayal; she is merely an instrument or extension of him, rather than a being in her own right. I will give only two examples. At a conference I attended in 1995, a young scholar argued that the Vajrayana *yab-yam* icon could never be liberating for women because of its obvious male-centeredness and male dominance. A more poignant memory involves conversations with some Zen Buddhist friends in Hawaii in

1980, which was very early in my career as a Buddhist feminist. As we looked at a *yab-yum* icon, they commented that whenever they saw it, they could not help but see mainly a male with a little extension of himself. "If that's not really what it's about, you're going to have to show that," they challenged me. It certainly is a challenge, given the centrality of this image to Vajrayana Buddhism. The male-centeredness of the icon is also evident in the fact that men rarely *see* or are troubled by the things I am pointing out. They tend either to see a magnanimous inclusion of the feminine—if they even notice there is a female in the icon—or to regard people who see any problems with the icon as "too sensitive"— what men have long said about women who notice male dominance.

Clearly, I could not have done *yab-yum* practices all these years if the internal feelings that arise while doing the practices evoked any of the above reactions. None of these issues actually arises during the practice *if* one has enough instruction at one's disposal. So something else must be going on. But before intimating what else is going on, I must admit that even having the text in one's hands isn't really enough. Reading most *sadhana* texts, by themselves, could reinforce rather than undercut the impression that this practice is about a *male* deity who *has* a female consort.

Whatever impressions the images and texts may promote, the *practice* itself is not about visualizing one's self as the male or as a *man* who has an external consort. That interpretation would be completely dualistic, whereas the whole point of Vajrayana Buddhism is nonduality, and *yab-yum* practices are intended to promote, not contradict, that vision. That one does not visualize one's self as a male with an external consort is in accord with the widespread Vajrayana Buddhist understanding of the coemergence, inseparability, nonduality, and equality of the masculine and feminine principles. However the icon may look to an uninitiated outsider, in Vajrayana symbolism, the relationship between the masculine and feminine principles is not hierarchical. One sees this more clearly when one remembers that the right hand is masculine and the left feminine and that the scepter (*vajra*) is masculine and the bell feminine. In Vajrayana ritual, they are always used together as equal mates. Even more forcefully important is the fact that wisdom and emptiness are regarded as manifestations of the feminine principle, while compassion and skillful means are regarded as manifestations of the masculine principle. One of the most important goals of Mahayana and Vajrayana Buddhism is the simultaneous development of wisdom and compassion, which are never ranked hierarchically.

Not only are the feminine and masculine principles equally emphasized; they are also inseparable. Even when the female or the male
yidam appears alone, her or his consort is represented in a covert
manner. For example, the *khatvanga* that Vajrayogini carries represents
her consort Cakrasamvara. Such knowledge makes impossible the
claim made by some that Indian images of divine androgyny are always
androcentric.

It should also be emphasized that men and women both perform this
practice, arising as the *yab-yum*, in exactly the same manner. It is crucial to understand that Vajrayana practice never suggests that men
embody the masculine principle while women embody the feminine
principle, though that point is often lost on outsiders. Each individual,
whether a man or a woman, needs to develop *both* wisdom and compassion; women do not specialize in wisdom nor men in compassion.
Because *sadhana* practice is regarded as an *upaya,* a skillful means to
quickly develop enlightened qualities in the practitioner, it is clear that
one would not regard the *yab,* or male deity, as somehow more real or
more important that the *yum,* or female deity, nor would one regard
oneself as the *yab* but not the *yum.*

Nevertheless, I also cannot avoid the conclusion that there is an
unfortunate disconnect between the *yab-yum* icon as traditionally represented and the core message of nonduality. It certainly does *look*
androcentric. If one had none of the insiders' tools and insights I have
outlined above, an androcentric reading of the icon would be very difficult to avoid. The insights about the core meaning of the icon that I have
just outlined are not easy to acquire. I have met more than one practitioner who had done considerable *yab-yum* visualization and still
thought of the practice as being about a male with a consort.

What can be done? Admittedly, one faces a difficult technical problem. How can one simultaneously portray sexual union and the faces of
the deities? Do we really need to see their faces? Over the years, I have
contemplated many solutions to this problem. At one point, I believed
that the conventional icon solved the problem as skillfully as could be
done. At that point, it seemed to me that seeing both deities full face
was essential. The only other way to portray both sexual union and
the faces of the deities would be to show their bodies in profile with
their heads turned toward the viewer—hardly a convincing pose for
sexual passion. I also heard of a traditional image with which I have
no personal acquaintance in which the image is reversed. One sees the
yab's back and the *yum's* front. I was intrigued with the idea, but never

considered it seriously as a solution to my problem. I have never believed that role reversal is the solution to feminist issues.

As I spent long, demanding days in strict retreat practicing a *yab-yum* self-visualization, I became less and less able to find the standard portrayal helpful or convincing, even though I had gone into the retreat thinking that the traditional portrayal was the only practical solution. I found myself using a modern greeting card with exquisite faces that avoided the "broken neck" syndrome and really featured both faces well, rather than a traditional *thangka,* as the support for my visualization. I found myself turning my three-dimensional *rupa* sideways on the shrine, which really did work better, that is to say, it seemed less misleading. I was clearly experiencing what one practitioner has called the inevitable inadequacy of the visual form, given that one is *not* looking at them when doing the practice, but *is* them—something that is impossible to portray visually. Nevertheless, why should the visual representation be so androcentric? Why the stubby legs? There must be a less androcentric solution.

(I do want to proclaim that I do not view this visual androcentrism as a deliberate attempt to thwart female practitioners or to aid male practitioners. I regard it only as an unfortunate side effect of the lack of feminist consciousness in Buddhist tradition and the fact that most authors of *sadhana* texts and most *thangka* painters have been men.)

For years, I tried, somewhat timidly, to discuss these issues with male leaders of Tibetan Buddhism, but either my concerns were dismissed or I was told that it is impossible to change traditional forms—a claim that I reject as a religious studies scholar. One *Rinpoche* told me that he understood my problem but that men had the same problems when they visualized themselves as a female *yidam* when doing Vajrayogini practice, so everything was even, equal, and fair—a comment I now regard as quite superficial. The main problem is that doing *sadhana correctly* is highly emphasized. Correct performance includes visualizing precisely, exactly as instructed. Thus, my dissatisfaction with the traditional representation of this icon and my proposed changes could have been considered rather heretical by these traditional teachers. However, calling a thoughtful criticism a "heresy" has always been the easy solution to real problems.

Meanwhile, I began to dream of a *thangka* that portrayed the *yab-yum* from the side, the partners of equal height, gazing intently into each other's faces—a mutually empowered passionate couple, as I later put it to the artist with whom I briefly discussed executing this *thangka.*

I had given up the notion that one needed to see their full faces, now convinced that profiles could also express passion, and that, whatever its drawbacks, my suggested design at least avoided the androcentrism that I had come to regard as so misleading and potentially damaging. (In part, I probably reached this conclusion after years of gazing at a cloth painting of the Hindu couple Radha and Krishna in my own collection. They are not portrayed in sexual union, and one sees their bodies almost in full frontal position, but they turn their heads to gaze intently into one another's eyes—passionate profiles.) I continue to regard this solution of the *yab-yum* in profile, rather than with either one facing out, as my preferred solution, or at least as one that should be tried.

Before going further with this analysis, a vital point must be made, especially given that the *yab-yum* image is always said to be an image in which the partners are in sexual union, and given the frequent use of the term *passion* in connection with the icon. (One of the most difficult things Vajrayana Buddhists have to explain to outsiders, even to other Buddhists, is why an image of "sex" is at the center of our symbolic universe. That could be the subject of a different chapter.) Though it may seem paradoxical and difficult to understand, this image, nevertheless, is not literally about sex, as in sexual intercourse. It is about nonduality, which is visually represented by the *yab-yum* icon. Without this understanding, if the image were taken too literally as being about sexual intercourse, it would not convey nonduality. It would convey the exact opposite—duality. I think most traditional Vajrayana practitioners would agree with me on this point. As strongly as I claim that the *yab-yum* icon is not about sex, I would also claim that it *is* about gender, though I think most traditional Vajrayana practitioners would disagree with me on this point. Because anthropomorphic imagery is crucial to the icon, it cannot avoid being about gender in my view. Because the *yab-yum* image cannot help but be about gender, it is so important to get the message right. Thus I continue to gnaw at this issue.

In fact, I have come to believe that continuing to raise this issue is a matter of basic Buddhist ethics. Because the *yab-yum* icon is so misleadingly androcentric and male-dominant, as is clear from the reactions of so many outsiders, it is important to continue to search for ways of representing this image that are more accurate and less misleading. Probably many potential practitioners, most of them women, have dismissed Vajrayana Buddhism out of hand because they do not want to be involved in a spiritual path that seems to be so male-dominant. Even more insidious, this image probably harms many women's abilities to take themselves seriously as practitioners, rather than as adjuncts to men. The harm would be done, not so much to women like me, who have some consciousness of what is going on and who fight back, but to women who take the traditional image for granted and are not all conscious of its subtle and insidious messages. These are very serious charges. It must be remembered, however, that I am not suggesting that there is any problem with the *yab-yum* icon, but only with the traditional way of *representing* it.

Why is this issue a matter of basic Buddhist ethics? Because, traditionally, Buddhist ethics recommend being very careful about appearances, about not doing things that would make ordinary people doubt the dharma. If teachers or monastics engage in improper behavior, for example, the effect is that many people become skeptical about the dharma they are teaching. What happens when aspects of the teachings themselves, such as the traditional way of representing the *yab-yum* icon, point in the wrong direction, away from nonduality and toward male dominance and androcentrism?

Regarding the *thangka,* things remained in stasis for some time, but in the fall of 1995, they seemed to come together. I was determined to meet a young woman teacher named Mindrolling Jetsun Khandro Rinpoche, who was then relatively new to North American audiences and had been getting rave reviews from Buddhist women whom I respected deeply. So I traveled to Boulder, Colorado, for the single purpose of meeting her.[6] Already familiar with my work, she told me she thought that feminism is necessary and encouraged me to continue with the work I was doing as a Buddhist feminist thinker. Obviously, this was an extremely empowering and encouraging meeting for me. Though I had many questions, the most important to me was the old question about *yab-yum* visualizations. Using my hands to represent the deities, I explained my problems and my proposed *thangka* to her. She also began using her hands and immediately tried out the various visualizations. Reaching her decision quickly, she asked me to try not to use my proposed visualization during practice, at that point in time, but also to proceed with having the *thangka* painted "for inspiration," as she put it. I asked her why not use the alternative visualization during practice, and she replied that at this point I was only working with thoughts anyway, so their content didn't matter too much.

It is hard to overestimate the kindness and understanding I received in this conversation. For the first time, my questions and concerns had been taken seriously by a highly trained Tibetan *Rinpoche* rather than being dismissed. Though I do not know for sure, I will probably always think this happened because it was a woman-to-woman conversation. Both of us work, in very different ways, in the same highly male-dominated environment. No wonder she took my questions seriously and understood me in a way that no one else had. Over the many years since this conversation, she has continued, very quietly but very effectively, to encourage me in my work as a Buddhist feminist critical and constructive thinker. The implications are obvious.

Regarding the *thangka,* for a while, everything seemed to be proceeding very rapidly. I called a *thangka* painter who had enough skill to be able to execute the painting, and she too was extremely excited about the project, though she also told me she would not have been willing to execute such an unconventional *thangka* if I had not already received Jetsun Khandro Rinpoche's blessing. The artist also told me later that after she had discussed the project with a male Tibetan lama, he immediately became very enthusiastic, saying that "you'd be able to see better with that visualization." We drew up a contract and I made a down payment on the *thangka*. A year passed and no drawings appeared. The artist had more work than she could handle, so I asked that my down payment be returned. Some years later we tried again, even taking photographs of a three-dimensional *yab-yum* icon that could serve as a model. But now the *thangka* painter has a much more important and prestigious patron than myself, Sakyong Mipham Rinpoche! I doubt I will be able to compete for her time anytime soon. That is where things stand, as of this writing. It's too bad. To the best of my knowledge, this will become a new image in the repertoire of Tibetan Buddhist images, if it is ever executed. In the thirteen-hundred-year history of Tibetan Buddhism, no one has thought of this alternative, or at least no one has given it form. I believe it would be a historic *thangka*. It all seems so simple, so obvious, in hindsight, and yet it is so difficult to finally bring it to fruition. However, even if the actual *thangka* does not take physical form for some time, the issue has been raised, and I do not believe it can be put off indefinitely.

Regarding my experiences contemplating this icon, I believe what is most instructive is how, on the one hand, I have struck out on my own into uncharted territory, but on the other hand, how I have worked with tradition and traditional authorities. It is clear from the way I work with images, especially in my informal practice of surrounding myself with icons and immersing myself in their contemplation, that I am striking out on my own. There is a good deal of innovative contemplation and exploration in my informal practice, and I believe this personal, idiosyncratic way of working with traditional approaches is essential for feminists at this point in history. Clearly, my envisioned new *thangka* is the product of years of working alone, on my own, engaging with the tradition through arousing my own contemplation and creativity.

As much as possible, for two reasons, I also want to work with tradition and traditional authorities. First, in my view, genuine spiritual breakthroughs are so rare that completely rejecting traditional religions because they are tainted by patriarchy is fairly dangerous spiritually and may leave one more bereft than ever. Just as some feminists choose to trust their own creativity as they reject traditional religions, I choose to trust my own ability to sift the wheat from the chaff and to forge a union between feminism and the invaluable spiritual insights of a long-standing, well-tested spiritual discipline. My second reason for making the choice to work with tradition and traditional authority as much as possible has everything to do with Buddhist ideas of *upaya,* or skillful means, of taking the actions that are most likely to get the job done. My feminist view is that a feminist society is more likely to come about if feminists work within institutions, such as the traditional religions, rather than abandoning them for less frustrating, clearly feminist alternatives. Though I cannot tell the stories in the context, over the years my work *has* made some major differences in the Buddhist systems within which I have worked. I believe that the story of the long process I have gone through to bring these changes into the realm of form demonstrates that not all traditional religious authority systems are completely unworkable. It also demonstrates that one does need a good deal of patience and persistence to work within them.

CHAPTER 13

Feminist Theology as Theology of Religions

Not long ago, I sat in a gathering of feminist theologians. The topic was "diversity"; numerous complaints about lack of diversity were being voiced, but it was clear that lack of diversity *among* the Christians, not absence of *religious* diversity, was being protested. I pointed out that the diversity among *Christians* represented was far greater than the diversity among *religions* and that the discussion presumed a Christian context, which I, a non-Christian, found problematic. The conversation paused momentarily to allow me to make my comment, then returned to its previous direction, as if I had never spoken. I felt as if I had momentarily surfaced from underwater in some giant ocean, only to have the waters submerge me again immediately. I also noted that I had felt this way before. In earlier days, it had not been uncommon for men to treat women's observations about religious studies or theology in the same way. One of the few other non-Christian feminists locked eyes with me and whispered, "They just don't get it, do they?" How many times had we said this about men when trying to explain to them what feminism is and why it matters? This was a profoundly discouraging moment for me, a non-Christian pioneer in the feminist study of religion who has spent my life and career as a feminist theologian and scholar of religions involved almost equally in feminist issues and in issues surrounding religious diversity.

Others have also noticed this strange development in feminist theology. As the editors of the recently published anthology *Is There a Future for Feminist Theology?* comment, "Although we have included diversity in terms of theoretical and methodological issues, what this volume lacks . . . is any dialogue with non-Western contexts. This on-going lack of engagement by feminist theology, and gender theory itself, with experience outside Western culture artificially limits the issues of gender and religion. From our perspective, this is the major task for the next millennium. The traditional dichotomy between East and West, a meta-narrative of a past age, needs to be dissolved to allow the vast plurality of global experience to take center stage."[1]

Ursula King has called feminism "the missing dimension in the dialogue of religions," noting that if more women became prominent and visible in "dialogue, this in turn might help to transform the oppressive patriarchal structures of religions." In the same article, she notes that Christian "feminist theology, though wide-ranging and internally very diverse itself, is not yet critically wrestling with the challenge of religious pluralism."[2]

"Theology of religions" is a relatively new term that has to do with noting the diversity among the religions of the world and developing conceptual tools for relating with and understanding that diversity. Critical to an adequate theology of religions is that it be knowledgeable about and conversant with the great Asian wisdom traditions; merely raising one's gaze to include other monotheisms does not constitute serious encounter with religious diversity. To date, theology of religions has been largely a Christian activity, but only because religious diversity is more theologically challenging to monotheisms than to nonmonotheistic religions.[3] In a religiously diverse world in which people of the various religions are in constant contact with each other, eventually all religions will have to develop ways of helping their believers understand and live peacefully with the religious diversity that is not going to disappear. In this enterprise of developing theologies of religions, many tools can be and have already been used, including comparative studies, interreligious exchange, and dialogue. As demonstrations of how these various tools can be used and to participate in the adventure of coming to terms with religious diversity in Christian perspective, two books, written by women but containing no explicitly feminist dimensions, are highly recommended: Diane Eck's *Encountering God: A Spiritual Journey from Bozeman to Benares* (Boston: Beacon Press, 1993) and Judith Berling's *A Pilgrim in Chinese Culture: Negotiating Religious Diversity* (Maryknoll, NY: Orbis Books, 1997).

Discussing feminist theology as theology of religions clearly presents problems, as the above experiences and quotations indicate. Three intertwined issues are involved: the current lack of religious diversity in most feminist theological forums, the lack of any theology of *religious* diversity in most feminist theology, and the relative lack of feminist participation in most formats for interreligious exchange. Indeed, the most extensive "interreligious" discussion in the literature of feminist theology to date is the relatively acrimonious debate on Christian feminist anti-Judaism, which hardly constitutes a theology of religions or an interreligious exchange by the above criteria.[4] A few early books are more inclusive, but studying their tables of contents quickly shows that the vast majority of the chapters speak from a Christian context, a few from a Jewish context, and even fewer from Muslim, Hindu, Buddhist, or other religious contexts.[5]

Thus, the tasks of this chapter must be largely constructive: discussing how or why the current situation regarding feminist theology and issues of religious diversity came to be, developing feminist grounds for serious feminist attention to religious diversity, and finally, suggesting how a feminist theology of religions might look. In this brief chapter, only an outline of those tasks can be undertaken.

Feminist theology, as I envision it, is a movement that cuts across tradition lines, influences all religious traditions, and is relevant to all of them. Indeed, in the early years of the feminist theological movement, that was the case, as Christian, Jewish, post-Christian, and Buddhist theologians worked closely together and were about equally visible in the feminist theological movement.

Nevertheless, struggle over diversity is not new to the feminist theological movement. "In retrospect, it is clear that diversity—of aims, concerns, and perspectives—was always present, even when feminist gatherings felt unified, exuberant, and triumphant in their stand against patriarchal religion and androcentric scholarship."[6] By the mid-1980s, cries of outrage about the watchword of early feminist theology, "women's experience," were widespread. The feminist theological movement had universalized "women's experience" as white, middle-class, heterosexual experience, it was claimed. Therefore, to be genuinely inclusive, diversity of class, race, culture, and sexual orientation must be taken seriously. Genuine and irreconcilable theological differences also emerged. Experiencing this breakdown of a perceived unified front against patriarchy was traumatic and painful. Why was, and is, it so difficult to deal with this diversity and disagreement? I suggest that in large part the difficulty is due to "a deeply entrenched tendency in Western thinking to turn difference into hierarchy. . . . If we are different, then one of us must be better."[7]

Because of deliberate efforts to be more genuinely inclusive and because excluded groups of women demanded that their voices be heard, many feminist theological gatherings are now more diverse regarding race, class, culture, and sexual orientation. But somehow, in that process, *religious* diversity was lost. For all their faults, the feminist theological gatherings of the early 1970s *were* more religiously diverse than they commonly are today. It is also worth noting that in most contemporary cultural discourse about diversity, religion is rarely mentioned.

I would argue that, in ignoring religious diversity, feminist theology has stopped short of its goal of genuine inclusivity, and even that it has lost ground. Though diversity is usually valued by feminist theologians, the kind of diversity promoted is intercultural diversity *within* Christianity.[8] "Feminist theology" and "Christian feminist theology'" have been conflated in many arenas of discussion. Unwittingly, Christian feminist theologians, who think of themselves as more inclusive than mainstream theologians, have been co-opted by one of the more archaic, out-of-touch aspects of mainstream theology—its tendency to equate "religion" with "Christianity." Furthermore, as one who works extensively in both feminist theology and in the theology of religions, in my experience, Christian feminist theologians are among the worst offenders in this regard. For non-Christian feminists, this exclusionary practice is insulting, maddening, and frustrating. The place I would least expect to encounter it is in the feminist theological movement to which I have given so much of my life and work. Personal feelings and experience aside, this development is also limiting for the development of feminist theology. Intercultural Christian diversity will not yield the stunning variety of religious options that would come with genuine *interreligious* study and dialogue that takes account of the variety *within* each religion.

Are there feminist grounds for developing theologies of religion and for learning about and thinking about religious diversity? The history of the feminist theological movement itself provides the first major feminist reason for being concerned with religious diversity. Feminist theology was born from the experience of being excluded by patriarchal religions and the resulting convictions that the voices of the excluded deserve to be heard and that adequate theology cannot be done on the basis of silencing many voices and limiting the theological forum to the chosen few. The landmark anthology of feminist theology, *Womanspirit Rising,* proclaimed in 1979 that "the *diversity* within feminist theology and spirituality is its strength" (emphasis added).[9] The second major *feminist* reason for such concern was also articulated already in that early anthology. Though the phrase "widening the canon" does not appear in that anthology, the concept is implicit throughout it, especially in its concerns with rejecting the binding authority of the past and in searching for new traditions. Since then, the issues of how to use the received canon in feminist ways and where to find new sources with which to do feminist theology have been important to most feminist theologians. For feminists, concern with religious diversity is necessitated by the most basic values of feminist theology—the importance of inclusivity and the necessity to widen the canon.

These feminist reasons for interest in religious diversity are different ways of expressing two reasons why a theology of religions is necessary today. One is ethical and the other is epistemological. The ethical reasons have to do with the facts that religious diversity is a reality, not a mistake, and that religious diversity is part of the experience of most contemporary people. Intolerance and exclusive truth claims may be unavoidable when religions are relatively isolated from each other, but they are lethal when religions must mix and mingle in a common environment, as is the case today. The moral reasons thus amount to the same thing as the feminist value of including the formerly excluded. The epistemological reasons have to do with the illuminating power of the "comparative mirror," with the truth of the slogan that "to know one religion is to know none."[10] They also have to do with the fact that religions other than one's own may well contain ideas and symbols from which feminist theologians might learn something useful. The epistemological reasons thus amount to the same thing as the feminist need to widen the canon, whether through rejecting received patriarchal interpretations or through utilizing formerly noncanonical sources.

In keeping with my understanding of feminism as a religious movement that crosses religious boundaries and has similar implications for all religions, I will propose a theology of religions that I believe would be an adequate feminist theology of religions. Though to date, theology of religions has been largely composed by Christian theologians, I do not believe that an adequate theology of religions would differ significantly from one tradition to another. Theologians of all traditions have to deal with the fact of religious diversity in a morally compassionate and theologically compelling manner; they all need to ask what can be learned from diverse perspectives. Insofar as possible, I will pose the conceptual alternatives and provide arguments for the positions I advocate. In just one chapter, of course, it will not be possible to fully discuss all possible alternatives and arguments; thus this chapter is an invitation to discussion, not a foreclosure of it.

MORAL ISSUES AND FEMINIST VALUES:
EVALUATING RELIGIOUS DIVERSITY POSITIVELY
AND INCLUDING THOSE WHO HAVE BEEN EXCLUDED

The first layer of a theology of religions is concerned with the problem of how to normatively understand that other religions besides one's own exist. To date, three positions have been proposed: exclusivist, inclusivist, and pluralist. Because these positions are already well known and developed in mainstream theology of religions, they will only be summarized very briefly here.[11] The exclusivist claims that her position alone among the world's religions has validity and would be the only religion in an ideal world. This position necessitates negative attitudes toward all other religions, and exclusivists often claim that nothing of any value can be found in other religions. The inclusivists say that there is some merit in other religions, that they are not wholly inadequate. But an inclusivist would also claim that, in the final analysis, these other religions are not completely adequate because they are waiting to be "fulfilled" by the teachings found in the inclusivist's religion. The other religions would be "better" religions if only they would adopt what the inclusivist most values about her own religion. (This use of the term *inclusivity* is not the same as that discussed as the feminist value of inclusivity. I use the term here because it is usual in mainstream theologies of religion.) The pluralist would say that no religion is either the only valid religion or the most valid among religions. Rather, each religion provides something valuable and interesting in a giant mosaic. We probably have personal affinities for one among the religions, but that does not elevate the worth of that religion for everyone else. A pluralist is also interested in dialogue with members of other religions and in learning from other religions, whether through the study of that religion or through dialogue.

For a feminist theology of religions, the only suitable candidate among these options is the pluralist position. It is inconceivable that a feminist theologian would go through all the heartache of being excluded from her own religion and doing the theological work required to include herself back in, only to turn around and make exclusive or inclusive truth claims about the religion that excluded her! Furthermore, as already pointed out, a major value of feminist theology is to include the voices that have not been heard, to widen the circle, to learn how to welcome diversity. It makes no sense for those values to stop when they hit the boundary of one's own religion and for another set of values to take over at that point. I do not think this would be a controversial point among feminist theologians, even though none has, to my knowledge, explicitly addressed the issue. Because this argument, in my view, holds for feminist theology, it follows that it also holds for "mainstream" theology.[12]

Other ethical reasons for preferring the pluralist position are not specifically feminist. Only the pluralist position provides ways for different religions to live together peacefully, without competition. The exclusivist or inclusivist positions, if held simultaneously by members of different religions, can only lead to mutual hostility. It is unreasonable to take for oneself a position regarding religious diversity that, if taken by others of a different persuasion, leads to suffering and away from peace, wholeness, and healing. If religions don't provide peace, wholeness, and healing, what good are they?

When the pluralist position is advocated, someone always brings up the specter of absolute relativism. Does anything go then? Are there no standards, theological or moral? Pluralists are not saying that one cannot evaluate religious phenomena; we are saying that no religion has a monopoly on either truth or falsity, relevant or harmful teachings and practices. Furthermore, every religion has some of each. In evaluating religious phenomena, I would claim that ethical behavior is far more important than theological doctrines. It is easy to demonstrate, if one studies world religions, that there are many cogent theologies; there is no particular need to rank or evaluate them against one another. If they can be evaluated or ranked at all, the only possible basis for such ranking would be the ethical consequences of theological ideas. When a theological doctrine, by itself, harms people who try to believe in it or when a theological doctrine translates directly into oppressive social practices, then it could be negatively evaluated. Many Jewish and Christian feminists have claimed that the exclusively male language and imagery of deity common in the monotheistic religions is one such example.[13] More generally, I would claim that if people who hold to a set of doctrines are transformed in ethically positive ways by their adherence to those doctrines, they can be evaluated positively, though that does not mean those doctrines are therefore of universal value. If, on the other hand, people are rigid, inflexible, hateful toward those who are different, wasteful of natural resources, or cruel to animals, then the religious doctrines they hold are not working, are not doing their proper job of transforming humans into gentler, kinder, more compassionate beings. According to this standard, all religions have both succeeded and failed, another reason to hold the pluralist position.[14]

The ethical dimensions of a feminist theology of religions are quite straightforward and uncontroversial, in my view. The more interesting, and potentially more challenging, dimension of any theology of religions is the epistemological dimension, which takes us from accepting the plurality of religions as theologically unproblematic to the necessity of actually learning something about, and possibly from, these religions. The epistemological reasons for developing a feminist theology of religions center on the effect it could have on one's *own* theological development, and thus the development of feminist theology in one's *own* tradition. There are two possible and interdependent ways of going about this task: learning about and from the various religions through academic study of them and engaging in dialogue with members of these traditions.

Can one claim to do adequate constructive theology, feminist or otherwise, if one knows little or nothing about religions other than one's own? At least in a time such as ours, in which religious diversity is everywhere and information about world religions is readily available, I would claim that one cannot. The theological imperative has always included taking account of the contemporary culture, which now includes what the modern disciplines and modern knowledge tell us about the world. Included in that knowledge is detailed information about the phenomenon of religion in general, as well as information about a great variety of religions. In a pluralistic and postcolonial era, it is inappropriate to proceed with one's constructive work as if that revolution regarding our knowledge about world religions had not occurred. If theologians are not at least somewhat familiar with this material, they are not operating with a full deck and are constructing theology in a vacuum. How could a theologian, feminist or otherwise, make any claims about religion when operating with a sample of one?

I would also make this claim because of the power of the "comparative mirror" to illumine self as well as other. It is hard to imagine looking at religion through the lens of only one religion after one has begun to study and think about religion comparatively, not only because of what has been learned about the possibility of other religious perspectives, but also because one has so many more tools with which to see one's own religion. The phrase "comparative mirror" denotes not only learning some information but using that information in a certain way. A mirror is reflexive, whereas information by itself is not. In the comparative mirror, we see ourselves in the context and perspective of many other religious phenomena, inviting, even necessitating, self-reflection about our own religious and cultural systems. In that process, "our own world, instead of being taken for granted, becomes exposed as *a* world, its contents held up to the comparative mirror and we become a phenomenon to ourselves."[15] For theological reflection, feminist or otherwise, nothing is so useful as becoming a phenomenon to oneself, because in that process, we see and understand ourselves much more clearly. Part of that seeing includes seeing the strengths and weaknesses of the perspectives we take for granted. As we begin to experience that there really are religious *alternatives,* our own perspective must also become an *alternative,* not merely the only viable theological position or something with which we are stuck.

Furthermore, by really looking into the comparative mirror, we will undoubtedly find many alternatives that we would be unlikely to imagine on our own. For example, most feminist theology takes it for granted that we will speak of deity in some way, even if we are very dissatisfied with the symbolism of deity named and spoken of as male-only. But what of a nontheistic religious alternative, such as that modeled by Buddhism? It would be useful to feminist theologians used to working in theistic contexts to contemplate such a possibility, to contemplate the pros and cons of theism itself. Theism looks different in the comparative mirror than it does when one takes it for granted and does not regard it as an alternative.

Unlike a beginning student of religion, an experienced constructive theologian will probably begin not only to learn about but to learn from the material revealed in the comparative mirror relatively quickly. This process of learning from the data in the comparative mirror needs to be discussed carefully, because it contains many potential pitfalls. It must also be admitted that a feminist theologian will face challenges when looking into the comparative mirror that may not be faced by a conventional theologian.

Feminists sometimes object to looking into the comparative mirror because all the religions they see there are patriarchal to some degree, and people are tired of studying patriarchal religion. In and of itself, this complaint is true; all major world religions are patriarchal to some extent. However, there is little place else to go for alternatives with which to imagine religion anew. It would be enjoyable to find some religion that fulfilled one's feminist dreams, but that is unlikely. Such religious visions have to be pieced together from the available parts, combined with imagination, stubbornness, and courage. Why limit oneself to the familiar patriarchies in that quest? There are very interesting and very useful religious ideas and practices in other traditions. Furthermore, feminist theologians, especially Christian and Jewish feminist theologians, are more than adept at finding inspiration and reason for going on, despite and within familiar patriarchies. Why should it be different with unfamiliar patriarchal religions? The benefits of finding a really useful and interesting symbol, concept, or practice are greater than the discomfort generated by encountering patriarchy in unfamiliar places.

Nevertheless, for a feminist, one of the trickiest tasks of looking into the comparative mirror is dealing with material that is not only patriarchal in familiar ways but also seemingly immoral and irredeemably oppressive. Western feminists, religious and secular, have sometimes been eager to criticize and condemn practices that strike them as completely cruel and unbearable for women. Unquestionably, when a feminist studies some unfamiliar religious contexts, she is likely to heave a sigh of relief that she does not live in that culture. Some practices, such as African genital operations on women, cannot be evaluated as anything but completely horrific by feminist standards. Nevertheless, we must ask if vocal outrage is the most effective way of responding to such practices.

Quick condemnation of unfamiliar religious or cultural beliefs and practices is one of the great pitfalls of cross-cultural studies in general. The purpose and the promise of such study is not to feel smug and superior. Long experience in teaching unfamiliar religions has given me certain insights about how best to proceed. First, the ground rules of looking into and learning from the comparative mirror require suspension of judgment at first, until one is thoroughly familiar with the situation being studied. One must first try to understand why such practices exist and what purposes they serve, according to the viewpoint of the religion being studied. Empathy is the most critical tool for looking into the comparative mirror in ways that do not create further mutual entrenchment and scorn. It must be applied in all cases, even the most unsavory, before appropriate judgments can be made. If, rather than jumping to conclusions about how certain religious or cultural

phenomena are experienced, one takes more time to reflect on a particular practice, there may be some surprising conclusions (see chapter 3
of this volume).

In other cases, seemingly undesirable conditions are not really very
different from what Western women experienced until very recently, or
even today. In particular, statements about the inferiority of women and
the requirement that women should be subject to male authority stem-
ming from other religious contexts should not sound too different from
the homegrown variety.

Finally, outsiders' judgments about women's situations are often
made on the basis of *public* observation, of what goes on in public
spaces. Women do not usually have authority in public spaces, including
religious public spaces; indeed, they might not even be present.
However, if one knows the situation more intimately, one will discover
that women often have a great deal of power behind the scenes, and
everyone knows that and takes it for granted. As we have become familiar with the cultural and religious system of India and China, this point
has been demonstrated time and again.

However, some religious ideas and practices remain deplorable to a
feminist even after much consideration. Then what? Cross-cultural
public denunciations from first-world countries and former colonists
probably only entrench the situation further. Then resisting changes to
women's situation becomes part of national pride and resistance to
Westernization. It does little good to talk about African genital *mutilation* rather than African genital operations, or to decry Muslim practices
surrounding gender, to name two of the most inflammatory feminist
causes. It would probably be far better to work quietly with *women* from
these situations and to support them financially and emotionally.

Though it may seem that we have strayed from a feminist theology of
religions into the ethics of cross-cultural studies, that is not the case.
Theologians are perhaps more apt to make judgments about what they
study than are social scientists and scholars of religious studies.
Therefore, as theologians become more competent in their knowledge
about the vast diversity of religious phenomena and in their thinking
about religious diversity itself, it is crucial for them to be able to make
comparisons and judgments in ways that are not offensive or naive.

Feminists also sometimes object to looking into the comparative
mirror because of all the difficulties entailed in becoming somewhat
conversant with the materials revealed in the comparative mirror and
developing an accurate understanding of them. In my experience, this

reluctance has occurred at all levels of scholarly development, from professional scholars who do not attend presentations on feminist topics if they are about an unfamiliar religion, to students in a Goddess seminar who tuned out when we came to the book on Hindu goddesses. When I asked my students, who were all women studies minors and eager to study material on goddesses, why they were not so willing to make more of an effort to learn about the Hindu materials, I got the same answer from them that I receive from more established scholars. "Too many foreign words," they said. The apprenticeship required for being able to use the comparative mirror effectively and adequately can be daunting. One *is* required to learn a good bit of terminology (perhaps even a foreign language), and one must empathize one's way into rather different worldviews.

On the one hand, an extremely sensitive issue regarding cross-cultural knowledge and exchange is inappropriate appropriation without an adequate apprenticeship. Segments of the feminist spirituality movement have been especially criticized by Native Americans for indiscriminate and unauthorized borrowing from their traditions.[16] Caution is better than plunging ahead on the basis of insufficient knowledge. On the other hand, though the process of learning about other traditions is never-ending in a certain sense, it is essentially no different from the process by which theologians first learn the ancient texts and languages and all their theological variants, which are prerequisites for competence and theological literacy within their indigenous tradition. Theologians are not born with that information already imprinted in their brains; they learn it, usually relatively early in their training. But why stop there? My claim is twofold. First, to do adequate theology in a pluralistic world, one needs information about the whole world, not just one's corner of it. Second, the additional perspective on one's own tradition that one gains by this process of looking into the comparative mirror is well worth the effort.

I have already offered the example of studying and contemplating a nontheistic religion like Buddhism to refine one's understanding of the utility and limits of theistic symbolism. Hinduism offers the example of well-nuanced ways of alternating personal and impersonal imagery of the Ultimate, which is an issue with which many feminist theologians are concerned. At least as provocative are the many goddesses of Asia, with their colorful symbolism and intricate mythologies. They provide a living example of goddesses as integral parts of ordinary people's religious lives, not merely as the construct of a small number of Western religious thinkers. I can think of no reason to exclude those materials from the widened canon, to stop short at the borders of Western history and culture.

When feminist theologians do let a wider canon speak to them, there are two ways it can influence their theology. One is by osmosis, and the other is by deliberately altering one's theology on the basis of what has been learned from the comparative mirror. By "osmosis" I mean that study and contemplation of various unfamiliar ideas, symbols, and practices gradually begins to affect how one thinks and how one views the world, which of course spills over into one's theologizing. A good example of the process would be the post-Christian theology of Carol Christ, who has studied ancient goddesses, especially those of Greece, very thoroughly, but who does not simply import wholesale the goddesses she has studied into her theology. Rather, she constructs a systematic theology of the goddess based on this study and a good bit of creative imagination.[17] In certain ways this process is more authentic and involves less chance of total misunderstanding and misrepresentation of unfamiliar materials.

The process of direct borrowing and deliberately altering one's theology is more difficult, which is probably one reason why most academically trained theologians avoid it. If academically trained theologians do deliberately alter their theology on the basis of what they see in the comparative mirror, they are more likely to look at marginalized materials from their own tradition than to look at symbols or practices from completely different traditions. A good example of a feminist theologian who engages in this kind of use of the comparative mirror is Rosemary Ruether, especially her books *Sexism and God-Talk: Toward a Feminist Theology* (Boston: Beacon Press, 1983) and *Women and Redemption: A Theological History* (Minneapolis: Fortress Press, 1998). These books demonstrate clearly how material that was omitted from the official canon of Christianity can be used in deliberately constructing alternative theologies.

Making theological use of materials from outside one's own culture or religion is much more difficult and challenging because it is so easy to use them in inappropriate or superficial ways. Sometimes those whose symbols and practices we might like to learn from do not wish to share them. Native American resentment about how the New Age and feminist spirituality movements "borrow" their symbols and practices has already been noted. A wise rule of thumb in such cases might be to look elsewhere if we are told that we are not welcome to those symbols and practices, no matter how attractive they might be to us. In other cases, the materials are so wrenched out of context and reinterpreted that the new theology lacks credibility. Or, as people shop here and there for goddesses and religious practices they like, the result is a "good parts" synthesis that is superficial.

Most problematic, however, is simply not doing justice to the materials one is borrowing. For example, as a long-time practitioner of Vajrayana Buddhism, I am not thrilled by most appropriations of "Tantric goddesses" because they miss the whole point of the practice and the symbolism. My own theology is, of course, deeply influenced by these materials, but I have studied them closely for more than twenty-five years. Thus we find ourselves back to the question of what constitutes a proper apprenticeship. Time and again, I have found this question of apprenticeship to be crucial; religious teachers of many backgrounds, including Native American, are happy to teach committed students willing to serve the apprenticeship.

On the other hand, clearly religious symbols can cross cultural frontiers, change, develop, and become deeply incorporated into new religious contexts. We know this because it has happened. The goddesses of the ancient world became the Virgin Mary. Kwan-yin broke loose from her Buddhist moorings and her former male gender as an Indian bodhisattva to become one of the most popular and beloved goddesses of China and Japan. There is no reason that, over time, this process could not happen to Western religions, both Christian and post-Christian, as Asian goddesses become more familiar and more beloved. At this point in time, the most likely candidate for finding a home in the West is the Hindu Goddess Kali, though Kwan-yin is also receiving more attention from Westerners longing for goddesses.[18] In Western appreciations and appropriations the meanings of Kali and Kwan-yin and their impact on devotees are quite different from what they are in Asian contexts. However, with enough time and with widespread veneration of these goddesses, that will not matter. They will have transformed into Western goddesses with Asian roots, who will still be worshipped in Asian contexts as well. This process will be especially interesting, because Asian devotees of Kali or Kwan-yin and their European and American devotees can interact with each other easily, if they choose to do so.

Even though feminist theologians do not often engage in the *study* of other religions, this possibility has been discussed at some length because of its potential impact on the development of feminist theology. However, at present, most of the few feminist theologians involved in learning about and learning from other religions do so through the practice of interreligious dialogue, of which Buddhist-Christian dialogue is probably the most developed. In some ways, dialogue is probably an easier and quicker method by which to learn about and learn from unfamiliar religions than study. In dialogue, one is interacting with members of another religious tradition who are usually very well educated and very articulate in that tradition. They serve as a living library ready to correct one's misinterpretations and misunderstandings of the other religion. However, dialogue between relative amateurs without thorough academic grounding in their own tradition could well become a detour.

To those unpracticed in dialogue, it is important to understand what genuine dialogue is and is *not*. It is not a covert missionary activity in which each side tries to prove the superiority of its religion. It is not a debate, with all the adversarial connotations of the term *debate*. Nor is it an attempt to find some commonality between religions, an attempt to discover that at the bottom line, in an esoteric way, all religions really are the same.

Many people have the misconception that, in conversations or dialogue with people of other religious persuasions, one could not help but try to demonstrate the superiority of one's own position to one's partner. "After all," they say, "you are committed to this religious perspective; you have devoted years to studying and practicing it. Clearly you must think that it is the best position." The question in response is, "Best for whom?" A pluralistic theology of religions easily accommodates love of and enthusiasm for one's own religious position with deep appreciation of other positions. One does not have to be very psychologically sophisticated to realize that religion cannot be a one-size-fits-all phenomenon. There is no reason to expect that the religious symbols and practices to which I can deeply relate have the same resonance for everyone. Being defensive about one's own perspective is the stance least likely to result in successful dialogue. For this reason, participation in dialogue almost requires a pluralistic theology of religions, or at least a broadly inclusivist theology of religions. One of the major problems in interreligious dialogue is that the people who need it most are the least likely to engage in it.

Debate is also less than ideal as a format for dialogue, and in fact, it is never used as a format for dialogue, to my knowledge, even though some might think that dialogue would be a debate. Debate is an exercise in which the most skilled debaters "win," which does not prove the truth of their position, and the agenda of debate is to score points for oneself, not to understand the other. Furthermore, a skilled debater needs to be able to argue either side of the debate, which makes debate better suited for fine-tuning one's understanding of the intricacies of various theological positions within one's own tradition than for understanding a radically different alternative. Unless both debaters were highly skilled in discussing both traditions, debate as a format for interreligious dialogue simply would not work. Even then, it would not prove as fruitful as conversation on a common topic.

Probably the most widespread misconception about interreligious dialogue is that its purpose is to find common ground, areas of agreement between the religions, so that mutual suspicions and hostilities can end. After all, if all religions really teach the same things in the long run, what is there to fight about? This understanding of dialogue carries a covert theology of religions with it. Genuine religious diversity is still seen as a problem if this is one's concept of the purpose of dialogue. It is felt that there must be some common meeting point for all the religions, if we could only find it, and that finding it would promote better relations between the religions. But why do we need a common meeting point? Can't we just appreciate the diversity of religions? Most people who have specialized to some extent in interreligious dialogue do not hold the view that there is a common ground upon which all the religions can agree, nor do they think that it would be preferable for there to be a common ground for all religions.

Why, then, should one engage in interreligious dialogue? In the long run, the purpose of dialogue is the same as the purpose of studying other traditions: to enrich one's own theology with input that one would probably never think of by oneself. The foremost theoretician of dialogue, John Cobb, states that the attitude one brings to dialogue is willingness to listen completely and carefully, and to change as a result of dialogue. He, and many others, would claim that any genuine encounter changes one; therefore, entering interreligious dialogue means being open to theological growth. Nor are the changes predictable ahead of time. Programmed change and genuine encounter are mutually incompatible.

It is important to realize that while theological growth and change is an assumed outcome of dialogue, the change with which one is concerned is internal change in oneself, not affecting the theological thinking of the other. That is the other's prerogative and issue. For example, in discussing Jewish-Christian dialogue, John Cobb suggests that, while Christians might hope that someday Jews could integrate the story of Jesus into their history and would feel that such a change would enrich Judaism considerably, the reason for Christians to engage in Jewish-Christian dialogue is not to make that case. "The Christian purpose in dialogue with Jews must be to change Christianity."[19]

This principle does not mean that dialoguers cannot make suggestions to each other, especially when trust has developed. Dialogue can also provide a way to see ourselves as others see us, if we are open to hearing about the impressions our theologies make on other people. Genuine dialogue produces the reaction "I never would have thought of that" regarding assumptions and givens of our own position. But that process is reversible. In genuine dialogue, when mutual trust is established and it is clear that there is no covert missionary agenda, one is free to say to one's dialogue partners, "You know, I just don't get that belief or that practice. It doesn't make any sense to me. What does it offer you?" One can also make suggestions to one's partners. "Why don't you consider these ideas or practices? It seems to me that they might be helpful to you." Finally, of course, one of the genuinely enjoyable aspects of interreligious dialogue is discussing comparisons and contrasts between religions with truly knowledgeable people of good will.

That feminism is the missing dimension in religious dialogue was one of the jumping-off points of this chapter. But that voice is missing because the feminists aren't there! In the dialogue contexts in which I participate, Christian feminists' seeming lack of interest in dialogue is often noted and regretted. As with studying other religious traditions, probably feminists hesitate to become involved in such dialogues because they involve dialogue among patriarchal religions. But, at least in some dialogue contexts, there is a great deal of sensitivity to feminist issues and the men are as unaccepting of religious sexism as are the women. For example, the Society for Buddhist-Christian Studies wrote into its bylaws the principle that its board and its officers, as well as speakers in its programs, will always include, not only parity between Christians and Buddhists, but also between men and women. That happened in part because feminists participated in the founding of the society. Granted, other dialogue contexts are more sexist and less welcoming of women. But the academic study of religion and Jewish and Christian theology were not very welcoming either when feminists first demanded entry. Because feminism is a major movement in many religions today, its voices need to be heard in the dialogues among these religions. But feminists themselves are the only ones who can add that voice.

SUMMARY

Feminist theology's lack of serious attention to any dimension of a theology of religions, to religious diversity, is its most serious failing, in my view. This lack of attention is truly difficult to understand, given feminism's emphases on including the unheard voices, on not trying to speak for others, and on the need for new sources for theology. Feminist theologians could benefit greatly from exposure to religious systems that are truly different, that are not just culturally diverse variants of Christianity or monotheism. Furthermore, this lack of attention to the theology of religions and to interreligious dialogue isolates and marginalizes feminist theology in the academy and in the world. If we want to change the world, we can hardly do it by retreating to our feminist enclaves and never seriously encountering the rest of the religious world. Ignoring even our feminist colleagues whose feminist theologies may be religiously different is even more peculiar. If feminists of the various religions are not talking with each other, one wonders what has gone wrong with religious feminism. The claims and arguments put forth in this chapter are all challenging and controversial. But I do not believe they are more challenging and controversial than were the feminist study of religions or Jewish, Christian, and post-Christian feminist theologies when they were first proposed. Besides, someone has to go out on a limb when something important has been ignored!

PART FIVE

Buddhist Feminism

Feminist Buddhism

THE FOLLOWING CHAPTERS NEED LITTLE introduction; enough stories giving their background and context have been told throughout parts 1 through 4 of this garland. However, because I have written so much on Buddhism, even on women or feminism and Buddhism, this section is highly selective. I will explain the principle of selection.

Part 5 begins with the most current version of what I have always considered to be my most important reflection on Buddhism and feminism, my comments on the transmutation of anger into clarity and peacefulness that was the unexpected, totally surprising first result of the Buddhist meditation practices that I had begun some years earlier. The first paper and talk I ever gave on Buddhism and feminism occurred in 1980 at an early International Buddhist-Christian Dialogue conference. I had offered a paper on Buddhism and feminism, and the conference organizers responded with an invitation to present one of the plenary addresses. I wrote a very, very long paper simply to collect all my thoughts, but in the end, I had to give my address from notes and the heart, in a darkened, amphitheatre-type hall. I had also been given a long time to speak. It was not only my first address on Buddhism and feminism, but also one of the first ever given anywhere. No one knew what to expect, including myself. I also knew that for the first time, I would address an academic audience as a Buddhist practitioner, something that I now do routinely, but this first experience was quite frightening. In the darkened theater I was able to see a few academic types looking puzzled and leaving, but my primary reference point in the audience was Bob Aitken, Roshi, whom I saw grinning from ear to ear. I knew I was onto something. The response was overwhelmingly positive, more than I could ever have hoped for, though, I must say, it *was* a good talk as well.

This conference marked another major change in my life. It was my first immersion in interreligious exchange and dialogue. Over the years, I have only become more involved in that enterprise, as I took on various leadership roles in the Society for Buddhist-Christian Studies, including coediting its journal for ten years. I really welcome the chance to take part in an enterprise where my input is valued, being a woman is neither an obstacle nor an advantage, and feminist controversies can be on the back burner, rarely needing direct attention. Unfortunately, as noted in the part 4, very few other feminists have deigned to participate in discussions of this issue that is so critically important to a world and a nation in which inability to deal satisfactorily with religious diversity threatens us all.

The comments on the transmutation of anger and the unworkability of feminist rage were selected (not by me) for publication as the most memorable part of the paper and the address. Perhaps they were selected because they seemed to indicate a remarkable turnabout on my part by those who knew me. Remember, this was still the "rage stage" of feminism, when most feminists thought that intense anger expressed toward men and patriarchy was not only justified but praiseworthy. This address led to an early spate of publications and speaking engagements on Buddhism and feminism, or feminism from the perspective of Buddhist practice. Many feminists were, quite understandably, upset to have one among their ranks suddenly making a critique of feminism from the point of view of an unknown religious tradition that most of them (correctly) considered to be quite patriarchal.

I have long regarded the surprising discovery that anger about one's own perceived unjust situation is not helpful to anyone as the most significant statement about Buddhism and feminism that I have ever made. I have given this address many times as a dharma talk, and it has been reworked and republished a number of times over the years. When I was invited to make a feminist contribution to the book *Mindful Politics,* I wanted to rework these comments. This is the most complete statement I have ever made regarding these concerns.

Chapter 15, however, is the other side of these comments. I have never implied or stated that, simply because anger against oppression and injustice does not work, that, therefore, one should simply accept the status quo as impossible to change. Engaged Buddhists do need to care about gender (and other social issues). The problem is that engaged Buddhists usually do *not* include gender among the issues they care about.

Chapter 16, "The Dharma of Gender," is my current philosophical statement regarding Buddhist gender analysis, though it is supplemented by the introduction to this garland of reflections. I intend eventually to expand this topic into a book, a sequel to *Buddhism after Patriarchy,* to be written some twenty years after the first version.

Chapter 17, "Yeshe Tsogyel: Enlightened Consort, Great Teacher, Female Role Model," written in 1984 and virtually unchanged for publication here, is one of the oldest of the writings in this book. I wanted to include this piece precisely because it is one of my oldest works on gender and Buddhism that still stands on its own, rather than being part of an evolving discussion of gender analysis and Buddhism. I also include it because it is the first article in which I introduced my concern with what I consider to be *the* key feminist issue in Buddhism—the presence or absence of women dharma teachers, which is then explicitly addressed in the much newer chapter 18. I was amazed to discover, as I reread the chapter on Yeshe Tsogyel, how many issues that I later expanded upon were already dealt with in summary form in this very early work. I include this chapter also because it is about a good story that deserves to be more widely known.

In retrospect, as noted earlier, all the discussions presented in this garland of reflections were begun in the brief five or six years between 1975 and 1980. The first versions of chapters 2, 8, 10, and 14 were written during this period. Those four chapters represent a remarkably diverse set of offerings. No wonder some scholars criticized me for my seeming inability to settle on one topic or issue. For me, there was an internal consistency that others could not see. The consistent feature is the thread on which all the beads of this garland have been strung—the thread of feminist reflection.

CHAPTER 14

The Clarity in the Anger

When dualistic worldviews prevail, Buddhist political thinking and acting become very difficult, if not impossible. Fundamentally, Buddhism discourages "us and them" analyses as much as it discourages evaluating complex situations as "black and white" dichotomies. Buddhism claims that all beings are equal in the sense that they share the same basic nature, whether they are friends or enemies. Sharing the same basic nature is more important than status as friend or enemy, which is impermanent in any case. Though duality and the difference between friends and enemies, between those who are right and those who are wrong, can feel very real, Buddhist analytical meditation always shows that such feelings, though temporarily real, are ultimately illusory. Acting upon them leads to grief, regret, and suffering.

By contrast, politics, at least as frequently practiced, easily divides the world, the country, the neighborhood, or the dharma center into those who are right and those who are wrong. Common political practice also encourages passionate belief that one's own cause is just and good, and that following the views of the other side would bring disaster. Decisive choice is required, we are told. Therefore, many involved in politics who try to befriend those on both sides of a conflict experience the same fate as that of Thich Nhat Hahn in Viet Nam. Both sides regard them as disloyal enemies. "If you are not for us, then you are against us," a common current political slogan, is the epitome of dualistic thinking. Such dualism is antithetical to Buddhist ways of viewing reality.

As a result, many Western Buddhists are deeply suspicious of "causes," of being involved too much in politics, or of having seemingly political issues, such as justice and peace, be discussed at dharma centers. (The engaged Buddhist movement is a notable exception, but its overall impact on Western Buddhism is somewhat limited.) Asian and historical forms of Buddhism are often perceived as deeply apolitical and without significant social involvement by many Westerners, both scholars and practitioners. This perception may not be accurate, but that question cannot be discussed in this context.

The widespread Buddhist suspicion of "causes" has always been a difficult issue for me. I was a feminist before I became a Buddhist and have never been convinced that Buddhists' reluctance to take its feminist critics seriously is appropriate. While I have learned much about the perils and pitfalls of involvement in a cause such as feminism through my Buddhist practice, I also have learned that continuing involvement in a cause can teach one much about the dharma. What I have learned and how I learned it is the subject of this chapter.

Early in my life as a Buddhist practitioner, I was repeatedly told that concern with feminism and gender issues was not in accord with Buddhist dharma. I was told that involvement in a political cause inevitably involves attachment, while Buddhism and enlightenment are about detachment. I wasn't the only practitioner to receive this advice, and it is a long-held position in dharma debates. On many occasions, I have heard newer meditation students ask about their feelings of frustration and anger concerning environmental destruction, social injustice, racism, sexism, or impending war. Usually their concerns were dismissed with the slogan, "Just sit more," said in a way to imply that if their practice were better, they would not care about such things. Sometimes they were told that because enlightenment is the only ultimate solution to people's woes, formal practice was the only useful response to political issues and social problems, which is one traditional Buddhist position.

But Buddhism, despite its deep loyalty to nonduality, also emphasizes ethics as the basis of the spiritual path and a prerequisite for the successful pursuit of meditation and wisdom. Do not ethics, by their very nature, involve the duality of discriminating right from wrong, the duality of knowing what to cultivate and what to avoid? Does not politics involve a similar duality? Political issues minimally call for discriminating between better and worse alternatives and occasionally require discriminating right from wrong in a more absolute sense. Because both politics and ethics involve discriminating between better and worse, it would be difficult not to see a connection between ethics and politics. So how can Buddhists hide behind ultimate metaphysical nonduality as a justification for avoiding the ethical issues brought up by politics?

Many Buddhists would probably argue that Buddhist ethics are directed toward individual choices and behaviors, whereas politics involves struggles for power and material wealth between groups of people. As a result, ethical uprightness is much more difficult in politics. Furthermore, clashes for power and wealth easily intensify the polarization and demonizing of others that so often characterizes politics.

Other Buddhists concerned to bring individual and group ethics together, would respond that those political struggles often have a great deal to do with individual well-being, including having enough time and money to practice spiritual disciplines. Especially given the Buddhist claim that all things are interdependent, it is not so easy to separate individual choices from group decisions. Indeed, one of the most cogent modern criticisms of traditional Buddhist thought is that, though Buddhism is adamant in asserting nonharming as its most basic ethic, it lacks an understanding of structural violence. Buddhist thought has not usually noted the harm wrought by a *social system* that automatically favors some, such as men, over others, such as women. It should be noted in passing that traditional Buddhism cannot be faulted too much for this lack of awareness. All traditional religions regarded political and social systems as inevitable fiats rather than the results of choices made by many human beings over many years.

Nevertheless, some Western Buddhists justify their opposition to political involvement by arguing that political action is only an attempt to "fix samsara," to rid it of its pain, which is impossible. Changing group fates through politics, they tell us, is only an attempt to subvert karma, which controls people's positions in samsara. The poor deserve to be poor, by virtue of their karma; women deserve to be dominated by men by virtue of their karma, and so on.

But in Buddhist thought, karma is not predestination. If it were, there would be no point to practicing Buddhist spiritual disciplines, because the development of awareness, insight, and compassion would have no effect on predestined outcomes. If karma were predestination, one might as well sleep and engage in frivolous activities as practice meditation, because the predetermined outcomes would be the same in any case. But Buddhists have never rejected the possibility that individuals can change their future karma through present choices. Why should it be different for groups, which are only collections of individuals seeking to change their karma?

It is true that Buddhist thought can seem ambiguous, sometimes claiming that the best course of action is to avoid taking sides, because no real differences can be found between one thing and another, while at other times clearly urging that choices be made between what to cultivate and what to avoid. This line, so difficult to discuss, runs between absolute and relative truths, however, not between ethics and politics. Balancing absolute and relative truths and properly honoring their inseparability is one of the most difficult issues in Buddhism, both to discuss and to accomplish. That balance cannot be achieved by cultivating individual ethics, which is a necessary discipline in Buddhism, while abjuring causes devoted to peace and justice, such as feminism, because they too easily degenerate into name-calling and polarization.

Rather, two difficult tests of individual attainment confront the Buddhist concerned about the politics of peace and justice. Accomplishing them could be considered the *siddhis,* or "powers," of Buddhist social action. One must be able to retain equanimity and awareness while caring about a "cause" and in the midst of conflict. One must also be able to maintain contentment and cheerfulness in the midst of failure, and seemingly unending obstacles to any real attainment of justice and peace. Advice about and practices leading to this delicate but essential state of mind are the most important contributions Buddhists can make to political discussions, including discussions of feminism.

For a Buddhist another fact deserves attention. In my long experience of being involved with gender, a peace-and-justice issue that many Buddhists prefer to ignore, I have found that the most interesting dimension of politics for a Buddhist is the way caring about a "cause" provides constant fuel for working through the three poisons of aversion, attachment, and ignoring. Given that these three are at the very hub of the wheel of cyclic existence (samsara), it is no wonder that they are the constant pitfalls besetting Buddhists concerned about political causes. However, against those who decry Buddhist political involvement, one must realize that the three poisons cannot be avoided merely by avoiding politics.

Practitioners of Vajrayana Buddhism understand that, like any unenlightened energy, each of the three poisons includes the potential for its transmuted form. Aversion contains muted clarity; attachment contains unrealized compassion; and ignoring contains complete, all-inclusive spaciousness.

Because one can learn so much about the most profound dimensions of Buddhist realization by carefully contemplating one's actions and reactions to political and social concerns, I simply cannot agree that serious Buddhists should avoid politics as a diversion from serious practice. Rigid dualities are always conceptual mistakes in Buddhist practice, and perhaps the most inappropriate duality of all is that between "real practice" and politics.

I do agree with more conservative Buddhists who claim that Buddhist attainment is primarily about individual transformation rather than social change. I also agree with those Buddhists who claim that until one has enough attainment to sustain equanimity and awareness through distractions, one should perhaps limit one's involvement in causes. One may well do more harm than good if the three poisons immediately take over when conflict or frustration occurs. Having heeded such warnings, I explore what one can learn about the dense interweaving of aversion, attachment, and ignoring, as well as the possibility of their transmutation, through devotion to a cause such as feminism.

At least in Western contexts, aversion takes the lead among the three poisons that beset those who work on "causes," but its enlightened counterpart, clarity, is not far behind. I claim that aversion takes the lead for at least three reasons. First, one is devoted to a cause only because of aversion to some well-established practice, such as the straitjacket of traditional gender roles. Second, no matter how well or poorly one voices feminism, one will be on the receiving end of aversion from those who despise this cause. Third is the extreme aversion, expressing itself as aggression toward "the other side," so frequently found among those who espouse a cause. While examining each of these forms of aversion, we will see one of the three poisons usually brings the others in tow, as well as how each transforms into its enlightened aspect through greater awareness and equanimity.

The whole thing began, at least for me, with intense aversion to the male-dominant gender practices of my society and my chosen profession. My aversion was intense and unremitting. I tried to control expressing my anger, because for women, such expression was disapproved completely. But I felt completely justified in my rage and did express my aggression whenever such expression seemed "safe," that is to say, when the social consequences would not be too high. I also experienced some seeming satisfaction, some relief from my intense emotion, whenever I could express my anger, and I even experienced some satisfaction simply from mentally skewering my tormentors.

Then I began to practice meditation, never expecting that such practice could change my relationship with feminism. After all, I was very sure of the correctness of my analyses. After several years, I could no longer dredge up the same feelings of release and emotional satisfaction by aggressive expressions of my frustrations and rage. I also began to see that little was being accomplished by these expressions and that, if anything, I was only causing mutual entrenchment.

Over the long term, what changed was not my analyses, which were largely correct, but the emotionalism and attachment with which I expressed those analyses. That change has had mixed results. While I have been much more successful in convincing people that sexism of any stripe is simply inappropriate and not in accord with Buddhist dharma than would ever have been possible if my intensely angry expressions had continued, nevertheless, many people remain hostile to these analyses and prefer to ignore them. Unpacking this short story reveals the many dense links between the three poisons and their enlightened counterparts.

The utter accuracy of regarding clarity as the enlightened, transmuted form of aversion has been intensely vivid to me since these early days. In Vajrayana Buddhist psychology, every negative emotion contains some enlightened energy which can be unleashed through meditation practice. Anger transmutes into clarity, or more accurately, when angry expressions subside, underlying clarity can shine through. Water is the element associated with anger; murky water veils what is in its depths, while clear water both allows those depths to be seen and reflects perfectly what is on its surface. That is how political analyses are. Even the seemingly most misguided contain some intelligence and accuracy; even the most angry are right, in least in part.

For example, male-dominant institutional forms simply cannot be made to square with Buddhist dharma, no matter what arguments may be enlisted by male-dominant traditions. The most frustrated, unskillful, out-of-control feminist has that much straight. Aggression, anger, and aversion mask clarity, but the clarity is there nevertheless. Friends mistakenly assured me that as my practice matured, my caring about feminism would vanish, but what vanished was my own rage, leaving the clarity of what I had already seen much sharper and more vivid.

In people lacking deep spiritual discipline, usually anger overwhelms clarity, making the clarity indiscernible to others and often a minor part of one's own awareness. Instead, one experiences pain and grief about the perversions of peace and justice one sees so clearly. Directing verbal (or physical) attacks at others seems to bring satisfaction. It is so tempting to lash out with sarcasm and angry humor when one sees clearly but is powerless to do anything to bring real change. At least one can yell and make cutting remarks, but these reactions only temporarily mask the pain one feels, soon making another outburst necessary. Meanwhile, others can be excused if aggression is more evident to them than the clarity contained in these outbursts.

The interplay between anger and clarity has never been more adequately demonstrated than by an interchange I witnessed some years ago between Jetsun Khandro Rinpoche and a student. The student asked what one should do about things that made one angry. Khandro Rinpoche replied quite sharply, "Anger is always a waste of time." The student, looking shocked, blurted out, "But what about things you should be angry about, like abuse?" Without losing a second, Khandro Rinpoche replied, "I didn't tell you to give up your critical intelligence. I told you anger is a waste of time." (Notice that she did not tell the student just to "sit more.") So the trick is to tame anger while not losing critical intelligence. To tame anger by disconnecting one's critical intelligence would be to fall into apathy and ignoring, not to attain realization.

"But what about the things about which one *should* be angry" was this student's expression of critical intelligence, phrased in perhaps poorly chosen words. "Should" is a word more connected with attachment and passion than with aversion. Though one's devotion to feminism may be triggered by aversion to existing practices, it also contains a strong element of passion and desire. "I hate the way things are and I desire them to be different." Outsiders to Buddhism are often mystified by the way Buddhists see hope and fear as two sides of the same coin, not radically opposed emotions, and the same analysis applies to aversion and attachment. They are not as opposed to each other as we often think.

Devotion to feminism involves great passion as well as great aversion. One is passionately devoted to an alternative vision of how things could be. Like every other expression still involved in dualism, political passion is double-edged. In Vajrayana Buddhist psychology, the enlightened expression of attachment *is* compassion—concern for the entire matrix not based on the distinction between self and others. I have always regarded my activities as a Buddhist feminist as an attempt to fulfill my bodhisattva vows, not a worldly diversion from those vows.

Without the gentling effects of deep spiritual discipline, attachment prevails and expresses itself as ideological fixation—an expression deeply tinged with aggression. Nothing is so repellant as a good idea held to without flexibility, gentleness, and humor. What makes involvement in political causes and organizations nearly impossible for many Buddhists is the self-righteousness of so many people who have good ideas. Their good ideas are expressed in an entirely dualistic manner, with no awareness of the basic goodness of those on the other side. I now find it difficult to be involved with many of my feminist colleagues because of their ideological rigidity and prefer the company of colleagues who are less self-consciously feminist in their outlook, but whose compassion does include concern for gender justice.

Some might ask, "But if you *really* care about something, will you not have strong and fixed opinions on that issue?" With careful attention, it becomes evident that cogent analysis and clarity of expression are not the same as aversion or attachment. Telling the difference between them is not so easy. Usually the actual words used are not so critical; rather, tone of voice and body language communicate whether fixation or clarity is driving the expression. It is possible both to care about something and to be nonideological and nonfixated in that caring. If it were not possible, the Buddhist ideal of nondual compassion would be an illusion.

Gradually, one's speech and expressions are tamed and one can talk about difficult issues without reeking of aversion and attachment. When that happens, communication is possible and one may succeed in getting one's message across. There is a middle path between fighting with others and simply turning numb and passive, deaf and dumb to clearly evident injustice and violence.

Avoiding the pitfalls of aversion and attachment, both in oneself and in others, is only the beginning. One may practice never speaking out on an issue if the murky emotionalism of aversion or attachment still clouds one's mind, and such a practice is essential. Even with this practice well in place, however, one will still be widely ignored and will often be the recipient of aggression and aversion from others. Clear analysis does not always penetrate, and even when it does, many people prefer to ignore the analysis or may even become hostile because clarity makes them uncomfortable.

The intermingling of willful ignoring and hostility that greet clear analysis presented without aversion or attachment is evident in a conversation I once had. I had just presented a talk in which I discussed that many Buddhist liturgies do not actually include any references to women or any feminine imagery, even though we women are supposed to feel that the liturgies include us. With some amazement, the woman with whom I was speaking said that she enjoyed Buddhist liturgies a great deal and had never noticed that they really did not include her. "You spoiled it for me!"

she said somewhat angrily. Apparently she preferred inaccurate, though pleasant, ignoring to deeper insight and greater clarity.

Such a reaction is not at all uncommon. It is the usual reaction to Buddhism's most profound teachings, such as teachings about egolessness. Ignoring is always the deepest and most intractable of the poisons, the root out of which the others grow. Amazingly, even in many Buddhist contexts, the response to unfamiliar but cogent feminist analyses is some variant of "I don't like the message, so let's kill the messenger." Ignoring quickly is displaced by aversion to the message and attachment to what is familiar. I could recount countless examples of being blamed for the information about gender inequity in Buddhism that I brought to people. People often say, not in so many words, that if only I didn't bring them information about traditional male dominance in Buddhism, it would not exist. And, in a certain sense, those of us who carry feminist messages do make information exist for those who were formerly ignorant. The only difference is that after the message has been delivered, unconscious ignoring is replaced by willful ignoring, a far more violent and aggressive act.

Thus we see the utter cogency of regarding clarity and aversion as the enlightened and deluded forms of the same energy. A message containing unwelcome clarity *feels* aggressive to those who prefer ignorance. As we know from elementary Buddhist psychology, the conventional response to feeling attacked is to attack the source of those feelings, which we conventionally believe lies with someone outside ourselves. Thus, someone who works on issues of social and political awareness must also learn to develop equanimity and accommodation regarding the indifference and rejection with which one's work is greeted. One could probably be more accepted and honored in one's community if one did not draw attention to things the community prefers to ignore. This dimension of being able to greet distasteful situations with equanimity rather than aversion is especially important and difficult.

When a Buddhist cares about feminism long enough, one begins to see, as I put it in one of my more recent slogans, that "being correct is not enough." In fact, being correct is the easy part. How does one express righteousness nondualistically? It is easy to be clear that male dominance is unjust and harmful. How does one express that conviction and caring skillfully, without alienating people? How can one really accommodate disagreement concerning issues about which one cares deeply and has great conviction? Do I really think that people who would argue that male dominance is necessary and is good for everyone, including women, might have a case? I don't think so. That clarity is the easy part. Going further with such an insight is the hard part. Contemplations about political involvement help us understand certain deep insights of the Buddhist tradition. When a Buddhist works long enough on a political issue, one begins to understand why Skillful Means (*upaya*) is the seventh paramita and Discriminating Wisdom (*prajna*) is the sixth paramita. One also begins to understand why clarity is useless without an ability to express clarity skillfully, why in Vajrayana Buddhist symbolism and practice, clarity is never invoked alone but only in partnership with skillful means.

Buddhism has two things to contribute to those involved in feminism. One is the immediate need for the skillful means of developing and maintaining equanimity and peacefulness in the face of opposition, oppression, and conflict. What of the long term? After people have expressed their outrage long and forcefully enough, they often burn out. Exhaustion replaces aversion as the chief outcome of caring about a cause. How does one keep going, year after year, when things do not get better, and even seem to be getting worse, as is the case with many of the issues feminists have cared about for years?

The second great gift of Buddhism to political processes is its ability to develop staying power in those who practice its spiritual disciplines. To stay concerned about social issues, one has to develop the ability to keep on working cheerfully year after year without hope of success and fear of failure. In my own case, I cannot imagine still caring about and working on feminist issues after forty years if I had not discovered Buddhist practices. Or if I were still concerned, I would probably also be filled with the pain of bitterness and frustration, which I am happy to report is not at all the case. This discovery too is in deep accord with fundamental Buddhist teachings, especially Mahayana Buddhist teachings on the paramita of patience.

Buddhist realization is about seeing deeply into the fundamental nonduality of experience, but politics seems rife with duality. I have argued that part of one's practice as a Buddhist might be to practice the inseparability of spiritual disciplines and politics. As we know, practicing nonduality is practicing the inseparability of absolute and relative truths. It could be tempting to think that when we practice spiritual disciplines, we are practicing on the absolute level, and when we practice politics, we are practicing on the relative level. But that would be much too dualistic an assumption. With true inseparability, we learn much about deep Buddhist insights through involvement with causes, and our immersion in Buddhist practices teaches us how to remain involved in politics—skillfully.

CHAPTER 15

Why (Engaged) Buddhists Should Care about Gender Issues

It seems to me that if Buddhists really followed their central claims about gender, engaged Buddhists would not need to be concerned about gender issues. But we live in a situation that is far from the Buddhist ideal or norm regarding gender; therefore engaged Buddhists do need to care about gender issues among their many other concerns. In this brief chapter honoring Sulak Sivaraksha, I will try to explain why I continue to focus on gender in my work as an engaged Buddhist, even though it would be far more pleasant and easier to give up that work, and giving up that work would probably also result in less hostility toward me from many in the Buddhist world.

I cannot count the number of times some supposed authority or elder in the Buddhist world has tried to explain to me that the work I have done as a Buddhist deeply concerned about gender equity in the world in general, and especially in Buddhism, is unnecessary and beside the point because Buddhists say that ultimately gender is irrelevant and enlightened mind is neither male nor female. Therefore, my bringing up the topic of reforms concerning gender practices in the Buddhist world is divisive and perhaps heretical. "You should be beyond gender," I am told. "Gender is irrelevant, so you should stop focusing on gender."

There is a twisted logic in the above summary of hundreds of discussions that both amuses and pains me. Basically, the question is, who's focusing on gender, and who wants to ignore it? Traditionalists may say that they are ignoring gender and I am focusing on it, but I think that assessment is actually the reverse of what is really going on. If traditionalists had no interest in maintaining or defending Buddhist institutions that, in fact, do focus on gender, usually to women's disadvantage, they could more reasonably claim that they are beyond gender. Then, for example, there would be no opposition to restoring the *bhikshuni* ordination, nor would it be expected that men, but not women, would be Buddhist teachers. But traditionalists *do* defend and maintain such gender-based institutions. Nevertheless, they accuse *me and other so-called feminists* of incorrectly focusing on gender when we call for the dissolution of gender-based practices. It seems to me that *we* are the ones who want to ignore gender and go beyond gender, but that we are forced to continue to bring up gender issues because traditionalists continue to assume that gender is a meaningful basis upon which to organize Buddhist social and religious institutions. I'd love to ignore gender, to go beyond gender, but by that, I mean truly ignoring gender, not continuing traditional gender-based practices, which often exclude women from the most meaningful and highly valued aspects of Buddhist life, while claiming that not talking about such gender-based practices is the same as transcending gender.

Therefore, I argue that, though Buddhists really shouldn't need to care about gender, engaged Buddhists must care about gender. In this short chapter, I will focus on two main reasons why engaged Buddhists must care about gender issues: first, among all the social concerns upon which engaged Buddhists generally focus, internally, Buddhism's record on gender is far worse that its record on racism, colonialism, economic injustice, or militarism; second, of all the issues that engaged Buddhists care about, gender alone is within the control of Buddhists, at least within our own Buddhist world. We, as Buddhists, may not be able to avert warfare, global capitalism, or environmental devastation. But, at least within our own Buddhist world, our social and religious institutions, only we Buddhists maintain the gender practices that have been so disadvantageous for Buddhist women. No outside force is making us set up our world the way we do.

Let us look at each of these claims in turn. Happily, when I survey Buddhism in general, it seems to me that overall our record as perpetrators of militarism, racism, or economic exploitation is relatively positive. Buddhists who have any control over the world usually do not call for or enact socially oppressive or aggressive measures. Throughout history, many Buddhists with power are famous for having improved social conditions, the best-known being, of course, Emperor Ashoka in ancient India. Even when not in power, Buddhists often are strong advocates for economic generosity that would promote the well-being of society at large, and they frequently point out the futility of expecting counteraggression ever to solve problems in any enduring way. In the modern world they have become highly respected peace leaders and advocates for social justice, environmental sanity, and interreligious cooperation.

Sadly, however, when I look at the broad history of Buddhism's actions regarding gender, I see a much less sanguine record. I often interact with non-Buddhists who simply cannot understand why a woman would be attracted to Buddhism, convert to it, and work intensely to understand and practice Buddhism; to them, it seems obvious that Buddhism is entirely male-dominated and does not really afford women much respect or opportunity to develop our potentials. Unfortunately, they can make a strong case that their impressions are accurate. Granted, Buddhism does have key teachings, such as egolessness and emptiness, that proclaim the irrelevance of gender. Indeed, I have often claimed that these teachings are central and normative within Buddhism, and traditional texts also make such claims. But these teachings have been honored at least as much in the breach as by being observed. As one of my Buddhist friends commented to me recently, "Buddhism has an incredibly strong basis in its teachings for deconstructing gender, but it's never come to much." It seems to me that Buddhism's overall record on gender is its greatest failing, its most obvious blemish. On other major social issues that engaged Buddhists care about, Buddhism's own track record is relatively positive; on gender its track record is horrible. This, then, is reason enough for engaged Buddhists to care about gender issues.

Sometimes it is claimed that concern for gender justice and gender equity is only a modern or a Western evaluation imposed from the outside on Buddhism. But a reading of Buddhist history does not substantiate that claim. In the very earliest days of Buddhism, women objected to being excluded from the monastic *sangha* and persisted until they were granted ordination. These are hardly Western feminist women importing a foreign idea into Buddhism; they were among the most important early practitioners of Buddhism. In contemporary times, Asian Buddhist women have insisted upon and gained a greater degree of gender equity than was the norm in recent times. Who cares if "Western feminism" had some role this development, as I believe it did. The changes that have happened in modern Asian Buddhism regarding women are important if Buddhism is to live up to its liberative and transformative potential. The women and men who promoted these changes are modern engaged Buddhists, as much as Buddhists engaged in any other cause.

The other major reason for engaged Buddhists to care about gender issues is that, at least within the Buddhist context, nothing is stopping us from initiating and implementing appropriate policies regarding gender, policies that actually promote basic Buddhist claims about the irrelevance of gender rather than policies that depend on strong gender differentiation and gender roles that usually are disadvantageous to women. With some major exceptions, in the modern world, Buddhists do not actually control the societies in which they live, a fact that is perhaps more noticeable to me as a Western Buddhist than to many in more traditionally Buddhist societies. We can advocate and persuade about the things engaged Buddhists care about: peace and justice in the world at large. But that is all we can do. Others will make the decisions about war and peace, about economic policies, about racial and cultural diversity, and about environmental survival. In non-Buddhist institutions, others also make the decisions about gender practices, and all we can do is advocate and protest, nonaggressively, of course. But within Buddhist institutions, whether in contexts where Buddhism has been practiced for centuries or in new Buddhist communities in the West, only Buddhists control practices surrounding gender. We could undo all the practices that depend on the relevance, rather than the irrelevance, of gender tomorrow, if we wanted to. No one outside Buddhism dictates policy regarding our monastic or educational institutions. No outside authorities determine our imagery or our liturgical language. We Buddhists alone are responsible for the kind of attention we give gender within our own world. However, it has been my experience over the years that rhetoric about the irrelevance of gender has been used far more frequently to justify ignoring current gender discriminations than to actually transcend gender. Certainly this mistake is something engaged Buddhists should care about.

I have heard many excuses for this state of affairs, but the one I find most problematic in the context of engaged Buddhism is the claim that gender is a minor issue compared with war, race, economic justice, or the environment. It is claimed that those issues involve real suffering, whereas gender issues can wait because they are not as cataclysmically imminent and do not harm people in the same way as do war, poverty, racism, or environmental destruction. But I would answer that this argument involves a rather superficial assessment of the suffering caused, not just to women, but also to men, by male-dominant gender practices. In any case, how do we rank suffering? Do we say that those who are aware of great suffering caused by gender injustice should simply look the other way and agree that other things are more important? What then happens to the Buddhist virtue of telling the truth and avoiding lying?

Perhaps if we have enough determination, we can live to see the day when the appropriate title of this chapter would be "Why Buddhists Need Not Care about Gender," rather than "Why (Engaged) Buddhists Should Care about Gender Issues." That would be an auspicious development.

CHAPTER 16

The Dharma of Gender

A classic meditation practice in Vajrayana Buddhism, called the Mahamudra Investigations, invites the meditator to search for the nature of unfettered mind by exploring several pithy questions. Does the mind have a color? Does the mind have a shape? Is the mind inside the body? Outside the body? The meditator is instructed to search diligently, exhausting all possibilities, instead of concluding on the basis of knowledge of Buddhist doctrine that unfettered mind could not possibly be found in any of these places. These investigations are more like Zen koans—baffling puzzles that have no unvaryingly correct intellectual or conceptual answer.

Here, the English word *mind,* generally used to translate various Tibetan terms used in this context, does not mean the brain or the sixth consciousness, or even the eighth consciousness. As with the Zen phrase, "dropping body and mind," language is being used to point to a state beyond language. Though meditation instructions to explore whether one can find mind anywhere may seem different from meditation instructions to drop body and mind, I suggest that these are two ways of expressing the same insight about where meditation practice leads.

One pithy question, however, is not part of these Mahamudra Investigations. Does the mind have a gender? Furthermore, this question does not appear to have been relevant to those who formulated the Investigations. Two seemingly opposite reasons might explain why this question does not occur. On the one hand, it could be contended, and often has been contended in Buddhist traditions, that gender is obviously not relevant to discussions of unfettered mind, making it unnecessary to investigate whether mind has a gender. If the question were to arise, some might claim that it has already been included in the question of whether mind has a shape, thus finding another way to avoid troublesome questions about gender.

But I think it is as least as likely that the question about mind having a gender is unasked because it was simply assumed that the person doing the investigations would be a male, or at least not someone whose life was bound up in the traditional female gender role. The extent to which the presumed subject of Buddhist philosophy and meditation is a male is shocking to someone with heightened awareness of how much difference gender makes in human affairs. I think it is quite likely that the question about whether mind has a gender is unasked, not because gender has been transcended, but because its determinative impact on people's lives is being ignored. The assumption that only men would take on certain roles such as public teaching, a widespread practice in Tibetan Buddhism, suggests willful ignoring, rather than transcendence of the extent to which people attribute absolute, not relative, meaning to gender. And there is a huge difference between ignoring and transcending, a difference which is of utmost importance in Buddhism.

I will suggest that gender identity and concepts about what gender entails are among the strongest hooks for ego-clinging in most people, which means that they become one of the more enduring bonds to samsara. Gender identity, I would claim, is more basic for most people than identification in terms of color, shape, or even culture, and is far more addictive. In this regard, I've always been struck by an argument used by some Roman Catholics against the ordination of women to the priesthood. The priest must mirror Jesus, it is claimed, and that means the priest must have a male body. I remember one commentator who claimed that Jesus could have been a Chinese rather than a Jewish male, but as a male, he would still have been essentially the same person, whereas if he had been a (Jewish) woman, he would have been an entirely different person. I wonder how many Buddhists feel the same way about the Buddha? After all, it is noteworthy in his rebirth stories that his female rebirths stopped before his animal rebirths.

Many who have become certain of the view that the self has no real or inherent existence still talk and act as if that nonexistent self harbors a truly existing gender. Such people nurture and act on many preconceptual,

unconscious, and unexamined assumptions about gender and also
expect others to conform to those assumptions. To put my claim at its
starkest, I will contend, based on my many experiences of talking about
gender and Buddhism, that while most Buddhists do not believe in the
existence of a permanent, abiding self, nevertheless, their attitudes and
actions indicate that they do believe in the real existence of gender. In
other words, the self that does not inherently exist nevertheless pos-
sesses gender that is regarded and acted upon as if it truly existed; or at
least that is the way many Buddhists talk and act, despite their beliefs
about the centrality of egolessness to a Buddhist view and way of life.
Their slogan seems to be "The self does not exist, but it has gender."
But such a view is illogical in the extreme; if the self lacks inherent existence, no attribute of that self, such as gender, color, or shape, could be
said to have inherent existence.

If this sounds confusing, it must be remembered that I am always
using the term *existence* in its precise Buddhist meaning, which denotes,
not that something appears, but that the appearing "something" is
unconditioned, uncaused, and independent of its matrix, that it exists
independently rather than interdependently. The appearance of gendered
individuals is not disputed; that such appearances should be assigned
automatic and invariant weight is disputed. The matter is more serious
because the meanings assigned to gender almost always involve an automatic second-class existence for some people in the worlds of practice
and study. Other factors, such as intelligence and a desire to practice
dharma, were trumped by gender norms and made little difference.

Another way of talking about the same issue involves the dispute over
gender essentialism. Many systems of thought, including certain strands
of feminism, have claimed that there are invariant traits or behaviors
essential to each gender. Many traditional claims about what makes
women inferior, such as their purported emotionalism and lack of
rationality, are based on such gender essentialism. In the same way,
some strands of feminism which are no longer in favor posited a gender
essentialism that elevated women above men. The claim that women are
more oriented to relationships and inherently less violent than men was
one common feminist essentialist claim. Notice that there are two components to this way of thinking. There are invariant, essential traits for
each gender which are almost always seen as the opposites of each other.
Furthermore, most systems of gender essentialism also posit an ethical
hierarchy between the opposites, even though what traits are associated
with men or women, and which gender is viewed as "better," varies

from one cultural situation to another. It is impossible to posit a gender essentialism that is not imprisoning, that does also involve imposing a prison of gender roles on people, which is why this view is rejected by most feminists. This conclusion about the imprisoning nature of gender roles would hold even in cases where it is maintained that the different gender roles are "equally valued." Traditional religions and cultures often make this claim about gender complementarity, but usually it is just another gloss on male dominance. Even if we could find a situation of genuine complementarity, that would not undo the imprisoning quality gender role assignment has on individuals.

One can easily find Buddhist texts espousing both essentialist and nonessentialist views of gender, but that does not mean that both views are equally cogent in expressing the fundamental Buddhist view. It only indicates how easy it is to exempt gender from Buddhism's usual reluctance to attribute inherent existence to anything, how easy it is to regard gender alone among many aspects of one's phenomenal existence as "really real." Attributing real existence to gender is doubly problematic— on feminist grounds and on Buddhist grounds.

The definitive Buddhist view of whether gender exists as anything more than a conventional label is found in the famous "Goddess" chapter of the Vimalakirtinirdesha Sutra. In this episode, a woman—the so-called Goddess—had been studying dharma in Vimalakirti's palace for twelve years when she was challenged by Shariputra, a famous first-generation disciple of the Buddha who is often portrayed in Mahayana scriptures as not understanding things very well. Impressed by her level of understanding, he challenges her: "Why don't you change your female sex?" To understand his challenge in context, it must be remembered that in many Mahayana texts, highly realized women *do* change their sex to prove that mind has no gender. Skeptical male Buddhists who had essentialized gender so much that they believed a female body renders one incapable of realizing unfettered mind could respond to no other demonstration of the fluidity and nonexistence of gender. But the Goddess does not buy into this logic. Instead, she says to Shariputra, "I have been here twelve years and have looked for the innate characteristics of the female sex and have not been able to find them," and she challenges him about what he could possibly mean by the innate traits of the female sex. Then she changes Shariputra into a woman and herself into a man, whereupon she challenges him (now her) to find her innate female traits. After she changes the befuddled Shariputra back into a man, he concedes that the female form does not possess innate characteristics.

This story says it all. I know that I have a female body or shape, but that doesn't really mean much. It does not mean that I must bear children, or even that I can. It does not mean that I necessarily have a gentle, nonaggressive demeanor, as opposed to a violent or nasty temperament. It does not even guarantee my primary sexual orientation, which has been guessed wrong almost as often as it has been guessed right by observers, both women and men. My female sex is not a reliable guide to my interests and concerns. I care little for many of the things that are supposed to interest women, but I also am interested in some things that are generally thought to be of more interest to women than to men. In short, though my sex may be the first fact about me that registers, it tells people relatively little about me. Nevertheless, though my female body doesn't translate into anything essential, a great deal has been projected onto it by society, by religions, and by individuals who think that the shape of my body reveals something intrinsically existing, something on which it is valid to pin all sorts of meanings and limitations. Gender designations as conventional, agreed-upon labels are harmless and somewhat useful. However, they are rarely left as mere labels and instead become hooks upon which to attach a prison of myriad expectations and demands.

Despite this definitive proclamation of the Goddess to Shariputra and its irrefutably correct Buddhist logic, Buddhist texts, institutions, and individuals are just as likely to believe in gender as a fixed, rigid, determinative, and limiting trait as anyone else. Their allegiance to the view that there is no permanent abiding self that is fixed, rigid, determinative, limiting, or inherently existing in any other way does not protect them from believing and acting upon an imputed real existence of gender. For this reason, I claim that, shocking as it may be, Buddhist logic about egolessness, or *anatman,* the third mark of sentient existence according to the Buddha, has never been thoroughly and consistently applied to gender. "There is no permanent abiding self, but it has gender. Furthermore, gender has an invariant and valid hold on people's lives. It truly exists, whatever else may be said about the lack of a permanent abiding self in doctrinal Buddhism." That seems to be the message and conclusion rampant in much of the Buddhist world.

For example, the Mahayana philosopher Asanga explains why a "completely perfected Buddha" is not a woman: "All women are by nature full of defilement and of weak intelligence. And not by one who is full of defilement and of weak intelligence is completely perfected Buddhahood attained."[1] The claim that something has certain samsaric qualities "by nature" seems very strange in a Buddhist context, given that emptiness (*Shunyata*) and Buddha nature (*tathagatagarbha*) are the only qualities posited as intrinsic to beings. Nor does this statement seem to be a generalization to which there could be exceptions, the kind of statement that might be offensive but does not totally go against the usual Buddhist view that nothing phenomenal is self-existing. I suspect that such claims that certain beings have specific samsaric qualities "by nature" would not be made concerning anything other than gender, and also would only be made about women, but not men. Such comments are made about individual men, but never about all men, or about men as a class. However, it is not difficult to find similar statements in other Buddhist texts. The sex segregation and male dominance of traditional Buddhist institutions, which also encourage belief in the reality of gender, are so well known that there is no necessity to do more than remind ourselves of their existence.

As I go about my work in the Buddhist world, I cannot avoid the impression that, while most Buddhists I encounter would not endorse Asanga's misogynistic statement, they also do not really believe the Goddess when she proves to Shariputra that gender has no essence or nature that is self-existing. Even in the context of discussing that very text, in the midst of making the point that egolessness and gender essentialism are mutually incompatible, I find that people *want,* desperately want, to believe that gender means something, definitively determines something, is real in some way. They have intellectually convinced themselves that there is no permanent abiding self, but they are averse to applying the same logic to its gender.

Two tactics are especially common among people who want to retain some belief in the enduring and definitive relevance of gender. The first is to appeal to the gender symbolism so prominent in Tibetan Buddhism or to talk about the "feminine principle" as ways to avoid looking into whether a prison of gender roles prevails in the midst of such positive female symbolism. The second is to become angry with those who point out that Buddhism contradicts itself when it essentializes gender in its institutions and practices, a response with which I am all too familiar!

It never ceases to amaze me that people think one can answer questions about how gender affects *people*—men and women—by appealing to "the feminine principle," which is positively evaluated and central to Tibetan Buddhism. But the presence of a positively valued feminine principle tells us nothing about how gendered people fare, nothing about whether they live in social systems of gender equity and nondiscrimination. People easily slip from talking about themselves as men and women to talking about "feminine energy" as if it is something that pertains especially to women or the "masculine principle" as if it is the property of men. They seem not to realize that there is no necessary correlation between men and the masculine principle or between women and the feminine principle, either doctrinally or experientially. In Vajrayana Buddhism, the symbolism associated with femininity and masculinity is fixed and precise; it is also balanced and complementary. One simply could not say that one is more elevated or important than the other, and both are necessary to balanced, full living. That is why it is so problematic to assume that the masculine principle somehow pertains to men in ways that it does not pertain to women, and vice versa. Such an assumption turns liberating images of how to balance and blend our human potentials into another version of the prison of gender roles.

It is equally problematic to presume that the presence of balanced, complementary gender *symbolism* means that human genderedness is dealt with satisfactorily. Positive symbolism of femininity combined with difficult lives for women is very common worldwide, but the fact that positive feminine symbolism does not necessarily translate into dignified lives of freedom for women usually does not register. I remember a very early gathering at which Mary Daly read one of her papers.[2] This was even before she had abandoned Christianity. Several Roman Catholic priests present asked her, with obvious frustration, what Catholic women could possibly lack or want, given that Catholics revered the Virgin Mary.

It is insufficient to revel in beautiful symbolism of the "feminine principle" while not checking how women (or men) are faring. Are women even allowed to emulate the strength and dignity of beings symbolizing the feminine principle? I automatically distrust those who discuss symbolism of feminine and masculine principles but do not make crystal clear their views on gender and human beings. They are often oblivious to the prison of gender roles coexisting with beautiful symbolism of the feminine.

For example, a book on the feminine principle in Tibetan Buddhism claims, "By virtue of having a female body, a woman radiates the feminine qualities more strongly, and it is natural for her to yearn for the masculine qualities. Similarly, it is natural for a man to yearn for the feminine qualities."[3] Because this kind of statement is repeated so frequently, it seems that the statement is meant as a claim about women's and men's natures, not a generalization to which there would be many exceptions. Such a statement may even be empirically true as a generalization that pertains to many people. However, when it becomes a normative statement about how people should feel or a metaphysical claim about some invariant "nature" that is different in women and men, it is no longer a harmless bit of folklore but a dangerous ethical and philosophical prison. Because talk of gender is so slippery, it is important always to be clear on such matters. In this case, it is unclear whether this author is speaking for herself or is representing the Tibetan lamas who were her primary informants, but the absence of any critique of the gender essentialism found in such comments is noticeable. We certainly have moved far from the insight of the Goddess who told Shariputra that she had searched unsuccessfully for her female nature for twelve years. Furthermore, I would claim that appreciation of the form of emptiness, so characteristic of Vajrayana Buddhism, is quite different from attributing inherent existence to those forms. One cannot excuse such talk about men's and women's natures by appealing to Third Turning teachings about the importance of seeing the form in emptiness.

However, programs on "the feminine principle" are far more popular these days than programs exploring Buddhism and human genderedness, because they put a spin on gender issues that is far more comforting and less stressful than exploring gender itself. People are tired of talking about gender; it causes discomfort, and audiences often avoid or turn on those who keep suggesting that gender is still an issue. Direct and accurate discussion of gender leaves no hook for ego to settle upon, whereas it is easy to feel better and more affirmed by pleasant talk of feminine and masculine qualities. In the context of this rather sharp critique of confusion between gender symbolism and gender as it pertains to men and women, it must be understood that I have no quarrel with traditional Tibetan gender symbolism and am not suggesting that we would be better off without such symbolism. In fact, I think such symbolism is useful and inspiring. Rather, I am objecting to the misuse of such symbolism to bolster vague beliefs in qualities that are inherent to men or to women, and thus to reinforce rather than undercut ego-clinging.

Reactions to those who promote awareness of gender are also telling. Somehow, we become the culprits, the villains, rather than those who do not question conventional gender arrangements. I could tell many stories by now, of course, but I will focus on two. In one case, I gave a talk that, among other things, pointed out that the consistent use of "he" in common (Shambhala) Buddhist liturgies was part of a much larger pattern of leaving women out. One listener was amazed that she had never noticed the clear implications of this language before, but she also was upset. "You spoiled it for me," she said. In the other case, I was seated at a table at Karme Choling during a large gathering of senior students, talking with a man who claimed he had been eager to meet me and said that I wasn't anything like he had expected. (That comment always makes me suspicious.) Suddenly he was standing, leaning over me, saying he had written to the *Shambhala Sun,* complaining that they had published my work. He claimed it shouldn't be published because "you always reference the dharma with gender. Why do you do that!" Clearly, he was quite angry. Spontaneously, I did something I would never do in my own persona. I tilted my head back, batted my eyelashes, and said in a throaty whisper, "Somebody's got to do it." The question is, who's referencing the dharma with gender? If dharma had not already been referenced by gender throughout Buddhist history and in all traditional forms of Buddhism, there would be nothing for me and other feminist critics to point out. Why do we get maligned for shining a light on what's always been there, especially given that traditional gender practices are highly questionable if the Buddhist view is taken seriously?

I've often been told that I should be beyond gender, by which my critics mean that I should look past the gender norms so evident in Buddhist thought and institutions because they really don't mean anything anyway. But what about the reverse? Shouldn't people who are uncomfortable with having basic facts and information pointed out also be challenged to go beyond gender? Even if truly going beyond gender entails dismantling many traditional forms? It is so illogical that those who notice facts about how gender operates in the Buddhist context are accused of fixating on gender while those who conveniently ignore the same information want to be thought of as beyond gender and unmoved by it. If they were truly beyond gender, challenges to current male-dominant gender practices would not bother them. At least they would be able to discuss the issues without becoming defensive and needing to claim that whatever Buddhism has done or the Buddha is purported to have said must be good and true. Ignorance, and most especially willful ignoring, which is far more pernicious in Buddhist terms, has nothing in common with transcendence and equanimity. Yet it is very easy to confuse ignoring and transcending, especially because it is comforting to one's conventional ego to claim transcendence while actually practicing ignoring. Those who insist upon and are attached to living their lives in accord with conventional practices regarding gender need to carefully examine whether these habitual patterns have anything to do with Buddhism and the life of Buddhist practice.

Furthermore, I would claim that, by and large, those who endorse gender essentialism and thus endorse a form of ego-clinging fare much better in the Buddhist world, including the world of Western Buddhism, than those who defy all the institutions and generalizations dependent on gender essentialism. In this one case, ignorance seems to be preferred over insight. Many with the power to determine Buddhism's future are extremely defensive on the topic of gender, being unwilling even to discuss it, let alone concede that some common Buddhist practices concerning gender may reinforce rather than undercut ego-clinging.

But what about commonsense relative truth, some may be screaming by now. Surely gender matters a lot. Surely some generalizations about women and men make sense. Indeed, I sometimes indulge in such generalizations myself in conversation, but I never take them too seriously or expect them to hold in all cases. There is a huge difference between a lightly held generalization, which may be useful for negotiating the phenomenal world, and a rigidly held doctrine about differences between women and men which must be enforced at any cost, even deforming individuals emotionally to make them fit gender expectations that have been laid out for them. The issue is not whether there are such generalizations but the rigidity and fixation with which they are held. Strong, rigidly held opinions and a stubborn fixed mind indicate immaturity of practice and should be tolerated at best, rather than cultivated. Why would any Buddhist want to hang on to generalizations and traditional practices surrounding gender, or be uncomfortable when they prove to be inaccurate or in need of change?

Indeed, why the need for gender as an immediate, easily assignable reference point? Rather than being uncomfortable when I cannot immediately assign gender to someone whom I see or with whom I am corresponding, I now delight in the spaciousness and freedom of such moments. Even in the majority of cases in which the grasping mind immediately labels a person by gender, I cultivate the flavor of going beyond the label. Such open-ended nongrasping awareness is much more in accord with Buddhist sensibilities and teachings than constantly pigeonholing people by their gender and then presuming a great deal about them. Even if we are not well enough trained to hold such open awareness, as Buddhists, we should train in that openness rather than solidifying our reference points.

The advantages of not relying so much on gender as a reference point were forcefully brought home to me recently while sitting in a meeting concerned with promoting proper sensitivity to gay men, lesbians, bisexuals, and transgendered people. I became somewhat impatient as I realized that if we weren't so used to seeing people first and foremost in terms of their gender and then assuming certain behaviors on that basis, sexual orientation wouldn't even be an issue. Things could be so much simpler. I have also been corresponding repeatedly with people who do not use titles and whose names do not indicate their gender to me. It is an instructive exercise in how little we actually need to know a person's gender in order to interact with that person. It occurred to me that the only occasion on which gender might be absolutely relevant is when someone who is not bisexual is seeking a sexual encounter.

Instead, we are constantly bombarded with information highlighting people's genders, and in the case of women, also sexualizing them to an extreme degree. It is ironic that at the same time as women's work lives are less dictated by conventional gender roles, they are dressed at work in ways that show off their sexual wares to an extreme that men would never tolerate for themselves. Short, tight-fitting outfits seem almost as essential to the successful woman as her skills, especially as she is portrayed by the media. It does not seem appropriate for men to be able to wear nonsexu-ally revealing formal attire to play in a symphony orchestra, for example, while the women playing violins next to them have their upper bodies on display. The same is true of business meetings or proceedings in a court of law. Such attire is problematic, not only because it blatantly advertises one's gender, but even more so because of the extreme degree to which it sexualizes women. We simply do not need that much information about each other's gender and sexuality to live successfully in the relative world. Constantly being bombarded with extraneous information about gender and with sexually provocative attire makes it far more difficult to remem-ber that unfettered mind is beyond gender.

But if mind is truly beyond gender, why make such a fuss about gender? That is an argument I have often heard, usually from those who do not favor changes in liturgies or institutions that would make them more gender-inclusive, gender-free, and gender-neutral. The issue of gender is rather like the issue of self or ego in Buddhism. We are in the paradoxical situation of being burdened by our attachment to self at the same time as we know that the burdensome self has no inherent exis-tence of its own. But how do we dismantle that self? Not by ignoring it and pretending it does not exist, but by studying it very carefully. Very few people would figure out that cherishing the nonexistent self is the cause of all suffering without being instructed in that knowledge, without studying the Buddhist view that makes such a conclusion inevitable and without significant practice of meditation and contemplation. To be able to forget the self, it is first necessary to study the self, as Dogen said. "To study the Buddha way is to study the self. To study the self is to forget the self."[4] But what good does it do to try to forget the self if one is always remembering gender? Indeed, I would claim it is impossible to truly forget the self unless one also truly forgets gender. Unfortunately, gender seems to be more remembered than forgotten in much Buddhist practice. So what does that say about truly forgetting the self?

Truly forgetting gender requires studying gender intensely rather than willfully ignoring existent gender practices that cause suffering while claiming that gender doesn't matter. Because gender discriminations can and have caused so much suffering, we must study very carefully whether we are still caught up in fixed or rigid beliefs about gender despite our Buddhist outlook. As we have inherited ego-clinging by virtue of our karma of ceaseless habitual patterns, so we have inherited strong attachment to notions of gender. As we need to overcome our attachment to ego, so we need to overcome our attachment to gender. We should not fall prey to the common practice of proclaiming, by actions or words, that there is no permanent abiding self, but that it has gender. And we do that every time discriminations based on gender in any way harm or limit any being.

To study gender involves looking at all our Buddhist practices to see if they might in fact attribute inherent existence to gender and then finding ways to correct that attribution. Sometimes we may need to remove gendered language, but in other cases it might be helpful to retain or add specific references to gender.

As an example of removing gendered language, I will recount the turmoil surrounding the translation and retranslation of a specific text. In Shambhala Buddhism, important *terma* texts composed in Tibetan by Chögyam Trungpa have been used for many years in some of the meditation programs important to that lineage.[5] They were first translated into English in the late 1970s, before the paradigm shift regarding the use of generic masculine pronouns had fully transpired. Verse after verse of this much-loved and much-used text talked about the practitioner as "he." Gender stuck out like a sore thumb all over the text; it was genuinely impossible to avoid thinking of gender when contemplating the text.

Those of us who objected to the translation were told, predictably, that we, not the translators, were the ones with the problem, that we were being overly sensitive and should not notice trivial things like pronouns. Theoretically, gender was being ignored because of its irrelevance, but in actuality, it loomed large, causing suffering and alienation until it was extensively studied. Many years and many frustrated practitioners later, it was finally conceded that the intent of the text was not to alienate and exclude half of those who tried to take the text to heart, and that if such alienation and grief were occurring regularly, it would be better to retranslate the text to be more in accord with its basic intent. The new translation, which uses the plural to replace the generic pronoun "he," reads beautifully. Gender truly can be forgotten when reading this text now. It simply does not occur to anyone to wonder about gender, to wonder whether they are truly included in the message of the text, whereas the earlier translation required the exhausting mental gymnastics of trying to forget about gender when it was glaringly present. Why it took so much effort to make such a simple and obvious change is something I will never understand. That the changes were made is evidence that if gender is studied honestly and thoroughly, eventually, it can be forgotten.

In this case, one could truly forget gender by taking out gender-specific language and replacing it with gender-inclusive language. But one does not need to remove all references to gender. Gender references can also be used to include and to comfort. I am thinking of a practice common in Tibetan Vajrayana liturgies in which certain beings, such as bodhisattvas or *yidam*s, are explicitly listed as "male and female bodhisattvas." They could just be listed without the adjectives "male" and "female," but I find this rather unusual practice quite comforting. In a world that has often left me out because of my gender, it is as if those who write liturgies want to make it crystal clear that I am not being left out. That too is a way of studying gender so as to be able to forget it.

But shortcuts, like trying to ignore the presence of gender or claiming that ignoring is the method for going beyond gender, only make things worse. It is like trying to forget the self while constantly feeding it. First we must study gender very carefully so that we can figure out how to forget it rather strengthening it further. We must always be alert that we are not attempting to forget the self while at the same time we are strengthening the hold that gender has on us, for if we do that, we will never forget the self either. I fear that it is rather easy to practice the slogan "the self does not exist but it has gender" and that it is done far more frequently than we would like to know.

CHAPTER 17

Yeshe Tsogyel

Enlightened Consort, Great Teacher,
Female Role Model

Two English translations of Yeshe Tsogyel's biography constitute an important resource for those interested in Tibetan Vajrayana Buddhism who do not read Tibetan.[1] Yeshe Tsogyel, probably Tibet's most influential and famous female religious teacher and one of the world's most significant female religious exemplars, lived in the eighth century CE. An important teacher in her own right, she was also, in her early life, the student of Padmasambhava as well as one of his principal consorts until he left Tibet. Padmasambhava is a semilegendary figure, the first great tantric master to come from India to Tibet to teach Vajrayana Buddhism.

This text is so provocative and intriguing that scholars and theologians with many interests can profitably study it, thereby enriching their reflections and their scholarship. I come to this text as a historian of religions, a feminist theologian, and a practitioner of Vajrayana Buddhism. I am primarily interested in the text as hagiography, and I will be using it in the way the hagiography traditionally functions—as inspiration to student practitioners who look to the great teachers as role models.

However, many of my concerns and conclusions are not traditional. The text is both difficult and provocative. Despite many years of the study and practice of Tibetan Buddhism, I often found the text difficult because of the inevitable Vajrayana technical language that preserves the inner secrets of the oral tradition while revealing the outer level of information. If this text is difficult for someone with some access to Vajrayana oral tradition, I do not know what it would be like for someone with little knowledge, especially practical knowledge, of Tibetan Vajrayana Buddhism. At times, when Tsogyel's various practices and initiations are described, the text may read to an outsider like the book of Leviticus. On the other hand, in terms of the sheer story line, I have never read a similar story and find it quite fascinating.

Anyone familiar with the basic mythic outline of the hero's life and with the life of Siddhirtha Gautama and other great Buddhist exemplars will immediately recognize that Tsogyel's life story manifests those patterns.[2] In addition, the biography is characterized by a strong element of the kind of sacred history typical of Tibetan historical writing. In sacred history the story is told from the point of view of enlightenment and narrates the emergence of primordially enlightened mind into phenomenal reality. Thus many events in Tsogyel's biography are told on two levels—on a "mythic" level, narrating the life of a great human religious teacher, and on the level of "sacred history," narrating how enlightenment manifested in the form of Tsogyel. These two forms of the story can seem far apart, and the "sacred history" is often based on esoteric concepts.[3]

Tsogyel's biography is divided into eight chapters. Their titles, paraphrased or quoted from Tarthang Tulku's translation, summarize her life history well. (1) "Yeshe Tsogyel sees that the time has come for her to teach and appear in the world," which narrates, on the esoteric level, the story of her conception. (2) "The arrival and manifestation of Yeshe Tsogyel in the land of Tibet," which narrates Tsogyel's exoteric human conception and birth. (3) "Yeshe Tsogyel recognizes the impermanence of all things and relies upon a teacher," which narrates Tsogyel's failed attempts to avoid conventional marriage, her suffering within conventional marriage, and her eventual union with her guru, Padmasambhava. (4) "Yeshe Tsogyel asks her teacher for instruction in the Dharma," which narrates Tsogyel's early training and her acquisition, by buying him out of slavery, of a principal consort, Arsara Sale. (5) "The manner in which Tsogyel did her practices," which narrates Tsogyel's solitary three-year practice in a cave at the snow line of a Himalayan mountain, the incredible austerity and discipline of those years, and the sexual and other fantasies that were part of her experience in those years. (6) "A summary of the auspicious signs which occurred as Yeshe Tsogyel practiced and the siddhis she manifested after achieving realization." (7) "The manner in which Yeshe Tsogyel acted to benefit sentient beings," which narrates Tsogyel's enlightened compassionate activities throughout her life. Finally, (8) "How Yeshe Tsogyel reached her goal, achieved Buddhahood and entered the expanse of all that is" (Tulku, pp. xi–xii).

Out of the wealth of her story, I have chosen to focus here on Tsogyel's relational life, especially on how her relational life intersects with her practice and her eventual achievement of enlightenment and Buddhahood. Initially, I had thought I would focus only on her relationships as consort, but I found her relationships with women so interesting that I also want to include them in my discussion.

In my reading, the single most dominant theme in the story of Tsogyel's relational life is the single-mindedness with which relationships are seen, not as ends in themselves, but as aids or detriments on the path of practice to Tsogyel's eventual realization of Buddhahood. When Tsogyel is portrayed as consort to Padmasambhava, the emphasis is on how the relationship fosters her spiritual training and development, not on their hypothetical erotic relationship or on how she meets Padmasambhava's needs. Similarly, her relationships with various other consorts foster her own spiritual development as well as theirs. They are not primarily erotic encounters to meet quasi-instinctual needs. The consort relationship develops both partners in their spirituality, which, though no different from ordinary physical existence, nevertheless pushes people beyond conventional habitual patterns into luminous awareness of the sacredness inherent in ordinary experience. Tsogyel's relationships with women were similarly oriented to practice and realization. She is seen either as the discoverer and teacher of talented female practitioners or as a sister-adept of other highly developed women. In several episodes of her biography Tsogyel and other female adepts meet, share teachings with one another, and delight in each other's dharmic company.

This overarching theme in Tsogyel's relational life is foreshadowed already in the esoteric story of her conception. "Tsogyel saw the need for beings to be instructed and manifested in the world" (Tulku, p. 13). Seen from the viewpoint of enlightenment narrated in sacred history, Tsogyel is a multilayered being. Her *Dharmakaya* manifestation is Samantabhadri—primordial Buddhahood; her *Sambhogakaya* manifestation is Vajrayogini, one of the most important *yidams* (personal, nontheistic deities) of Tibet; in the *Nirmanakaya,* the apparition-body of ordinary human form, she is Yeshe Tsogyel, eighth-century Tibetan woman, great teacher, enlightened consort (Tulku, p. 5; Dowman, p. 3).[4] Seen from the other side, this Tibetan woman who exerted herself on the path of practice and attained Buddhahood in a single lifetime man-ifests the inherent *Sambhogakaya* and *Dharmakaya* qualities of all beings and all experience. To appreciate Tsogyel's life, it is necessary to read and hear the story on many levels at once, especially on the levels of both myth and sacred history.

According to the narrative of her prehistory, Tsogyel, as a lady-merchant appeared before a previous Buddha and expressed her vow never to be reborn except to benefit beings. Eventually she became the (Hindu) Goddess Ganga, revered Shakyamuni Buddha, and the (Hindu) Goddess Sarasvati. Then, according to the text, Padmasambhava reflected, "Now is the time for the Goddess Sarasvati to manifest and help me spread the Mantrayana teachings" (Tulku, p. 12), which led to Yeshe Tsogyel's human conception and birth. At the same time, on another level, her *Sambhogakaya* level, Tsogyel is quintessentially under-stood as the speech emanation of Vajravarahi (a slightly more esoteric form of Vajrayogini). Vajravarahi, like most *guru*s and *yidam*s, takes five emanations: body, speech, mind, quality, and action. Padmasamb-hava, who "worked through appropriate and mystic consorts in order to spread the Mantrayana doctrine" (Tulku, p. 7), had consorts who were emanations of each of these five aspects of Vajravarahi. In addition, there was a sixth "essence *Dakini*," who was also an important consort, as well as "appropriate and mystic consorts more numerous than the sesame seeds it would take to fill the four walls of a house" (Tulku, p. 7). Tsogyel is the speech emanation and one of two major consorts. Some of the other consorts are important in the unfolding of Tsogyel's relational life history.

Having seen the need for Tsogyel's manifestation in the world, the *guru* and *dakini* (Padmasambhava and Tsogyel in supramundane form) meet in supramundane realms to engender Tsogyel. The story of her conception is told on two levels. On one level, "the vajra of the *Yab* joined the Lotus of the *Yum* and together they entered the state of great equanimity . . . The Great Bliss of the *Yab-Yum* penetrated everywhere in all realms of the world, and great tremors and earthquakes shook the universe. Light rays burst forth like shooting stars from the union of the *Yab* and *Yum*. The red letter 'A' came into view, and from it spiraled a garland of white vowels. The white letter 'VAM' appeared and from it spiraled a chain of red consonants. The lights and letters penetrated into the world, striking the ground . . . in Tibet" (Tulku, p. 13). Meanwhile, on another level, "One day when the Prince, my father, was twenty-five years old, while he and his queen, my mother, were enjoying the pleasures of love-making, my mother had a vision" (Dowman, p. 10). Extraordinary visions continued throughout the night for both. Nine months later the queen gave birth painlessly to a female baby with unusual abilities. Almost immediately, it was predicted that either she would become a great religious teacher or the consort of an emperor, an obvious parallel to the Buddha's life story.

Despite this extraordinary conception and birth, as is typical of many mythic biographies, the parents had absolutely no appreciation for Tsogyel's extraordinary potentialities and were concerned primarily with making a proper marriage for her. This marriage was very difficult to arrange because Tsogyel's mundane beauty aroused intense jealousy between the mundane kings. Finally her parents simply sent her away, with the edict that whatever man caught her first could have her and no one else could wage war over that event. Tsogyel's desire not to enter such a marriage was not taken into account by anyone. When captured, she resisted to the extent that her feet sank into a boulder as if it were mud, and only after being whipped "until my back was a bloody pulp" (Dowman, p. 16). did she submit. However, she kept her resolution to obtain enlightenment in a single life and escaped while her captors celebrated her capture in a drunken stupor. Living in a cave, subsisting on fruit, she was found out, and the wars over her threatened to continue. To end the turmoil, the emperor took Tsogyel as wife. The other suitors had to submit, and soon thereafter the emperor, who was eager to learn the Buddhist teachings, gave Tsogyel to the *guru* as part of his *mandala*-offering.

This turn of events suited Tsogyel perfectly, since she cared only to learn the teachings, and her *guru* was willing to teach her. However, she did not receive the full teachings at this point. Her guru consort, Padmasambhava, told her, "without a consort, a partner of skillful means, there is no way that you can experience the mysteries of Tantra. . . . So go to the valley of Nepal where there is a sixteen-year-old youth with a mole on his right breast. . . . find him and make him your ally" (Dowman, p. 44). Tsogyel found her consort, after a long, harrowing journey, but she found him in slavery and had to purchase his freedom. She did so by raising from the dead the son of an important Nepali family. They paid her with gold, which she used to purchase the freedom of her consort. Soon thereafter Tsogyel matured her practice with a three-year solitary retreat at the snow line. Well into the retreat, among the many illusions she found it necessary to experience were projections of

charming youths, handsome, with fine complexions, smelling sweetly, glowing with desire, strong and capable, young men at whom a girl need only
glance to feel excited. They would begin by addressing me respectfully, but
they soon became familiar, relating obscene stories and making lewd suggestions. Sometimes they would play games with me: gradually they would
expose their sexual organs, whispering, "Would you like this, sweetheart?"
and "Would you like to milk me, darling?" . . . all the time . . . trying all
kinds of seductive foreplay. Overcome by the splendour of my *samadhi*,
some of them vanished immediately; some I reduced to petty frauds by
insight into all appearances as illusion. (Dowman, p. 78)

However, during later stages of her practice, Tsogyel practiced "the last
austerity practiced for my own benefit. . . . The austerity of the 'seed-
essence of coincident Pleasure and Emptiness'" (Dowman, p. 85) with
three consorts, including the redeemed slave. Very soon after completing this practice, she returned to her guru Padmasambhava. He praised
her dharmic accomplishments lavishly and extensively:

O *yogini* who has mastered the Tantra,
The human body is the basis of the accomplishment of wisdom
And the gross bodies of men and women are equally suited.
But if a woman has strong aspiration, she has higher potential.

(Dowman, p. 86)

After this point the narrative focuses more on Tsogyel's accomplishments and her activities to benefit others, though she continues further
advanced practices as well. Immediately after Padmasambhava had
praised her accomplishments and made the above comments about
female practitioners, he suggested that she find a certain youth who
would be her consort in the Yoga of Immortality Practice. She replied
that she also wanted the initiation of Vajrakilaya or Dorje Phurba, the
Remover of Obstacles, specifically because of obstacles from the outside
world that she, a woman, faced. She complains that women incur everyone's hostility, no matter what they do. "The lot of a woman on the path
is a miserable one. To maintain our practice is virtually impossible, and
even to stay alive is very difficult" (Dowman, p. 89). After receiving the
Vajrakilaya initiation, she quickly found the required new consort and
together they quickly "achieved identity with Dorje Phurba, . . . had a
vision of the deities of Phurba's *mandala* and gained Phurba's siddhi"
(Dowman, p. 92).

We are now at the last two chapters of Tsogyel's biography concerning her activities in "establishing, spreading, and perpetuating the teaching" and her "fruition and Buddhahood." She gains innumerable

disciples, both female and male, and brings many of them to high levels of realization. She also leaves many *terma* texts in various places to be rediscovered later, when the time is ripe.[5] These activities occurred both while she was with Padmasambhava and after his departure, when she remained behind, "because of her superiority to work for the welfare of beings and to fill the earth with the Guru's teaching" (Dowman, p. 125).

After Padmasambhava's death, Tsogyel performed her final austerity, "the exchange of my karma for that of others"[6] in which she took on or worked with the extreme sufferings of others. She extricated from hell an official who previously had given her extreme trouble. She says, "I gave my body to ravenous carnivores, I fed the hungry, I clothed the destitute and cold, I gave medicine to the sick, I gave wealth to the poverty stricken, I gave refuge to the forlorn and I gave my sexual parts to the lustful. In short, to benefit others I gave my body and life" (Dowman, p. 135). In this phase of her practice, two especially difficult challenges came to her. She chose to accept both of them without being coerced in any way. She gave her body parts to another person to be used in a transplant operation. She also lived as wife with an extremely repulsive, diseased man who cried out for companionship.

After these accomplishments Tsogyel began to manifest throughout the universe in different forms, satisfying whatever were people's needs—food, wealth, clothing, and the like. "To the childless I appeared as sons or daughters, bringing them happiness; to men desiring women I appeared as attractive girls, bringing them happiness; to women desiring husbands I appeared as handsome men, bringing them happiness" (Dowman, p. 146). The list continues, dealing with those afflicted by anxiety and frustration, those wandering in the *bardo*, in short to those in every difficult situation.[7] She explains: "In short wheresoever is sentient life, there are the five elements; wheresoever are the five elements there is space; insofar as my compassion is coextensive with space, it pervades all human emotion. Appearing first as one emanation and then as another, I remained . . . for twelve years" (Dowman, p. 147).

Immediately thereupon the narrative concludes with Tsogyel's death. Yeshe Tsogyel "composed [her] self in the *samadhi* that brings all things to extinction" (Dowman, p. 150). In a long concluding narrative, her students ask for further teachings and receive final teachings and predictions. "With this farewell she ended, and light, shimmering, sparkling iridescently in splendid vivid colours, streamed towards the South-West and vanished from sight. All of us who witnessed this final departure prostrated countless times after her. . . . Then our minds full

of grief, our hearts heavy, our stomachs in our mouths, our tears flood-
ing the path, staggering, unable to control our bodies, panting and heav-
ing, we retreated to the meditation cave . . . where we spent the night"
(Dowman, p. 186).

Before going on to comment on these facets of her story, I want to
briefly narrate several more incidents exemplifying other variants of the
relational theme.

Not all of Yeshe Tsogyel's relationships with men are "positive," at
least in the conventional sense. What is notable about these episodes is
the way they are turned into dharmic events by Tsogyel, promoting
either her own practice or the realization of her very tormentors. The
first negative episode involves her attempts to avoid conventional marriage and the cruel treatment she receives from her captors. But she
transforms this into her first lesson in basic dharma, concerning the pervasiveness of suffering and impermanence. A predharmic initiatory
ordeal necessary to motivate one toward the path of dharmic practice
and an important event in any Buddhist biography. After she meets
Padmasambhava she says,

> I am young, but not inexperienced
> For suffering was revealed to me at the age of twelve
> When my parents denied me my request for celibacy
> And gave me as a bride in a lay marriage.
>
> (Dowman, p. 26)

And he replies, confirming her assessment of her experience.

> You, a woman of sixteen years
> Have seen the suffering of an eighty-year-old hag.
> Know your pain to be age-old karma,
> And that the residue of that karma is erased.
>
> (Dowman, p. 26)

Because of this coincidence of her suffering and her meeting the teacher,
Tsogyel is able to hear and practice Buddhism and the Vajrayana. Two
other events stand out. While on her journey to the Nepal valley to find
her consort Atsara Sale, seven thieves sought unsuccessfully to steal her
gold (Dowman, p. 44). Many years later, after completing most of her
practices, including the Vajrakilaya practice for removing obstacles, she
was robbed and raped by seven bandits (Dowman, pp. 118–19). In both
cases, her speech to her tormentors converted them to the path of
dharma and transmuted their energies from their previously aggressive
and unenlightened expression to dharmic, enlightened pursuits. In all

fourteen cases the formerly depraved men became her students when she unlocked for them some insights into the sources of their destructive energies and how to work with those energies more effectively. I find these examples quite provocative and challenging.

Finally, in terms of biographical episodes, I want to present a few examples of Tsogyel's relationships with women. In the narrative, she has many, many women students, of whom a few stand out. One of them was thirteen when she began to bring offerings to Tsogyel during Tsogyel's three-year retreat. Tsogyel asked the girl's father, a Bhutanese king, to allow the girl to accompany her, which he agreed to do. The girl, named Tashi Chidren, became the Activity Emanation of Vajravarahi and one of Padmasambhava's six main consorts. She was with Tsogyel until the end, one of her eleven root disciples. Another of Tsogyel's eleven root disciples, with her until the end, was Kalasiddhi, who became Tsogyel's disciple much later. She also was recognized as an emanation of Vajravarahi, the Quality Emanation, and became one of the six major consorts. Among the eleven root disciples are also two other women, one of the queens, Liza Jangchub Dronma, and Shelkar Dorje Tsomo. (Incidentally, faithful Atsara Sale, the redeemed slave, was also there at Tsogyel's death.)

More extended discussions of Tsogyel's companionship with the other two women, who are major emanations of Vajravarahi, are given. Early in her practice, just after meeting Atsara Sale, they go to visit Sakya Dema, the Mind Emanation of Vajravarahi. At that point Sakya Dema is probably more accomplished than Tsogyel, who asks Sakya Dema for teachings. Sakya Dema then asks Tsogyel to give her any teachings she can pass on. The two women also acknowledge each other as consorts of the *guru*. "Then our finite minds united in the Buddha's mind and we exchanged precepts and instructions" (Dowman, p. 56). Near the end of her life, in the last story narrated before Tsogyel's last instructions and prophecies, "the flower Mandarava came from India. Emerging from the sky with her six disciples, she greeted me. She stayed with me for thirty-nine human days and we exchanged and tightened our precepts, making endless discussions on the dharma" (Dowman, p. 147). Mandarava was the Body Emanation of Vajravarahi and the major consort of Padmasambhava in India. The two women exchanged advanced teachings with each other and wrote encomiums to one another. Both expressed their unity with one another and resolved to work to enlighten all sentient beings. Mandarava ends her poem to Tsogyel thus:

> May I be one with you, Mistress of Powerful Magic.
> Hereafter, purity suffusing the sphere of purity

In your field of lotus-light,
You and I will project emanations of Buddha's karma
As light-forms of Guru Pema Skull-Garland's compassion:
May we empty the depths of the three realms of samsara.

(Dowman, p. 150)

To conclude the condensation of Tsogyel's relational biography, I quote a passage describing her essential relationship with Padmasambhava, her root *guru* and her consort. "The Guru and Dakini, mystic partners, having identical ambitions, serve all beings with skillful means and perfect insight; with the same activity of speech we expound sutras and tantras; with the same apparitional projections we control the phenomenal world; with the same knowledge and talents we work for the good of the teaching and all living beings; with the same karmic activity we utilize the four karmas of transformation at will. Ultimately Pema Jungne and Yeshe Tsogyel are identical to [*Yab-Yum* of the Absolute (Tulku, p. 145)]: our Body, Speech, Mind, Activity, and Quality are coextensive with all-pervasive space" (Dowman, pp. 122–24).

This account of Tsogyel's relationships is haunting, provocative, and appealing to me. I know of no similar story of a woman whose relational life and spiritual journey are so intertwined and support each other so thoroughly. I would like to sort out several themes important to that assessment.

First, a sharp differentiation exists between conventional relationships and dharmic relationships, relationships between *sangha* members on the path. Tsogyel bitterly fights against conventional marriage and suffers greatly within it. Many other times, including the two encounters with thieves discussed earlier, she encounters aggression, violence, and attempts to restrain her from her spiritual practice by malicious or misguided outsiders. These attacks are based on the neurotic passions or *klesa*s, rather than on the enlightened passions, or on mindfulness practice and compassion. Tsogyel, because of her high spiritual attainments, provides a model in working skillfully with these situations and transforming difficult circumstances into spiritual practice, both for herself and often for her tormentors as well. Bringing such difficulties into one's spiritual practice rather than merely launching into an outburst of neurotic passion is a very important practice and skill in Vajrayana Buddhism.

Dharmic relationships are different. Not based on neurotic or unenlightened passions, they are neither mutually exploitative nor exploitative of one or the other of the partners. Regardless of who is the leading or

more developed partner, the relationship serves to develop both partners more fully, to mature them both in spiritual practice. Though one
partner may be the more advanced practitioner, that person's practice
still needs the support of the less developed consort. Tsogyel's consorts
are often referred to as her "supports," as are Padmasambhava's consorts. Furthermore, these roles are not gender-fixed; they depend on
levels of development. Padmasambhava is Tsogyel's guru; she is his consort during periods of training. But she is also guru to both female and
male students; some of the male students are also her consorts, supporting her practice. In the long run, Vajrayana Buddhism presents a
balance of feminine and masculine energy, both on the ultimate level
and on the empirical level.[8] During the period of development and training to achieve that ultimate balance, sometimes the leading role is taken
by a man, sometimes by a woman. When such status or authority is
devoted to enlightening all beings rather than to aggrandizing one's own
position, exploitation cannot happen. Thus the power plays so common
in conventional relationships are not present in Tsogyel's dharmic relationships. And the neurotically compulsive insanity that so often
plagues relationships is not part of Tsogyel's relationships with her
dharmic consorts and friends.

This rather different quality of relationship comes through especially
clearly in the unconventional and nonpossessive conduct of the relationships. Though Tsogyel is Padmasambhava's consort, much of the
time she is not with him. Often she is doing solitary practice or is practicing with her other consorts. When she is with him, the narrative concerns the practices they did together and their activities to teach and
spread the dharma. Tsogyel's other consorts became Padmasambhava's
students and attendants; her female students sometimes become
Padmasambhava's consorts. Various combinations of these dharmic
friends often travel and practice together. Furthermore, Tsogyel's most
vibrant encounters with women occur with Padmasambhava's other
major consorts, Sakya Dema and Mandarava, her equals on the path.

An aspect of this nonpossessive and nonneurotic mode of relation-
ship involves the way sexuality is integrated into these relationships.
They are not primarily erotic encounters; they are primarily dharmic
encounters to which there seems to be a sexual aspect. In fact, the sexual
level of these relationships is so much not the focus of the narrative that
I bring up the topic at all only because of stereotypes about the
Vajrayana and the importance of consorts in some aspects of Vajrayana
Buddhism. This is not because Tsogyel's sexuality is ignored or

repressed; working out an enlightened version of her sexuality was apparently an important part of Tsogyel's training during her retreat. In that narrative her sexual fantasies—still based somewhat on wanting-ness, desire, and ego orientation—are dealt with very explicitly. I found the passage quite interesting, both because it reverses the more usual motif of women tempting men, and because, as far as I know, spiritual biographies of women usually do not portray the women as having strong sexual desires themselves, but mainly as having to fend off the lust of men.

It is interesting that the most explicit discussion of Tsogyel's sexuality involves her inner world. As many feminists have pointed out, such an inner life is usually based on rejecting aspects of one's own psyche, which are then projected onto others, turning them into objects. Those objects then become, in terms of Buddhist psychology, the objects of desire, grasping, and fixation, and the whole cycle of samsaric suffering is kept spinning. When Tsogyel has integrated her psyche, has become more realized, men are not such objects of grasping and fixation. Then all aspects of experience, including sexuality, are in proper relationship with one another, a situation which cannot happen when sexuality is an end in itself, engaged in with an ego-orientation of self-gratification and clinging. When sexuality no longer involves a process of objectification, it does not demand special comment or description. Tsogyel's integra-tion of spirituality and sexuality provides an important paradigm for understanding the proper connection between relationship and dharma practice. This topic is important for contemporary women, because dharma, in the extended sense of concern for truth and social service, is often difficult for women to integrate with their conventional role expec-tations and their natural longing for companionship.

What is the connection between relationship and spiritual or intel-lectual discipline? Which one is or should be the leading element in one's life? Which one promotes which? What mishandling or unbalanc-ing of the two would cause destruction of one or both? These are impor-tant questions, especially because so frequently relationship is the most difficult and frustrating arena of life, much more so than one's liveli-hood, profession, or spiritual practice. This occurs because of unbal-anced priorities and unrealistic expectations of relationship as the solution to existential anxiety and suffering. What Tsogyel's relational biography shows is that relationships carried on in the context of a spir-itual discipline can dissolve clinging, grasping, and fixation and need not involve the anxiety, neurotic passion, and jealousy of conventional relationships. So often in conventional relationships, expectations, needs, and neurotic passions cause the relationship to increase rather than to ease suffering. The only way out of this situation is to dissolve the unrealistic expectations surrounding the relationship. These ego-fixations and ego-orientations dissolve through spiritual discipline. Tsogyel's "vision-quest" all her life was to dissolve the confusion and clinging in her mind, not to find the relationship that would make her feel better.[9] Her biography demonstrates a proper balance or prioritization of relationship and spiritual practice. She seeks enlightenment and gains both enlightenment and enlightened relationships.

In her ability to integrate enlightenment with enlightened relationships, Tsogyel provides a provocative, challenging, and untypical model for women and companions of women. Tsogyel, in her relational life, is consort, not wife and not nun. In order to undo the fixations of conventional relationships, it is not necessary for her to renounce relationship. The way she combines relationship and dharmic achievements presents a significant model, in my view. As consort, she provides an unusual model, contrasting with the much more typical Buddhist roles for women as either wife or nun. The consort model, as exemplified by Tsogyel, is very inspiring despite its rarity and unconventionality, particularly for contemporary women whose vision-quest is enlightenment and dharmic service. In many ways, this model is much more workable than either of the conventional models—wife or nun. Conventionally, at least in patriarchal societies (and all Buddhist societies have been patriarchal), wives are essentially servants to their husbands and children. It is not a role that fundamentally promotes realization, though many women manage to circumvent the liabilities of the role. On the other hand, male companionship, heterosexual experience, and the presence of male energy are important to some women as a component of the total path of spiritual discipline they tread. The nun role, despite its liberating potential, does not allow this kind of male companionship. Tsogyel as consort, though unusual in the repertoire of roles for women found in Buddhist literature, is inspiring to contemporary women and is worthy of emulation.

Particularly noteworthy and exemplary about Tsogyel's role as consort are the nonmonogamous and nonpossessive nature of her relationships, combined with her ability to be a companion to her consorts while not losing her vision of her own reason to live—enlightenment and service. This model is inspiring and comforting to women; it is also challenging to companions of women. Not only are women called upon and challenged to become a Yeshe Tsogyel; their companions are challenged to become a Padmasambhava, willing to engage in an intense relationship with a woman without the safety of monogamy, on either her part or his, or the subservience of the wife-role in patriarchal society.

Tsogyel's and Padmasambhava's essential complementarity and equality also provide a model of female-male relationship far more appropriate than the conventional patriarchal model of male superiority or the separatist and female supremacist version of current feminist theory. I began this study of Tsogyel's biography curious about whether her story indicated the existence of any traits, qualifications, or dilemmas that are intrinsic to women on the spiritual path and not shared by men. To answer this question adequately it would be necessary to compare Tsogyel's biography carefully with other biographies in the same genre.[10] Because I have not yet conducted this study to my satisfaction, my speculations are preliminary and subject to change.

However, at this point, my conclusion is that Tsogyel's biography, compared with biographies of other similar spiritual heroes in Vajrayana Buddhism, does not point to essential, basic differences based on gender that affect or enhance one's spiritual practice, though some more superficial differences probably occur.

Two statements, one from Padmasambhava and one from Tsogyel, on this question are found almost side by side. Both have already been referred to. After Tsogyel's completion of her three-year retreat her guru says,

> The human body is the basis of the accomplishment of wisdom
> And the gross bodies of men and women are equally suited
> But if a woman has strong aspiration, she has the higher potential.
>
> (Dowman, p. 86)

A few paragraphs later, Tsogyel complains: "Inadequate women like me with little energy and an inferior birth incur the whole world's hostility. When we go begging the dogs are hostile. If we possess food or wealth then thieves molest us. If we are attractive we are bothered by fornicators. If we work hard the country people are hostile. Even if we do nothing at all the tongues of malicious gossips turn against us. If our attitude is improper then the whole world is hostile. Whatever we do the life of a woman on the path is a miserable one. To maintain our practice is virtually impossible and even to stay alive is very difficult" (Dowman, p. 89). Probably Tsogyel is exaggerating because she is making her case to receive the Vajrakilaya—Remover of Obstacles—practice. The more obstacles, the more need for the practice, because in Vajrayana Buddhism one must always justify receiving a new practice rather than demanding it or simply beginning to do it.

It is interesting that both Tsogyel and Padmasambhava attribute the better situation to the other sex, though Padmasambhava does not dwell on the difficulties of the male role. Such cross-sex curiosity and jealousy is actually very common in the literatures of many disciplines and cultures. Such comments probably indicate that everyone recognizes superficial differences between women and men and one often feels that she or he is missing something. Superficially, whichever sex one is, there are some disadvantages and some advantages, and one is missing something because one can be only one sex.

Nevertheless, spiritual biographies like Tsogyel's seem to me to emphasize that these differences are rather unimportant on any absolute or ultimate level, though certain ways of giving social form to these differences can be completely unjustifiable and cruel. On the path of spiritual discipline, women and men face the same essential difficulties of overcoming conventional lifestyles. Men too must often circumvent parental pressure to marry and continue the family enterprise. They must equally overcome neurotic passions such as aggression, ignorance, clinging, pride, or jealousy.[11] They equally experience discouragement, resistance, and many other such obstacles intrinsic to spiritual practice. The portrayals of enlightened, compassionate activity also betray no essentially different activities. Both teach, debate, discover students, give initiations, practice, edit and compose texts, and travel about the country giving whatever help is needed. And there is no evidence that the enlightened state of mind, the mind of Buddha, is different in a male than a female body. In fact, it is self-contradictory to imagine that One Mind could be different in different bodies—leading to the common statement that Enlightenment occurs neither in a male body nor in a female body. Gender is not a category that is of ultimate significance.

This conclusion, if correct, is important, since not only does it contradict conventional patriarchal thought, including those strands of Buddhist thought which state that womanhood is an inferior birth,[12] but also it counters some currents in contemporary feminist thought, which posit an intrinsic female superiority based on female body experience, states of mind, or both.[13] This separatist feminist train of thought has been produced by an overevaluation of the relative uniqueness of women's experiences. The conventional generic masculine, which sometimes treated women as men and sometimes as nonexistent, is certainly inaccurate; therefore all the literature exploring women's experiences is a needed corrective.[14] However, this correction does not require a conclusion of innate essential differences between women and men, with its consequent claims for the intrinsic moral superiority of women. Recognizing and exorcising the evils of patriarchy does not depend on defining women as innately and essentially biophilic while men are necrophilic.[15] In fact, this conclusion and the essential impetus of feminism toward an enlightened society are incompatible with each other.[16] If the sexes are that innately different, if sexual and moral dualisms are that deep, there is no hope for humanity and it makes little difference which gender is theorized to have the "right" or "better" attitudes and values. If roughly half the human species were unhuman, lacking in basic goodness, how would we ever achieve an enlightened society?

My conclusion, of course, raises as many questions as it answers. If women and men are not so different, why have sex roles and gender stereotypes been so dominant, and so often so patriarchal and advantageous to men? In this context, I do not wish to explore historical and cross-cultural answers to that question, but to bring the question back to Tsogyel's biography and to Tsogyel as role model. Is Tsogyel a token, so rare as to be worthless as a role model? Worse, is Tsogyel's experience so much like that of other great spiritual models, many of whom are men, because essentially she is one of the few women who made it in a male system and is a male-identified woman?

A positive answer to the latter question would, I believe, depend on a prior philosophy of feminism with which I do not agree. Therefore, I would not interpret Tsogyel as a male-identified woman. The former question, about Tsogyel as token because of the imbalance between numbers of women and men of her caliber is much more significant, disturbing, and provocative. If women and men are equally suited for enlightenment, why are there so few women like Tsogyel, especially considering the numbers of men like her?

Actually, for the time and place described in the text, I was surprised to have the opposite reaction: there were a lot of women like her! Four of her eleven root disciples were women, and the text constantly narrates her interactions with female students, both laywomen and nuns. Things seem to have become more male-dominated later. We may be seeing another of the "first generation phenomena," so familiar to women's studies.[17]

Actually, when we ask whether Tsogyel can be a role model because there are so few women like her in her time and place, we are not asking whether Tsogyel can be a role model, but whether Tsogyel's society can be a model society. The presumed negative answer may be depressing in some ways, but it is not determinative of anything and should not be given too much importance. "There are no fully adequate models in the past" has become a slogan for feminism. That slogan has been used to liberate from past authority; it has also been used as an expression of poverty mentality or frustration with the past. I suggest instead that "there could be no fully adequate models in the past." I would argue that technological conditions prohibited fully adequate models in the past. But on a deeper level, an adequate model in the past would be useless if not realized and actualized in the present. It would even cease to be a model if it were only past; it would become a memory or a dogma. But if one is seeking to realize and actualize the present moment, the present situation, then one has an adequate model somewhere, somehow. Models are much more our inspiration than they are something that once existed separately from us.

Still, the "numbers question" has troubled me for many years and has been my most serious misgiving about and feminist criticism of Buddhism. I have questioned where in Buddhist thought or institutions would lie explanations for this disparity in numbers. It is not found in the basic and essential Buddhist thought or worldview, which is profoundly nondualist and therefore nonmisogynist. A genderized deity, gender hierarchy, and hierarchical dualism simply are not characteristic of core Buddhadharma, at least as expressed in the Mahayana and the Vajrayana; therefore, the feminist Buddhist critique requires different categories of explanation than does the feminist Christian critique. Currently, I am exploring an explanatory nexus of institutions, karma, and social reform, both to explain the past and as a wedge for a contemporary challenge to change. Briefly put, though the Buddhist worldview is exemplary, classical Buddhist institutions are not. Furthermore, I am suggesting that a certain interpretation of the notion of karma prevented the rise of social criticism and social reform as a dominant Buddhist issue. (This is, I believe, a subtly mistaken view of karma, but it is impossible to discuss the issue fully in this context.) Therefore, Buddhists did not notice the contradiction between their nonmisogynist worldview and their patriarchal institutions. Rather, they explained that everyone's situation, including women's relative difficulties, and even their female gender, was due to their karma.

Under then prevailing conditions, empirically, women's lives were harder than men's and, empirically, it was more difficult for women to study and practice formally. That much was conceded, even appreciated. Unfortunately, these difficulties were then explained as due to the karma of the beings currently reborn as women, rather than to social institutions in need of reform. Given the severe demands of intensive agriculture, high infant mortality rates, limited life expectancy, and lack of birth control, it may have seemed more reasonable to attribute the harshness of women's lives to karma than to imagine that humans could control or change those conditions. However, those conditions do not prevail today; therefore, the institutionalized social roles and life plans that coped with those conditions are out of date. The karma of women's lives has changed drastically, and there are no adequate models in the past. Thus, rather than discouraging social criticism and social reform, an understanding of karma promotes them. Institutions must change in order to accommodate the drastically changed possibilities of women's lives. There are no adequate models in the past, including Tsogyel's society. But Tsogyel herself, enlightened consort and great teacher, remains a wonderfully inspiring female role model.

CHAPTER 18

Buddhist Women and Teaching Authority

The primary feminist criticism of Buddhism is that most often, dharma teachers are men. Feminists have responded with two solutions to this problem. One obvious solution would be to make structural changes to ensure that women are trained as teachers, and then to make sure that women are promoted as teachers. Other feminists have proposed a different solution, stating that giving dharma teachers any real authority is itself a patriarchal practice which cannot be redeemed by encouraging women to become dharma teachers.

Many Westerners are deeply suspicious of the authority a Vajrayana or Zen dharma teacher has over his or her students. Especially after scandals involving abuses of power that rocked North American Buddhism in the 1980s, suspicions about unlimited teaching authority increased. Nevertheless, from the point of view of Buddhist practice, there are limits as to how egalitarian and democratic Buddhism can become. While power has been and can be abused, some aspects of Buddhist life *do* require the authority of a lineage and a teacher. It is important to sort out which issues can be decided by group consensus and which aspects of Buddhist life cannot be subjected to majority rule.

It is dangerous for people who do not understand Buddhist teachings well and who have not practiced for many years to decide what should be taught or what meditation technique to use. Many fundamental Buddhist teachings, such as the Four Noble Truths or Egolessness, go so much against the grain of people's ordinary hopes and fears that they would never be the result of a popular vote, which is why democracy is a poor tool for deciding what should be taught at a Buddhist dharma center. Authoritative teachers are unlikely to become unnecessary in genuine Buddhism any time soon.

On the other hand, the authority of dharma teachers pertains to dharma, to the teachings and practices of Buddhism, not to a *sangha's* institutional life, which can be decided by the community. Even though dharma teachers have spiritual authority, they must be subject to judgment by the community if they engage in inappropriate behavior, such as sexual misconduct, misappropriation of funds, or other undharmic conduct.

Because dharma teaching is so important in Buddhism, the acid test for whether Buddhism has overcome its male-dominant heritage is the frequency with which women become dharma teachers. There is no logical reason why about half the dharma teachers should not be women. That historically men nevertheless have monopolized teaching roles can be traced to two factors: (1) the male-dominated cultures in which Buddhism was founded and in which it has always been practiced, and (2) some of the rules of Buddhist institutional life.

Some people think that this historical generalization is no longer relevant because of the visibility and popularity of some North American women dharma teachers, such as Pema Chodron, and the fact that many North American women are senior teachers. Buddhism, however, is a much larger and longer-lived phenomenon than Western convert Buddhism, and those historical norms are still widespread in much of the Buddhist world. Even among North American Buddhists, a disproportionate percentage of the most respected and authoritative teachers are men, especially among those who follow various forms of Tibetan Buddhism. This claim can readily be verified by looking at teachers' ads in North American Buddhist publications. In a recent issue of *Buddhadharma,* thirteen teachers were pictured in ads for dharma programs they were leading; twelve of them were men. The *Shambhala Sun* ads pictured nineteen male teachers and no female teachers. In *Tricycle,* the ratio was fifteen male teachers to two women teachers. That magazine was advertising its own "Tele-Teachings" series, featuring six male teachers and one female teacher. North American Buddhists tout the fact that roughly half of the people teaching at most dharma centers are women. Nevertheless, a phenomenon I have long observed still prevails. Within the hierarchy of those who have teaching titles and authority, men dominate at the top ranks while women often do most of the teaching at the lower ranks. Given these facts, premature self-congratulations and denial of the relevance of the issue of female teachers are probably unwarranted. Instead, we should question more deeply why women teachers are so important, what institutional forms promote or discourage their presence, and what about the contemporary situation, at least for North Americans, could promote an actual presence of women teachers that would be more in accord with dharma than are the historical precedents.

Some modern people are truly mystified about why the Buddha seemingly concurred with the male dominance of his culture, but there is little question that he did, or least that he is portrayed as having done so in stories told about him that became authoritative. Historical records, which may or may not go back to the Buddha himself, not only portray the Buddha as concurring with the male dominance of the times but also as initiating rules that ensured male dominance in his *sangha* and made it difficult for women to attain the status of a major dharma teacher. Monastic rules declare that all nuns are junior to even the most recently ordained monk. (Laypeople, of course, are junior to monastics.) It is recorded that when Prajapati, the first nun, suggested that seniority should be reckoned by how long one has been ordained, not by one's gender, the Buddha replied that even in sects with poor leadership, men never regarded women as their superiors, so how could such behavior occur in his *sangha?*

Some have argued that women are not harmed if they do not become dharma teachers, so long as women receive the same training as men. Such commentators claim that the point of Buddhism is to practice meditation and to attain enlightenment, not to attain a prestigious reputation as a teacher. Some have even argued that institutional male dominance actually benefits women. With no hope of attaining status and fame as a dharma teacher, women are free to practice sincerely and well, unencumbered by the eight worldly concerns. Men, by contrast, it is claimed, often take up monastic life as a career path and become more concerned about their prestige and position than about their practice and attainment, which perverts the purpose of Buddhist study and practice. But if things really worked out this way, women should definitely be the dharma teachers because their attainments would be more genuine!

I argue that institutional arrangements, dominant in most Buddhist cultures for most of Buddhist history, that make it difficult, if not impossible, for women to become highly respected dharma teachers *do* harm women, in at least five ways. Additionally, in most Buddhist cultures, the path to teaching authority lies in monastic institutions; thus, if women's path to monastic life is blocked, as was the case in many forms of Asian Buddhism, women usually will not become teachers.

First, there is sheer practicality. It has been argued that even though nuns' hierarchal subordination to monks does not limit their practice and attainment, nevertheless, that subordination may well explain the demise of the nuns' order in many parts of the Buddhist world. The immediate cause of the decline of the nuns' order was economic; nuns simply didn't receive much economic support, which made it difficult for them to survive. Because throughout the traditional Buddhist world, the merit earned by making donations is thought to be dependent on the worth of the recipient, lay donors prefer to support the most prestigious teachers—all of whom, because of monastic rules regarding seniority, were monks. Even an excellent woman teacher simply could not gain the same kind of following a monk would have, given that she would still be regarded as inferior to monks and, in most cases, would not be allowed to teach monks. Consequently, she would attract less economic support for herself and her nunnery. This was a large part of the downward spiral that doomed the nuns' order in some parts of the Buddhist world.

Second, when combined with cultural beliefs about women's intellectual and spiritual inferiority, the fact that women were not going to be dharma teachers anyway led to the view that women didn't really even need to receive much training. For example, Tibetan Buddhist nuns were usually not taught philosophy and debate, or how to draw sand mandalas, on the grounds that they wouldn't be using those skills anyway. Recently, Tibetan nuns have received training in such skills, but I know of no instance of women being taught the so-called lama dances for which Tibetan Buddhism is so famous. This logic for not even teaching women represents not a downward spiral but a vicious circle. Because women are thought to be intellectually and spiritually inferior, it is said that they don't need to be trained. Their lack of attainments, due to their lack of training, is then used as justification for not giving women high teachings or advanced practices.

Third, given lack of economic support and the common prejudice that women—nonteachers by definition—did not need to be well educated, it is not surprising that the option to become a nun was not attractive and nuns had little prestige. A family might well be embarrassed to have a daughter become a nun, whereas when a son became a monk, he brought great honor to the family. As a result, women were often discouraged from becoming nuns or taking on serious spiritual discipline. By and large, it seems clear that most Buddhists preferred women to become wives and mothers rather than nuns, or even lay retreatants practicing solitary renunciation. This was true even in the Buddha's time. Glowing praises of generous female lay donors contrast significantly with the reluctance with which the Buddha is reported to have allowed women to become nuns. Thus, women who had a genuine spiritual vocation often found no support for their calling, a state of affairs which certainly harms women.

The fourth way the lack of women dharma teachers harms women is particularly devastating. Women practitioners have no role models. I have often been told that because the dharma is beyond gender, such issues are irrelevant. I have been told that since the dharma is the same whether it is taught by a woman or by a man, it couldn't possibly make any difference if there are no women dharma teachers. I have been told that it is trivial and undignified even to bring up such concerns. But I have replied that if the dharma is truly beyond gender, then there should be no disparity between the number of women and men teachers. I also claim that if dharma is genuinely gender-free and gender-neutral, but, nevertheless, there have been so few women teachers historically, the fault lies elsewhere. It lies with the Buddhist tendency to uncritically buy in to whatever social arrangements it finds in the surrounding culture.

It is impossible to argue that role models who look like oneself make no difference. From the point of view of absolute truth, of course, role models who look like oneself are irrelevant. But students do not begin at the level of absolute truth. We begin at a very confused level of relative truth—not even accurate relative truth, but at the level of simple mistakes, thinking that the rope is a snake, to call upon a common Buddhist teaching analogy. It is very easy to see Buddhism as a snake that is not helpful to women when most or all of the teachers are men. An intelligent and perceptive student would naturally ask if people like oneself benefit from this particular path. Is it worthwhile to become deeply involved in Buddhist study and practice if one is told that one has little chance of success because of one's gender? If these low chances of any real attainment are demonstrated daily by the lack of anyone who looks like oneself in Buddhism's most valued roles, one wonders why women should take Buddhism seriously. I certainly experienced this dilemma myself.

Regarding most other basic questions about the path, Buddhists are much less defensive and show great concern for finding the most effective skillful means for helping people see that the supposed snake is really a rope—and that the rope itself is illusory. As I have already narrated, people like myself are often reprimanded for even bringing up questions of gender. But if gender is irrelevant, the only way to demonstrate that irrelevance is the skillful means of empowering women teachers. Of course, for women to be empowered as teachers, they must first be trained completely, which is difficult when all women are defined as subordinate to any man, whatever their relative accomplishments and seniority may be.

The fifth way that making it difficult for women to become dharma teachers harms women may be the most devastating of all. If there are few or no women teachers, the experiences and viewpoints of women are forever lost to history, and the women who do achieve high levels of realization despite all the obstacles they face are obliterated in historical records. This difficulty intersects with the fourth difficulty, the lack of role models for women practitioners. The role models may well have been there, but they were not recognized and, therefore, not recorded. If women are not recognized as dharma teachers, their spiritual biographies will not be available to illuminate the path. Some Buddhist traditions rely heavily on the life stories of great teachers as inspiration for contemporary students. Stories of women dharma teachers are needed by men to counter their own culturally based feelings of superiority, and women need these biographies for inspiration.

What is the path for a woman who has been taught that her rebirth is less free and well favored than that of a man, who has few role models, and who was probably discouraged from thinking of herself as a serious practitioner? Gender may be ultimately irrelevant, but that ultimate irrelevancy is situated in a relative and samsaric world. How does she come to a realization of the irrelevance of gender, and what does her experience of conventional gender norms mean in her path? Her specific experiences as a woman in a male-dominated world and a male-dominated religion will be different from those of a man and are worth recording as a guidepost for other practitioners, both women and men. But who records the experiences of an unrecognized teacher? Because she is not recognized and her experiences are not recorded, the example of her path to realization, those specific experiences, are lost, furthering the impression that women are, indeed, less free and well favored than are men because so few of them seem to achieve much success on the path.

Sometimes the fault for losing these stories and role models lies, not with the Buddhists of a specific era, but with those who keep the records. Women may be known in their own contexts as highly competent practitioners and teachers, but no one thinks to record their teachings, as they would think to record the teachings of a similar male teacher. Or, if the records are kept, they may not be remembered as frequently as the records of male teachers. For example, highly accomplished women were relatively common in Tibetan Buddhism, but the first teachers Western students of Tibetan Buddhism heard about were all men. Western practitioners of Zen Buddhism recite daily a lineage pedigree devoid of female names—until some women painstakingly reconstructed a lineage of female dharma teachers.

Thus, we must conclude that although gender is ultimately irrelevant, until sexist and male-dominated conventions and institutional practices are eliminated from Buddhism, gender does matter in the relative world. As I have argued many times, the Buddhist view may be gender-neutral and gender-free, but Buddhist practices and institutions are not. And the view and practice should be in line with each other, not in contradiction with each other. Among the Buddhist practices that honor gender far more than it deserves to be honored, none is more devastating than the omnipresent tradition of not honoring and recognizing women as dharma teachers, which is founded on the equally devastating practice of not training women competently and completely. And that practice, of course, traces its parentage to sexist notions of female inferiority and the need for men to be ranked as superior to women in each and every case.

Because many Western Buddhists are completely unfamiliar with Buddhist history and the way Buddhists usually accepted the social practices of their cultural matrix, it is important to circulate this information more widely. There are valid reasons why so many non-Buddhists regard Buddhism as a highly patriarchal religion that is quite disadvantageous to women, and we should be familiar with our own dark side.

Although it would be unwise for Buddhists to conclude that gender inequities are a matter of history because in the recent past among Western Buddhists more women are teaching dharma, much has changed for Buddhism worldwide in the past thirty years. There is a flourishing Buddhist women's movement, and much progress has been made in reestablishing the nuns' *sangha* and in upgrading the training nuns receive. The training available to laywomen has also improved greatly, and Western Buddhism is almost entirely a lay movement at this point. Among Western Buddhists, many women have also been recognized as lineage-holding dharma teachers, more so in the Zen and Vipassana communities than among Westerners who practice Tibetan Buddhism. Most observers would claim that something unprecedented in Buddhist history is happening among Western Buddhists. If we count all teachers teaching dharma, rather than only the best-known and most-recognized Western dharma teachers, almost half the Western dharma teachers are women. This situation could represent a glass half-empty if reactions to this fact are complacency, but it would represent a glass half-full if taken as indication that appropriate changes can be made.

To what do we owe these vast changes in Buddhist practice? Certainly to the fact that they are more in line with fundamental Buddhist teachings than were traditional sexist and male-dominant practices. Understandably and justifiably, those of us who advocate greater gender equity in Buddhist practice always look to Buddhist teachings for our warrant for what we advocate, and we also look to past exemplars, such as Yeshe Tsogyel, for inspiration. If classic Buddhist teachings contradicted practices of gender equity, we would not have much of a case (and I, for one, would not be a Buddhist). However, those teachings have always been part of Buddhism, without having made a significant impact on Buddhist practices surrounding gender in the past. So something in addition to Buddhism's gender-neutral and gender-free teachings must be contributing to the current changing situation.

Western Buddhists tend not to explore the impact that their Western heritage may have had on how they practice Buddhism. But I suggest that aspects of our Western heritage are extremely valuable to our Buddhist practice and that we discard or denigrate our Western roots to our peril. Would we feel so comfortable abandoning the religions of our parents and families without Western concepts of individual choice and freedom of religion? For most of human history, in most parts of the world, such conduct would have been unthinkable and nearly impossible. We Western Buddhists sometimes tend to decry "individualism," human rights, and other ideas of the European enlightenment, or question their relevance to Buddhist practice, but without their large-scale acceptance in the society we live in, I doubt that Western Buddhism would flourish as it does.

The major thinkers of the European enlightenment did not necessarily extend their proclamations of individual liberty and dignity to women, but women quickly picked up on the cues and made the logical implications themselves. Famous early female heroes who made the case for women's equity and equality include Mary Wollstonecraft, Ann

Hutchinson, and Abigail Adams. That premier document of the European enlightenment and the charter of the United States, the U.S. Constitution, did not consider women to be citizens and did not grant to us the right to vote. But again, women quickly drew the logical conclusions. By the mid-nineteenth century, led by the Grimké sisters, Susan B. Anthony, Elizabeth Cady Stanton, and others, many were advocating that women be recognized as human beings by granting to women the same rights that were granted to men, including the right to vote. Finally, less than one hundred years ago, in 1920 the U.S. Constitution was amended to grant women the right to vote. Concern about gender equity and equality lessened after this victory and became completely dormant during the 1950s; women had been dismissed from their vital factory jobs after the end of World War II and had been sent home to have babies. The 1950s perhaps represent a nadir of awareness that women might want to have lives not bounded by the gender roles assigned to them by a patriarchal culture. As someone socialized in the 1950s, I often suggest that those of us who remember how horrible things were then need to explain why the second wave of feminism arose in the first place. By the late 1960s and in the 1970s, both women and men were again fully aware of how much conventional gender arrangements cripple women and were advocating more equitable gender arrangements. This is the environment in which Buddhist teachings first became available to North Americans of non-Asian descent on a large scale.

Though they often will not acknowledge their debts to the second wave of feminism, I would argue that most of the current leading female teachers of Buddhism owe at least part of their success to that movement. Whether or not they are personally poised to acknowledge that influence, most highly regarded contemporary North American women teachers benefited greatly from the feminist insistence that if men deserve human rights, then women equally deserve human rights. Had Asian Buddhist teachers first brought Buddhism to the West during the 1950s, when the cult of domesticity was at its height and conventional gender roles were rigidly enforced, women would have been staging bake sales rather than meditating and studying side by side with men, preparing to become teachers. Thus, apart from the milieu produced by feminism, it is unlikely that many of the most noted North American female teachers would have been prepared to teach and even more unlikely that they would have been accepted as teachers. Therefore, I suggest that at least some of the inspiration and motivation for changes in the contemporary acceptance and elevation of some Western women teachers of the dharma is the result of the second wave of feminism, which has changed everything about our lives for the better, forever.

We would do well to delight in the auspicious coincidence (*tendrel*) that brought Buddhist teachers and feminist consciousness to us at the same time. And when we trace our ancestry as practitioners, it would be accurate to thank not only our overt lineage ancestors, those whose connections we chant every day, and not only the more obscure female Buddhist ancestors whom we painstakingly research and discover, but also the generations of women and men who taught us the practical, everyday, institutional meaning of that simplest, most radical, and most accurate of feminist slogan—"women are human beings." If in waves of backlash and complacency we do not lose what we have recently gained, we may live to see the day when not only will women teach dharma, but it is just as likely that the most honored lineage holders will be women as that they will be men. At that point, Buddhism would finally be actualizing its teachings and its vision, rather perpetuating the current undharmic contradiction between gender-free and gender-neutral teachings and institutions that favor men over women.

CHAPTER 19

Is the Glass Half-Empty or Half-Full?

A Feminist Assessment of Buddhism at the Beginning of the Twenty-first Century

Even relatively casual observers of Buddhism often note that doctrinally Buddhism is free of the myths and symbols that make some other religions so intractable to feminist reforms. There is no Ultimate Reality spoken of as a male, no Ultimate Father or Male Savior; there is no myth of a rebellious female starting the world on its downward spiral. Those same observers also comment that, nevertheless, Buddhism and Roman Catholicism or Eastern Orthodoxy *look* quite similar: many men in elaborate costumes in positions of authority, with very few women to be seen. Why? What is being done about this contradiction at the heart of Buddhism?

In less than thirty years, we have gone from a situation in which almost nothing had been written about Buddhist women for many years to a situation in which books and articles appear regularly. In 1979, Diana Paul published her helpful and well-annotated collection of texts, *Women in Buddhism: Images of the Feminine in the Mahayana Tradition.*[1] In 1980, I gave my first talk (and probably *the* first talk) on Buddhism and feminism at an international conference on Buddhist-Christian dialogue, to the bemusement of some Japanese delegates who couldn't understand how there could be a feminist critique of Buddhism.[2] After all, they said, Buddhists had taken care of all those issues long ago by reassuring everyone that "deserving women would be reborn as men." In the mid-1980s, Sandy Boucher was conducting the interviews that led to her book *Turning the Wheel: American Women*

Creating the New Buddhism.[3] In 1987, Karma Lekshe Tsomo organized the first of many Sakyadhita conferences, which led to the first of many publications emanating from those conferences.[4] *Buddhism after Patriarchy: A Feminist History, Analysis, and Reconstruction of Buddhism,* the first somewhat complete feminist survey of Buddhism, was published in 1993.[5] There is now a worldwide Buddhist women's movement, many women Buddhist teachers, at least in North America, and a growing consensus that the traditional male dominance of Buddhism is a problem, though I would argue that institutional changes are still very slow.

So is the glass half-full? Are we well on the way to recasting Buddhism in ways that make it more adequate for its female followers? Perhaps, if burnout, backlash, and complacency do not take too high a toll. Is the glass half-empty? Is Buddhism still a religion that works better for men than for women, despite the changes of the past thirty years? Many coffee table picture books about Buddhism would certainly give that appearance. And certainly the glass is half-empty and leaking the rest of its contents if premature self-congratulations lead to complacency.

A colleague and friend once commented to me that in its philosophical views and it meditation practices, Buddhism has tremendous potential for deconstructing gender, but all that potential has led to very few results. In looking at the half-full, half-empty glass, I will consider three topics: first, Buddhism's potential for deconstructing gender; second, some reasons why this potential did not come to fruition historically; and third, some of the changing situations in the contemporary Buddhist world, both Asian and Western.

TARA'S VOW: GENDER AND DHARMA IN BUDDHISM

One of my favorite stories for illustrating many of the points that need to be made when discussing Buddhism and gender are found in a seventeenth-century Tibetan text that narrates how Tara, one of the favorite Tibetan female meditation deities, came into existence. Like all the exalted beings in Buddhist mythological universes, she was at one time a human being engaged in the same meditation practices we do. After much practice, she finally experienced awakened mind. The monks around her suggested that she could (and should) now take on a male rebirth. Instead of doing so, she told them, "In this life, there is no such distinction as 'male' and 'female' . . . and therefore, attachment to ideas of 'male' and 'female' is quite worthless. Weak-minded worldlings are always deluded by this." She then vowed to take female form continuously through her long career as an advanced Bodhisattva, what some would call a female Buddha.[6]

This story illustrates all the issues. The distinctions, the labels "male" and "female," are declared to be quite worthless. They are declared worthless by a female who becomes enlightened, proving her very point, and the point made by all Buddhist teachers: enlightened mind is beyond gender and cannot be labeled "male" or "female." Therefore, it makes no sense to claim that females can't attain enlightenment. Nevertheless, people do become attached to those labels and give more value to the label "male," as is shown by Tara's attending monks, who expect that now she would take on male form. Tara has to point out to them that "weak-minded worldlings are always deluded by this." She is heroic and extremely unusual in her resolve to remain in a female body throughout her entire Bodhisattva career of endless lifetimes spent working for the well-being of all. It is also worth pointing out that Tara, who presumably had been a student of the monks who advise her to transform into a man, is wiser than her teachers and has to correct them. I make this point because at this time in the Buddhist world, actual critiques of Buddhist male dominance are more likely to come from students than from teachers, even though all the teachers would say that enlightened mind has no gender, and that gender has no ultimate reality.

It is also important to remember that this story and the concerns expressed in it are not the product of Western feminism. To claim that feminism is a Western concern artificially imposed on Buddhadharma simply will not hold. Texts from every period of Buddhist history and every school indicate that Buddhists have always thought about the disconnect between their gender-free and gender-neutral teachings and the male-dominant world they live in.

"THE DHARMA IS NEITHER MALE NOR FEMALE": WHY BUDDHISTS SHOULD NOT BE SEXISTS

Without exception, Buddhist teachings and teachers are insistent and consistent that at the ultimate level, gender is irrelevant. Buddhism may be the only religion which makes this claim so unambiguously and with such force. This is a very strong but accurate statement.

It is important to understand why, whenever the matter is subjected to rigorous analysis, Buddhists agree that gender has no ultimate significance or reality. What is that tremendous potential for deconstructing gender, noticed even by casual observers of Buddhism? The recognition that gender is irrelevant and cannot be used to make any meaningful distinctions among people is built into the very fabric of Buddhism's most fundamental and basic insights and teachings. Buddhist teachings on interdependence, egolessness, and emptiness mean that nothing exists by itself or has inherent, independent reality, which is what Buddhists mean when we claim that things are illusory and dreamlike. Buddhist analysis is first deconstructive. We take things that we assume to be real and subject them to analysis. When we do that, we find that what we take to be permanently existing entities actually are infinitesimally brief constellations of components that come together and fall apart, propelled by causes and conditions. Therefore, there is no enduring phenomenon to be clung to and such clinging will produce nothing but sorrow. Therefore, gender has no real existence; it is illusory and dreamlike. Logically, gender cannot be excepted from the reality that pertains to everything else. That is the basis for Tara's claim that there is "no such thing as 'male' and 'female.'"

Though the analysis is blindingly clear, the implications of interdependence, egolessness, and emptiness for our lives are not easily wrapped up in a few words and communicated to the outsider, or even to aspiring Buddhists. On the other hand, the matter is utterly simple. Find something that exists apart from causes and conditions. You won't. That's interdependence. Find an aspect of yourself (something that is really you, not something abstract and imaginary that you call your "soul") that has never changed, that endures through all changes, and that is independent rather than interdependent. You won't. That's egolessness. Extend that search. Find an aspect of the world, of your environment, that is not subject to causes and conditions, that is unchanging, and that is unrelated to its matrix. You won't. That's emptiness.

The seemingly nihilistic connotations of the words *egolessness* and *emptiness* have thrown off many Western commentators, but most Western commentators work from a spiritual framework that assumes ultimate duality; Buddhists do not. *Egolessness* and *emptiness* are not negative terms and certainly are not nihilistic in their meanings. Rather, though this point can be difficult to grasp, things can exist (in the relative sense, of course) only because they lack inherent, unchanging, independent, uncaused being. Such inherent, permanent existence would prevent life, which is nothing if not dynamic and fluid. Egolessness and emptiness are simply descriptive of reality, of "things as they are," to quote a favorite Buddhist phrase.

However, out of that description of reality flow many implications, including the fact that there is "no such thing as 'male' and 'female.'" It is impossible, if one understands the basics of Buddhism, to attribute anything intrinsic, invariant, or essential to maleness or femaleness. As is often said, such labels are convenient designations, agreed-upon names, but to attribute any reality to them, or to require people to conform to what has been defined as "male" or "female" is to completely miss the point. When we do, we become, as Tara puts it, "weak worldlings who are always deluded by this."

HOW "WEAK WORLDLINGS" BECOME DELUDED

Most Buddhists know about teachings such as interdependence, egolessness, and emptiness, but many of them still attribute reality to gender, become attached to conventional implications of gender, and become defensive and uncomfortable when the reality of gender is challenged. In effect, both Buddhist individuals and Buddhist institutions seem to operate by the slogan "Of course there is no ego, but gender is real." Or put even more illogically and starkly, "There is no ego, but egolessness is gendered." Why does that happen? This question can be answered on many levels.

Buddhist teachings must not only point to the truth and reality of interdependence, egolessness, and emptiness, but also explain how people so often miss those realities and instead cling to an illusory world of seemingly real entities, including illusory maleness and femaleness, assumed to exist inherently. At rock bottom, people miss interdependence, egolessness, and emptiness, not because they are abstract and remote, but because these basic realities are so simple, so easy to access, and so near at hand. Buddhist teachings never talk about nirvana or enlightenment as being somewhere else, far away or in the distant future. Enlightenment is here and now—if we don't miss it. This also means that enlightenment is fundamentally a change of attitude, a deeper insight. The world does not especially change for enlightened beings; rather their attitude toward it and methods of dealing with it change. People would not become sexless, they would still look the same, but we would no longer fixate on or limit ourselves or others by the gender labels we use in conventional communication.

How we stray from that primordial brilliance moment by moment is one of the great mysteries, according to Buddhism, perhaps the only real mystery. There is no absolute beginning point. Analysis starts in the present, in which confusion is rampant, in which "weak worldlings" have already become deluded. The strong tendency to reify things, including ideas about what gender means, and then to cling to these ideas, is often called "habitual patterns." Habits, as is well known, are nearly impervious to change. According to Buddhism, the habits of reifying things, believing in self-existence, and dividing people into male and female are incredibly deep-seated and have been reinforced by countless lifetimes spent making those mistakes over and over again—millions and millions of moments in which, instead of recognizing the boundless space of unfabricated freedom, we clung to a bit of illusory, self-created identity, thus reinforcing that habit and making it even stronger. One of the greatest problems with habits is that after a time it no longer seems possible that things could be any other way; we simply define ourselves as someone who has a certain good or bad habit, as if it were an unalterable part of our essential being. That is how the meanings we attach to gender identity become so strong and why gender roles and gender norms seem "normal," seem to be part of reality itself.

One of the strongest and most persistent habitual patterns is to attribute invariant and fixed meaning to gender. In fact, this habitual tendency is so deep that even though many Buddhists are aware that belief in permanent, independent ego is a problem that causes them great suffering, and even though they try to undermine their stubborn belief in self-existence, nevertheless, it rarely, if ever, occurs to them that a large part of this troublesome ego is their gender identity, or that attributing significance to gender or clinging to gender identity is causing them suffering. Attributing importance or invariant meaning to gender must be located either in the ego or in the fundamental egoless nature. No Buddhist teacher would locate gender identity in the realm of egolessness, which means the gender identity must be an aspect of ego. Though teachings about ego and egolessness are constant, staple fare in Buddhist education, teachers very rarely discuss gender when they teach about ego and egolessness. In some cases, I fear that may be because they still attribute significance to gender themselves, like the monks attending Tara when she definitively uncovered egolessness.

At least as strong as the habitual tendency to fixate on gender identity is the habitual pattern of evaluating men as superior to and more important than women, which is the basis for setting up social and

religious institutions that favor men over women, and the basis for
describing the world from the point of view of their experience while
ignoring the experiences of women, defined as inferior, and also uninteresting. It takes no imagination at all to realize that this habitual pattern is alive and exceedingly healthy in the Buddhist world. It endures
from the narrative relating the Buddha's reluctance to allow women to
join the monastic community to the assumption that the newest Tibetan
tulku, or reborn teacher, would, of course, be a boy. Between these
moments in time, all nuns were defined as inferior to even the newest
and youngest monks and had to sit behind them at all assemblies.
Though the Buddha did not honor the caste hierarchy that prevailed in
the India of his day, he did retain its gender hierarchy, setting up rules of
monastic discipline that clearly made nuns dependent on monks in
many ways. (Other rules did protect nuns, however. For example, nuns
could not be asked to cook or sew for the monks.) Nuns were often educated much more poorly than monks, and large segments of the
Buddhist world allowed the nuns' order to die out completely. Being
reborn as a woman was said to be the result of negative karma and
countless thousands of women prayed and did practices to help them
attain a male rebirth. Seeing this picture, it is understandable why feminists would ask why any woman would ever choose to be a Buddhist.
How could a religion that has such a clear understanding of nonduality,
such a strong realization that gender is illusory and unreal, get things so
completely wrong on the ground, in the everyday world, and in its institutional life?

It is fair and reasonable to point out that, regarding gender,
Buddhists did things more or less like all other religions and cultures,
despite holding ultimate views that completely undercut such practices.
Furthermore, Buddhists themselves long ago noticed this disconnect, as
the story of Tara and many other texts point out. Is there something
about the relative world that constrains us into fixed gender roles and
gender hierarchy, even when we know better? For Buddhists, giving an
accurate account of the relative world is also important.

Buddhists accounted for the gender disparities so evident in the relative world by appealing to karma, a notion so basic to the Indian worldview that even the Buddha accepted it without question. *Karma* refers
to the fact that any action produces an appropriate reaction, both physically and morally. Thus, karma can refer to both cause and effect. An
action sets something in motion; in that sense karma is a cause. But
what results, an effect, is also called karma. Everything experienced in

the relative world is the result of karma, or causes and conditions. That does not, however, mean that everything is foreordained or fated, as many Westerners often assume. The *present* constellation of events is the result of past actions; it cannot be changed. However, *how one deals with the present is not predetermined; choice is involved at that point.* Those choices are important because *present choices* determine *future outcomes.* The only caveat that must be interjected here is the reminder that habitual patterns, especially unconscious ones, can drastically limit the arena of choice. The prison of gender roles perpetuates itself so easily because living in it is one of those largely unconscious habitual patterns for most people.[7]

To illustrate these points, let us use as an example the subject of this chapter. Because of past karma, I was reborn a woman in this life. I have no idea what that karma was, and there is no reason to try to figure out why I was reborn as a woman in this life. The present is what makes a difference. What I do with my female rebirth is up to me. I could follow the gender norms of my culture unquestioningly, or I could write *Buddhism after Patriarchy.* I received a great deal of pressure to fall into the female gender role, and no support for becoming the person who would write *Buddhism after Patriarchy.* Which of those choices I make determines a great deal about my future and also has an impact on the world around me. Though I suppose some traditional Buddhists might disagree, I assume that writing *Buddhism after Patriarchy* results in better karma for the future than willingly following repressive gender norms.

The traditional Buddhist account of women's situation in a male-dominant world must be phrased correctly and understood precisely. Starting in the present, as does all Buddhist analysis, Buddhists looked around themselves and saw that most women were living in undesirable, unpleasant situations. They were subject to the authority of others, usually men, had little or no independence, usually had little opportunity for study and practice, experienced heavy reproductive demands with no fertility control, frequently died in childbirth, frequently lost infants and children, faced demands for heavy physical labor in addition to their reproductive difficulties, and often had to endure having co-wives as well. Who would choose or want such a life? The only logical conclusion was that these beings were suffering from the results of unfortunate choices in the past. The only compassionate response was to offer them ways to change their situation positively in the future. This is why female rebirth is said to be unfortunate or woeful, the result of unfortunate karma, and why women are told to aspire to become men in the future.

Western women usually experience these teachings as extremely hurtful, but there is more to them than is evident at first glance. Because Westerners have such different metaphysical assumptions from those of Buddhists, they usually hear in these statements things that are not really part of their message. Westerners tend to hear these teaching as saying that women *are* bad, but that is not at all what Buddhists are saying. Buddhists would not say that women *are* bad, but only that they *carry* unfortunate karma in their karmic continua. Carrying unfortunate karmic seeds is completely different from having a defective or an evil nature, something often attributed to women in many other religious traditions. For one thing, negative karmic seeds work themselves out or are burned up; they are not an enduring, intractable part of one's nature. One is not defined or constituted by these negative seeds; they are adventitious, temporarily obscuring something more basic.

Second, because Buddhists are not talking about an enduring essence or nature, as is much Western discourse, not all women are necessarily conditioned or constrained by the situation in which most women find themselves. There are no metaphysical barriers to women doing anything or taking on any role. It would not occur to Buddhists to say that women's nature prevents them from becoming ritual leaders or teachers, which is quite different from the position of many Christians, who see women as metaphysically, inherently incapable of being priests. Another important implication of the fact that Buddhists are not attributing women's woes to an intractable, enduring nature, but to karmic, historical factors, is that gender roles are not divinely or cosmically ordained. One of the most imprisoning doctrines, found in many religions, is that current gender roles are necessary, inevitable, and unchangeable because of divine command or cosmic requirements. Buddhists could say that not only are women's woes the result of unfortunate karma, but also that our current system of gender roles is nothing but the result of an impermanent nexus of cause and effect. There is nothing inevitable about it; it is only maintained by force of habit. Even deep-seated habits are not binding or inevitable in the ways that a divine command, a cosmic law, or an immutable, eternal nature would be.

Finally, behind the unpalatable suggestion that women solve their problems by becoming men and the equally unpalatable claim, made anonymously to me in 1980, that feminism is irrelevant to Buddhism because "deserving women are reborn as men" lurks a remarkable admission. To be a woman in a male-dominated world *is* unfortunate and painful! Buddhists admitted that long ago, defining the woes of female rebirth as, among other things, being subject to male authorities and having to work hard taking care of their husbands.[8] Buddhists do not ask us to try to believe that male domination is good for everyone or that everyone should be happy under its aegis. They know better than to claim that male dominance actually benefits women or that women should be happy and grateful that men have authority over them. One of the key elements of feminism has been admitted by Buddhists for a long time. If only we could get contemporary societies and people to arrive at a similar consensus that male dominance is painful for women and for human beings in general!

The primary purpose of Buddhist discipline and practice is to eliminate suffering, so if it is determined that something causes suffering, Buddhists should try to overcome that obstacle.[9] That is why Buddhists held out the promise of rebirth as men to women suffering under male dominance. Traditional Buddhists could not imagine what contemporary feminists do—a society and Buddhist institutions that are not male-dominated. To them, it seemed easier and more possible to turn women into men, which indicates that many of the things that made female rebirth seem woeful were, at that time, deemed intractable. But if things changed, so that women's lives were no longer governed by those same factors, there would be no Buddhist grounds for continuing male dominance. According to Buddhism, male dominance is grounded in karma, cause and effect, or historical circumstances, not women's inherent nature, the will of God, or cosmic necessity. If the karma, the historical conditions change, the situation of women not only can change; it will.

So the question becomes, have conditions changed sufficiently to undo male dominance, both in society and in Buddhist institutions? In my analyses, I have always attributed historical male dominance less to the inherent nastiness of men and more to the material circumstances, technology, and medical knowledge of the times. I would agree with the assessment that women's live *were* woeful in the circumstances that prevailed when Buddhists offered rebirth as a man as the only solution to male dominance. I certainly would not want to be a woman subject to the conditions most (Buddhist) women have endured throughout most of history. In fact, I spent much of my youth dreading growing up to be a woman. I would also suggest that two fragile but real contemporary circumstances can change women's lives drastically and dramatically. They are reproductive freedom and the ability to make personal, individual choices about one's life. These conditions are far from securely or widely available. But they are definitely possible and offer a far more adequate way to undo the disconnect between Buddhism's gender-neutral and gender-free vision and its male-dominant institutions than offering "deserving women" future rebirth as a male.

UNDOING THE DELUSION

The first step in undoing the delusions of "weak-minded worldlings" regarding gender is more consistent, more honest, and better teaching concerning gender. Paradoxically, Buddhism's exemplary views on gender sometimes short-circuit real awareness of the problems caused by traditional male dominance in Buddhist institutions. For example, though the story of Tara is known to every Tibetan Buddhist teacher, few respond to students' persistent questions about male dominance in Buddhism with the insights promoted in this story. Traditional teachers simply dismiss feminist criticisms and questions with the statement that enlightened mind is utterly beyond any conventional qualities and dichotomies, including that of male and female. That is true, of course, but the real questions, "Why is Buddhism so male-dominated?" and "What can be done about it?" have not been answered. Thus, instead of transcending gender, which is what the teacher intends to do, the reality of gender and the suffering caused by it are simply ignored.

Furthermore, the way teachers work with students who question Buddhist male dominance often includes a hidden, or even an overt, rebuke to the student for even asking such questions, for having such concerns. The teacher does not say, "Yes, you are right. Weak worldlings *are* always deluded by these things, but don't let their mistakes become an obstacle in your path." Instead, their answers imply that because, ultimately, gender has no relevance, it is shortsighted to be concerned about how gender works in the relative world. There can be a subtle insinuation that students who bring up such questions are lacking in sincerity and devotion. They are chided for being "too sensitive" and told to "practice more" because being angry and upset are not conducive to enlightenment. (That very last snippet of the advice is correct.) The teacher's response may be even more abrupt—something like "Aren't you over that yet?" "Why are you still asking these questions?" In other words, many times, teachers' responses to these questions are seriously lacking in the skillful means that is supposed to be the specialty of a good teacher.

Sometimes, accusations go further, claiming that the student who is concerned about gender inequities in the world of Buddhist institutions is the one who is "genderizing the dharma," thus implying that male-dominant institutions would, in fact, be gender-neutral and gender-inclusive if only those pesky feminists would stop noticing and making a fuss about male dominance. Then the opinion that people who "genderize the dharma" should not be allowed to publish or teach about those concerns sometimes follows. This has happened to me, though this rather extreme and angry comment came from another student, not a teacher. One can only reply that dharma is genderized by those who create and maintain male-dominant institutions, not by those who *notice and point out* those male-dominant institutions. Buddhism is about overcoming ignorance, not about promoting the status quo by encouraging ignorance of it.

In the past thirty years, around the world, Buddhists have been breaking down the prison of gender roles, undoing the delusion of "weak worldlings" that gender means anything ultimate or has any great significance for how one lives one's life.

For many Asian Buddhists, the dichotomy between monastics and laypeople is at least as pronounced as the male-female distinction. For them, a key issue has been restoring or upgrading the nuns' order.[10] Because of the prestige accorded to monastics in Asian Buddhism, it would be difficult for any other issue to upstage that of nuns' existence and status. Nothing could more forcefully demonstrate male dominance in Buddhist institutional life than the loss of the nuns' order in some parts of the Asian Buddhist world and its degradation in other parts.

For the Theravada Buddhist world, which had initially transmitted nuns' ordination to Mahayana Buddhists but then lost that lineage themselves, restoring the nuns' order was a difficult and controversial issue. Many opposed it on many grounds. Some claimed that, though Theravadins had originally transmitted the lineage to Mahayanists, the purity of that lineage could no longer be trusted because its transmission among Theravadins had been lost. Apparently, Mahayanists were not considered to be capable of transmitting monastic standards from generation to generation, because of doctrinal innovations which Theravadins did not approve of. Others claimed that women themselves did not want to be ordained as nuns. Throughout Theravadin countries, women did take informal ordination and lead a renunciant lifestyle. Though they had very low status and lacked many of the privileges accorded to monastics, they were self-governing, largely because they were not considered to be genuine monastics. Some claimed that these women did not want to be ordained as nuns because then, as nuns, they would be subject to the authority of monks, as monastic codes specified. However, it is hard to understand how these low-status, informal nuns could have been independent, in any meaningful sense of that word, given that monastics were so highly revered but these "nuns" were not considered to be real monastics by most. In any case, some Buddhists have taken matters into their own hands. The first nuns' ordination held in a Theravadin Buddhist country in over a thousand years took places in Sri Lanka in 1998, and more have followed. Most reports indicate that, whatever the opinion of monastic authorities about their ordinations, Theravada nuns are being accepted in many Theravada contexts.

In other Asian contexts in which nuns, whether fully ordained or not, were more common and more accepted, the main issue was about their education. In Korea, Taiwan, and other parts of the Chinese diaspora, and in parts of Vietnam, the nuns' ordination lineage had not been lost. Obviously, there could be no controversy about whether there should even be nuns in these contexts, as there was in the Theravada countries. Nuns were an accepted part of the Buddhist institutional world and thus were in a much better position to take advantage of economic and educational opportunities that became available in the late twentieth century. In East Asia, as the economy boomed, nuns benefited in many ways. In Asian cultures, rich laypeople have always wanted to patronize religious renunciants as a way to make merit for themselves, and also to ensure their continued prosperity. (In many Asian contexts, it is believed that stinginess leads to poverty while generosity leads to wealth. A rich person who is not generous is despised.) Thus, a great deal of money was available to religious institutions, but rather suddenly, the number of monks began to decline and the number of nuns to rise, so that today, by most estimates, there are six nuns for every monk. It is easy to imagine why this imbalance has happened; the secular economy affords great opportunities for men but many fewer for women. Women seek out the nuns' lifestyle for the same reasons they always have: because of genuine spiritual vocation, to avoid patriarchal marriages, and to receive an education, which might not otherwise be available to girls. With plentiful economic resources, the nuns are flourishing. Their monastic institutions are not second-class imitations of the monks' institutions, as they have often been, and nuns receive a complete classical Buddhist education in both philosophy and meditation. In addition, many of them receive doctoral degrees from Western institutions while being supported by their home monasteries. Probably this combination of generous economic support and many nuns receiving such support has never before occurred in Buddhist history. Most of the time, there were plenty of monks, and because it is thought that the merit earned by giving donations depends in part on the virtue of the recipient, monks, by definition more worthy than nuns, always received the lion's share of donations. I have visited nunneries in both Korea and Taiwan. I was very impressed with the feistiness, dignity, and self-confidence of the nuns, as well as by their well-equipped facilities.

Tibetan Buddhism presents yet another picture. (When discussing Tibetan Buddhism, it must always be remembered that this tradition was severely disrupted when Tibetans lost their homeland to the Chinese in 1959. Contemporary Tibetan Buddhism is known mainly from its refugee communities in India.) Nuns' novice ordination was transmitted to Tibet, but if the full ordination lineages made it into Tibet, they did not survive there. However, among Tibetan Buddhists, both novices and fully ordained monastics wear the same maroon robes and live very similar lifestyles, so the lack of the full ordination did not hamper Tibetan nuns as much as it hampered the informal Theravada "nuns," who could not wear robes of the monastic color to indicate their lack of true monastic status. In fact, in some Theravada countries, especially in Thailand, it is extremely controversial, even dangerous, for nuns who have received full, final ordination to wear monastic robes of the traditional color. What hampered Tibetan nuns was the familiar lack of economic support, leading to limited educations and meager institutions. In addition, the belief that female rebirth is much inferior to male rebirth was (and probably still is) quite robust in popular Tibetan Buddhist culture. On the other hand, both historically and in the present, Tibetan Buddhists also did recognize some extraordinary women as great practitioners and teachers; such women are very highly regarded.

For the Tibetan situation specifically, and probably to some extent for Asian Buddhism in general, a detailed, poignant account of historical difficulties and current changes is found in Kim Gutschow's well-researched and well-written book *Being a Buddhist Nun: The Struggle for Enlightenment in the Himalayas,* which is the result of many years of fieldwork living among Ladakhi nuns.[11] At the beginning of her research, Gutschow found that all women and men, without exception, regarded female rebirth as a liability, as something negative and to be avoided. The local nuns were few and had to struggle economically, often having to hire themselves out to do housework or heavy labor to earn enough funds for the year's supplies, or to slowly build their monastery. Many of the nuns had completed the required preliminary meditation practices. Still, they were not allowed to perform the more advanced aspects of their cycle of practices, despite the main meditation deity of their cycle of practices being Vajrayogini, one of the foremost female meditation deities of Tibetan Buddhism. In the 1990s, as the area opened up more to modern and outside influences, things began to change. An aristocratic local woman became a nun—something that aristocrats, especially women, rarely did. Tsering Palmo studied medicine in Dharamsala and began to study and practice Buddhism seriously. She became the foremost local leader for change in the treatment of nuns. In 1995, a Sakyadhita conference was held in Ladakh, attended by Buddhist nuns and laywomen from all over the world, electrifying "local audiences with their deportment and teachings."[12] The Dalai Lama did not attend, but sent a message commending Buddhist women for "casting off traditional and outmoded restraints to dedicating themselves to implementing and promoting Buddhist practice."[13] In the years that followed, local people both sought to upgrade the situation of the nuns and opposed Tsering Palmo's work because they were fearful of what would happen if they subverted the monks' privileged status. Finally, in 1998, the Dalai Lama accepted her invitation to give a public talk on women and spoke to a "thronged audience about how men and women have an equal capacity for enlightenment."[14] After that, local attitudes changed, though certain difficulties still persisted. As in East Asia, the number of monks is dropping and the number of nuns is growing.

This narrative includes elements found in many accounts of Asian Buddhist women in the twentieth century. The nuns' order was nonexistent or severely curtailed by the monks' order. (This was less so in East Asia). International education and an international Buddhist women's movement brought new awareness to local women about the problems with their situation and about potentials for improvement, whether full ordination, better education, better facilities, or better economic support were needed. Many local people, both men and women, both lay and monastic were opposed to, or at least uneasy about upgrading the nuns' situation. Usually, powerful Asian Buddhist leaders, (males by definition) but not always from the local region, gave their support to the women and nuns, which usually aided the women and the nuns greatly. Change is slow, but it also seems inevitable that Asian Buddhist women's and nuns' situations will continue to improve.

Obviously, these changes are the result of a complex blend of Asian and Western influences and female and male leadership. It is not necessary to sort out these influences further.

If the story about Asian Buddhist women is mainly the story of nuns, the story of Western Buddhist women is mainly the story of laypeople and their concerns,[15] whether the Buddhists are converts or Asian Americans. Outside of Asia, there is no economic basis for the monastic institutions that were always thought to be essential to Buddhism by Asian Buddhists. There simply are not enough rich lay Buddhists to support monastic institutions in the West and many more people who want to practice meditation seriously than can be supported by donations to Buddhist institutions. While more traditional Buddhists might find this situation untenable, many commentators see this new development of lay Buddhists who are also serious meditators as exciting and promising. What would Buddhism be like if serious practitioners of meditation also had jobs and families? Throughout most of its history, Buddhism had promoted a division of labor: monastics pursued the accumulation of wisdom by engaging in meditation and philosophical studies; laypeople pursued the accumulation of merit by supporting them, but were not expected to be able to engage in serious study and practice because of time constraints. Western convert Buddhists are attempting to undo this neat division of labor.

Western Buddhism in a complex phenomenon. The majority of Buddhists in Western countries, especially the United States and Canada are Asian Americans, some of whom have been in the West for generations and many more of whom are recent immigrants. But the Western Buddhists who get the most attention are the converts, in part because they are the most recent converts to one of the world's most successful missionary religions, and in part because they are extremely articulate and have already made many contributions to Buddhism worldwide.

Beginning in the late 1960s and increasing exponentially in the 1970's, Asian teachers from some the major Buddhist denominations began teaching in North America and North Americans, mainly well-educated Caucasians, began practicing meditation and converting to Buddhism in large numbers. Many Asian meditation teachers, frustrated with the relative lack of interest in serious meditation practice in their home countries, were happy to teach these eager new meditators, about half of whom were women. For men and women to be engaging in intensive practice together as lay practitioners was an innovation. It led to significant developments.

One development involved what happened to Buddhist meditation centers when these young converts married and began to have children. Before they had families and careers, the long retreats common in forms of Buddhism that emphasize meditation were not a problem, assuming that somehow the economics of the situation could be worked out, and in the early days, creative financing was common in convert Western Buddhism. But by the middle 1980s, these converts began to have children. That would have been un-notable, except for the fact that half the convert students were women who were not willing to retire from their lives as serious students of Buddhadharma to take sole responsibility for childcare.

Instead, they asked for at least two things. First, meditation centers should provide child care, so that parents of young children could participate in the programs. This was unheard of in traditional meditation centers that cater mainly to monastics, childless by definition. Slowly, with many false starts, meditation centers did begin to offer child care programs. They are now a standard part of many meditation centers and many programs.

These convert Buddhist parents also wanted something more subtle. They wanted to hear teachings on how childcare and livelihood could be experienced as extensions of their meditation practice, rather than as distractions from it. After all, classic Buddhist texts talked about the identity of *samsara* or confused existence and *nirvana,* enlightenment, and about how bodhisattvas took on all worldly situations to help beings. Buddhist literature contains stories about people who attained had enlightenment while engaged in mundane activities, including stories about women whose families would not let them engage in formal practices, who then used their housework as an object of mindfulness meditation and attained realization by those methods.

So what about a layperson making a living and rearing children? Zen Buddhists, though not most other forms of Buddhism, already had some insight into regarding work as part of formal spiritual discipline. One of the great innovations of Chinese Ch'an (Zen) Buddhists had been requiring monastics to do daily work, growing their own vegetables. Mindfulness could be cultivated along with the vegetables. Zen literature also included great classics on cooking and a meditator aspiring to become a major teacher was required to take a turn as head cook as part of that journey. Zen Buddhist centers in North America under the leadership of the great Suzuki Roshi became famous for their organic gardens, the vegetarian restaurant, Greens, which they founded in

San Francisco, and their sulfur hot springs resort, Tassajara, a desirable resort that serves gourmet vegetarian food during the summer and becomes a meditation center for intensive practice during the winter. Students who work at the resort in the summer earn credits to stay at the monastery for the winter retreats, which are otherwise quite expensive. Other North American Buddhist groups have also adopted the practice of requiring manual and service work during meditation programs. Partly this is done for economic reasons, to make the programs more affordable, but partly it is done to teach people how to carry mindfulness into everyday life. I consider that the many hours I have spent chopping vegetables in kitchens at practice centers were just as important as the hours I spend in formal meditation and in listening to talks about meditation. The issues involved in developing similar practices regarding jobs in the secular world are more difficult, of course. But there is great possibility for further development in this area, and Buddhists would only be adding to commentary on the category "Right Livelihood," which is the fifth element of the Eightfold Path, Buddhism's fourth Noble Truth, and goes back to the origins of Buddhism.

Regarding motherhood and parenting as a form of meditation practice has been more difficult. In many a classic Buddhist tale, women lament that they cannot follow their heart's desire to do intensive practice because they have to take care of their children. Monks, who wrote virtually all the major Buddhist literature, simply did not encounter the need to combine childrearing with their lives as meditators. Monks may have learned how to cultivate mindfulness with their vegetables, but there were no young children at monasteries. Monasteries often served as orphanages, but the young boys in them were ordained as monks and expected to follow the monastic routine. I am familiar with one nunnery in India that includes many young girls. But there are no infants; all the girls are old enough to be in classes, so the nunnery is more like a boarding school than a day care center. A few women who are also regarded as great meditators and teachers did have children, but they left no reminiscences about combining formal meditation with motherhood.[16] When North American Buddhists, both women and men, who had spent years moving from meditation center to meditation center, began to have children, a huge outcry when out. Where was the Buddhist literature discussing parenthood as path, the teachings on how to practice mindfulness in the midst of dirty diapers and screaming children? By the late 1980's some literature dealing with this question began to appear[17] and recently, a Zen Buddhist woman has written a book specifically on motherhood as path.[18] As the first generation of children born to convert Buddhist parents has grown to young adulthood, they have also to record their experiences, so that in the future, others will be able to find out about what it was like to be a first generation Buddhist child in the Western world.[19]

Whether for Asian or for Western Buddhists, however, the most significant step in undoing the delusions of "weak worldlings" regarding gender is empowering and honoring women as teachers. My most persistent and consistent feminist critique of Buddhism is that throughout Buddhist history, and even in the contemporary world, most teachers are men. The most honored and important role in the Buddhist world is that of the teacher, guru, Rinpoche, Roshi, or whatever other title may be used. Yet throughout Buddhist history, and even in the contemporary world, it has been very difficult for women at attain any of those titles. Why is this a problem? Isn't dharma the same whether taught by a man or a woman? That challenge has been thrown at me many times. But for many reasons, it matters whether or not women are teachers. For one thing, Buddhist texts and institutions would probably not exhibit such a pervasive preference for men and maleness if more women could have become revered teachers. For another, women would have had role models, something that all educators agree is important for students. Most important, the experiences of women would not have been lost to the tradition if women had been teachers and had written about their practice, as male teachers have always done.[20] Had that happened, we might not have encountered the situation of Western practitioners asking desperately for meditation instruction on parenting as path and as part of their spiritual discipline. But most important, Buddhism's exemplary views regarding the irrelevance of gender are rendered completely meaningless if all or most of those teaching that exemplary view have male bodies.

As we move into the twenty-first century and Buddhism's twenty-sixth century, the situation is changing. For one thing, persistent historical explorations, largely undertaken by Western students, have uncovered more female teachers and role models than were commonly known about earlier. The *Therigatha* (Songs of the Female Elders),[21] barely known to earlier students of Buddhism has become well-known. More Tibetan female teachers are being discovered all the time. Zen students have painstakingly brought to light a hidden record of female lineage ancestors.

More important, currently women teachers are being recognized and authorized to teach much more regularly. Among Tibetan teachers, Jetsun Khandro Rinpoche,[22] who was recognized as a *tulku* and trained from an early age, is teaching publicly in a way that is unprecedented for an Asian female teacher. She has many Western students and a center in North America. She also heads a nunnery in India and plays a large role in the day-to-day operations of Mindrolling monastery, her father's monastery and one of the great Tibetan monasteries in exile. However, Asian women teachers, especially those who travel and teach in the West, are still relatively rare.

Many Western converts to Buddhism now have been practicing and studying for thirty or more years and have begun to teach. In Zen and Vipassana lineages, women have been given full transmission and permission to teach as independent teachers. In the Tibetan lineages, almost no Westerners, men or women, have been given such teaching authority. Nevertheless, even in centers that follow some form of Tibetan Buddhism, Westerners do a great deal of the teaching. From the beginning, about half of these Western teachers of the dharma have been women. These were the same women who began preparing for that role, probably without intending to, when they sat with the men at the feet of Asian dharma teachers in the 1960's and 70's, instead of confining themselves to preparing food and cleaning up afterward, as their mothers would have done in the 1950's. Some of these women are now among the best-known and most highly respected Western dharma teachers. This development—the percentage of dharma teachers who are women, the independence with which some of them teach, and the respect they receive—is an unprecedented, momentous development for Buddhism, which hopefully will change Buddhism forever. I have often commented about the extreme good fortune that, for various historical reasons, Asian Buddhist meditation masters began to teach Western students in large numbers in the late 1960's and in the 1970's—at exactly the same time that the second wave of feminism was transforming Western society to its core. Some people might be inclined to see this as a mere random happenstance, but Buddhists affirm that things do not happen by chance. They happen because of karma, because of causes and conditions. When two lines of cause and effect come together in ways that are mutually beneficial, Tibetan Buddhists refer to that as *tendrel,* auspicious coincidence. This term is often used to name the meeting of teacher and student, the most important event in the life of a student. Similarly, I have long claimed that the coincidence of Buddhism and feminism was auspicious, extremely auspicious for both. Surely Tara would regard this meeting as very helpful to overcoming the delusions of "weak worldlings."

CHAPTER 20

Being a North American Buddhist Woman

Reflections of a Feminist Pioneer

In this final chapter I would like to reminisce about some of my key experiences and insights as a North American Buddhist woman and scholar-practitioner. How did I become a Buddhist in the first place? What was it like thirty years ago to be both a Buddhist and a feminist? Why do I think that Buddhists still need to be feminists? What has been most important to me about being a Buddhist? I would also like to reflect on what I have always considered the most important topic for Buddhist women—the presence of women teachers.

One may well wonder, given Buddhism's dismal record on equity and equality for women, why a Western woman already well grounded in feminism would choose to become a Buddhist.[1] Indeed, after I began serious Buddhist practice in 1976 and took refuge in the Three Jewels in 1977, most of my feminist friends and colleagues were totally mystified.[2] They could understand Jewish and Christian feminists who would decide to work for change within their inherited traditions, but they could not understand why someone would convert to a foreign tradition not known for its support of women's equality.

My involvement with Buddhism actually began much earlier. I first began to study Buddhism as a graduate student at the University of Chicago in 1965, but its doctrines did not compel me very much. It was not that I disagreed with those doctrines; I was just trying to learn a lot about a lot of religions, fast, and to learn Sanskrit at the same time. Buddhism as a doctrinal system did not stand out. Nevertheless, I had been extremely taken by what I had learned of "Tantra" in my graduate school classes, and read everything available at that time on Tantra and Tibetan religions. They somehow made a deep impression on me, and years later, I found that that the stories that had drawn me the most were precisely the stories of the Tibetan lineages with which I had the most karmic affinity and whose practices I later took up with great enthusiasm.[3]

In the meanwhile, feminist issues consumed me much more. I had always been keenly aware of the subservient position of women in Western religions and had quietly rebelled and tried to work for change. As I moved further into my doctoral studies, I became aware of the pervasive androcentric (male-centered) methodology of my chosen field of study, which always thought of men as the more interesting and only important subjects of research. It may be hard to believe now, when there is so much research about women and religion, but only forty years ago, there was no information about women's participation in religion in any of the major sources, and the topic was completely "off limits." I was told that studying women was unnecessary because men were already being studied and "the generic masculine includes the feminine, making it unnecessary to focus specifically on women."[4] Given how pervasive gender roles are in most traditional cultures and the sexual segregation so characteristic of most, it still baffles me how learned scholars could have made such uninformed deductions, but such was the conventional wisdom of those times.

Buddhism caught up with me in the fall of 1973. I was teaching a college-level survey course on Buddhism for the second time, struggling to understand its basic doctrines more adequately. I was also extremely unhappy. I had just moved to Eau Claire, Wisconsin, where I have lived for more than thirty years, and had quickly realized it was going to be a very lonely place for me. I was also mourning the terminal illness of my lover, whom I had seen for what I knew would be the last time just days earlier. As I walked to my class on a beautiful fall day, trying to better understand the Four Noble Truths, which I was about to teach, I only longed to be able to appreciate the beauty of that day unburdened by my misery. Suddenly things became very clear. I could not appreciate the beauty of my immediate surroundings because I so desperately wanted things I could not have. Buddhism's second Noble Truth, that desire is the cause of suffering, became completely clear. I did not need to be convinced of the first Noble Truth, that suffering pervades conventional life. But the third Noble Truth, that suffering ceases when its cause—attachment—is given up, also became utterly clear in a vivid instant of complete detachment and openness. I stood still and said to myself, "The Four Noble Truths are true!" Unlike most academics, who might hold ideas philosophically without taking their practical consequences to heart, I immediately thought that if the first three truths were actually true, then the fourth truth, which details Buddhism's specific path, must also be true. That would mean that I should learn to meditate, something not easily accomplished in northern Wisconsin in 1973.

I did find a way to learn to meditate, and several years later, in 1977, I finally found my way to one of the major centers for Buddhism in North America—Boulder, Colorado—to receive deeper training in meditation. I had decided before I left Wisconsin that, while meditation was valuable, I would not become a Buddhist. The main reason was that I had already been through two sexist religions (Christianity and Judaism) and didn't need a third trip through a religion that preferred men to women and limited women severely. So what happened? I can only say that the experience of living in a Buddhist environment thoroughly captivated me. I remember crying as I decided that Buddhism was simply too profound to let the patriarchs have it without protest. But I went into Buddhism with my eyes wide open. I knew that taking refuge in the Three Jewels meant that I would also be writing *Buddhism after Patriarchy*.[5]

It was not easy then, nor is it especially easy now, to be both a Buddhist and a feminist. The North American feminist theological establishment is not especially attuned to issues concerning religious diversity, despite its sensitivity to cultural diversity within Christianity. Many seem to believe that a white North American cannot authentically be a Buddhist, a viewpoint my Tibetan woman teacher scorns. They hold this viewpoint even while asserting that Africans and Asians who have become Christians are simply exercising religious choice. Buddhists generally are no more sympathetic to feminism. Many North American Buddhists, having little knowledge of Buddhist history or of Asian Buddhism, deny that Buddhism has any patriarchal baggage, citing the usual naive claim, "I've never been discriminated against." To them, somehow this claim seems to prove that, therefore, male dominance has never existed in the past or the present. In addition, Buddhists have problems with "causes," especially when they are voiced in an aggressive manner that suggests self-clinging and attachment. However, issues of equity for women and women's equality are especially avoided. Even the engaged Buddhist movement, which self-consciously takes up contemporary political, economic, and social issues, almost never concerns itself with gender analysis or women's issues.

Sometimes people try to corner me into declaring a primary loyalty. But to me, the Buddhist way of hyphenating its most profound wordings about reality solves that dilemma. Rather than prioritizing deep insights, Buddhists usually claim that, though different, they are of equal value. Thus, we talk of the inseparability of form and emptiness as emptiness-luminosity. Neither word by itself really captures what Buddhists say about the ultimate nature of our experience, and both are necessary. But the hyphen makes them, in a sense, one word. I would say the same of Buddhism-feminism. When both are properly understood, there can be no hostility or division between them.

Having taught and written about Buddhism so much for so many years, it is difficult to pinpoint exactly what about Buddhism makes me so committed and enthusiastic. It would be easy to say, as do so many Western Buddhists, that Buddhist meditation practices are what makes Buddhism so appealing. A meditation practice involving silent sitting for considerable periods of time was the completely new ingredient in our lives. Early on, it *was* meditation that made all the difference. It had a profound effect on me in only a few years, making my rage over sexist injustice unworkable.[6] But one doesn't really have to be a Buddhist to practice the basic discipline of mindfulness-awareness, or *samatha* meditation. Many Christians also practice that form of meditation, which was common in India before the Buddha's time.

In the long run what brings joy to me and what keeps me in Buddhist orbit is what is unique to Buddhism—*vipashyana*. This term is impossible to translate accurately, though "special insight" is a common translation. For most people, Special Insight does not occur without the formal meditation practice of *samatha*, without the many types of mindfulness-awareness practice, but Special Insight is not limited to times of formal meditation. The experience that first turned me to Buddhism was an experience of Special Insight, a penetrating and clarifying breakthrough to a different level of understanding. For me, a verbal person, those experiences cry out to be put into words, but the pith of Special Insight is always beyond words and concepts, which is not to say that verbal, conceptual formulations are useless. Buddhism has an immense repertoire of verbal, conceptual modes of pointing to the contents of Special Insight, all of which delight me because of their profundity and the way they point to what really does matter, what really is real. Initially, the Buddhist view illumined my suffering, an experience that is not an unusual route into Buddhist practice. Along the way, it provided a great deal of insight into how to think about gender issues effectively. Now it provides me with cogent ways to think about one of the pressing issues of our time, religious diversity.[7] In all cases, the words and concepts that can be so helpful arise out of experiences of utter stillness and equanimity that are so central to Buddhist sensibilities. This process—the insights that arise when one practices Buddhist disciplines and the way these insights illumine core issues of human existence—is, for me, the enduring delight of being a Buddhist.

That enduring delight, however, comes from something quite different from the sheer intellectual agility that dominates many academic contexts. Verbalizations of Special Insight are not quite the same as debating points, nor is their purpose to solve intellectual puzzles in which one is not personally invested. Rather, they are the tradition's best distillation of the experiences of its best minds—to be contemplated and investigated thoroughly, until one knows for sure, for oneself, whether they ring true or not. The process of contemplating and the encouragement to investigate for oneself mean that Buddhism is alive and that its insights can be applied to any situation or problem one might encounter. Thus, as I intimated earlier, I find Buddhist teachings too profound for me to be deterred by Buddhism's historical male dominance. And, in the long run, it has always been the Buddhist view that compels me to continue the journey, whatever other frustrations, especially reluctance even to acknowledge that Buddhism has gender issues, may continue to accompany me on my path.

In authentic Buddhism, that profound view and the accompanying practices are transmitted by a teacher. Nowadays, most or all of these teachings and practices are also available in books, but without personal instruction from a teacher, it is difficult to grasp these teachings at a deep level. Anyone in the teaching profession should understand this immediately; individual attention and oral instruction are often critical if a student is to comprehend the material. Like many other wisdom traditions, Buddhism doubts the ability of written materials, by themselves, to convey deep insights and does not give final authority to texts. They are too easily perverted by the self-interest of the naive reader, as any consideration of the religious fundamentalisms common today in religions that give ultimate authority to a text should quickly indicate. Relying on their texts, religious leaders claim to have direct access to the mind of God and seek to dominate all people on the basis of their conviction that they have the truth for everyone. Buddhist teachers do not operate in this manner.

Buddhist teachers, including myself, often say that Buddhist teachings are extremely simple and basic—so simple that they are easily missed. Thus, it is as difficult to overestimate the importance of teachers in Buddhism as it to overestimate the importance of personal verification of the relevance of what one has been taught. Though Buddhists regard teachers very highly, the purpose of a teacher is to help one discover what one is unlikely to discover on one's own, not to provide beliefs or ideologies for the student. (Buddhism is not a creedal religion turning on correct beliefs in any case.) Without personal verification through examining one's own experiences, any profound teachings remain fundamentally irrelevant to the student. Thus, in Buddhism, as in many religious traditions that emphasize personal transformation through spiritual practices, the teacher-student relationship is subtle and profound. It is up to the student to discern that the teacher is trustworthy, not a spiritual fraud, and then to practice assigned disciplines seriously; the teacher has the responsibility to discern the student's needs accurately and not to gratify her or his own ego needs through having disciples.

In my work as a Buddhist feminist, I have always emphasized the importance of women teachers, for many reasons.[8] I have argued many times in the past, and I would still argue today, that the most serious indicator of male dominance in Buddhism historically has been the relative absence of female teachers. I would also argue, as strongly as possible, that the bottom line determining whether Buddhism has overcome its patriarchal tendencies is the presence of female teachers. It has been argued that because the dharma is beyond gender, it doesn't matter whether women or men are the teachers of that timeless, genderless dharma; the message would be the same in any case. But I would argue that because the dharma is beyond gender, therefore, one should expect that there would be about equal numbers of women and men dharma teachers unless humanly constructed social barriers are placed in the paths of women (or men). No other manifestation of the claim that dharma is beyond gender makes sense. Why would there be more men than women teachers of the timeless dharma that is beyond gender? Yet throughout Buddhist history, women dharma teachers have been relatively rare, though in contemporary North American Buddhism about half the teachers of Buddhism are women.

In my own life as a Buddhist practitioner, I have worked with both women and men teachers, though early in my practice life, my primary teacher was a man whose activities were problematic to many women, Chögyam Trungpa, Rinpoche. My own position has always been that while theoretically I would like to work with a woman teacher, ideology does not determine my choice of teachers. I would always become a student of the teacher with whom I felt the closest relationship, the teacher I felt offered the clearest and most profound instruction in dharma, rather than seeking out a woman teacher simply because she was a woman. *In Buddhism, it is the student's responsibility to choose a teacher carefully, so that one can then trust the teacher. Ideology, even feminist ideology, is a poor guide to finding someone worthy of trust.*

Nevertheless, I was curious about the few women who did teach in the Tibetan tradition and made an extra effort to meet them. Contrary to ideology, but consistent with good sense about dharma, I did not initially feel especially compelled by these women *as* teachers. This pattern persisted even when I met the woman who is now my principle teacher, and for whom I now function as a senior teacher, Her Eminence Mindrolling Jetsun Khandro Rinpoche. Now the relationship fits the classic description of the teacher-student relationship in Tibetan Buddhism, and I am very happy about this development, which really did not occur with either of my primary male teachers, despite years of serious study and practice. But, despite my feminist viewpoint that the presence or absence of women teachers determines whether Buddhism is overcoming its heritage of male dominance, I am not convinced that my relationship with Jetsun Khandro Rinpoche developed *because* she is a woman, but because she *is* the teacher that she is, as well as because of an apparent karmic link between us. That is as it should be.

I went to considerable effort to meet Khandro Rinpoche, because, like the dharma itself, she was not going to come to Eau Claire, Wisconsin. Another of many trips to Boulder, Colorado, took me to meet her, and I was excited about the person I met, as well as about the fact that she strongly encouraged me to continue my work as a Buddhist feminist and promised she would help me with my practice. From that point on, I regarded her as one of my teachers, though my primary loyalties remained with the Shambhala Buddhist organization in which I had grown up. She assumed the same thing about my primary identification, and I actually became much more involved in the Shambhala organization while I also began to study seriously with Khandro Rinpoche, doing a major retreat with her every year. I was somewhat surprised, given my views about the importance of women teachers, that I continued to feel strongly connected with my male teachers even after I had found an ideal female teacher, but honesty is more important than ideology in Buddhist practice.

Eventually many things converged, and somewhat against my earlier expectations, I began to realize how much I had learned from Khandro Rinpoche, how much major issues had been transmuted, and how much I was really in her world. At that point I began to consider her my primary teacher, though my other teachers also remain important. I think that this whole process is highly instructive regarding the actual relationship between ideology and authentic experience. It was good for me to learn that, whatever my belief system might be, I could regard a male teacher as my primary teacher even when a female teacher was also present. It is also good to know that when I came to regard Khandro Rinpoche as my primary teacher, it was because of her being the teacher she is, not because she is a woman. I am also delighted finally to have the kind of relationship with an authentic teacher for which I had always longed.

In sum, what is it about being a Buddhist that delights me so much? The profundity of its view, the transformative power of its spiritual disciplines, and the results—real change, a transformation from unhappiness to contentment. On the one hand, Buddhist disciplines bring taming of ideology and anger; and on the other hand, they bring a deepening of nonfixated passion for liberation—at all levels. Who could ask for more?

Notes

INTRODUCTION

1. Nancy Auer Falk and Rita M. Gross, eds., *Unspoken Worlds: Women's Religious Lives*, 3rd ed. (Belmont, CA: Wadsworth, 2001); Gross, *Buddhism after Patriarchy: A Feminist History, Analysis, and Reconstruction of Buddhism* (Albany: State University of New York Press, 1993); and Gross, *Feminism and Religion: An Introduction* (Boston: Beacon Press, 1996).

2. Innumerable books about the visual dimensions of Tibetan Buddhism are easy to find. Two books containing useful basic information are Jonathan Landaw and Andy Weber, *Images of Enlightenment: Tibetan Art in Practice* (Ithaca, NY: Snow Lion, 1993); and Rudy Jansen, *The Book of Buddhas: Ritual Symbolism Used on Buddhist Statuary and Ritual Objects* (Diver, Holland: Binkey Kok Publications, 1990).

3. Though I had picked my title before I was aware of this new book, another Buddhist author has recently chosen the same analogy for his lifework. See Khenpo Nyoshul, *A Marvelous Garland of Rare Gems: Biographies of Masters of Awareness in the Dzogchen Lineage (A Spiritual History of the Teachings of Natural Great Perfection)* (Johnson City, CA: Padma Press, 2003).

CHAPTER 1

1. Rita M. Gross, "Three Strikes and You're Out: An Autobiography at Mid-Life," in *A Time to Weep, A Time to Sing: Faith Journeys of Women Scholars of Religion*, eds. Mary Jo Meadow and Carole A. Rayburn (Minneapolis: Winston Press, 1985), pp. 30–46; and Rita M. Gross and Rosemary Radford Ruether, *Religious Feminism and the Future of the Planet: A Buddhist-Christian-Feminist Conversation* (London and New York: Continuum, 2001), pp. 25–47.

2. Gross and Ruether, *Religious Feminism*, pp. 33–5.

3. *Rebirth* could mean literal physical rebirth, but it just as easily connotes a psychological style or mind-set in Buddhist psychology. Such a mind-set could last for a few moments, for an entire physical life span, or for many lifetimes.

4. Rita M. Gross, "'Finding Renunciation and Balance in American Buddhism: Work, Family, Community, and Friendship," in *Soaring and Settling: Buddhist Perspectives on Contemporary Social and Religious Issues* (New York: Continuum, 2000), pp. 94–107; and Gross, "Some Reflections on Community and Survival," *Buddhist-Christian Studies Journal* 22 (2003): 3–19.

5. Rita M. Gross, "Impermanence, Nowness, and Non-Judgment: Appreciating Finitude and Death," in *Soaring and Settling*, pp. 140–51.

PART TWO

1. For example, at some point in the mid- to late 1980s, by which time every scholar should have been able to assimilate the changes required by feminist scholarship, including gender-inclusive language and examples of how women practiced their various religions, a textbook publisher asked me to quietly "fix up" a prominent textbook on world religions. This textbook was multiauthored; each chapter on each of the different world religions had been written by a prominent male scholar of that religion. Each chapter had been written in generic masculine language, using a completely androcentric model of humanity to select examples to be included in its description of the religion portrayed. The textbook was due for a revision, and by that time, professors and students would no longer accept a textbook that had not assimilated changes required by the emergence of women's studies scholarship. Hence, I was asked to "revise" the book. Puzzled, I asked the publisher why he didn't just require the authors of the various chapters to bring their own writings up to date. The publisher replied that that request had been made, but the authors had replied that "they just couldn't do it; they didn't know how." Tolerating such incompetence on the part of established scholars and covering for them has always seemed to me to be quite problematic. Why not simply withdraw their book from publication and commission a new textbook by authors capable of writing in gender-inclusive and gender-neutral ways? And why did the publisher assume that I had no scholarship of my own that needed tending to? Why the assumption that I would gladly revise a male-authored book so that it would conform to the new scholarly standards of the day?

2. The first book I read after completing my dissertation was Simone de Beauvoir's *The Second Sex*. I was amazed and furious. I had duplicated her conclusions about men viewing themselves as subjects and women as objects in the prevailing discourses of the day. Reading her book earlier could have given me many clues and saved me a great deal of work. The fact that none of my mentors even mentioned such an important book is indicative of how androcentric the established scholars of the day actually were.

3. Rita M. Gross, *Buddhism after Patriarchy: A Feminist History, Analysis and Reconstruction of Buddhism* (Albany, NY: State University of New York Press, 1993), pp. 291–317; and Gross, *Feminism and Religion: An Introduction* (Boston: Beacon Press, 1996), pp. 5–28.

4. One of the conference organizers did point out in his concluding comments that my question had not been taken up at all by the conference participants. See Kari Mikko Vesala and Heikki Pesonnen, "Religion and Relations: The Social Dimension of Methodological Arguments," in *How to Do Comparative Religion? Three Ways, Many Goals,* ed. Rene Gothani (Berlin and New York: Walter de Gruyter, 2005), p. 207.

CHAPTER 2

This chapter, which was written in 1975 and presented at the 1975 national meetings of the American Academy of Religion, is based on methodological conclusions reached in my doctoral dissertation, *Exclusion and Participation: The Role of Women in Aboriginal Australian Religion,* for which I was awarded a PhD from the University of Chicago in 1975. It was published once, in Rita M. Gross, ed., *Beyond Androcentrism: New Essays on Women and Religion* (Missoula, MT: Scholars Press for the Academy of Religion, 1977), pp. 7–21, and has been out of print for many years.

1. The best discussion of woman as "the other" in androcentric culture is Simone de Beauvoir's classic *The Second Sex.*

CHAPTER 3

This chapter was written in 2001 in response to an invitation to present the keynote address at the conference Methodological Innovations in the Study of Religion and Gender, held at the University of Bristol, England, in April 2001. It was published in *Gender, Religion, and Diversity: Cross-Cultural Perspectives,* eds. Ursula King and Tina Beattie (London and New York: Continuum, 2004), pp. 17–27.

1. I have told the story of my adventures as a graduate student writing one of the first dissertations on women and religion in a book coauthored with Rosemary Radford Ruether: *Religious Feminism and the Future of the Planet: A Buddhist-Christian Conversation* (New York: Continuum, 2001), pp. 39–44.

2. According to information provided by Ursula King, the term *androcentric* was invented in 1903 by U.S. sociologist Leslie Ward in his comments on Johann Jakob Bachofen's gynocentric theories about early society. But it did not come into widespread usage until the women's studies movement, and to my knowledge, the term was reinvented rather than borrowed from Ward's work.

3. I used the term *androgynous* to mean "both male and female," its clear etymological meaning, rather than the more popular meaning of "vague and undifferentiated sexuality." That usage still prevails in my 1996 book, *Feminism and Religion: An Introduction* (Boston: Beacon Press). However, because that terminology was not adopted by others in the field, I have now given up my preferred terms and use the more cumbersome "gender-neutral and gender-inclusive models of humanity" instead.

4. Gross, "Androcentrism and Androgyny in the Methodology of History of Religions," in *Beyond Androcentrism: New Essays on Women and Religion,* ed.

Rita M. Gross (Missoula, MT: Scholars Press, 1977), pp. 7–19, and chapter 2 of this volume.

5. For example, let us look at the literature on Engaged Buddhism. Two major anthologies, Christopher S. Queen and Sallie B. King, eds., *Engaged Buddhism: Buddhist Liberation Movements in Asia* (Albany, NY: SUNY Press, 1996), and Christopher S. Queen, ed., *Engaged Buddhism in the West* (Boston: Wisdom Publications, 1999), discuss a wide range of social issues and Buddhist movements that address these issues. There is no discussion of feminist issues in Buddhism in either volume, though the book about Asian Engaged Buddhism does contain a chapter on the movement to restore the nuns' ordination in those Asian lineages in which it has been lost, certainly not the only issue for Buddhist women. My work is mentioned several times in the volume on Engaged Buddhism in the West. I am identified as a feminist theologian, but my work on feminism is not cited. Instead, several articles I have written on Buddhism and ecology are misidentified as Buddhist approaches to the population problem. Clearly, for these editors, gender issues, especially those regarding equity for women, are a separate conceptual category. It is quite common to regard war and peace, racism, economic justice, and the environment as "real" social issues and to think of gender issues as less central to the project of social justice.

6. See especially the methodological appendix "Religious Experience and the Study of Religion: The History of Religions" in Rita M. Gross, *Buddhism after Patriarchy* (Albany, NY: State University of New York Press, 1993), pp. 305–17.

7. The most complete argument is Rita M. Gross, "The Place of the Personal and the Subjective in Religious Studies," in *The Researcher Experience in Qualitative Research*, eds. Susan Diemert Moch and Marie F. Gates (Thousand Oaks, CA: Sage Publications, 2000), pp. 163–77, which is also reprinted here as chapter 4 of this volume.

8. I first emphasized this distinction in the other methodological appendix of *Buddhism after Patriarchy* (pp. 291–304). My book *Feminism and Religion: An Introduction* (Boston: Beacon Press, 1996), one of the very few books genuinely about women and *religion*, not women and *Christianity*, is built on this distinction, and developing the distinction is central to the book's first chapter.

9. See references to specific examples in Gross, *Feminism and Religion*, pp. 66–79.

10. Rita M. Gross, "Hindu Female Deities as a Resource in the Contemporary Rediscovery of the Goddess," *Journal of the American Academy of Religion* 46, no. 3 (September 1978): 269–91.

11. Grace G. Burford, "Issues of Inclusion and Exclusion in Feminist Theology," *Journal of Feminist Studies in Religion* 16, no. 2 (Fall 2000): 85.

12. Deborah F. Sawyer and Diane M. Cutler, eds., *Is There a Future for Feminist Theology?* (Sheffield, England: Sheffield Academic Press, 1999), p. 24.

13. The term *Eurocentric* is not used to contrast European and North American thought, but rather to differentiate symbol systems and religious teachings that derive from a non-European source, such as Asia or Africa, from systems of thought that trace their intellectual ancestry to European thought. Thus, North America is included as part of the "Eurocentric" orbit.

14. For a fuller discussion of these issues, see Rita M. Gross, "Feminist Theology as Theology of Religions," *Feminist Theology* 26 (January 2001): 83–101; and chapter 13 of this volume.

CHAPTER 4

This chapter, written in the late 1990s, was commissioned by a colleague in the social sciences at the University of Wisconsin, Eau Claire, for an edited book she was compiling on the experience of a researcher doing qualitative research in the social sciences. It was published in Susan Diemert Mock and Marie F. Gales, eds., *The Researcher Experience in Qualitative Research* (Thousand Oaks, CA; London; New Delhi: Sage Publications, 2000). It has never been available to an audience of scholars in religious studies.

1. Wendy Doniger O'Flaherty, *Other People's Myths* (New York: Macmillan Publishing Company, 1988), p. 18.

2. Rita M. Gross, *Buddhism after Patriarchy: A Feminist History, Analysis, and Reconstruction of Buddhism* (Albany, NY: Sate University of New York Press, 1993); and Gross, *Soaring and Settling: Buddhist Perspectives on Contemporary Social and Religious Issues* (New York: Continuum, 1998).

3. Rita M. Gross, *Buddhism after Patriarchy: A Feminist History, Analysis and Reconstruction of Buddhism* (Albany, NY: State University of New York Press, 1993); and Gross, *Feminism and Religion: An Introduction* (Boston: Beacon Press, 1996).

4. Gross, *Feminism and Religion*, p. 76.

5. For example, see Cheris Kramarae and Dale Spender, *The Knowledge Explosion: Generations of Feminist Scholarship* (New York: Teachers College Press, 1992).

6. Kunkum Sangari and Sudesh Vaid, eds., *Recasting Women: Essays in Colonial History* (New Delhi: Kali for Women, 1989).

7. Nancy Auer Falk and Rita M. Gross, *Unspoken Worlds: Women's Religious Lives* (Belmont, CA: Wadsworth, 1989). The currently available third edition was published in 2001.

8. For a critical discussion of feminist discussions of prehistory, see chapter 9 of this volume, "The Prepatriarchal Hypothesis: An Assessment."

9. William E. Paden, *Religious Worlds: The Comparative Study of Religion* (Boston: Beacon Press, 1988).

10. Ibid.

CHAPTER 5

This chapter was written in 2002 in response to an invitation to present a keynote address at the international conference Approaches in Comparative Religion Reconsidered, held in Helsinki, Finland, in November 2002. It was published in Rene Gothoni, ed., *How to Do Comparative Religion? Three Ways, Many Goals* (Berlin: Walter de Gruter, 2005), pp. 149–66, and has been revised and shortened for publication in this volume.

1. See chapter 13 of this volume, "Feminist Theology as Theology of Religions," and Rita M. Gross, "Excuse Me, but What's the Question? Isn't Religious Diversity Normal?" in *The Myth of Religious Superiority: A Multi-Religious Exploration,* ed. Paul Knitter (Maryknoll, NY: Orbis Books, 2005), pp. 75–87.

2. When I began my study of religion at the University of Chicago in 1965, there were about four hundred students in the Divinity School, twelve of whom were women. Six of the twelve women had entered with the class of 1965, and the professors were concerned about what they could do with "so many" women who wanted to study religion. Some of them confessed to changing the content of some of their lectures because there were women present.

3. Kathryn Young, "Having Your Cake and Eating It Too," *Journal of the American Academy of Religion I* 61, no. 1 (March 1999): 167–84. My response follows her comments in the same issue of the journal.

4. Ray L. Hart, "Religious and Theological Studies in American Higher Education," *Journal of the American Academy of Religion* 67, no. 1 (March 1991): 715–827.

5. Though many books and articles could be cited, two important and comprehensive books were published in 1979 and 1980. For feminist theology, the important early collection is Carol P. Christ and Judith Plaskow, *Womanspirit Rising* (San Francisco: Harper and Row, 1979). The first edition of Nancy Auer Falk and Rita M. Gross, eds., *Unspoken Worlds: Women's Religious Lives,* was published in 1980 by Harper and Row. The current third edition was published by Wadsworth in 2001.

6. Because many people are unclear about what feminism entails, short, simple definitions remain essential. I define feminism in two ways. Feminism seeks "freedom from the prison of gender roles," and it involves "radical practice of the cohumanity of women and men." The essential point of both definitions is that women are fully, equally human. They are not a separate quasi species about which men have opinions and for whom they make the rules, even though these assumptions about women were the clear, though unstated, implication of almost all prefeminist talk about women and gender.

7. Rita M. Gross, "Where Have We Been? Where Do We Need to Go? Women's Studies and Gender in Religion and Feminist Theology," in *Gender, Religion, and Diversity,* eds. Ursula King and Tina Beattie (London: Continuum, 2004), pp. 17–27; and chapter 3 of this volume.

8. See "Androcentrism and Androgyny in the Methodology of History of Religions," chapter 2 of this volume.

9. Mircea Eliade, *Patterns in Comparative Religion: A Study of the Element of the Sacred in the History of Religions* (Cleveland and New York: World Publishing, 1963).

10. Mircea Eliade, *Rites and Symbols of Initiation: The Mysteries of Birth and Rebirth* (New York: Harper and Row, 1958).

11. An example of the politics of research far removed from religious studies involves the Atkins diet, which claims that a diet far different from the high-carbohydrate, low-fat diet recommended by the medical establishment for years is actually healthier in some ways and helps people lose weight relatively easily.

Proponents of this diet claim that a high-carbohydrate diet actually causes obesity. For thirty years, no research was done on this diet, despite much anecdotal evidence of its effectiveness. Any scientists contemplating doing such research quickly gave up the project because they would have lost all credibility and respectability in their profession for undertaking such research. See Gary Taubes, "What If Fat Doesn't Make You Fat?" *New York Times Magazine*, July 7, 2002, pp. 22–27.

CHAPTER 6

This chapter was written in 2000 and delivered as a plenary address at the Sixth International Buddhist-Christian Dialogue Conference held in Tacoma, Washington, in August 2000. It was published in *CrossCurrents* 53, no. 1 (Spring 2003), pp. 8–20.

1. Elie Wiesel, *The Town Beyond the Wall*, trans. Stephen Becker (New York: Avon Books, 1969), p. 190. See also Carol P. Christ's feminist quotation and retelling of this story in her book *Laughter of Aphrodite: Reflections on a Journey to the Goddess* (San Francisco: Harper and Row, 1987), pp. 20–21.

2. *Newsweek*, June 12, 2000, p. 56.

3. Review of *Gladiator*, Eau Claire *Leader-Telegram*, Thursday, May 18, 2000, sec. C.

4. Wiesel, *Town Beyond the Wall*, p. 190.

PART THREE

1. The cumbersome phrase "gender-neutral and gender-inclusive models of humanity" replaces what I called "the androgynous model of humanity" for much of my career and is found in many other articles in this volume. My reason for this change in terminology is explained in chapter 3, note 3.

2. While I was completing my dissertation, I contacted my long-term colleague Nancy Auer Falk to suggest that we coedit an anthology of articles on women's religious lives, in non-Western religions for the first edition, and in global perspective for the second and third editions. We knew that there was almost nothing then in print that could be used in such an anthology and that we would have to seek out scholars who could do such research in their areas of specialization. In the summer of 1975, immediately after receiving my PhD, I drove to Nancy's home and we spent about a week trying to figure out how we could possibly construct such an anthology. We actually advertised for scholars who might be contributors in several academic newsletters and solicited others whom we knew. Gradually we gathered a list of contributors. The editing process was extremely painstaking and time-consuming in a precomputer age. It is almost impossible to imagine how we did that editing, but it did involve another trip to Nancy's home and about a week of painstaking word-by-word coediting of a final manuscript. The first edition of *Unspoken Worlds* was published in early 1980. The second edition was published in 1989, and the third in 2001. Publishers would gladly accept a fourth edition, but Nancy and I have agreed that we have completed our work on this topic.

3. Eleanor McLaughlin, "The Christian Past: Does It Hold a Future for Women?" in *Womanspirit Rising: A Feminist Reader in Religion,* eds. Carol P. Christ and Judith Plaskow (San Francisco: Harper and Row, 1979), pp. 93–106.

CHAPTER 7

The research which led to this chapter was begun in 1967 and was incorporated into my doctoral dissertation, "Exclusion and Participation: The Role of Women in Aboriginal Australian Religion," for which I was awarded a PhD from the University of Chicago in 1975. A longer version was presented at the American Academy of Religion meetings in 1976 and published in the *Journal of the American Academy of Religion* (December 1977, pp. 1147–81). The condensed version, published here, has been the concluding chapter of all editions of *Unspoken Worlds: Women's Religious Lives,* from the first published by Harper and Row in 1980, to the most recently published revised third edition: Nancy Auer Falk and Rita M. Gross, eds., *Unspoken Worlds: Women's Religious Lives* (Belmont, CA: Wadsworth, 2001), pp. 301–10. I also published a more comprehensive survey article on the materials discussed in my doctoral thesis: Gross, "Tribal Religion: Aboriginal Australia," in *Women in World Religions,* ed. Arvind Sharma (Albany: State University of New York Press, 1987), pp. 37–58.

1. W. Lloyd Warner, *A Black Civilization: A Study of an Australian Tribe,* rev. ed. (New York: Harper and Row, Harper Torchbooks, 1958), p. 384.

2. A.P. Abbie, *The Original Australians* (New York: American Elsevier, 1969), p. 125.

3. C.H. Berndt, "Women and the 'Secret Life,'" in *Man in Aboriginal Australia* (Sydney: Kegan and. Robertson, 1964), p. 274.

4. R.M. Berndt and C.H. Berndt, *Sexual Behavior in Arnhem Land,* Viking Ford Publications in Anthropology 16 (New York: Viking, 1951), pp. 89–90.

5. K. Langloh Parker, *The Euahlayi Tribe: A Study of Aboriginal Life in Australia* (London: Archibald Constable, 1905), pp. 56–58.

6. R. Piddington, "Karadjeri Initiation," *Oceania* 3, no. 1 (1932): 83.

7. Phyllis Kaberry, *Aboriginal Woman: Sacred and Profane* (Philadelphia: Blakiston Co., 1939), pp. 242–45.

8. Ursula McConnel, *Myths of the Munkan* (Melbourne: Melbourne University Press, 1957), pp. 135–43.

9. R.M. Berndt and C.H. Berndt, *The World of the First Australians* (Chicago: University of Chicago Press, 1964), p. 237; Berndt and Berndt, *Man, Land, and Myth: The Gunwinggu People* (East Lansing: Michigan State University Press, 1970), p. 116.

10. The fullest account of the Djanggawul myth cycle is found in R.M. Berndt, *Djanggawul: An Aboriginal Religious Cult of North-Eastern Arnhem Land* (London: Routledge and Kegan Paul, 1952).

11. R.M. Berndt, *Kunapipi: A Study of an Australian Aboriginal Religious Cult* (New York: International Universities Press, 1951).

12. Berndt and Berndt, *World of the First Australians,* p. 221.

13. Warner, *A Black Civilization,* p. 318.

14. Berndt and Berndt, *World of the First Australians*, pp. 144–45.

15. M. F. Ashley-Montague, "The Origin of Subincision in Australian," *Oceania* 8, no. 2 (1937): 204–7.

16. Berndt and Berndt, *World of the First Australians*, p. 146.

17. Warner, *A Black Civilization*, p. 268.

18. R. M. Berndt, *Djanggawul*, p. 41.

19. R. M. Berndt, *Kunapipi*, p. 55.

CHAPTER 8

The idea that eventually led to this chapter is mentioned in chapter 2, "Androcentrism and Androgyny in the Methodology of History of Religions." The chapter was finally written in 1995 and presented at the seventeenth Congress of the International Association for the History of Religions, Mexico City, 1995. It was published in *Religion: An International Journal* 28, no. 4 (October 1998): 319–27. For publication in this volume, I have not attempted to update the review of the literature. This chapter is not primarily a review of the literature but an attempt to rethink how best to present a complex, difficult, and culturally unfamiliar phenomenon.

1. Rita M. Gross, "Menstruation and Childbirth as Ritual and Religious Experience in the Religion of Aboriginal Australians," in *Unspoken Worlds: Women's Religious Lives*, 3rd ed. (Belmont, CA: Wadsworth, 2001), pp. 301–10; and chapter 7 in this volume. See also "Primal Traditions: The Example of Aboriginal Australia," in *Women and World Religions*, ed. Arvind Sharma (Albany: State University of New York Press, 1987), pp. 37–58.

2. Among others, see Elisabeth Bernard, *Chinnamasta: The Aweful Buddhist and Hindu Tantric Goddess* (Delhi: Motilal Banarsidass, 1994); C. Mackenzie Brown, *God as Mother: A Feminine Theology in India* (Hartford, VT: Claude Stark and Co., 1974); Brown, *The Triumph of the Goddess* (Albany: State University of New York Press, 1990); Thomas B. Coburn, *Devi Mahatmya: The Crystallization of the Goddess Tradition* (Delhi: Motilal Banarsidass, 1985); and Coburn, *Encountering the Goddess: A Translation of the Devi-Mahatmya and a Study of its Interpretation* (Albany, NY: SUNY, 1991); Kathleen M. Erndl, *Victory to the Mother: The Hindu Goddess of Northwest India in Myth, Ritual, and Symbol* (New York: Oxford University Press, 1993); John Stratton Hawley and Donna Marie Wulff, eds., *The Divine Consort: Radha and the Goddesses of India* (Berkeley, CA: Berkeley Religious Studies Series, 1982); Pupal Jayakar, *The Earth Mother* (New Delhi, India: Penguin Books, 1980); David Kinsley's *Hindu Goddesses: Vision of the Divine Feminine in Hindu Religious Tradition* (Berkeley: University of California Press, 1986); Leonard Nathan and Clinton Seely, trans., *Grace and Mercy in her Wild Hair: Selected Poems to the Mother Goddess* (Boulder, CO: Great Eastern, 1982); Tracy Pintchman, *The Rise of the Goddess in Hindu Tradition* (Albany, NY: SUNY, 1994); and William S. Sax, *Mountain Goddess: Gender and Politics in a Himalayan Pilgrimage* (New York: Oxford University Press, 1991).

3. William Paden, *Religious Worlds: The Comparative Study of Religion* (Boston: Beacon Press, 1988), p. 164.

4. Max Müller was one of the founders of the academic study of Indian religions and a proponent of *religionswisssenschaft*, the claim that religions could and should be studied like any other observable object using scientific methods. He coined the term *henotheism* as an attempt to understand how a religion could take seriously the existence of a multiplicity of deities. His explanation was that the religious person accepted many deities as "real," but in the religious experience, the only deity that was "real" psychologically was the deity being worshiped in the present moment.

An older, very highly recommended exception to this generalization is Alain Danielou, *Hindu Polytheism* (New York: Random House, 1964). This book includes poetic and cogent arguments for the profundity of "polytheistic" theology.

5. A very recent Western theological challenge to Western fixation on the number "one" and attempt to work out a theology of multiplicity is Laurel C. Schneider, *Beyond Monotheism: A Theology of Multiplicity* (London and New York: Routledge, 2008).

6. It is very interesting that the gesture I am describing, called "anjali," is one of the most common gestures in both Hinduism and Buddhism. It is used, among other things, as the most common gesture of greeting and of showing respect. In Vajrayana Buddhist ritual, this *mudra* is very common and is often interpreted as expressing a nondual joining of seeming opposites without minimizing or obliterating either of them. The right hand symbolizes many things, as does the left. They are joined without losing their individuality—an extremely potent but simple gesture representing the coincidence of opposites, or nondual "union."

CHAPTER 9

This chapter was primarily written as part of a chapter in my book *Feminism and Religion* (Boston: Beacon Press, 1996), pp. 151–69. Along the way, it was also presented at the seventeenth Congress of the International Association for the History of Religions in Mexico City in 1995 and published in *Gender/Bodies/Religions: Adjunct Proceedings of the XVII Congress of the International Association for the History of Religions*, ed. Slyvia Marcos (Cuernavaca, Mexico: Aler Publications, 2000), pp. 73–91.

1. Cynthia Eller, *Living in the Lap of the Goddess: The Feminist Spirituality Movement in America* (New York: Crossroad, 1993), pp. 150–84. The phrase "creation of patriarchy" is taken from the book title *The Creation of Patriarchy* (New York: Oxford University Press, 1986), written by Gerda Lerner.

2. Lionel Tiger, *Men in Groups* (New York: Random House, 1969); George Gilder, *Sexual Suicide* (New York: Quadrangle, 1973).

3. Riane Eisler, *The Chalice and the Blade: Our History, Our Future* (San Francisco: Harper and Row, 1987), pp. 24–28.

4. David Kinsley, *The Goddesses' Mirror: Visions of the Divine Feminine* (Albany: State University of New York Press, 1989), p. xviii.

5. Peggy Reeves Sanday, *Female Power and Male Dominance: On the Origins of Sexual Inequality* (Cambridge: Cambridge University Press, 1981), p. 4.

6. M. Kay Martin and Barbara Voorhies, *Female of the Species* (New York: Columbia University Press, 1975). p. 190.

7. For a fuller discussion of this and other issues, see Margaret Ehrenberg, *Women in Prehistory* (Norman: University of Oklahoma Press, 1989), pp. 38–76.

8. For example, see Sanday, *Female Power,* pp. 113–20, 135–43.

9. Ehrenberg, *Women in Prehistory,* p. 173.

10. Ralph Mannheim, trans., *Myth, Religion, and Mother Right: Selected Writings of J. J. Bachofen* (Princeton, NJ: Princeton University Press, 1967).

11. Elizabeth Gould Davis, *The First Sex* (Baltimore: Penguin Books, 1973); Merlin Stone, *When God Was a Woman* (New York: Harcourt, Brace, and Jovanovich, 1978).

12. Anne Barstow, "The Prehistoric Goddess," in *The Book of the Goddess: Past and Present,* ed. Carl Olson (New York: Crossroads, 1983), pp. 7–28.

13. Marija Gimbutas, *The Language of the Goddess* (San Francisco: Harper and Row, 1989); and Gimbutas, *The Civilization of the Goddess* (San Francisco: Harper and Row, 1991).

14. Elinor Gadon, *The Once and Future Goddess* (San Francisco: Harper and Row, 1989); Anne Baring and Jules Cashford, *The Myth of the Goddess* (New York: Penguin, 1991).

15. Carol P. Christ, *Laughter of Aphrodite* (San Francisco: Harper and Row, 1987).

16. Eisler, *Chalice and the Blade,* p. 24.

17. David Kinsley, *The Goddesses' Mirror: Visions of the Divine from East and West* (Albany, NY: SUNY Press, 1989), pp. xi–xix; Katherine K. Young, "Goddesses, Feminists, and Scholars," in *The Annual Review of Women in World Religions,* eds. Katherine K. Young and Arvind Sharma (Albany, NY: SUNY Press, 1991), pp. 105–79; Joan B. Townsend, "The Goddess: Fact, Fallacy, and Revitalization Movement," in *Goddesses in Religions and Modern Debate,* ed. Larry W. Hurtado (Atlanta: Scholars Press, 1990), pp. 180–203.

18. Townsend, "The Goddess," p. 197.

19. Rosemary Ruether, *God and Gaia* (San Francisco: Harper and Row, 1992), pp. 143–65.

20. Townsend, "The Goddess," p. 194; Young, "Goddesses, Feminists, and Scholars," p. 146.

21. Thornkild Jacobsen, *Treasures of Darkness: A History of Mesopotamian Religion* (New Haven, CT: Yale University Press, 1976), pp. 77–84.

22. Lerner, *Creation of Patriarchy,* pp. 15–53; Ehrenberg, *Women in Prehistory,* pp. 99–107.

23. Hans J. Nilssen, *The Early History of the Ancient Near East: 9,000–2,000 B.C.* (Chicago: University of Chicago Press, 1988), gives an overview of the process of urbanization and population density leading to heightened warfare, rather than the other way around.

24. Robert Ellwood, "Patriarchal Revolution in Ancient Japan: Episodes from the *Nihonshoki* Sujun Chronicle," *Journal of Feminist Studies in Religion* 2, no. 2 (Fall 1986): 23–37.

25. Sanday, *Female Power,* p. 165.

26. Ibid., p. 8.

27. Barstow, "The Prehistoric Goddess," p. 14.

PART FOUR

1. Rita M. Gross, "Hindu Female Deities as a Resource in the Contemporary Rediscovery of the Goddess," *Journal of the American Academy of Religion* 47, no. 3 (1978): 269–91.

2. *Forms of Prayer for Jewish Worship*, vol. 2, *Prayers for the Pilgrim Festivals of the Reform Synagogues of Great Britain*, 2nd rev. ed. (London: Reform Synagogues of Great Britain, 1995), pp. 617–19.

CHAPTER 10

This chapter has a long history. The first thing I wrote after I completed the final draft of my doctoral dissertation in 1974 was an essay titled "Female God Language in a Jewish Context." That version, which did not include the role-reversal fantasy or any suggestions about female *imagery* (as opposed to *language*) for deity was reprinted in the classic anthology Carol P. Christ and Judith Plaskow, eds., *Womanspirit Rising: A Feminist Reader in Religion* (San Francisco: Harper and Row, 1975), pp. 167–73. In that form, the article had considerable influence. Meanwhile, I was also exploring how Hindu images of goddesses might inspire Western feminist reconstructions of deity. When asked to contribute an article to Susannah Heschel's anthology *On Being a Jewish Feminist: A Reader* (New York: Schocken, 1983), pp. 234–47, I combined the two approaches and added the role-reversal fantasy. This was my last attempt to write in a Jewish voice.

1. For a longer, more detailed statement of this argument, see Rita M. Gross, "Female God-Language in the Jewish Context," in *Womanspirit Rising*, eds. Carol P. Christ and Judith Plaskow (New York: Harper and Row, 1979).

2. For a more detailed discussion, see Rachel Adler, "The Jew Who Wasn't There: *Halakhah* and the Jewish Woman," in *Response: A Contemporary Jewish Review* 7, no. 2 (Summer 1973): 77–89; and Rita M. Gross, "On Being a Religious Jewish Woman," in *Ancient Roots and Modem Meanings: A Contemporary Reader in Jewish Identity*, ed. Jerry Diller (New York: Bloch, 1998).

3. I am indebted to Nelle Morton's Christian role-reversal fantasy in *Sexist Religion and Women in the Church: No More Silence* (New York: Association Press, 1976), pp. 29–31, for inspiration for this role-reversal fantasy. Several sentences have been quoted directly from that work.

4. The English translation of this very familiar traditional prayer, as given in *Forms of Prayer for Jewish Worship*, vol. 2, *Prayers for the Pilgrim Festivals* of the Reform Synagogues of Great Britain, 2nd rev. ed., (1995), p. 211, is "Blessed are You our God and God of our ancestors, God of Abraham and God of Sarah, God of Isaac and God of Rebecca, God of Jacob and God of Rachel and Leah, the great, the mighty and the awesome God, God beyond, generous in love and kindness and possessing all. You remember the good deeds of our ancestors and

therefore in love bring rescue to the generations, for such is your being. Sovereign who helps and saves and shields. Blessed are You God, the shield of Abraham and Sarah." Because Hebrew involves much more genderized grammar than does English, gender is much more obvious in the Hebrew version in the role-reversal fantasy than in the English translation. On page 210, the same prayer book provides a Hebrew alternative that does reverse the gender inflections of most traditional words, such as "you," from masculine to feminine. Hebrew prayer intimately addresses deity as "you," but as in many languages, there is a masculine "you" and a feminine "you," though there is no distinction between a formal and familiar form of "you."

5. For a fuller discussion of these images as well as all the issues involved in rediscovering female imagery of deity and utilizing non-Western resources as a tool, see Rita M. Gross, "Hindu Female Deities as a Resource in the Contemporary Rediscovery of the Goddess," *Journal of the American Academy of Religion* (September 1978): 269–91.

6. For a brilliant demonstration of this point, see Carol Christ, "The Liberation of Women and the Liberation of God," in *The Jewish Woman,* ed. Elizabeth Koltun (New York: Schocken Books, 1976), pp. 11–17.

CHAPTER 11

This chapter resulted from an invitation to participate in a panel discussion at the 1994 meetings of the American Academy of Religions. It was published in Alf Hiltelbeitel and Kathleen M. Erndl, eds., *Is the Goddess a Feminist? The Politics of South Asian Goddesses* (Sheffield, UK: Sheffield Academic Press, 2000), pp. 104–12.

1. Rita M. Gross, "Hindu Female Deities as a Resource in the Contemporary Rediscovery of the Goddess," *Journal of the American Academy of Religion* 47, no. 3 (1978): 269–91.

2. Fatima Mernissi, "Women, Saints, and Sanctuaries in Morocco," in *Unspoken Worlds: Women's Religious Lives,* 3rd ed., ed. Nancy Auer Falk and Rita M. Gross (Belmont, CA: Wadsworth, 2001), pp. 144–53.

3. This distinction, which has been made by some anthropologists, is very useful. Authority, which is men's prerogative, is the right to command and to be obeyed. Power is the ability to influence how things happen, even though one does not have the formal authority to determine what is done. Women often have considerable power in patriarchal societies, even though they have little or no authority.

4. In a situation of "mythical male dominance," both men and women *say* that men control society. But when the society is observed, women actually have considerable influence, which is not acknowledged openly by either men or women.

5. Susan Wadley, "Hindu Women's Family and Household Rites in a North India Village," in Falk and Gross, *Unspoken Worlds,* pp. 103–13.

6. For example, see Lina Gupta, "Kali, the Savior," in *After Patriarchy: Feminist Reconstructions of the World's Religions,* eds. Paula Cooey, William R. Eackin, and Jay B. McDaniel (Maryknoll, NY: Orbis Press, 1991), pp. 15–38.

7. Gross, "Hindu Female Deities."

8. See chapter 10, "Steps toward Feminine Imagery in Jewish Theology."

9. Appropriate "apprenticeship" for such cross-cultural "translation" is discussed in depth in chapter 13, "Feminist Theology as Theology of Religions."

CHAPTER 12

This chapter was written in response to an invitation to deliver a presentation at the conference The Feminization of Ritual, held in 1996 in Victoria, British Columbia. Though that version was published in my book *Soaring and Settling: Buddhist Perspectives on Contemporary Social and Religious Issues* (New York: Continuum, 2000), it has been substantially revised for publication in this volume.

1. It might seem strange to claim that psychological transformation, whether individual or collective, is a side effect of ritual. Very often individuals report experiences of greatly heightened consciousness during ritual, and effective rituals can promote or even create group cohesion. Yet these transformations are the *effect* of ritual being performed precisely and regularly, whether or not the ritual happens to be inspiring on any specific occasion. In this sense, individual or social transformation is a side effect of ritual performance, rather than the reason for such performance.

2. See chapter 10, "Steps toward Feminine Imagery of Deity in Jewish Theology," and chapter 11, "Is the (Hindu) Goddess a Feminist?"

3. For an excellent discussion, see Diana Eck, *Darshan: Seeing the Divine Image in India* (Chambersburg, PA: Anima Books, 1985).

4. Rita M. Gross, "Female God-Language in a Jewish Context," in *Womanspirit Rising: A Feminist Reader in Religion*, eds. Carol P. Christ and Judith Plaskow (San Francisco: Harper and Row, 1979), pp. 167–73; Gross, "Steps Toward Feminine Imagery of Deity in Jewish Theology," in *On Being a Jewish Feminist*, ed. Susannah Heschel (New York: Schocken Books, 1983), pp. 234–47.

5. For an account of my own experience with Vajrayogini practice, see Rita M. Gross, *Soaring and Settling: Buddhist Perspectives on Contemporary Social and Religious Issues* (New York: Continuum, 2000), pp. 211–22. See also Miranda Shaw, *Buddhist Goddesses of India* (Princeton, NJ: Princeton University Press, 2006).

6. In the long run, this meeting turned out to be extremely important for me. See chapter 20, "Being a North American Buddhist: Reflections of a Feminist Pioneer."

CHAPTER 13

This chapter was initially invited as a contribution to *Cambridge Companion to Feminist Theology* (Cambridge: Cambridge University Press, 2002), pp. 60–78. It was also published in the *Journal of Feminist Theology* 26 (January 2001): 83–101, and was the focus paper for a panel discussion titled Feminist Theology as Theology of Religions at the 2002 meetings of the American Academy of Religion.

1. Deborah F. Sawyer and Diane M. Cutler, eds., *Is There a Future for Feminist Theology?* (Sheffield, UK: Sheffield Academic Press, 1999), p. 24.

2. Ursula King, "Feminism: The Missing Dimension in the Dialogue of Religions," in *Pluralism and the Religions: The Theological and Political Dimensions*, ed. John May (London: Cassell, 1998), pp. 40–55.

3. For a survey of Christian theologies of religion, see Paul F. Knitter, *No Other Name? A Critical Survey of Christian Attitudes Toward the World Religions* (Maryknoll, NY: Orbis Books, 1985).

4. Katherina von Kellenback, *Anti-Judaism in Feminist Religious Writings* (Atlanta, GA: Scholars Press, 1994); Leonare Siegle-Wcnschwitz, Judith Plaskow, Marie-Theres Wacker, Fokkelien van Dijk-Hemmes, and Aspodeld P. Long, "Special Section on Feminist Anti-Judaism," *Journal of Feminist Studies in Religion* 7, no. 2 (Fall 1991): 95–125.

5. Diana Eck and Dcvaki Jain, eds., *Speaking of Faith: Global Perspective on Women, Religion, and Social Change* (Philadelphia: New Society Press, 1987); Virginia Ramey Mollenkott, ed., *Women of Faith in Dialogue* (New York: Crossroad, 1988).

6. Rita M. Gross, *Feminism and Religion: An Introduction* (Boston: Beacon Press, 1996), p. 49.

7. Ibid., p. 51.

8. For a more detailed discussion of this process, see Gross, *Feminism and Religion*, pp. 49–58.

9. Carol P. Christ and Judith Plaskow, eds., *Womanspirit Rising: A Feminist Reader in Religion* (San Francisco: Harper and Row, 1979), p. 15.

10. William Paden, *Religious Worlds: The Comparative Study of Religion* (Boston: Beacon Press, 1988), p. 164.

11. A clear, accessible discussion is found in D. Eck, *Encountering God: A Spiritual Journey from Bozeman to Benares* (Boston: Beacon Press, 1993), pp. 166–99.

12. For a detailed presentation of my discussion of these arguments, see Rita M. Gross, "Religious Diversity: Some Implications for Monotheism," *Crosscurrents* 49, no. 3 (Fall 1999): 349–66.

13. For example, see Carol Christ's famous essay "Why Women Need the Goddess: Phenomenological, Psychological, and Political Reflections," in Christ and Plaskow, *Womanspirit Rising*, pp. 273–87.

14. For a fuller development of these arguments, see Rita M. Gross, "The Virtues and Joys of the Comparative Mirror," *Boston University School of Theology Focus* (Fall 1999): 9–16.

15. Paden, *Religious Worlds*, p. 165

16. Cynthia Eller, *Living in the Lap of the Goddess: The Feminist Spirituality Movement in America* (New York: Crossroad, 1993), pp. 74–81.

17. Carol Christ, *Rebirth of the Goddess: Finding Meaning in Feminist Spirituality* (Reading, MA: Addison-Wesley, 1997).

18. Rachel Fell McDermott, "The Western Kali," in *Devi: Goddesses of India*, eds. John Stratton Hawley and Diana M. Marie Wulff (Berkeley: University of California Press, 1996), pp. 281–313; Sandy Boucher, *Discovering Kwan-Yin, Buddhist Goddess of Compassion* (Boston: Beacon Press, 1999).

19. John Cobb, *Beyond Dialogue: Toward a Mutual Transformation of Christianity and Buddhism* (Philadelphia, Fortress Press, 1982), p. 49.

CHAPTER 14

This chapter has a very long genesis, beginning with a paper, presentation, and publication occurring in 1980 titled "Feminism from the Perspective of Buddhist Practice." Over the years, it has gone through many versions as dharma talks and other publications. I have chosen to reprint the latest and most complete version in this garland. That version was titled "The Wisdom in the Anger" and was published in *Mindful Politics: A Buddhist Guide to Making the World a Better Place*, ed. Melvin McLoed (Boston: Wisdom Publications, 2006), pp. 225–36.

CHAPTER 15

This chapter was originally an invited contribution to *Socially Engaged Spirituality: Essays in Honor of Sulak Sivaraksha on His Seventieth Birthday* (Bangkok: Sathirakoses-Nagapradipa Foundation, 2003), pp. 70–74.

CHAPTER 16

This chapter was prepared in response to an invitation to give a talk at the San Francisco Zen Center in 2002. It was later published in *Encounters with the Word: Essays in Honor of Aloysius Pieris, S.J.*, eds. Robert Crusz, Marshall Fernando, and Asanga Tilakaratne (Colombo, Sri Lanka: Ecumenical Institute for Study and Dialogue, 2004), pp. 257–79, and in *Contemporary Buddhism: An Interdisciplinary Journal* 5, no. 1 (May 2004): 3–13.

1. Quoted in Rita M. Gross, *Buddhism after Patriarchy: A Feminist History, Analysis, and Reconstruction of Buddhism* (Albany: State University of New York Press, 1993), p. 61.

2. Mary Daly is one of the best known and most controversial figures in Western feminist religious and philosophical thought. While she began her career as a Roman Catholic reformist theologian, she abandoned Christianity as hopelessly patriarchal and began her long career as a "feminist philosopher." Her most influential books include *Beyond God the Father: Toward a Philosophy of Women's Liberation* (Boston: Beacon, 1973) and *Gyn/Ecology: The Metaethics of Radical Feminism* (Boston:; Beacon, 1978).

3. Judith Simmer-Brown, *Dakini's Warm Breath: The Feminine Principle in Tibetan Buddhism* (Boston and London: Shambhala, 2001), p. 216.

4. Kazuaki Tanahashi, *Moon in a Dewdrop: Writings of Zen Master Dogen* (San Francisco: North Point Press, 1985), p. 70.

5. *Terma* is the term applied to certain texts that are said to have been hidden by great teachers of the past to be discovered in the future at the point in time when they are needed. The practice of "discovering" *terma* is relatively common in Tibetan Buddhism.

CHAPTER 17

This chapter was first written in 1984 and presented at the meetings of the American Academy of Religion in that year. It was published in *Feminine Ground: Essays on Women and Tibet*, ed. Janice Willis (Ithaca, NY: Snow Lion Press, 1989), pp. 11–32.

1. Keith Dowman, trans., *Sky Dancer: The Secret Life and Songs of the Lady Yeshe Tsogyel* (London: Routledge and Kegan Paul, 1984), hereafter cited in text; and Tarthang Tulku, trans., *Mother of Knowledge: The Enlightenment of Yeshe Tsogyal* (Oakland, CA: Dharma Press, 1983), hereafter cited in text. Since this chapter was written, a third translation has appeared: Gyalwa Changchub and Namkhai Nyingpo, *Lady of the Lotus-Born: The Life and Enlightenment of Yeshe Tsogyel*, trans. the Padmakara Translation Committee (Boston: Shambhala Publications, 1999).

2. The most well-known source for this basic mythic motif is Joseph Campbell, *The Hero with a Thousand Faces* (Cleveland and New York: World Publishing Company, 1956).

3. This terminology is used to distinguish the two levels often found in Tibetan narratives. The more exoteric level of the story can well be handled by the term *myth* as used in history of religions. But it is helpful to have another term to distinguish the same story, being told from another level or from another point of view. Some use the term *sacred history*, though there is no consensus as yet.

4. This passage discusses Tsogyel from the ultimate point of view by discussing her ultimate existence in terms of the *trikaya*, the three bodies of the Buddha. A good discussion of this difficult concept is found in Bhikshu Sangharakshita, *A Survey of Buddhism* (Boulder, CO: Shambhala, 1980), pp. 240–55. Relatively detailed information about Vajrayogini can be obtained in Chögyam Trungpa, "Sacred Outlook: The Vajrayogini Shrine and Practice," in *The Silk Route and the Diamond Path: Esoteric Buddhist Art on the Trans-Himalayan Trade Routes*, ed. Deborah E. Klimburg-Salter (Los Angeles: UCLA Art Council, 1982).

5. *Terma* texts are especially known or important in the more esoteric forms of Tibetan Buddhism. Supposedly, recognizing the need for them in future ages, great teachers encode the appropriate messages and hide them. Later, they are mystically rediscovered by another great teacher, who makes them much more widely available. This concept could be compared to the stories found already in the beginnings of Mahayana, to the effect that Shakyamuni Buddha himself taught the Mahayana sutras during his own historical life but then hid them with the *naga*s when he realized people were not yet ready to hear them. Both stories, on one level of analysis, function to show that "new" religious developments and texts are not really deviations.

6. This term and the stories narrated at this point seem connected with the Mahayana emphasis on compassion and to be examples of perfected *tonglen* practice. As a meditation practice, on the medium of the breath, one gives away all one's positive experience and qualities to others and then takes on their negativity and suffering. The fact that Tsogyel takes on these experiences as her "final austerity" and really is able to relieve the suffering of others only after

years of intense Vajrayana practice demonstrates an important and often missed point about the Vajrayana—it is an *upaya*, the skillful means quickly to attain the Mahayana so as to manifest Buddha-activity in the world.

7. *Bardo* is the intermediate period between death and taking on a new body at conception. It is said to be extremely confusing and frightening to those of small attainments. For a translation and commentary on the classic text about the *bardo*, see Francesca Fremantle and Chögyam Trungpa, trans., *The Tibetan Book of the Dead: The Great Liberation Through Hearing in the Bardo* (Boulder and London: Shambhala, 1975).

8. A full discussion of the feminine and masculine principles in Vajrayana Buddhism would be a vast undertaking, especially since much of the material is part of the esoteric teachings. My statement here summarizes my article "The Feminine Principle in Tibetan Vajrayana Buddhism: Reflections of a Buddhist Feminist," *Journal of Transpersonal Psychology* 16, no. 3 (1984): 179–92.

9. The term *vision quest,* from the Native American traditions, refers to an initiation in which young people go out alone to "cry for vision from the other world." It also refers, more metaphorically, to the lifelong quest for a deeper vision of reality. For a short, beautiful, and authentic first-person narrative of a vision quest, see Arthur Amiotte, "Eagles Fly Over," in *Parabola: Myth and the Quest for Meaning* 1, no. 3 (September 1976): 28–41.

10. Extensive hagiographic literature is now found in translation. The only other text addressed specifically to the hagiography of women is Tsultrim Allione's *Women of Wisdom* (London: Routledge and Kegan Paul, 1984). Padmasambhava's life story, traditionally attributed to Yeshe Tsogyel, is translated as *The Life and Liberation of Padmasambhava* (Berkeley, CA: Dharma Publishing Co., 1978). Other important biographies include Herbert Guenther, trans., *The Life and Teachings of Naropa* (London: Oxford University Press, 1963); Nalanda Translation Committee, trans., *The Life of Marpa the Translator* (Boulder, CO: Prajna Press, 1982); and Lobsang P. Lhalungpa, trans., *The Life of Milarepa* (New York: E.P. Dutton, 1977).

11. The list "aggression, ignorance, clinging, pride, or jealousy" actually enumerates the five root-*klesa*s, or defilements, in Vajrayana Buddhism. They transmute into the Five Wisdoms of the Five Buddha families. See Chögyam Trungpa, *Cutting through Spiritual Materialism* (Berkeley, CA: Shambhala, 1973), pp. 217–34.

12. Diana Paul, *Women in Buddhism: Images of the Feminine in Mahayana Tradition* (Berkeley, CA: Asian Humanities Press, 1979; Berkeley: University of California Press, 1985). Though much Mahayana literature contains highly positive images of women, one also finds quite negative ones. The texts here are well arranged and explained so that one can readily see the various strands of Mahayana attitudes toward women.

13. Succinct statements of this thesis in feminist theory can be found in Charlene Spretnak, ed., *The Politics of Women's Spirituality: Essays on the Rise of Spiritual Power Within the Feminist Movement* (New York: Anchor Books, 1982), pp. 510–28, 565–73.

14. The methodology condensed into this statement is more completely explained in Rita M. Gross, "Women's Studies in Religion: The State of the Art,

1980," in *Traditions in Contact and Change*, ed. Peter Slater and Donald Wiebe (Waterloo, Ontario: Wilfrid Laurier Press, 1983), pp. 579–91.

15. This terminology pervades Mary Daly's *Gyn/Ecology: The Metaethics of Radical Feminism* (Boston: Beacon Press, 1978). See especially pp. 252–55 and 360. For a review of this position from the Buddhist point of view, see Rita M. Gross, "Bitterness and Effectiveness: Reflections on Mary Daly's *Gyn/Ecology*," in *Anima: An Experiential Journal* 7, no. 1 (Fall 1980): 47–51.

16. This use of the term *enlightened society* is a cryptic but direct reference to the tradition of Shambhala, the once and future enlightened society of Tibetan tradition. For some Buddhists, this tradition is completely alive and significant. See Chögyam Trungpa, *Shambhala: The Sacred Path of the Warrior* (Boulder, CO: Shambhala, 1984).

17. Though not yet, to my knowledge, systematically studied, it is commonly noted that new, or "frontier," situations tend to allow women greater equality and freedom than is later found in the same situation. This thesis could easily be documented for the origins of Buddhism, Christianity, and Islam. But it is also noticeable in many reform movements within religious traditions and even in secular situations. For example, in many western U.S. states, women could vote before women's suffrage forced its allowance throughout the country.

CHAPTER 18

This chapter was written in 2004 and presented at the Sixth Sakyadhita International Conference on Women and Buddhism in Seoul, Korea. It has been published in a number of places, most recently in *BuddhaDharma: The Practitioner's Quarterly,* vol. 6, no. 2 (Winter 2007): 32–37.

CHAPTER 19

This chapter was written at the request of the *Journal of Feminist Theology* and will be published there in 2008. It was presented in Taipei, Taiwan, in 2007 at the International Conference on Religion and Gender Ethics.

1. Diana W. Paul, *Women in Buddhism: Images of the Feminine in the Mahayana Tradition* (Berkeley, CA: Asian Humanities Press, 1979).

2. Rita M. Gross, "Feminism from the Perspective of Buddhist Practice," *Buddhist-Christian Studies* 1 (1981): 72–82.

3. Sandy Boucher, *Turning the Wheel: American Women Creating the New Buddhism,* rev. ed. (Boston: Beacon Press, 1993).

4. Karma Lekshe Tsomo, an American nun who practices in the Tibetan tradition, lived and studied for many years in Asia before she earned a PhD and began university-level teaching. She founded and is president of Sakyadhita, an international organization for Buddhist women. In that capacity, she has organized many conferences on women and Buddhism, most of them held in Asia. At this point, these conferences are held every two years. For information about them, see www.sakyadhita.org.

5. Rita M. Gross, *Buddhism after Patriarchy: A Feminist History, Analysis, and Reconstruction of Buddhism* (Albany: State University of New York, 1993).

6. Ibid., p. 110.

7. I have long defined the goal of feminism as "freedom from the prison of gender roles," because I think that prescribed gender roles are themselves the problem. This problem cannot be alleviated by coming up with a more equal set of gender roles, or by attributing greater value to women's assigned roles. If there are gender roles, there will be suffering caused by the constraints of being hammered into a role that does not fit. This definition of feminism is as relevant for men as it is for women, one of its many virtues.

8. Buddhists catalog what makes a woman's life miserable. One list is called the "five woes": menstruation, pregnancy, childbirth, having to leave one's parental home at marriage to live with the husband's family, and having to work hard taking care of one's husband and his family. Feminists would point out that three of these are male evaluations of female biology; women might well not share this assessment. The other two are social expectations that are part of the "prison of gender roles." The other major catalog is called the "three sub-serviences." They are the need for women always to be under the authority of some male: in youth the father, in midlife the husband, and in old age the son. Obviously, these are also part of the "prison of gender roles," which I am claiming is a deep-seated karmic habit rather than anything given in the nature of "things as they are."

9. One of the most persistent misunderstandings about Buddhism is that it regards suffering as inevitable and intractable, probably because its first two Noble Truths are about suffering and the cause of suffering. The third truth, however, is about the cessation of suffering. The second truth claims that suffering is caused by attachment and the third that when the cause of suffering—attachment—is renounced, suffering ceases. That is to say, in enlightenment, things don't change; *our attitudes* change, and that makes all the difference between confusion and enlightenment.

10. For historical information on Buddhist nuns, see Nancy Auer Falk, "The Case of the Vanishing Nuns: The Fruits of Ambivalence in Ancient Indian Buddhism," in *Unspoken Worlds: Women's Religious Lives*, 3rd ed., eds. Nancy Auer Falk and Rita M. Gross (Belmont, CA: Wadsworth, 2001). For contemporary information, see Karma Lekshe Tsomo, ed., *Sakyadhita: Daughters of the Buddha* (Ithaca, NY: Snow Lion, 1988).

11. Kim Gutschow, *Being a Buddhist Nun: The Struggle for Enlightenment in the Himalayas* (Boston: Harvard University Press, 2004).

12. Regarding Sakyadhita, see note 4. Gutschow, *Being a Buddhist Nun*, p. 239.

13. Ibid.

14. Ibid., p. 242.

15. For a fuller account of Western Buddhist women, see Rita M. Gross, "Women's Issues in Contemporary North American Buddhism" in *The Encyclopedia of Women and Religion in North America*, ed. R. Keller and R.R. Ruether (Bloomington: Indiana University Press, 2006), pp. 1207–14.

16. Machig Labdron, a great female teacher of eleventh-century Tibet, did have several children. For her traditional biography, see Jerome Edou, *Machig Labdron and the Foundations of Chod* (Ithaca, NY: Snow Lion, 1996).

17. Sandy Eastoak, ed., *Dharma Family Treasures: Sharing Buddhism with Children* (Berkeley, CA: North Atlantic Books, 1994).

18. Karen Miller, *Momma Zen: Walking the Crooked Path of Motherhood* (Boston: Shambhala, 2006).

19. Sumi Loundon, ed., *Blue Jean Buddha: Voices of Young Buddhists* (Boston: Wisdom Publications, 2001).

20. See chapter 18 of this volume.

21. C.A.F. Rhys Davids and K.R, Norman, trans., *Poems of Early Buddhist Nuns (Therigatha)* (Oxford: The Pali Text Society, 1989).

22. Her Web site is www.vkr.org.

CHAPTER 20

This chapter was first presented as the keynote address at the First Midwest Conference on Women Practicing the Dharma in March 2006 in Chicago and was published in various languages in *Concilium: International Review of Theology* 42, no. 3 (August 2006).

1. Over the years, I have found it critical to define what I mean by feminism, given the preconceptions and stereotypes about it that prevail, especially in times of backlash. I have used two general definitions for many years. First, feminism is about freedom from the prison of gender roles, from the notion that women automatically want certain things and behave in a certain way, while men automatically behave in a different way and want different things. Second, feminism is about the radical practice of the cohumanity of women and men. This means that all human options must be available to both women and men, without regard for cultural gender roles and expectations. This definition of feminism liberates men at least as much as it liberates women.

2. To formally become a Buddhist, one must take Refuge Vows in the presence of a preceptor and a witnessing *sangha* (community). The Three Jewels are Buddha, as example, Dharma, as reliable teachings, and Sangha, as community of companions.

3. The topic of *karma* is easily misunderstood. Basically, it is about cause and effect, not only in the physical realm, but also in the moral realm. Karma is more about the negative effects of misconduct on the doer of those deeds than about the sufferings of unfortunate people, as is so often supposed. *Karmic affinity* means that for some reason, unexplainable by the theories of Western science and social science, I have an incredibly strong affinity with some lineages of Tibetan Buddhism (and not with others). The traditional Buddhist explanation for such otherwise inexplicable affinities would invoke karma, the effects of relationships made in past lives.

4. This statement was made to me in the fall of 1968 by one of the professors of the history of religions at the University of Chicago, which was then premier program in comparative religions in the world.

5. Rita M. Gross, *Buddhism after Patriarchy: A Feminist History, Analysis, and Reconstruction* (Albany: State University of New York Press, 1993), the first book-length feminist analysis of Buddhism in general, is one of the most

influential books on Buddhism and gender. It has affected both academic Buddhist studies and the practice of Buddhism.

6. This process is described in Rita M. Gross, "The Female Body and Precious Human Birth: An Essay on Anger and Meditation," in *Soaring and Settling: Buddhist Perspectives on Contemporary Social and Religious Issues* (New York: Continuum, 2000), pp. 7–12.

7. For example, see Rita M. Gross, "Excuse Me, but What's the Question? Isn't Religious Diversity Normal?" in *The Myth of Religious Superiority: A Multifaith Exploration*, ed. Paul Knitter (Maryknoll, NY: Orbis, 2005), pp. 75–87.

8. See Gross, *Buddhism after Patriarchy*, pp. 252–55.

Text:	10/13 Sabon
Display:	Sabon
Compositor:	International Typesetting and Composition
Printer & Binder:	Maple-Vail Book Manufacturing Group